THE TEMPLE
OF JERUSALEM

THE TEMPLE OF JERUSALEM

Past, Present, and Future

John M. Lundquist

Westport, Connecticut
London

Library of Congress Cataloging-in-Publication Data

Lundquist, John M.
    The Temple of Jerusalem : past, present, and future / by John M. Lundquist.
        p. cm.
    Includes bibliographical references and index.
    ISBN-13: 978–0–275–98339–0 (alk. paper)
    1. Temple of Jerusalem (Jerusalem) 2. Jerusalem in Judaism.
    3. Jerusalem in Christianity. 4. Jerusalem in Islam. I. Title.
    DS109.3.L86 2008
    296.4'91—dc22   2007031910

British Library Cataloguing in Publication Data is available.

Library of Congress Catalog Card Number: 2007031910
ISBN-13: 978–0–275–98339–0

First published in 2008

Praeger Publishers, 88 Post Road West, Westport, CT 06881
An imprint of Greenwood Publishing Group, Inc.
www.praeger.com

Printed in the United States of America

The paper used in this book complies with the
Permanent Paper Standard issued by the National
Information Standards Organization (Z39.48–1984).

10   9   8   7   6   5   4   3   2   1

To My Family

Contents

Acknowledgments

This book, and everything else I have written on temples and on the Temple had their genesis in a course titled "Early Oriental History," taught by Professor Hugh W. Nibley at Brigham Young University in the Fall of 1959. From that day to the present, very few days go by without my feeling the influence, the example, and the force of Hugh Nibley's scholarship and personality. Only a slightly less forceful impact on me comes from my teacher at the University of Michigan, Professor George E. Mendenhall, whose influence only began in 1973. In addition to Professor Mendenhall, I was deeply influenced by Professor David Noel Freedman at the University of Michigan, and, at Brigham Young University, by Professor Truman G. Madsen, who gave me my second publishing opportunity for a temple-themed article in 1984. Additionally, I enjoyed many memorable talks with Dr. Raphael Patai in New York City in the years before his death. His writings, ideas, personality and his encouragement of me have had a deep impact on me.

I also want to thank my beloved parents, of blessed memory, and my sister, Carolyn.

I want to thank my editor at Praeger, Ms. Suzanne I. Staszak-Silva. Without her I could not and would not have completed this book.

I want to thank Mee Kyung, who will know why.

My family has always supported me and given me so much love. I want to thank and express my love to Sue, Jennifer, Scott, Aidan, Emily, Dietert, Leif, Kjella, Eric, Margaret, Peter, and Jack.

John M. Lundquist

Introduction

The temple is a sacred, demarcated place. The English term derives from Latin *templum,* a place set aside for the purpose of augury. The English word "contemplate" comes from the same root, thus that which the ancient Roman augur "saw" within his range of vision was that which he "contemplated," was a vision that encompassed and was based upon the temple. A Greek cognate *temenos,* was a precinct, a piece of land marked off from common uses and dedicated to a god; the term now means the platform on which the temple stands—an architectural structure that separated the building off from common, everyday activities.

The Babylonian temple united the three primary world regions in the cosmos—sky, earth, and underworld—with a central pillar connecting the three zones. The Egyptian term for temple *hwt ntr* signified the manor or mansion where the god lived and where his ritual worship took place. Inscriptions call the Ptolemaic period temple of Edfu in Egypt the "Foundation Ground of the Gods of the Beginnings." The inner sanctum itself was called the "High Seat," the mythical mound of primordial creation, the most powerful and sacred earthly place imaginable. Several Hebrew words designate the temple in the Bible. Hebrew *heikal* (related to Akkadian *ekallu,* from Sumerian *e-gal,* "great house," thus "palace"), is frequently used for shrines, high places, and so on, prior to the building of the Temple of Solomon, but also for the heavenly sanctuary (Isa. 6:1). Most common in the Old Testament are *bet YHWH*, House of Yahweh," and *bet Elohim*, "House of God." Hebrew *miqdash* is used for the Jerusalem temple (2 Chr. 36:17, *Beit ha-Miqdash*, "House of Holiness").

Sacred space became so regarded because it is where the primordial acts of creation occurred and where a prophet or king met with deity. Because the earthly temple is built on the pattern of a heavenly model, it represents the heavenly prototype established on earth. The earthly temple incorporates, encompasses, and encloses this space, and passes on its power to humankind through their contact with the temple. In general this occurs through ritual, a highly prescribed, detailed set of instructions and actions, controlled by priestly functionaries, possessed of the authority of deep antiquity, and requiring exactitude and care in its performance. The temple cannot be approached or entered casually, without proper authority and without extensive ritual preparations, such as washing, anointing, and dressing in clean, usually white, ritually proper clothes.

"Temple" means an association of symbols and practices connected in the ancient world with both natural mountains or high places and built structures. These symbols include the cosmic mountain (Psalms 48:1–2), the primordial mound (Isaiah 28:16), waters of life (Ezekiel 47:1, 12), the tree of life, sacral space, the celestial (heavenly) prototype of the earthly sanctuary (Exodus 25:9). These practices, which can be called the temple ideology, emphasize spatial orientation and the ritual calendar; the height of the mountain or building; revelation of the divine prototype to the king or prophet by the deity; the concept of "center," according to which the temple is the ideological, and in many cases the geographical, center of the community; the dependency of the well-being of the community on proper attention to the temple and its rituals; initiation, including the dramatic portrayal within the temple of the cosmogonic myth as the primary vehicle of ritual; extensive concern for death and the afterlife, including burial within the temple precincts; sacral (covenant-associated) meals; revelation in the holy of holies to the king or prophet by means of the Tablets of Destiny; formal covenant ceremonies in connection with the promulgation of laws, such as the famous ancient Near Eastern law codes (for example the Code of Hammurabi, which came about from a commission that King Hammurabi received in the Esagila temple); animal sacrifice; secrecy; and the extensive economic and political impact of the temple on society.

Of all the important features of temples enumerated above, two in particular stand out for special mention and elucidation: the symbolism of the mountain and heaven. In the Babylonian creation account, *Enuma Elish*, when the waters of chaos subsided following their defeat by the forces of cosmos (the god Marduk), there appeared a mound of earth, the primary and primordial mound of creation, where the deity first appeared. This mound became transformed into the sacred mountain, the most holy place on earth, the archetype of the temple. In virtually all cultures, temples are either the architectural representation of the primordial mound, or of a world mountain, or some combination of the two.

The mountain and the temple are inseparable: "It shall come to pass in the latter days that the mountain of the house of the Lord shall be established as the highest of the mountains, and shall be raised above the hills; and all the nations shall flow to it, and many peoples shall come and say: 'Come, let us go up to the mountain of the Lord, to the house of the God of Jacob....'" (Isa. 2:2–3). All of the features that cause/create/determine the sacredness of the mountain are attached to the temple, and determine its architecture, symbolism, and ritual. The Egyptian Step Pyramid of Zoser was an architectural realization of the primordial hill or mound of creation, later modified into the true pyramid. The canonical, prescribed ritual foundation ceremonies for temples in ancient Egypt included the ritual of "hoeing the earth," which is directly related to the concept that the temple is the upward architectural extension out of the primeval waters of creation, leading up into the sky above the primordial mound.

In ancient Judaism, a foundation stone appears in the place of the primeval mound. According to the ancient Jewish Midrash the foundation stone is in front of the ark, which is considered the foundation of the world.

> Just as the navel is found at the center of a human being, so the land of Israel is found at the center of the world. Jerusalem is at the center of the land of Israel, and the temple is at the center of Jerusalem, the Holy of Holies is at the center of the temple, the Ark is at the center of the Holy of Holies, and the Foundation Stone is in front of the Ark, which spot is the foundation of the world. (Midrash Tanhuma, *Qedoshim* 10)

This foundation stone played the same role as the primordial mound in Egypt: it was the first solid material to emerge from the waters of creation, and it was upon this stone that God effected creation. According to Jewish legend, it was the primordial rock on which Jacob slept, at the place he subsequently named Bethel (Gen. 28). This same rock then came to be placed in the Holy of Holies (*debir*) of Solomon's Temple. According to

Islamic tradition, it is this same rock from which the Prophet Mohammed ascended into heaven over which the Dome of the Rock is built.

The mountain, a powerful earthly center and point of contact with the heavens, became a gathering place for the celebration of seasonal rituals and for renewal ceremonies at the New Year. A main purpose of the New Year festivals was to rededicate the temple, to reestablish and reaffirm the people's connection with the gods in the heavens. Numerous reliefs depict the processions of kings and nobles, approaching the city in order to attend the New Year festivals, where the rededication of the temple would signal the resumption of cosmic union and harmony.

The vegetation that the creative waters of life produced, which can be equated with the "trees of life," was luxurious, pristine, and life giving. This symbolism is exceptionally vivid in Hebrew Bible references to the messianic temple of the end of time:

> Then he brought me back to the door of the temple; and behold, water was issuing from below the threshold of the temple toward the east (for the temple faced east); and the water was flowing down from below the south end of the threshold of the temple, south of the altar. . . . And on the banks, on both sides of the river, there will grow all kinds of trees for food. Their leaves will not wither nor their fruit fail, but they will bear fresh fruit every month, because the water for them flows from the sanctuary. Their fruit will be for food, and their leaves for healing. (Ezekiel 47: 1, 12)

Other sources indicate that these waters flowed out from under the holy of holies, and were in fact kept in place or capped by the foundation stone. Temple architecture, paintings, and reliefs depict the "primordial landscape," the world as it was in the beginning—mound, water, and trees of life (or other vegetation) in or near the most holy place.

Not only do creation and life come up out of the depth; they come down from the sky, from the heavens, the dwelling place of deity. The basic idea is that there exists in the sky a perfect place, the "city" of the gods. The goal of human life is both to establish contact with this place and to return to it after death, thus to share in the life of the gods. The primary way by which the gods share with humans knowledge of this place, and information on how one gets there, is through the temple.

The god reveals to a king or prophet the architectural plan for the earthly temple, which is a replica of the heavenly temple. Exodus 19 and 25 provide the classic pattern: the prophet ascends the holy mountain, where he is shown a pattern (Hebrew *tabnit*) of the heavenly temple to examine: "According to all that I show you concerning the pattern of the tabernacle, and of all its furniture, so you shall make it" (Exodus 25: 9).

The Apostle John the Revelator was transported to a sacred mountain to view the heavenly city of Jerusalem, which in the context of the Book of Revelation is one vast temple: "And in the Spirit he carried me away to a great, high mountain, and showed me the holy city of Jerusalem coming down out of heaven....And he who talked to me had a measuring rod of gold to measure the city and its gates and walls" (Revelation 21: 10, 15).

The innermost sanctuary of the temple, the most holy place, is a model on earth of the place where God lives. He does not live in the earthly temple's most holy place; this is clear from Exodus 19: 18, 20, where the Lord descends out of heaven onto the mountaintop. The deity offers a glimpse into this heavenly place through the inner sanctum of the temple, where his presence is experienced by the prophet or the king on special occasions.

> Hezekiah received the letter from the hand of the messengers, and read it; and Hezekiah went up to the house of the Lord, and spread it before the Lord. And Hezekiah prayed before the Lord, and said: O Lord the God of Israel, who are enthroned above the cherubim, thou art the God, thou alone, of all the kingdoms of the earth; thou hast made heaven and earth. Incline thy ear, O Lord, and hear; open thy eyes, O Lord, and see; and hear the words of Sennacherib, which he has sent to mock the living God. (2 Kings 19: 14–16)

But how does one reach heaven? The answer is to be found in the mountain—the archetype and prototype of the temple. Exodus 19 points conveniently and profoundly in the right direction. The way up the mountain involves ritual, or rites of passage, through which the prophet mediates knowledge of God to the people who have been prepared by this ritual to approach the holy place. In many of the great religious traditions, the gods were thought to live on mountains, or to descend from heaven to a holy mountain, there to meet with those who have made the arduous journey to the center to be instructed. The mountain is the center because it was the first place of creation. It is the vertical pole connecting the heavens with the earth and with the underworld, the place that then becomes known as the "navel" of the earth. It is thus the "center" both because of the vertical relationship, connecting it with the heavens, and because of the horizontal aspect, drawing all peoples to it. To become one with God, one must join God at the mountain. The journey to the mountain and the ascent once one has reached that place are arduous and fraught with dangers and obstacles. This is the symbolism of Exodus 19–25.

The Temple of Jerusalem incorporates this entire body of symbols, and is indeed viewed as the very archetype of the Temple by people all over the world, in spite of the fact that it has not existed since 70 c.e. In the form of its present offspring, the Dome of the Rock, which stands upon the Temple Mount in Jerusalem, still stands as beacon to the world, a cosmic Center, the place on earth "nearest to Heaven."

Echoes of the influence of the Temple of Jerusalem are felt as far away as Japan, where persistent and ancient traditions claim definitive and formative influence of the Temple on the evolution of Shinto temples. But the influence of this Temple is felt far beyond the boundaries of the world's great religious traditions. The most widely heralded contemporary American artist, Matthew Barney set the third of his Cremaster Cycle films in New York City's Chrysler Building, where the central drama revolved around the symbolism and ritual of the Temple of Solomon, as mediated through traditional Masonic symbols and rituals. In Cremaster 3, the sculptor Richard Serra portrays the figure of Hiram Abif, the Phoenician master builder who supervised the construction of the Temple of Solomon (1 Kings 7:13–14; 1 Chronicles 2:13–14). The Barney film depicts Serra the sculptor, in his role of Hiram Abif, constructing the two gigantic bronze pillars, Jachin and Boaz, which stood in front of the Temple of Jerusalem (1 Kings 7:15–22). These two structures were part of the museum installation at the Guggenheim Museum during the Cremaster Cycle exhibition in 2003. I felt certain that only very few of the tens of thousands of visitors to the Cremaster Cycle exhibition at the Guggenheim Museum would have recognized these allusions to the Biblical Temple of Solomon, or would have understood or remembered their setting within the Hebrew Bible. And so, even though the Judeo-Christian-Islamic traditions, as well as significant portions of Western history and popular culture are permeated with the aura of the Temple of Jerusalem, still, there is widespread lack of knowledge and understanding of the details and meaning of the Temple.

It is ironic, given the immense influence of the Temple of Jerusalem on the world's religions, and on the intellectual, spiritual, and artistic traditions of humankind, that there are not any architectural or decorative or archaeological remains from this Temple known to have survived to the present time. Although this fact may seem to present impediments in the way of a book on this subject, there are abundant, chronologically diverse, scriptural and historical records, as well as eyewitness accounts from ancient times that allow us to reconstruct a highly accurate view of the Temple in its two major building phases: how it was constructed, its decorative and ritual patterns and processes, the events that led to the destruction of the Temple of Jerusalem at two separate historical periods, and the manner in which it influenced subsequent developments in the construction of sacred buildings within Judaism, Christianity, and Islam. Indeed, the way in which the Temple of Jerusalem continues to exercise its hold upon the religious views of vast numbers of the present-day population of the world in relationship to apocalyptic events that, in the prophetic literature of Judaism, Christianity, and Islam, will accompany the "end of the world." Throughout history, times of turmoil have brought to the surface the volatile theme of apocalypticism, and this apocalypticism has always had the Temple of Jerusalem at its scriptural and spiritual center.

In this book I am covering all aspects of the theme of the Temple of Jerusalem: its original construction in the time of King Solomon (the First Temple), its role in the spiritual and ritual life of ancient Israel, its destruction in 587 B.C.E. by Babylonian King Nebuchadnezzar, its reconstruction in 516 B.C.E. under the guidance of Zerubbabel, as a result of the commission of the Persian King Cyrus (the Second Temple), the vast enlargement that occurred during the time of the Idumean King Herod (around 20 B.C.E.), its final destruction in 70 C.E. by Roman general Titus, and then its dynamic and abundant afterlife as the leading influence in the construction of Jewish synagogues, Christian cathedrals, and Islamic mosques. Within this chronological setting, I have examined the efforts of archaeologists to identify, within the remains of archaeological excavations in the Syro-Palestinian cultural area, temples that are contemporary with the Temple of Solomon that allow us to attain the greatest possible idea of what the Temple of Solomon actually looked like. Furthermore, I have illuminated the archaeological and scriptural remains of the Essene community of Qumran, with particular emphasis on the Qumran Temple Scroll, to see what light this remarkable community throws on our understanding of the role of the Second Temple in the life of both ancient Judaism and of early Christianity.

This work emphasizes the symbolic nature of the Temple of Jerusalem, constantly examining its hold upon the adherents of the three great faiths that claim descent from the patriarch Abraham, and also examines the central role of the Temple and the Temple Mount in Jerusalem in the current political crisis, as well as views of the "Third Temple," the Messianic temple of the future, and how it would play out within the context of the three religions.

The book is based on the biblical texts (the Hebrew Bible and the New Testaments), the Qumran documents, the Apocryphal and Pseudepigraphal books of both Old and New Testaments, the Coptic Gnostic texts of Nag Hammadi, the Greek and Latin texts of such authors as Josephus and other inter-testamental travelers, scriptural commentators and historians, the Mishnah and the Talmud, Medieval Christian works documenting the construction of the great early cathedrals, early Islamic documentation of the constructions of the Dome of the Rock in Jerusalem, and the writings of Medieval Jewish, Christian and Islamic travelers and pilgrims. The Apocalyptic writings of the three religions, Judaism, Christianity, and Islam, are used to give a picture of "end of the world" expectations and the role of the Temple of Jerusalem in those speculations. In this same light, I have placed the Temple of Jerusalem within the context of the political crisis of the Middle East. I have both consulted and reflected in the book itself the latest historical and religious scholarship and political thinking on these issues.

CHAPTER 1

The First Temple

The Temple of Jerusalem came into being in ancient times within the same set of historical and religious circumstances as was the case with the neighbors of the biblical peoples as they built their great temples: the establishment of an empire, the establishment of a royal dynasty, and the linking together of this kingdom and dynasty with deity; and the selection of a location on which to build the universal cosmic temple which revealed a rich and ancient history as a sacred place. One of the most vivid, historically and theologically illuminating verses in the Hebrew Bible is that found in 1 Samuel 8:5: "now appoint for us a king to govern us like all the nations." In previous times, the nomadic Israelites of the post-Egyptian experience, followed by the village-dwelling Israelites of the period of the Judges, worshiped a deity whose shrine was carried about in a tent, with no fixed or permanent architectural structure to hold it. "To be governed like the other nations" meant to have a massive, luxuriously appointed, cosmic temple, sitting high atop the holy mountain, inhabited by a deity who had given his blessing to a royal dynasty.[1]

The empire in question was the Kingdom of Israel, which evolved out of the village-based Israelite political entity of Judges (in anthropological theory a chiefdom), and was cemented with the conquest of the Jebusites, a non-Israelite, Canaanite, people, and the citadel of their holy city, known as the "stronghold of Zion," which bore the ancient name Jerusalem (2 Samuel 5:6–7).

The royal dynasty was that of David, who had been anointed king of Israel by the prophet Samuel, following the downfall of Saul (1 Samuel 16:13). Then, following a period of continual warfare between David and his followers and the formally recognized King, Saul, and his followers, Saul was killed, and David became officially recognized as king, first, over the tribe of Judah (2 Samuel 2:7), and then over the remaining tribes of Israel (2 Samuel 5:1–5).

The Hebrew Bible connects David, his ancestors, and his posterity, with the dynastic god of the House of Israel, Yahweh, from earliest times. Following David's conquest of Jerusalem, and his uniting the entire House of Israel under his kingship, he proceeded to carve out a modest-sized regional kingdom, based on the military defeat of a number of neighboring peoples. The Hebrew Bible identifies the extent of that empire as encompassing ancient Moab, Edom, and Ammon (roughly modern-day Jordan), the territory of the Philistines (modern-day Israel and Palestine), and Aram (modern-day Syria—David put garrisons in Damascus) (1 Samuel 8: 10).

Kings build temples.[2] David, as the founder and consolidator of the Kingdom of Israel, should have been the one to build a monumental temple to the God of Israel. Once he had conquered "the stronghold of Zion," that is the citadel of Jerusalem, he built a palace there, calling it the "city of David" (2 Samuel 9), and also began expanding, widening, and strengthening the citadel, an area called *millo* in the narrative. *Millo* seems to have been a kind of fill or earthwork that possibly connected the southern slope with the northern.[3] As a matter of fact, the Bible states that the Lord determined that it would be Solomon, and not David, who would build the temple (2 Samuel 7:12–13; 1 Chronicles 28:3–6).

Once the city had been conquered and the king had built a palace there, his thoughts turned towards transporting into the city that object that would transform Jerusalem into a city of God, the sacred center of the kingdom. This was the Ark of the Covenant, the gilded acacia wood chest that held the Tablets of the Law from Mount Sinai, and that was carried with the Israelites during their wilderness wanderings. During the time of the wanderings, the Ark was kept within a tent shrine, called variously *mishkan* (dwelling), *'ohel mo'ed* (tent of meeting—Joshua 18:1), and *miqdash* (sanctuary). Following the conquest of the Land of Canaan in the time of Joshua, the Ark was placed in Shiloh, which became the *de facto* shrine city of the Israelite confederacy (Joshua 18:1).[4] The shrine is called "the tent of meeting" in this passage. However, according to Judges 20:27, the ark was located in Bethel: "And the people of Israel inquired of the Lord (for the ark of the covenant of God was there in those days)."

Then, at the beginning of the book of 1 Samuel, we are introduced to the father and mother of the prophet Samuel. The father, Elkanah "used to go up year by year from his city to worship and to sacrifice to the Lord of hosts at Shiloh" (1 Samuel 1:3). The priest of this shrine, Eli, is described as "sitting on the seat beside the doorpost of the temple of the Lord (*heikal Yahweh*) (1 Samuel 1:9). Later, in the same chapter, we read that Samuel's mother, Hannah, after she had weaned the infant, "brought him to the house of the Lord (*beit* Yahweh) at Shiloh" (1 Samuel 1:24). There must have been quite a substantial sanctuary at Shiloh, actually functioning as what we would understand to be a temple. In biblical usage a temple implies a built structure, with roof and walls, articulated rooms, a more formal structure than just an "altar." The temple would be furnished with cultic objects, including altars, and would be ministered to by a formal priestly class, as opposed to an altar, at which, in biblical times, any Israelite could function.[5]

During the interminable wars fought between the Israelites and the Philistines, as recorded in the book of 1 Samuel, the Ark of the Covenant, that most holy article of the biblical tabernacle, was removed from the temple at Shiloh and taken into battle against the Philistines by the Israelites (1 Samuel 4:3–4), to be used as a palladium, a magical amulet to secure victory. The Ark was seized by the Philistines (1 Samuel 4:11), bringing great calamity upon Israel. The Philistines set it up in the main temple of their god, but after experiencing the wrath of the God of Israel, determined to return it to the Israelites (1 Samuel 5–6). The Israelites received the Ark and installed it in the house of one Abinadab in the village of Kiriath-jearim (1 Samuel 7:1). It was from this same house that the Ark of the Covenant was brought by King David some 20 years later into the newly captured City of David. The Ark was carried on a cart with David offering up sacrifices, "girded with a linen ephod" (2 Samuel 6:13–14), leading a joyous procession, filled with wild dancing and shouting and the sounds of horns, until the Ark was placed "inside the tent ['*ohel*] which David had pitched for it" (2 Samuel 6:15–17).

We have now reached the point in time (approximately 1005 B.C.E.) when the stage is set for the building of a magnificent temple to the God of Israel. David himself dwelt in the "Stronghold of Zion" (2 Samuel 5:19), which he called the City of David, and "perceived that the Lord had established him king over Israel, and that he had exalted his kingdom for the sake of his people Israel" (2 Samuel 5:9–10). Indeed, the biblical narrative at this moment introduces us to what can be seen as the primary theme in our later attempts to understand the structural nature of the temple: the Israelites themselves do not have the technological expertise, nor the access to the necessary raw materials, to carry out the building of such a supremely important building. "And Hiram king of Tyre [on the coast of Phoenicia/Lebanon] sent messengers to David, and cedar trees, also carpenters and masons who built David a house [that is, a palace]." (2 Samuel 5:11). We will see later that it will be the same Phoenician craftsmen, along with the fabled raw materials from the coastal mountain ranges of the Lebanon, most famously cedar (2 Samuel 5:11), that will be crucial in building the temple, and that it will be partly in the direction of Phoenician culture that we will want to look in order to understand the architectural plan and the interior design of the temple.

In the meantime however, we must look at the final prerequisite that ancient temple builders had to consider in the choice of a site for a temple, as mentioned in the opening paragraph: the site must already possess an ancient history as a sacred place at the time it is chosen for the building of the temple. "Once sacred, always sacred." Throughout the world, temples, shrines, all types and manners of sacred places remain at the same place, over centuries, even millennia, with previous architectural plans usually embedded within later enlargements, irrespective of changes in religion or empire. Generally speaking, "irruptions of the sacred"[6] occur in locations that are already auspicious for some reason, but of course there are exceptions to this, where some immediate, new event at a particular site endows that place with sacredness for the first time.[7]

As an example of a long period of sacrality at the same site, the Cathedral of Chartres, completed in its present form in 1220, incorporated within its ground plan the remains of four previous churches, dating back to fourth to sixth centuries, which "fit inside each other like Russian dolls." According to legend the same site, in pre-Christian times, was a Druid grotto sacred to the Gaulish tribe, the Carnutes, and it is even possible that the site was sacred in megalithic times, around 2000 B.C.E.[8] If this latter were to prove to be accurate, that means that the site on which Chartres Cathedral sits today would have a 4,000-year history as a sacred place.

From within the Middle East itself, the most famous example of multiple-thousand-year continuity at one site of a sacred place is the ancient Sumerian city of Eridu, the southern Iraqi site of Tell Abu Shahrein. According to the Sumerian King List "When kingship was lowered from heaven, kingship was (first) in Eridu."[9] The excavators working at this site uncovered a sequence of 19 temples at the foot of the Ziggurat temple tower, dating from approximately 5000 B.C.E. to approximately 2000 B.C.E.

Successive kings continued to build shrines at the site, up to the time of Babylonian king Nebuchadnezzar II, (604–562 B.C.E.).[10]

What makes a place sacred? In Eliade's phrase, it is an "irruption of the sacred."[11] The sacred, the divine world, manifests itself in the world of humans, reveals itself, and the place where that revelation occurred becomes sacred. The temple itself then rises at that place, and for hundreds, or even thousands of years thereafter, shrines will stand there, often of new religions as the course of history brings in new peoples, new conquerors, and so on. The "irruption" typically occurs at places that are "naturally" sacred: mountains, caves, trees, wells, or rivers. Deities reveal themselves on the tops of mountains, in caves, at springs, or other natural areas.

The sacrality of the Temple Mount is based on a number of events, divine interventions, and appearances that I will describe before going on with the description of the building of the temple. The biblical narrative associates the origin and designation of the "Stronghold of Zion" as a sacred site with several ancient events dating to the time of Abraham, to that of his son Isaac, and to the encounter of King David with a Jebusite named Araunah.

To begin with, the archaic Biblical narratives centering on the Patriarchs associate Abraham with a "Melchizedek king of Salem [who] brought out bread and wine; he was priest of the Most High (Hebrew *El Elyon*—a Canaanite god)" (Genesis 14:18). The place name Jerusalem (the same as Salem of this narrative) is attested as a Canaanite city in the Egyptian Execration Texts, of around the nineteenth to eighteenth centuries B.C.E.[12] Melchizedek figures in Psalm 110 where King David is said to have become "a priest forever after the order of Melchizedek" (Psalms 110:4). Melchizedek was thus a Canaanite priest-king in Middle Bronze Age Jerusalem, to whom Abraham was a vassal, worshipping a Canaanite deity named El Elyon, "God most high."

The next crucial event in the process by which the Hebrew Bible confirms the great antiquity of the Temple Mount as a holy place comes in Genesis 22, the account of God's command to Abraham to "Take your son, your only son Isaac, whom you love, and go to the land of Moriah, and offer him there as a burnt offering upon one of the mountains of which I shall tell you" (Genesis 22:2). 2 Chronicles 3:1 confirms that this place, Moriah, is the place on which the Temple of Solomon was built: "Then Solomon began to build the house of the Lord in Jerusalem on Mount Moriah, where the Lord had appeared to David his father at the place that David had appointed, on the threshing floor of Ornan the Jebusite" (2 Chronicles 3:10). Thus, "one of the mountains of…the land of Moriah" of Genesis 22:2, the Mount Moriah where the temple was built, and the threshing floor of Ornan, both of 2 Chronicles 3:10, are all one and the same place, from the perspective of the Hebrew Bible.[13]

The next link in the historical chain of documentation of a holy place is introduced in the final phrase of the preceding verse: the threshing floor of Ornan (called Araunah in 2 Samuel 24:16). King David purchased this threshing floor from Araunah for 50 shekels of silver, and erected an "altar to the Lord, and offered burnt offerings and peace offerings" (2 Samuel 24:24–25). The account of the purchase by David of the threshing floor of Araunah/Ornan given in 1 Chronicles 21:15–30, is a classic case of Eliade's "irruption of the sacred." Israel was threatened with a pestilence, and the destruction of Jerusalem by the Lord because David improperly declared a census of the people of Israel. Just at the moment of the onset of the destruction, the Lord stayed his hand, and sent an angel to David, specifically to the threshing floor of Ornan. The angel stood with a drawn sword, causing David and his followers to dress in sackcloth and to fall upon their faces. "Then the angel of the Lord commanded Gad to say to David that David should go up and rear an altar to the Lord on the threshing floor of Ornan the Jebusite." (1 Chronicles 21:18). David approached Ornan, who was threshing wheat with his sons, and initiated the process by which he would purchase the site. Following the purchase, "David built there an altar to the Lord and presented burnt offerings and peace offerings, and called upon the Lord, and he answered him with fire from heaven upon the altar of burnt offering" (1 Chronicles 21:26). At this point David is quoted as saying: "Here shall be the house of the Lord God and here the altar of burnt offerings for Israel" (1 Chronicles 22:1).

It is obvious that the threshing floor itself has great significance here as an integral part of the sacrality of the site. A threshing floor is a place, still seen in the Middle East today, where the harvested grain is brought, usually on the outskirts of a village, and stored in stacks. Then, a team of oxen drags a flat-bottomed sledge, the bottom of which is sometimes equipped with metal tacks or nails, around the stack, breaking the sheaves down to prepare for the final threshing process, where the peasant tosses the grains into the air with a wooden pitchfork, separating the wheat from the chaff. The threshing floor is thus the locus of a basic early technology in the threshing of grains. But what else is it?

Threshing floors are known in ancient Greek religious texts, from ancient Egypt, and from Medieval Middle Eastern sources to have been sacred places, numinous places, where a variety of religious rituals were carried out. Grain is obviously associated with first-fruits offerings, with the celebration of harvest festivals, with fertility and human and animal sexuality, and temples to gods and goddesses are associated with threshing floors, such as the temples of Demeter in ancient Greece. In ancient Egypt the mystery plays to the god Osiris, celebrating his revivification, were carried out on threshing floors, and the Egyptologist B. H. Stricker has traced the origins of Greek (and thus, by extension of Western) theater to the threshing floors of Egypt and early Greece, and to the temples closely associated with and built next to them.[14] Threshing floors were also places of prophecy, as in 1 Kings 22:10, where the prophets were prophesying in front of the kings of Israel and Judah, "at the threshing floor at the entrance of the gate of Samaria."

The final element identifying a site as sacred, found in temples worldwide, and in the Temple of Jerusalem is the mountain, the sacred mountain, the premier and primordial place of revelation. The "stronghold of Zion" (2 Samuel 5:7), the stronghold of the Jebusites conquered by David, the ancient holy place designated as such in the sacred stories of the Israelites, such as the account of Abraham and Isaac at Mount Moriah, the location of a numinous threshing floor, becomes, with the building of the temple there, THE holy mountain par excellence. Mount Zion is assimilated to the other holy mountain of Israelite experience, Mount Sinai, the Mountain of God, where Moses met with the deity and received the Law while all Israel waited below (Exodus 19–31; Exodus 18:5: "…when he was encamped at the mountain of God." Isaiah 2:3: "Come, let us go up to the mountain of the Lord, to the house of the god of Jacob"). This is particularly evident in the Book of Psalms, for example Psalms 133: "It is like the dew of Hermon [i.e., Mount Hermon], which falls on the mountains of Zion." "Zion possesses all the prerogatives of the cosmic mountain."[15] Even though the Temple Mount in Jerusalem is not literally the highest geographical point in that region[16] it becomes, through its innate sanctity and through the fact of the temple, the place where "in the latter days…the mountain of the house of the Lord shall be established as the highest of the mountains, and shall be raised above the hills" (Isaiah 2:2). "For out of Zion shall go forth the law, and the word of the Lord from Jerusalem" (Isaiah 2:3).

The concept of the holy mountain with its associated temple, or the humanmade mountain and its temples, as in the Mesopotamian Ziggurat complexes—or the mountain itself serving as the dwelling place of deity—with his temples situated below in the center of his holy city, is commonplace in ancient Near Eastern religions, and, most relevant for the religion of ancient Israel, in the religion of the neighboring Canaanites, with the city of Ugarit on the Syrian coast (destroyed ca. 1200 B.C.E.) the most influential parallel to the accounts of the Old Testament.[17]

In the Ugaritic texts, there are two primary deities, the old patriarchal god El and the young storm god Baal, and each has his own mountain, the mountain of El, where the god dwells in a tent, and Mount Zaphon, where Baal builds his palace. El lives at the "sources of the two rivers," the primeval waters of creation, from which his decrees issue forth. In the Hebrew Bible, Yahweh has two mountains, Sinai and Zion. The Hebrew Bible's descriptions of Yahweh includes archaic language in describing Yahweh, his personality, his manner of rule, and his relationship to the two mountains. This language echoes the style and vocabulary of the Ugaritic epics, and attributes to Yahweh roles and characteristics that echo those attributed to El and Baal in the Ugaritic poems. Examples of this archaic stage of Hebrew can be found in Exodus 15: 1–21, the Song at the Sea, Judges 5: 2–31, the Song of Deborah, and in many Psalms. These poems celebrate Yahweh's tent of dwelling on the sacred mountain of Sinai, the movement of the tent with the people of Israel in their Wilderness Wanderings, the role of the tent as a place of oracle, and the ultimate installation of the tent in the *debir* of the sacred temple on the second mountain, Zion in Jerusalem. "Yahweh is seen as moving his residence from Sinai by allowing the earthly copy of his tent, 'the tabernacle of the tent of meeting' (*mishkan 'ohel mo'ed*) shown to Moses on the mountain, to be carried to the land of Canaan...." which was "the portable tent shrine that was the predecessor of the temple on Zion."[18]

We thus now have in place all the various strands that come together to deepen our understanding of the place on which the Temple of Solomon rose, the place that has retained its sacred character to this day, approximately 4,000 years after the time of Abraham, according to traditional dating. Jerusalem was already a sacred city in the Middle Bronze Age, around 2000 B.C.E., ruled over by a Canaanite priest-king. The sacrifice (another ancient concept associated with threshing floors) of Isaac was commanded to take place upon the sacred mountain, Moriah, while finally David formally purchased the threshing floor that flourished on this same holy mountain, in order to bring the age-old sacred potential of this place to fruition.

This combination of primordial, sacred events associated with the site, along with the role of the Rock of Foundation, described below, combine to create what in the study of the temple is called a *temenos,* a platform intended to support a sacred edifice. We must here consider the topography of Jerusalem as it must have existed in the time of David and Solomon. David conquered the Jebusite stronghold, that is their citadel, which was situated along the southernmost ridge that extends south of the present-day Temple Mount, the ridge that, in its entirety, borders the Kidron Valley on the west. This became the "stronghold of Zion," the "city of David," the place to which David had the ark of the covenant brought from Kiriath-jearim and installed in a tent, where it stayed until the temple was completed. (2 Samuel 5:6–8; 2 Samuel 6). David, and after him Solomon, had terraces (the *millo* of 2 Samuel 5:9 and 1 Kings 9:15) constructed along the western side of the Kidron Valley, linking the Jebusite fortress area with the expanded, higher area that became the Temple Mount. It was the area of the threshing floor of Araunah that became the site of the actual Temple Mount, the sacred *temenos*.[19] This area, the *temenos,* the holy mountain of God, the sacred platform on which the temple was to stand, is, as is the case in all ancient Near Eastern temples, a highly restricted zone, off limits to the general populace, "set apart——both ritually by consecrating the ground on which it was erected and out of which it seemed organically to grow, and architecturally, by building an imposing series of progressively more restrictive walls to surround and protect it. The temple's ritual and architectural barriers repulsed the chaotic forces that continually threatened the ordered world within."[20]

There is one additional, very important aspect of the sacrality of ancient temples, which we must address before we come to the actual building of the Temple of Jerusalem. This is the concept that a king cannot, of his own knowledge or understanding, create or produce the architectural plan of the temple. It must be revealed to him by God, and this usually in a process called "incubation," whereby the king spends the night in a temple or shrine, there to receive the knowledge of the divinely ordained plan of the temple in an auspicious dream. The best-known example of this process from antiquity is the account of the building of a temple to the god Ningirsu in Lagash by the Sumerian king Gudea (2143–2124 B.C.E.). Gudea received the revelation that he should build a temple, and the plan for how it should be built, in a dream in the temple of Eninnu. He then went to another temple, that of the goddess Gatumdu, in order to have the dream interpreted.[21]

The Hebrew Bible establishes the concept of a heavenly temple in a number of places. It is this temple that provides the plan for how the earthly counterpart should be constructed. The clearest example of this concept is found in the accounts of the building of the Tabernacle in the Wilderness, by Moses, as found in Exodus. While Moses was on the holy mountain, receiving the revelations from God, he was told "According to all that I show you concerning the pattern of the tabernacle, and of all its furniture, so you shall make it" (Exodus 25:9). The Hebrew word for "pattern" is *tabnit*. The *tabnit* is the heavenly model, the place where the deity is enthroned, and it is this model that the prophet or king should follow, bringing the heavenly down to earth.[22]

Rabbinic literature speaks of an "upper Temple and a lower Temple, the latter "a true likeness of the original." The upper Temple is 18 miles above the lower.

> God showed Moses the heavenly Temple and said unto him: Make a likeness of it on the earth. The lower Temple is set against the upper Temple. The upper Holy of Holies is set against the lower Holy of Holies. The throne of below, that is, the Ark, is set against the throne above.[23]

While the High Priest is sacrificing in the lower Temple, the archangel Michael is sacrificing in the upper Temple. When the lower Temple was destroyed, sacrifice in the upper Temple, that is in Heaven, also ceased.[24]

Ancient Egyptian texts and temple reliefs give us another vivid example of how the process of bringing the plan of a heavenly temple was brought down to earth. The Temple of Edfu in Egypt, built between 237 and 71 B.C.E., contains on the walls of the pillared hall a series of reliefs depicting a ritual which is known as "stretching the cord." In order to determine the exact floor plan of the temple, the king, acting in his role as the god Horus, together with the goddess Seshat, "mistress of the ground plans and the writings," on a new moon night, first "stretched out" the sky, determining its borders, then transferred the plan of the perfect temple in the sky down to earth in a kind of "sacred surveying," thus establishing the four corners of the temple's plan.[25]

The idea of the heavenly plan being "measured" and thus transferred to earth, serving as the perfect model, appears in two places in the Bible. The first of these is found in Ezekiel, beginning in Chapter 40, the great messianic/apocalyptic section of this prophet's writings. In classic prophetic fashion, the prophet is taken in a vision to a high mountain, where he sees "a structure like a city opposite me" (Ezekiel 40:2). This "city" is obviously meant to be the heavenly city where God dwells. There the prophet encounters "a man, whose appearance was like bronze, with a line of flax, and a measuring reed in his hand." (Ezekiel 40:3). This man then proceeds to guide the prophet on a tour of the heavenly city, all the while measuring out the dimensions of the temple and of the city, which are recorded in Chapters 40–42. At the end of this process, the man announces to Ezekiel, "And you, son of man, describe to the house of Israel the temple and its appearance and plan" (Ezekiel 43:10). Here again we have the Hebrew word *tabnit*, "plan," implying the heavenly plan that serves as the prototype and model for the earthly version.

The second example of this concept in the Bible is found in the Book of Revelation in the New Testament. There, in Chapter 11, John is "given a measuring rod like a staff," and instructed to "Rise, and measure the temple of God and the altar" (Revelation 11:1). Then, in a vision of the millennial period, one of the seven angels "carried me away to a great, high mountain, and showed me the holy city of Jerusalem coming down out of heaven from God" (Revelation 21:10). Thus, during the period of earthly existence, in the divine chronology, an earthly temple will stand on the earth to represent the one in heaven. In the Messianic period, the heavenly temple will descend onto the earth, creating the perfect city of Jerusalem that will last forever.[26]

The counterpart of the process of the heavenly plan being revealed to the prophet or king is not as clearly spelled out in the Hebrew Bible as in the Gudea inscriptions, and in many other ancient sources, but scholars generally accept the account given in the first chapter of 2 Chronicles, related to Solomon, as the equivalent. There it is related to King Solomon, along with his assembly, "went to the high place that was at Gibeon; for the tent of meeting of God, which Moses the servant of the Lord had made in the wilderness, was there" (2 Chronicles 1:3). David brought the Ark of the Covenant from Kirjath-jearim into Jerusalem and installed it on Mount Zion, but the tent of meeting (that is, the Tabernacle, the portable sanctuary carried by Israel through the wilderness) had remained in Gibeon, an ancient "high place," a place of oracle and revelation. Solomon sought an oracle from God at this time and place: "Solomon went up there to the bronze altar before the Lord, which was at the tent of meeting, and offered a thousand burnt offerings upon it" (2 Chronicles 1:6). The key passage occurs in the next verse: "In that night God appeared to Solomon, and said to him, 'Ask what I shall give you'" (2 Chronicles 1:7). And then, in 2 Chronicles 1:13: "So Solomon came from the high place at Gibeon, from before the tent of meeting, to Jerusalem." Even though it does not expressly state it as such, many scholars agree that this is the equivalent of the Gudea incubation experience described above: it was here that God revealed to Solomon the heavenly plan of the temple, and the instructions on how it should be built. His visit to the high place at Gibeon, and his auspicious night of sleep there, during which God appeared to him to reveal the oracular message, fits in with the pattern outlined by Kapelrud.[27] The next chapter of 2 Chronicles, Chapter 2, begins with the words: "Now Solomon purposed to build a temple for the name of the Lord, and a royal palace for himself."

However, it is not quite that simple because the Bible also gives David a major role in the preparation of the building materials for his son (1 Chronicles 22, 29), and even states that he had received the plan for the temple directly from God, with the word for plan, *tabnit* (as in Exodus 25: 9, above) again used in the passage: "All this he made clear by the writing by the hand of the Lord concerning it, all the work to be done according to the plan" (1 Chronicles 28:19). This means that David received the heavenly plan by divine oracle, as did his son Solomon. However, David was forbidden from building the temple himself, because he had shed blood (1 Chronicles 22:7–8; 28:3). Instead "David gave Solomon his son the plan for the vestibule of the temple, and of its houses, its treasuries, its upper rooms, and its inner chambers, and of the room for the mercy seat; and the plan of all that he had in mind for the courts of the house of the Lord, all the surrounding chambers, the treasuries of the house of God" (1 Chronicles 28:11–12). This lengthy passage ends with a restatement of the crucial idea: "All this he [that is, David] made clear by the writing from the hand of the Lord concerning it, all the work to be done according to the plan (Hebrew *tabnit*)." (1 Chronicles 28:19). In any case, both kings, David and Solomon, are depicted as having sought out direct revelation from the Lord as to the architectural plans, the building materials, the interior design, and so on, before they could proceed. David is depicted not only as having received such divine instructions, but also as having made all the necessary preparations of Phoenician workers, craftsmen, and stonecutters of necessary building materials, such as dressed stone, bronze, iron, and cedar timbers (1 Chronicles 22:2–4).[28]

The biblical accounts of the building of the Temple of Jerusalem by King Solomon are found in 1 Kings, 6–8, and 2 Chronicles 2–4. The three sets of biblical records that record the history of ancient Israel in the period of time that we are following, the two Books of Samuel, the two Books of Kings, and the two Books of Chronicles are not to be taken as consecutive histories, as it appears from their placement in the Bible. Each was written at a different period, using different sources, and from differing theological perspectives. Although the Books of Kings and Chronicles appear to record the same historical material in the same order, they were written at dramatically differing time periods, and have quite differing theological points of view. The Books of Kings were compiled from a diverse set of dynastic records, annals, and stories, by two different Deuteronomic editors, one writing around the time of the death of King Josiah, 609 B.C.E., the second, writing in Babylonian Exile, bringing the record to its close with the destruction of the Kingdom of Judah by the Babylonians in 587 B.C.E. and the beginning of the Exile. The meaning of the Deuteronomic editing of the Bible relates to the reforms carried out by King Josiah, during whose reign a copy of the Book of Deuteronomy ("Book of the Covenant") was found in the temple during cleaning and restoration, following a long period of apostasy (2 Kings 22). The reforms that the king introduced as a result of this discovery were attempts to return the Kingdom of Judah to the purity of religious practice mandated in the Book of Deuteronomy. Thus the Deuteronomic History, that is the Books of Samuel and Kings, compiled at a much later date than that ascribed to the events themselves as they played out, colors, interprets, and modifies earlier events from the point of view of the later Deuteronomic editor.

The Books of Chronicles were edited by the Chronicler, an anonymous editor or editors living after the return from Babylonian Exile, not earlier than around 400 B.C.E. Chronicles is very idealistic, imposing upon the historical record certain key ideas, reinterpreting the reigns of David and Solomon in terms of this idealism, a point of view informed by the Exile as well as by exposure in Babylonian Exile to the fabulous and sophisticated religious and cultic achievements of the Mesopotamian peoples, imposing ideas and historical realities from the time in which he wrote or edited. Thus although the accounts of the plans and actual building of the Temple are contained within both sets of records, they come from very different periods of time and reflect very differing interpretations of Israelite religion. Where the two accounts differ, we have the choices of harmonizing them, seeing the one as a later, idealizing account, or as an account reflecting the time period of the Second, (Zerubbabel) Temple (see Chapter 3), the other as earlier and perhaps more accurate, or perhaps not being able to decide which is a more accurate account of the actual First Temple. Unless the two texts actually contradict one another, we will use them as a composite, in order to fill out the details as much as possible.[29]

According to 1 Kings 6:1, the building of the Temple of Jerusalem began in the fourth year of Solomon's reign, a date to which scholars assign the year 960 B.C.E. The Temple was completed in 953 B.C.E. In the records of King Gudea of Lagash, mentioned above, he states that

> Gudea, the en priest of Ningirsu, made a path into the Cedar Mountain which nobody had entered before; he cut its cedars with great axes. With axes he fashioned (them) for the *sar.ur*, the "Right Arm of Lagash," the "Floodstorm-Weapon" of his king. (Like) giant snakes, cedar rafts were floating down the water (of the river) from the Cedar Mountain, pine rafts from the Pine Mountain.[30]

We read in 2 Chronicles 2: 3–4: "And Solomon sent word to Huram [= Hiram] the king of Tyre: 'As you dealt with David my father and sent him cedar to build a house to dwell in, so deal with me. Behold, I am about to build a house for the name of the Lord my God and dedicate it to him for the burning of incense of sweet spices before him.'" And in the same chapter, verses 8 and 9: "Send me also cedar, cypress, and algum timber from Lebanon, for I know that your servants know how to cut timber in Lebanon. And my servants will be with your servants, to prepare timber for me in abundance, for the house I am to build will be great and wonderful."

The kings of the ancient Middle Eastern kingdoms, Sumer, Babylon, Assyria, Egypt, Aram, and now, Israel, all went in person, or sent messengers or messages before them, to the "Cedar Mountain," to Lebanon, famed for its precious, aromatic woods, in order to obtain this wood for the building of their temples. Without such timber, along with vast quantities of other luxury building materials that we will mention in due time, their gods could not be housed properly, nor would proper glory accrue to the king or to his kingdom. This expedition to the Cedar Mountain was both a ritual requirement for the king related to his universal dominion, and a religious one, requiring him to obtain the ultimate building materials.

No architect is named, but we have already seen that in the ideology of that time, kings are temple builders, and they receive architectural direction and guidance directly from on high. But of course Solomon received technical help from experienced builders such as Hiram, and others whom Hiram sent, such as the craftsman/architect Huram-abi (the Hebrew of this name is literally "Hiram my father.") of 2 Chronicles 2:13–14, called simply Hiram of Tyre in 1 Kings 7:13, whose legend, as Hiram Abif, flourished during the European Middle Ages and up to the present time in the form of Rosicrucian and Masonic myths. The descriptions the Bible gives of this man fulfill all information we would like to have as to who was responsible for the ultimate structure: 1 Kings 7:14 describes him as "the son of Naphtali, and his father was a man of Tyre, a worker in bronze; and he was full of wisdom, understanding, and skill, for making any work in bronze. He came to King Solomon, and did all his work."[31] However the account in 2 Chronicles 2:14, goes far beyond this description: "the son of a woman of the daughters of Dan [thus of Israelite ancestry, of the tribe of Dan!], and his father was a man of Tyre. He is trained to work in gold, silver, bronze, iron, stone, and wood, and in purple, blue, and crimson fabrics and fine linen, and to do all sorts of engraving and execute any design that may be assigned him, with your craftsmen, the craftsmen of my lord, David your father." We have here a description of what constituted the profession of architecture in ancient times, and in some ways up to pre-modern times, for example to the Gothic era in Europe. "The medieval bishop or abbot could rely on his mason to take care of the practical problems of the task; the ideas he himself provided were not of a technical but rather of an aesthetic and symbolic kind."[32] All of the technologies that we know were employed in the building of the Temple of Solomon are specifically named in this verse.

The preparations King Solomon made for the building fit in well with other ancient records of temple building. I would like to compare here two lists of luxury products gathered together for the building of a temple, that of David, found in 1 Chronicles 29:5, with that of the Sumerian King Gudea of Lagash, mentioned above. First the list of Gudea, who dates to a much earlier time (2143–2124 B.C.E.): Following the enumeration of the cedar and other precious woods, partially quoted above he goes on to enumerate:

[In the quarries which nobody had entered (before), Gudea], the *en*-priest of Ningirsu, ma[de] a path and(thus) the stones were delivered in large blocks. Boats (loaded) with *haluna* –stone, boats (loaded) with *nalu* –stone, they brought to Gudea, *en*-priest of Ningirsu, also bitumen (filled) in buckets, *igi.engur* –bitumin and gypsum from the mountains of Magda as (if they be) boats bringing barley from the fields. Many other precious materials were carried to their *ensi,* the builder of the Ninnu-temple: from the copper mountain of Kimash—(after) the soil had been prospected (for copper ore)—its copper was mined in clusters; gold was delivered from its mountain as dust for the *ensi* who wanted to build a house for his king, for Gudea they mined silver from its mountain, delivered red stone from Melluha in great amounts. In the *sir*-quarry, they mined *sir*-stone (alabaster) for him.[33]

Now, the account of David's preparations for the temple, from 1 Chronicles 29:2–5:

So I have provided for the house of my God, so far as I was able, the gold for the things of gold, the silver for the things of silver, and the bronze for the things of bronze, the iron for the things of iron, and wood for the things of wood, besides great quantities of onyx and stones for setting, antimony, colored stones, all sorts of precious stones, and marble. Moreover, in addition to all that I have provided for the holy house, I have a treasure of my own of gold and silver, and because of my devotion to the house of God I give it to the house of God: three thousand talents of gold, of the gold of Ophir, and seven thousand talents of refined silver, for overlaying the walls of the house, and for all the work to de done by the craftsmen, gold for the things of gold and silver for the things of silver. Who then will offer willingly, consecrating himself today to the Lord?

The mention of "talent" (Hebrew *kikar*), as the basic unit of measure, gives us an excellent opportunity to consider just how much gold and silver are claimed here. A single "talent" represented 35 kilograms or 75 pounds.[34]

I would now like to add one additional ancient account, from the annals of the Assyrian King Tiglath-Pileser III (744–727 B.C.E.), from about 200 years later than the time of the construction of the Temple of Solomon. The purpose of this account is to complement the accounts of the raw materials, the luxury products and the technical skills attributed in the Bible to the preparations for the building of the temple. This is an record of booty received by the Assyrian king on one of his campaigns:

> I received tribute from Kushtashpi of Commagene, Rezon of Damascus, Menahem of Samaria, Hiram of Tyre, Sibittibi'li of Byblos, Urikki of Qu'e, Pisiris of Carchemish, I'nil of Hamath, Panammu of Sam'al, Tarhulara of Gurgum, Sulumal of Militene, Dadilu of Kaska, Uassurme of Tabal, Ushhitti of Tuna, Urballa of Tuhana, Tuhamme of Ishtunda, Urimme of Hubishna (and) Zabibe, the queen of Arabia, (to wit) gold, silver, tin, iron, elephant-hides, ivory, linen garments with multicolored trimmings, blue-dyed wool, purple-dyed wool, ebony-wood, boxwood-wood, whatever was precious (enough for a) royal treasure; also lambs whose hides were dyed purple, (and) wild birds whose spread-out wings were dyed blue, (further-more) horses, mules, large and small cattle, (male) camels, female camels with their foals.[35]

We can see from these parallel ancient Near Eastern records how well the biblical accounts fit in to the overall pattern of luxury goods, precious metals, dye-stuffs, semi-precious stones, animal hides, fine woods, and fine stones that were commonplace in ancient times in the building of temples and in royal households and treasuries. This gives a picture of fabulous wealth, of highly developed technologies in these materials, of extensive technical and crafts skills, and of wide spread trade in, exchange of, and looting of these materials across a vast area.

There were regional centers that were rich in both raw materials and in related craft skills, such as the Phoenician states on the coast of Lebanon. The Lebanese coast was a center of vast cedar forests, as well as of the fabled murex shellfish, which supplied what was probably the most highly desired and costly raw material in antiquity, the dye color purple, mentioned in the 2 Chronicles 2:13 verse relating the skills of Huram-abi, as well as in the list of tribute of Tiglath-Pileser III, above. The purple dye had a value many times that of gold. According to Boyd, "Twelve thousand shells would produce less than 2 g. (.07 oz.) of dye."[36]

In the verse detailing King David's vast preparations for the building of the temple, 2 Chronicles 29:4, mention is made of "the gold of Ophir" (called "gold of Parvaim" in 2 Chronicles 3:6 and in 1 Kings 9:28). Ophir may have been located in the southern Arabian peninsula, modern-day Yemen, and was also a source for gold, woods, and precious stones.[37]

The most important fabric mentioned in connection with the Temple of Jerusalem is of course linen, which was used in the priestly garments as well as in the various hangings inside the temple. Linen is the product of the flax plant, which was highly treasured in antiquity, and was harvested in lowland areas such as the Jordan Valley.[38] However, the finest quality of this fabric was almost certainly imported from Egypt.[39]

I Kings states that Solomon and Hiram entered into a peace treaty (1 Kings 5:12), and that Solomon levied a corvee labor force of 30,000 Israelites, who went to Lebanon in relays of 10,000 men each, staying in Lebanon one month, in Israel two, while 70,000 debris carriers assisted 80,000 stone masons in the hill country (1 Kings 5:13–18). 2 Chronicles adds an important and interesting detail, namely that Hiram offered to have his workers cut the timber, which would be brought on rafts by sea to Joppa (modern-day Haifa), from there to be offloaded and taken "up" to Jerusalem (2 Chronicles 2:15–16). A detail that is contradictory to the account of 1 Kings, and is probably to be attributed to the late, Post-Exilic conditions in which the Chronicler wrote, is that non-Israelite aliens performed the manual labor (2 Chronicles 2:17–18).

The primary building material was finely dressed ashlars, prepared in an off-site quarry. However, no stone was seen within the temple; every surface was covered with wood paneling, the walls and ceilings with cedar, the floors with cypress. Gilded olive wood doors formed the entrances to both *heikal* and *debir*. According to the account in 2 Chronicles, a veil of blue, purple, and crimson linen, with cherubim embroidered on it, was hung immediately before the Ark of the Covenant, separating the *debir* from the *heikal* (2 Chronicles 3:14; see also Exodus 26:31–35—the Priestly account of the Tabernacle).

The temple was a tripartite structure, on a straight axis, which means that the worshipper entering the front door would theoretically be able to proceed in a straight line to the Holy of Holies in the back, the *debir*. The building consisted of three distinct architectural units. The three units or rooms were the *'ulam*, porch or vestibule; the *heikal*, cella or nave, the word that comes in Hebrew to be used for the entire building; and the *debir*, the inner sanctuary or Most Holy Place, the Holy of Holies. The *debir* is said to be a structure built entirely of cedar wood, embedded within the five-cubit thick exterior walls (Ezekiel 41:2). This apparent fact of the debir as a completely wooden room, attached to the rear end of the building, will return to our attention in Chapter 2.[40] All inner surfaces are said to have been gilded, although some restrict this gilding only to the *debir*.[41] Some scholars assert that only the cherubim were gilded.[42] There is widespread skepticism on the part of scholars as to the amount of gold overlay that should actually be accepted and admitted for the temple. As mentioned above in reference to 1 Chronicles 29:2–5, the amount of gold of Ophir and silver that David claims to have laid in store for his son's building program is absolutely stupendous (225,000 pounds of gold). We can add to this amount the amount mentioned in 1 Kings 10, in the context of the visit to King Solomon of the Queen of Sheba, from the southern tip of the Arabian peninsula (modern-day Yemen). The text states that the queen "came to Jerusalem with a very great retinue, with camels bearing spices, and very much gold, and precious stones" (1 Kings 10:2). Then, later in the same chapter we read that "Now the weight of gold that came to Solomon in one year was six hundred and sixty-six talents of gold, besides that which came from the traffic of the merchants, and from all the kings of Arabia and from the governors of the land" (1 Kings 10:14–15).

In addition to giving us extraordinary insight into the nature of trade in that period, and of the sources of much of the luxury materials that went into the construction of the temple, this figure for the amount of gold is fascinating in comparison with the amount stated for David's preparations in 1 Chronicles 29:4 (3,000 talents). Are these numbers realistic? Most scholars think they are not.[43] However, comparing David's number (3,000 talents) with Solomon's (666 talents), it would have taken only four and one half years to accumulate David's amount at the one-year rate of Solomon's mentioned in 1 Kings 10:14. In any case, it needs to be pointed out that, in the light of ancient Near Eastern temple building, using Egypt as an example, Lanny Bell has written that "The generally drab appearance of most temples today is due to their ruinous condition. They have lost the gold plate or leaf that covered the tops of obelisks, the tips of flag masts, and parts of the walls; the brilliant paints and polychrome faience tiles or glass inlays that adorned the walls; and the elaborate furnishings that filled the chambers."[44] Ancient temples, as well as contemporary temples in much of Asia, utilized vast quantities of gold and other precious and semi-precious metals in their construction.

The records of ancient civilizations are filled with accounts of vast temple treasures in gold and silver. Alexander the Great is reported by Arrian to have taken 2,600 talents of gold and 600 of silver from Damascus, 50,000 talents of gold and 40,000 talents of raw silver and gold from Susa, as well as 120,000 talents of gold from Persepolis.[45] A medieval Arab conqueror of the Indian city of Malli, in the Punjab, reportedly sent 120 million *dirhams* of gold to Arabia, while another temple treasure at Multan was said to equal 2,397,600 *mithqal* (a gold coin weighing one and one half drams).[46] From more recent times the Red Palace of the Potala Palace in Lhasa, the place of rule of the Dalai Lamas, houses golden tombs of eight Dalai Lamas. One of these alone, that of the Fifth Dalai Lama (1617–1682 c.e.) is embellished with 3,700 kilograms of gold "thick as a cow's hide," while at its top sits a solid gold statue of the Bodhisattva Chenresi.[47]

The length of the temple was 60 cubits (a cubit equals approximately the distance between the elbow and the fingertips). Biblical evidence indicates that there were two cubits, a long cubit (the royal cubit) and a short cubit (the common cubit). The long or royal cubit has been estimated by one scholar at approximately 20.67[48] [= 52.5 cm.] inches. Its width was 20 cubits, its height 30 cubits. The *ulam* was 20 cubits wide and 10 cubits long, the *heikal* was 40 cubits long, and the *debir* was a cube, 20 cubits on each side.

The inner sanctuary was thus five cubits shorter than the rest of the building, presumably because the inner sanctuary stood over the Rock of Foundation, the original place of creation in the Israelite cosmogony.[49] The *debir* housed the Ark of the Covenant, with typical Near Eastern protective cherubim standing over it, thus forming the cosmic throne of the deity : "So the people sent to Shiloh, and brought from there the ark of the covenant of the Lord of hosts, who is enthroned on the cherubim" (1 Samuel 4:4). The *debir* truly brings the cosmic, mystical, esoteric character of the temple into clear focus. The cube shape is itself expressive of perfection, the perfection of deity, and within the mythology of ancient temple building is the typical shape of the heavenly temple.[50] The cube stands over the primeval Rock of Foundation, covering the powerhouse dynamo of creation itself. The Ark of the Covenant contains the tablets of the law, the holy scriptures, the eternal law upon which all reality is based.[51] It is these features which, above all, symbolize the temple's role as the "meeting place of heaven and earth."[52] The temple plan originated in heaven, with the heavenly temple. Perfection is the primary quality of heaven. This perfection is brought down to earth, and placed in the most auspicious piece of the earth's geography, the very place of creation, the preeminent holy mountain. The Holy of Holies, the *debir* IS "heaven on earth," the location of heaven on earth, thus it is the "throne of God," on earth (1 Samuel 4:4), because the real and actual throne of God is to be found in heaven.

The most dramatic evidence that we have in the Hebrew Bible for the distinction between, and the significance of, the heavenly throne comes from the callings of two of the greatest Israelite prophets: Isaiah and Ezekiel. The call of Isaiah appears in Isaiah 6:

> In the year that King Uzziah died I saw the Lord sitting upon a throne, high and lifted up; and his train filled the temple. Above him stood the seraphim; each had six wings; with two he covered his face, and with two he covered his feet, and with two he flew. And one called to another and said: 'Holy, holy, holy is the Lord of hosts; the whole earth is full of his glory.' And the foundations of the thresholds shook at the voice of him who called, and the house was filled with smoke (Isaiah 6:1–4).

Isaiah is here depicted as experiencing a vision of the Most Holy Place, or alternatively actually present within the *debir* of the Temple of Solomon.

The call of Ezekiel, on the other hand, occurred during the Babylonian exile, "as I was among the exiles by the river Chebar, the heavens were opened, and I saw visions of God" (Ezekiel 1:1). Thus the Temple no longer stood. His call, which encompasses the entire first chapter, depicts heaven itself, with God enthroned there on his actual throne, and with the various beings and creatures circling around in the midst of fire below the actual throne. The throne itself, and the deity, are depicted in terms of crystal-like brilliance, constructed of semi-precious stones, in the midst of thundering sounds, and gleaming, blazing light, fire, and brightness (Ezekiel 1:1–28).

So we have in the account of these two prophetic callings the primary distinction between heaven and earth, and the relationship between heaven and its earthly counterpart, the temple. For similar, even more fantastically detailed accounts of heaven, the heavenly throne, and inhabitants of the highest of the heaven, ad the deity, we can refer to the much later, Pseudepigraphical literature, particularly the Enoch books.[53]

These features serve to give us a clear understanding and basis of the pilgrimage aspect of the temple. It is definitely essential that believers "go to the mountain," to the earthly counterpart of heaven. "Three times in the year shall all your males appear before the Lord, the God of Israel."[54] Pilgrimage played an enormous role in the worship revolving around the Temple of Solomon, as it does with all temples. During festival periods, the population of Jerusalem would have at least doubled. In addition to the vast economic implications of this phenomenon, the temple propelled Jerusalem, otherwise a provincial center, into one of the premier cities of antiquity.[55] The *heikal* housed 10 golden lampstands, five on each of the north and south sides, the golden table for the showbread (Exodus 25:23–30), and the horned, gilded acacia wood altar of incense

(Exodus 25–27; 1 Kings 7:48–50). It is in the P document that we find a description of the golden seven-branched candlestick (Exodus 25:31–40).

The people of Israel were to "bring pure oil from beaten olives for the lamp, that a light may be kept burning continually…. He shall keep the lamps in order upon the lampstand of pure gold before the Lord continually" (Leviticus 24:1–4; Exodus 27:20–21). The altar for incense was to stand "before the veil that is by the ark of the testimony, before the mercy seat that is over the testimony, where I will meet with you" (Exodus 30–6). The purpose of the altar of incense is that "Aaron shall burn fragrant incense on it; every morning when he dresses the lamps he shall burn it, and when Aaron sets up the lamps in the evening, he shall burn it, a perpetual incense before the Lord throughout the generations" (Exodus 30:7–8).

The altar of incense plays a role in the single most important ordinance of the Israelite ritual year: the Day of Atonement. This was the only time during the year when the High Priest was allowed to enter the *debir*. The purpose of the Day of Atonement was to expiate the sins of the people, the priests, and any impurity that had accrued to the temple itself. The High Priest enters the *debir* twice on this occasion, once to make atonement for the priests, and once for the people. He takes the blood of a sacrificed bull into the *debir,* and sprinkles the blood "on the front of the mercy seat," and "before the mercy seat" seven times with his finger, this for the purpose of atoning for the sins of "himself and for his house" (i.e., for the Aaronites). During this time, he fills the *debir* with incense by means of a censer, "that the cloud of the incense may cover the mercy seat which is upon the testimony, lest he die" (Leviticus 16, passim). He then carries out the same procedure with the blood of one of two goats, a sacrifice for a sin offering for the sins of the people and for the impurity of the sanctuary. At this time, he sprinkles blood of the bull and the goat upon the four horns of the altar of incense. "There shall be no man in the tent of meeting [i.e., the temple] when he enters to make atonement in the holy place until he comes out and has made atonement for his house and for all the assembly of Israel." (Leviticus 16:17). Following these rituals, the second of two goats, which was preserved alive due to a lot (that is, the Urim and Thummim) cast by Aaron, was "presented alive" [i.e., "before the Lord," facing the ark inside the *debir*]. Aaron laid his hands upon the head of the goat, in order to "confess over him all the iniquities of the people of Israel, and all their transgressions, all their sins; and he shall put them upon the head of the goat, and send him away into the wilderness by the hand of a man who is in readiness. The goat shall bear all their iniquities upon him to a solitary land; and he shall let the goat go in the wilderness" (Leviticus 16:20–22).

The purpose of the gold table of the showbread ("the bread of the Presence"—Exodus 25:30), located in the *heikal,* was to hold a cereal offering of 12 cakes, in two rows of six, with pure frankincense on each row, "that it may go with the bread as a memorial portion to be offered by fire to the Lord" (Leviticus 24:7). The Aaronite priests were to order this offering each Sabbath, "before me always" (Exodus 25:30). As was always, and obviously the case with ancient priesthoods, "it [i.e., the cereal offering] shall be for Aaron and his sons, and they shall eat it in a holy place, because it is for him a most holy portion out of the offerings by fire to the Lord, a perpetual due" (Leviticus 24:9).

A three-story annex surrounded the *heikal* and the *debir,* but not the *ulam.* The annex had an entrance on the south side, and was accessed through a staircase that connected all three levels. The annex was joined to the *heikal* and the *debir* by means of cedar beams that were offset from the main walls "in order that the supporting beams should not be inserted into the walls of the house" (1 Kings 6:6;1 Kings 6:5–10). This annex structure was 15 cubits high in total height, as against the height of 30 cubits for the "house"—that is, the main side walls of the temple— which means that the annex did not extend upwards to the full height of the temple. The "windows...splayed and latticed,"[56] were therefore located on the sides of the outer walls, high above the annex. These are doubtless analogous to the clerestory windows high up on the walls of Egyptian temples, and "were for providing light to the main hall of the Temple."[57] The *debir* itself was in darkness: "Then Solomon said, 'The Lord has set the sun in the heavens, but has said that he would dwell in thick darkness.' I have built thee an exalted house, a place for thee to dwell in for ever" (1 Kings 8:12–13).

The presumed purpose of the annex was as a treasury, and as storage for ritual garments and objects. "Treasuries of the House of the Lord" are mentioned in 1 Kings 7:51, which held "the things which David his father had dedicated, the silver, the gold, and the vessels." Egyptian King Shishak (Shoshenq I of the 22nd Dynasty) invaded Palestine in the fifth year of King Rehoboam and "took away the treasures of the house of the Lord" (1 Kings 14:26). Other references to the storage of treasure in the temple are found in 1 Kings 15:15 and 18, and 2 Kings 12:18.[58] Temples all over the ancient Near East were economic powerhouses, centers of economic activity, and repositories of vast treasure.[59] At the time of King Hezekiah, there was not sufficient treasure in the temple treasuries for Hezekiah to be able to pay Assyrian king Sennacherib the 300 talents of silver and 30 talents of gold tribute that he demanded: "And Hezekiah gave him all the silver that was found in the house of the Lord, and in the treasuries of the king's house." In order to make up the shortfall, "Hezekiah stripped the gold from the doors of the temple of the Lord, and from the doorposts which Hezekiah king of Judah had overlaid and gave it to the king of Assyria."[60]

Two hollow, cast-bronze pillars (described as having been 18 cubits high in 1 Kings 7:15–22, but 35 cubits high in 2 Chronicles 3:15–17) stood in front of the *ulam*, named Jachin (the southernmost) and Boaz (the northernmost). The pillars had capitals of bronze, five cubits in height. The capitals were fitted out with a checker-work mesh, into which were carved pomegranate designs. One of the great debates regarding the temple is the placement of these two pillars. The implication seems to be that they were free-standing, "at the vestibule of the temple" (1 Kings 7:21—RSV), "at the portico of the Great Hall" (JPS Hebrew-English Tanakh), that is, standing free on the porch (the *ulam*).[61] However, many scholars have viewed them as engaged, that is forming a structural part of the *ulam* or entry porch, as 1 Kings 7:21 could be seen to imply: "He set up the pillars at the vestibule of the temple," translated by Ouellette "He set up the pillars of the vestibule of the Temple."[62] This would make the building a *bit Hilani* type, well known and documented from the Syro-Anatolian cultural realm in that time, meaning that the columns stood *in antis,* that is were engaged on either side of the porch entryway, supporting the awning or the extended side walls that projected outwards, to form the porch. A well-known eighth to seventh century B.C.E. pottery stand of a temple to the goddess Astarte from the site of Idalion in Cyprus, shows two lotus or palm-crowned capitals, supporting a small porch entryway.[63] This ceramic stand has been invoked by many scholars as a possible model on which to better understand the relationship of the pillars to the *ulam.*

The two bronze pillars carried cosmic connotations, founding the temple in the underworld while uniting it with the heavenly sphere. The names of the pillars symbolized the cosmic, universal rule of Yahweh and of the Davidic dynasty that the building of the temple founded and legitimized: Jachin meant that Yahweh had founded the dynasty and the temple, while Boaz meant that Yahweh's power emanates from the temple.[64] It was in front of these pillars that King Josiah recovenanted the people of Judah following the cleansing and restoration of the temple (2 Kings 23:2–3). The pillars have also been viewed as analogous to Egyptian *djed* pillars, symbolizing stability, or even as the twin pylon gateways into Egyptian temples, or as obelisks, standing on either side of the monumental [gateway] entrance to the temple. They would thus serve as the massive pillars of stability and of eternity through and over which the sun would rise each morning,[65] confirming the cosmic implications of the temple. The pylons at the front of Egyptian temples were viewed as two mountains, between which the sun rose each morning, as in the Egyptian hieroglyph *3ht*, "horizon."[66] The eastward orientation of the Temple of Solomon would reinforce this interpretation.

The temple was oriented toward the east. We get a clear picture of the eastern orientation of the temple in Ezekiel 8:16 where, in a time of corruption and disobedience, 25 men are described as standing "with their backs to the temple of the Lord, and their faces toward the east, worshiping the sun toward the east." There has been considerable debate over hundreds of years as to where the temple would have stood on the present *temenos* (the Temple Mount). The choices are: directly over the rock outcropping which is encompassed within and covered by the *Qubbat es-Sakhrah*—the Dome of the Rock; the area north of *Qubbat es-Sakhra;* the area south of *Qubbat es-Sakhra.* The intuitive choice for the location of the Temple of Solomon would naturally be the present-day location of the Dome of the Rock. Although I will discuss early medieval Christian views of the location of the temple in Chapter 5, and Muslim views in Chapter 6, suffice it to say here that the Crusaders renamed the Dome of the Rock *Templum Salmonis* following their capture of Jerusalem in 1099.[67] In other words they, and medieval Christianity in general, regarded the Dome of the Rock as the ancient location of the Temple of Solomon. Arguments have been made placing the temple north of the Dome of the Rock, on the same line as the Byzantine-period Golden Gate (which, in turn, was built on a much earlier gate) located in the northern quadrant of the eastern wall of the Temple Mount.[68] Leen Ritmeyer has argued exhaustively and convincingly for placement over *as-Sakhra,* and thus that the *debir* or most holy place would have stood over the rock outcropping that the Dome of the Rock shelters today.[69] He gives extremely interesting and useful reconstructions of "How the Temple Mount Developed" and of the various theories since 1864 regarding the extent of the Temple Mount and of the placement of the temple upon it.[70]

The theory placing the Temple north of the Dome of the Rock is the work of Israeli physicist Asher S. Kaufman. First, he considers the *as-Sakhra* as being too large to have been contained within the *debir* of the Temple of Solomon. Furthermore, Jewish ritual, namely the ritual of the Red Heifer (Numbers 19), requires direct sight lines from the location on the Mount of Olives where the heifer was slaughtered, such that the priest performing the ritual could look directly into the *heikal* of the Temple when he was sprinkling the blood towards the Holy of Holies (Mishnah *Middoth* 2:4;

Mishnah *Parah* 3:9, 4:2). The walls of the Temple Mount at that point on the East side were shorter so that the priest would have the direct line of sight across the Valley. Asher Kaufman was able to fix the probable location of the sacrifice based on the above-named factors. The resulting axis across the Temple Mount stands at about 100 yards north of the Dome of the Rock. On this axis, just to the East of the Western-most line of the Temple Mount enclosure wall, stands a pillared cupola from the sixteenth century, the Dome of the Tablets or Dome of the Spirits. It covers a rock outcropping that Kaufman identifies as the Rock of Foundation of Jewish tradition, the place that the Holy of Holies, the *debir*, enclosed. This line stands directly East of the Byzantine-period Golden Gate, thus establishing a much earlier gate (not identified or excavated at this point), as the Eastern gate of the Temple of Solomon.[71]

The overall impression of the temple precinct, standing on top of the stronghold of Zion and commanding the attention of all who approached from below, was that of a Near Eastern cosmic temple, sitting on top of the sacred mountain—the ultimate architectural expression of the heavenly temple revealed on the mountain of God, and built after the pattern revealed there (Exodus 25:8–9). The primordial waters of the abyss from the time of creation were harnessed, present in the symbolism of the bronze sea.[72] Everywhere were sacred trees and life-giving vegetation, both real-life and decorative (the walls of the nave and inner sanctum were carved with cherubim, palm trees, and flowers, and then gilded). The temple was the pinnacle of an ascending processional sequence, from the city below, up, through the gates on the east, through the courtyards with their gates, constantly ascending to an ever more sacred, holy, limited, restricted precinct.[73] The Book of Psalms emphasizes the ascension theme: "Who shall ascend the hill of the Lord? And who shall stand in his holy place?" (Psalms 24:3). The temple gates also play a major role in the Psalms: "Open to me the gates of righteousness, that I may enter through them and give thanks to the Lord. This is the gate of the Lord; the righteous shall enter through it."[74] The idea of the Rock of Foundation upon which the *debir* or Most Holy Place rested, which plays such an important part in the theology of the temple in later ages, is nowhere attested in the Hebrew Bible, *per se*. It (that is, the Rock of Foundation) is assumed based on three factors: (1) the raised floor of the inner sanctuary itself; (2) the widespread presence of similar ideas, particularly in Egyptian temple theology; and (3) the presence on the Temple Mount of the rock outcropping over which the Dome of the Rock was constructed, which since late antiquity has been widely assumed to have been the locus of the *debir*.

The key passage from antiquity that refers to this idea comes from the Talmud:

> Just as the navel is found at the center of a human being, so the land of Israel if found at the center of the world. Jerusalem is at the center of the land of Israel, and the temple is the center of Jerusalem, the Holy of Holies is at the center of the temple, the Ark is at the center of the Holy of Holies, and the Foundation Stone is in front of the Ark, which spot is the foundation of the world. (Midrash Tanhuma *Qedoshim* 10)

In ancient Israel, this Rock of Foundation played the same role as the primordial mound in Egypt: it was the first solid material to emerge from the waters of creation, and it was upon this stone the deity affected creation. According to Jewish legend, it was this primordial rock on which Jacob slept (Genesis 28:10–22), at the place he subsequently named Bethel. The Holy of Holies was then built over this same rock, and, according to Islamic tradition, it is the same rock from which the prophet Mohammed ascended into heaven, over which the third most sacred place in Islam, the Dome of the Rock, was constructed.[75] As in Egypt, the temple was thought to have been built over this sacred mound or rock. According to Lanny Bell "Typically constructed over a hillock or symbolic mound, this elevated room [the sanctuary] was the mythological center of the universe, where the primordial event of creation had occurred."[76] This is what, more than any other factor, establishes the temple as the Center, the goal of all pilgrimage, the site of the most sacred encounters between humankind and God.

There is another major difference between the accounts in 1 Kings and 2 Chronicles regarding the structure that divided the *heikal* from the *debir*. 1 Kings states that olivewood doors, carved with cherubim, palm trees, and flowers, overlaid with gold, separated the two chambers and gave access into the *debir* (1 Kings 6:31–32). 2 Chronicles describes this same entryway as having been covered by a "veil" (i.e., a curtain) "of blue, purple and crimson fabrics and fine linen, and worked cherubim on it" (2 Chronicles 3:14). Here, again, we are dealing with the probability that the 1 Kings account is historically accurate, while the Chronicler is writing from a time in the Post-Exilic period, with a rebuilt temple, where there probably was a veil, and not wooden doors.[77] We come here to one of the most important, yet enigmatic features of the temple, a feature with which we are well acquainted, and that figures importantly in the Tabernacle in the Wilderness as well, the "cherubim." As we have seen in 1 Samuel 4:4 "So the people sent to Shiloh, and brought from there the ark of the covenant of the Lord of hosts, who is enthroned on the cherubim" and in 2 Samuel 6:2, "And David arose and went with all the people who were with him from Baale-judah [i.e., Kiriath-jearim], to bring up from there the ark of God, which is called by name the Lord of hosts who sits enthroned on the cherubim." The two accounts of the building of the temple in 1 Kings and in 2 Chronicles give essentially the same description of the construction of the cherubim, which were placed inside the *debir*. For, in spite of the fact that we will later see the Ark brought from the tent wherein it had been installed by David, and that, as in the passages just quoted, the cherubim seem always to be associated with the ark during the earlier period, new cherubim were fashioned for it. They are enormous, winged creatures, 10 cubits tall, made of olivewood, overlaid with gold, each with two wings that measured five cubits each, which stand, as it were, over the ark. One of the wings of each creature extends in front of the ark, where the two wings meet, and one each touched the wall. They thus almost completely filled the room, and dwarfed the ark, over which they stood.[78] Both accounts have them "standing," facing the *heikal* (1 Kings 6:23–28; 2 Chronicles 3:10–14). What are the cherubim? It is universally accepted by scholars that they are virtually the exact equivalent of mythical protective figures that are associated with temples all over the ancient Near East. The word is actually a loan word from the Assyrian, *karibu*, in its sense of "a deity represented as making a gesture of adoration."[79] Several references from Late Babylonian texts describing the Temple of Marduk in Babylon mention a *ilu karibu*, a favorable deity, which stands at the door of the innermost shrine of the temple.[80] According to the Chronicler, there were two courtyards in front of the temple, a "court of the priests," and the "great court" (2 Chronicles 4:9).

According to the Deuteronomic record of Kings as well as the prophet Ezekiel, there were also two courts, mentioned in 2 Kings 21:5, Ezekiel 40:28 (an inner court), and Ezekiel 40:20 (an outer court). These courts had gates (Ezekiel 40:20), which presumably explains 2 Chronicles 4:9: "He made the court of the priests, and the great court, and doors for the court, and overlaid their doors [i.e., gates] with bronze." There was a massive enclosure wall separating the sacred acropolis off from areas of lesser sacrality. The Hebrew Bible describes this wall as having "three courses of hewn stone round about, and a course of cedar beams; so had the inner court of the house of the Lord, and the vestibule of the house."[81] Thus each of the two courts, plus the *ulam* were surrounded with such a massive enclosure wall. And of course, each wall was pierced with a massive bronze gateway, as mentioned above.

There are excellent visual examples of the forging of bronze temple doors, and of massive bronze gateways from civilizations on either side of that of ancient Israel. From Egypt in the time of Thutmosis III (1479–1425 B.C.E.), we have the Tomb of the Vizier Rekh-Mi-Re', in which there is a scene of the smelting of bronze doors with the caption: "Bringing Asiatic copper which His Majesty carried off from his victory in the Land of Retnu [Syria], in order to cast the two doors of the temple of Amun in Karkak, its surfaces overlaid with gold which gleams like the horizon of heaven."[82] A decree of Egyptian pharaoh Seti I relating to the temple of Seti I at Abydos state, of the temple doors: "Its enormous doors are made of wood from the Lebanon, while they are gilt with djam-gold and overlaid behind with copper. One feels refreshed seeing their form."[83] No such doors have survived from Egypt.[84] From ancient Assyria, in the time of King Shalmaneser III (859–825 B.C.E.), much closer in time to Solomon, we have the magnificently preserved bronze gates of Shalmaneser's palace at Balawat (ancient Imgur-Enlil).[85]

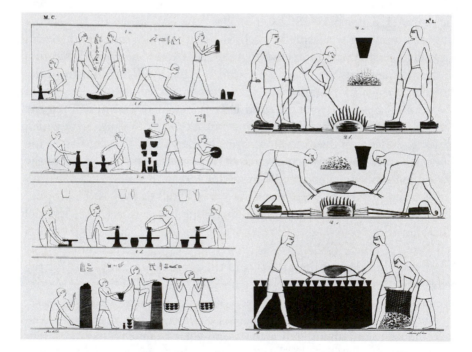

Carlo Lasinio, Engraver, Giuseppe Angelelli, Artist, Salvator Cherubini, Artist, Gaetano Rosellini, Artist, *Fabbricazione e cuocitura de vase testacei, Purificazione dell'oro* ("Fabrication of and firing of clay, and the purification of gold"). Right-hand side of plate: The process of casting a bronze door. Ippolito Rosellini, *I monumenti dell'Egitto e della Nubia*, Pisa: 1832–44. Vol. 2: *Monumenti Civili*, Plate 50. Asian and Middle Eastern Division, The New York Public Library, Astor, Lenox and Tilden Foundations.

Ezekiel states that the temple stood on a massive foundation, creating a sacred *temenos* that was six cubits thick (Ezekiel 41:8). Also, Ezekiel's vision of the Messianic temple, which was doubtless based on the temple as it existed in his time, records that 10 steps led from the pavement of the inner court to the entryway gate of the *ulam*. (Ezekiel 40:49).

The courtyard closest to the temple held a massive bronze ablution tank, the "molten sea" of 1 Kings 7:23, situated on the southeast corner of the temple. It was five cubits high, 10 cubits across, with a circumference of 30 cubits. A double line of gourd decorations encircled the sea just below the rim, and it stood on a base of 12 oxen, three each facing the cardinal directions, faces outward. Five wheeled bronze laver stands (ceremonial washing basins) stood at both the northern and southern corners of the

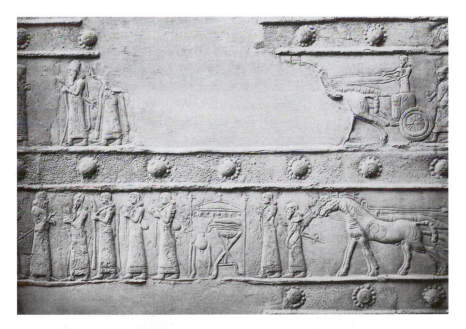

The Tribute of Unqu (Patinu). Samuel Birch, *The Bronze Ornaments of the Palace Gates of Balawat (Shalmaneser II [that is, Shalmaeser III], B.C.E. 859–825)*, Edited, with an introduction by Samuel Birch; with descriptions and translations by Theophilus G. Pinches. London: Society of Biblical Archaeology, 1880–[1902]. 5 fascs. In 1 volume, Plate E5. In the bottom register, middle, we see "…the royal pavilion—an elegant structure, the canopy of which is fringed with pomegranates, and the tops of the supporting columns ornamented with buds." (P. 5). [See also L. W. King, Editor, *Bronze Reliefs from the Gates of Shalmaneser, King of Assyria, B.C.E. 860–825*. London: Printed by the Order of the Trustees of the British Museum, 1915, Plate XXIX]. Asian and Middle Eastern Division, The New York Public Library, Astor, Lenox and Tilden Foundations.

temple. These stands were extremely elaborate, four cubits long, four cubits wide, and three cubits high. Panels set into the sides of the stands were carved with lions, oxen, and cherubim, while on a band at the top of the lavers were carved images of cherubim, lions, and palms. (1 Kings 7: 23–39). The "molten sea" doubtless plays the same role as the sacred lakes of Egyptian temples, such as Karnak. Water is a primary motif in temples all over the world, and is always present in the immediate precincts, as the waters of life, the fruit and trees of life, such as of Ezekiel's Messianic temple.[86] At the northeastern corner of the inner court, in front of the temple, was a wooden altar covered with bronze, used for burnt offerings, with horns at each of its four corners. This is the acacia wood altar of Exodus 27:1–2, five cubits long, five cubits wide, and three cubits high, which stood in front of the Tabernacle. David reconstructed this altar on the site of the threshing floor of Araunah, according to 2 Samuel 24:21, 25, and he (David) offered burnt offerings and peace offerings there in order to avert the Lord's wrath from the people of Israel. It was on this altar that Solomon offered up his prayer of dedication for the temple, first standing in front of it (1 Kings 8:22), then kneeling in front of it (1 Kings 8:54).[87]

The construction of the temple was completed in the Autumn of 953, but the dedication was postponed for 11 months to correspond with the Israelite New Year festivities (1 Kings 6:37–28; 1 Kings 8:2). At this point, as the final event in this massive, auspicious undertaking, the Ark of the Covenant, the tent that David had pitched for it (2 Samuel 6:12–17), and sacred objects that were inside the tent, were solemnly brought from their location in Zion, and the ark was placed within the *debir* "underneath the wings of the cherubim" (1 Kings 8:1–6). We have already seen that the Tent of Meeting, that is the Tabernacle, was located at Gibeon, where King Solomon went to consult it as an oracle before undertaking the building of the temple (2 Chronicles 2:3–5). Within this same sequence we are told that whereas David had taken the ark to Jerusalem, where he installed it inside a tent he had prepared, the Tent of Meeting, the Tabernacle, had remained in Gibeon (2 Chronicles 2:3). It is important to note that the "Ark which was brought by Solomon to the Temple was that of the Tabernacle."[88] Thus the ark was not fabricated anew for the temple at this time, as were for example the cherubim (1 Kings 6:23–28). The ark was a "primordial" object, part of the most ancient historical experience of the Israelites, originating in their wanderings period, at the time that it was housed within the Tent of Meeting. The ark was therefore now brought to Jerusalem and installed within the *debir* of the temple. Both the accounts in 1 Kings and in 2 Chronicles make reference to a puzzling detail regarding the ark. They state that its poles, that is the poles that carried and cushioned the ark, were so long that, once it was installed inside the *debir,* underneath the protective wings of the cherubim, that they "were seen from the holy place before the inner sanctuary; but they could not be seen from outside" (1 Kings 8:8; 2 Chronicles 5:9). The meaning of this passage is that the poles, which were never to be removed from the ark (Exodus 25:15), stuck out into the *heikal,* and that thus the ark was placed inside the *debir* length wise. This is an extremely important, though seemingly minor point, that has never been adequately discussed or explained. We will return to this issue in Chapter 2.

We come now to an issue not yet fully confronted, but one that must be understood in order to get a clear picture of the Temple of Solomon. That is the entire relationship of the Tabernacle in the Wilderness of Exodus 25–27 to the temple. The Tabernacle is a kind of proto-Temple, "The Temple building is understood as a permanent form of the original Israelite sanctuary, which had been a tent."[89] The wilderness experience of ancient Israel colors, influences, and hovers over all subsequent Israelite history and theology. We cannot understand the temple without an understanding of the events and experiences detailed in the books of Exodus, Numbers, and Deuteronomy. Of particular importance for us here are chapters 25–40 of Exodus, describing the construction of the tabernacle, ark, and the priestly garments.

This section of the Pentateuch, along with the Book of Numbers, is attributed to the Priestly writer (P) in the theory of the Documentary History of the Pentateuch. We have described above the Deuteronomic (D) content and date of the Hebrew Bible. The P source is generally assigned to the Post-Exilic Period, perhaps to somewhere around 515–450 B.C.E.[90] The Priestly writers are obviously priests, and have as their goal the presentation of the history of Israel from the point of view of the cult, and in particular to attempt to return Israel to the purity and holiness of the Mosaic period, and before that to the Covenant promises of Abraham, and to the cultic purity of the period of the wilderness wanderings, when the tabernacle and the ark signaled Yahweh's abiding presence among his covenant people.[91] Although the date of P is conventionally thus set so late in Israel's history, long after the Temple of Solomon had been destroyed, and although its primary focus is to establish the greater purity, holiness, and authenticity of the much earlier period, predating the period of the kings, it is not justified to use this late date as a reason to deny the historicity of the accounts of Exodus, Numbers, and Deuteronomy, as is the case with orthodox scholarship. Indeed, Menaham Haran dates all literary elements of the Pentateuch (J—the Yahwist, E—the Elohist, D, P) to the period of the First Temple. He writes "that P is the literary product of circles of the

Jerusalemite priesthood of the First Temple, not of the Second Temple period." And further

> It is maintained here, therefore, that all the sources of the Pentateuch—the most sacred part of the Old Testament canon—did in fact attain literary crystallization during the First Temple period, differing from each other only in character and dates of composition. P, written in the form of a treatise which covers the whole span of time from the primordial age until after the conquest of Canaan, actually parallels J and E, though it is later then them, while D is exceptional among them all in that it is cast in a rhetorical mold.[92]

To read the Hebrew Bible, and to immerse oneself in the histories, customs, and particularly temple building and cultic practices of the neighbors of the Israelites, is to convince one of the genuinely archaic, historically reliable, chronologically early authenticity of the Pentateuchal narratives, particularly, as we are concerned here, with the traditions of wanderings, the conquest of Canaan, the period of the Judges and early kingship, and of the period of the building of the First Temple. That is, although the final form that these various literary strands took is many centuries removed from the putative dates of the events themselves, and although the documents are colored and influenced by events of the times in which they were composed, and by theological issues that were prominent in the time of the final form of the document, the documents contain many elements, narratives, and so on, that are genuinely archaic, and actually date from the time of the events themselves, many centuries earlier.

Having said this however, it is necessary to state that virtually no mainstream scholar accepts the historicity or actuality of the Book of Exodus narratives regarding the construction of the ark, tabernacle, the priestly garments, and other cultic objects relating to the tabernacle (Exodus 25–39). The consensus of opinion regarding these narratives is that they are based on two elements, that is, within the P document: (1) the realities of the Temple of Solomon, as it existed in the time during which the P document was being formed, which were retrojected back onto a glorious past, the time of the wilderness wanderings, the time when Yahweh dwelt in a tent; and (2) authentic elements of the distant past, including the period of the wilderness wanderings, which had been preserved in historical memory, and as parts of books, archives, and traditions of the people of Israel.[93]

Thus, the ark and tabernacle and priestly garments of Exodus 25–39 are those of the Temple of Solomon. In fact, all the cultic objects, excluding the ark itself, are described as having been manufactured, including in different materials, in the 1 Kings and 2 Chronicles narratives of the building of the Temple of Solomon. For example, the cherubim of the ark of Exodus 25:18 are of pure gold, whereas those of 1 Kings and 2 Chronicles are made of gilded olive wood. The tables and lamp stands, of pure gold in Exodus 25–26, are fashioned in bronze in the 1 Kings and 2 Chronicles narratives.

There can be no doubt that the people of Israel wandered for a period of time in the Sinai desert and the areas of Edom and Moab, on the eastern side of the Jordan Rift Valley. Their chief shrine was doubtless a tent structure, and the primary cultic object of this tent was an ark. It was in this structure that they consulted their god, and the place where their god visited them:

> Now Moses used to take the tent and pitch it outside the camp, far off from the camp; and he called it the tent of meeting. And everyone who sought the Lord would to out to the tent of meeting, which was outside the camp. Whenever Moses went out to the tent, all the people rose up, and every man stood at his tent door, and looked after Moses, until he had gone into the tent. When Moses entered the tent, the pillar of cloud would descend and stand at the door of the tent, and the Lord would speak with Moses. (Exodus 33:9)

To get a complete understanding of this process we must add: "In the tent of meeting, outside the veil which is before the testimony, Aaron and his sons shall tend it from evening to morning before the Lord" (Exodus 27:21). In other words, the ark was inside the tent, in the most holy place. The purpose of the ark, and of the cherubim who stood over it, facing each other, their wings overshadowing the ark was "There I shall meet with you, and from above the mercy seat, from between the two cherubim that are upon the ark of the testimony, I will speak with you of all that I will give you in commandment for the people of Israel" (Exodus 25:22). The ark contained the tablets of the law (Exodus 25:21; 1 Kings 8:9).

We thus come now to a description of those aspects of the Temple of Solomon that are not described, or at least not in significant detail, in the Deuteronomic History (1 Kings) or by the Chronicler (2 Chronicles): the ark itself, the priestly garments, the priests themselves, and the temple festivals. For a description of these, we are dependent on P.[94]

The ark was constructed of acacia wood, two and one half cubits long, one and one half cubits wide, and one and one half cubits tall. That means a box, approximately 52½ inches long, and 31½ inches wide and tall, or about the size of a medium-sized office desk. It was gilded within and without. Golden rings were place at the four corners on the bottom, and gilded acacia wood poles, which were never to be removed from the ark, were constructed in order to carry the edifice. Scholars are divided as to the stance of the Ark within the *debir*, that is, whether its long side or short side could be seen from the *heikal*. Busink thought that it was placed with its long, or wide side showing, based on 1 Kings 8:7, and that the poles were in place at all times.[95] Ritmeyer assumes that the Ark was placed with its short side showing, the reason being that only in this way could the poles be removed.[96] I am assuming here that the poles were not removed (1 Kings 8:8), as Busink shows in his reconstruction.[97] The "testimony" (Hebrew *edut*—that is, the tablets of the law) was to be deposited inside (Exodus 25:10–16). A pure gold "mercy seat" (Hebrew *kapporet*—"cover") was placed on top, two and one half cubits long, one and one half cubits wide. The two golden cherubim, facing each other as they stood above the ark, spread out their wings, "overshadowing the mercy seat" (Exodus 25:17–21). "There I will meet with you, and from above the mercy seat, from between the two cherubim that are upon the ark of the testimony, I will speak with you of all that I will give you in commandment for the people of Israel" (Exodus 25:22).

The actual priestly functioning inside the temple, "before the Lord," was reserved to Aaron and his posterity. These are the Aaronites, the Aaronite priesthood, and it is to them that the high priesthood is assigned.[98] They alone may enter the temple,[99] and function in the holy place. Their core roles are described in two important places in the Hebrew Bible: (1) Deuteronomy 33:10, the Blessing of Moses: "And of Levi he said, Give to Levi thy Thummim, and thy Urim to thy godly one, whom thou didst test at Massah, with whom thou didst strive at the waters of Meribah; who said of his father and mother, 'I regard them not'; he disowned his brothers, and ignored his children, For they observed thy word, and kept thy covenant. They shall teach Jacob thy ordinances, and Israel thy law; they shall put incense before thee, and whole burnt offering upon thy altar." (2) 1 Samuel 2:28: "And I chose him out of all the tribes of Israel to be my priest, to go up to my altar, to burn incense, to wear an ephod before me." The three core functions are thus to wear an ephod, to burn incense, and to sacrifice burnt offerings, *before the Lord*.[100] These three functions can only be carried out by the Aaronites within the temple itself.

"For them there were prescribed the most elaborate, costly, beautiful, heavy garments, along with oracular instruments with which to inquire the will of the Lord."[101] The garments consisted of "a breastpiece, an ephod, a robe, a coat of checker work, a turban, and a girdle" (Exodus 28:4). All of the garments were to be constructed of gold, blue, purple, and scarlet yarns and fine linen. The ephod was a kind of apron, held on with shoulder straps tied around the back of the neck. To it was attached a band of the same material. Two semi-precious stones, each engraved with the names of six of the tribes of Israel, with gold frames, were attached, one each, to the straps of the ephod, upon the shoulders of priest. These stones are for "remembrance of the sons of Israel, and Aaron shall bear their names before the Lord upon his two shoulders for remembrance" (Exodus 28:12).

A "breastpiece of judgment (or decision)" a pouch that hung from the shoulder straps of the ephod by gold chain, had four rows of three semi-precious stones set into it, each one with a name of one of the tribes of Israel engraved into it, "So Aaron shall bear the names of the sons of Israel in the breastpiece of judgment upon his heart, when he goes into the holy place, to bring them to continual remembrance before the Lord" (Exodus 28:29).

The Urim and Thummim, oracular, mantic, divinatory stones of some type, were placed within the pouch. Two vivid, dramatic, and instructive instances of the use of the Urim and Thummim appear within the Books of Numbers and 1 Samuel. In Numbers, the Lord has chosen Joshua to succeed Moses. Moses is instructed to lay his hands upon Joshua, to impart to him some of Moses' authority. Then, Joshua must appear before the priest Eleazar, "who shall inquire for him by the judgment [i.e., the decision] of the Urim before the Lord." Thus the Urim was used to confirm a divinely ordained appointment.

In 1 Samuel 14 Saul used the Urim and Thummim to cast lots, to determine where guilt lay, whether with him and his son Jonathan, or with the people of Israel. "Therefore Saul said, 'O Lord, God of Israel, why has thou not answered thy servant this day? If guilt is in me or in Jonathan my son, O Lord God of Israel, give Urim; bit if this guilt is in thy people Israel, give Thummim." The lot favored the people of Israel, so Saul again had it cast between him and Jonathan, and it favored Saul.[102] The priest wore a blue robe underneath the ephod. The opening at the neck had a woven fringe. The garment had a fringe of pomegranates of blue, purple, and scarlet, with golden bells in between each pomegranate. Underneath this garment the priest wore a linen robe in checker work and a turban. A plate of pure gold was attached to the turban, at the forehead, with a piece of blue lace. The plate was engraved "Holy to the Lord," and served to "take upon himself any guilt incurred in the holy offering which the people of Israel hallow as their holy gifts" (for all of the above see Exodus 28).

The garments that the high priest wore on the Day of Atonement were different from those described here. They were of a simple linen fabric:

"He shall put on the holy linen coat, and shall have the linen breeches on his body, be girded with the linen girdle, and wear the linen turban; these are the holy garments. He shall bathe his body in water, and the put them on" (Leviticus 16:4). The type of linen described here is Hebrew *bad*, a plain weave, distinct from the finer grade of linen, *shesh*, mentioned for example in Exodus 28:5–8, in connection with the multi-colored brocades. According to Haran "The four plain linen vestments reflect a holiness transcending that of gold and wool-linen mixture, and the text finds it necessary to emphasize that 'they are holy garments' (Leviticus 16:4)."[103]

There was another category of priests, the so-called Levites, as in the phrase "Priests and Levites" (1 Kings 8:4). "Priests" refers to the Aaronite high priesthood, "Levites" to members of the tribe of Levi whose priestly task it is to serve the Aaronites, and to minister in the outer precincts of the temple:

> And the Lord said to Moses, Bring the tribe of Levi near, and set them before Aaron the priest, that they may minister to him. They shall perform duties for him and for the whole congregation before the tent of meeting, as they minister in the tabernacle; they shall have charge of all the furnishings of the tent of meeting, and attend to the duties for the people of Israel as they minister at the tabernacle. And you shall give the Levites to Aaron and his sons; they are wholly given to him from among the people of Israel. (Numbers 3:5–9)

"During the wanderings in the desert they had two tasks: first, the 'work,' *abodah,* and the portage of the tabernacle, that is, its dismantling, carrying, and reassembling in a new station; second, the guarding of the tabernacle and its appurtenances, by forming a barrier between the priestly holiness and the people, so as to prevent the Israelites from approaching too closely and from coming into contact with this holiness," the "contagious holiness" in the phraseology of.[104]

The Hebrew Bible constantly details and emphasizes the differing grades of holiness relating to the temple: the most holy place is the *debir.* As one moves away from that sanctuary, the level of holiness decreases, until one would be totally outside the temple precincts. There are two classes of priests to minister to this holiness, one of whom alone is worthy to enter the temple. The temple furnishings and temple clothes also reflect this differentiation.[105] The articles of furniture in the temple itself, that is inside the *heikal* and the *debir* are of gold or gold covered wood, while those in the courtyard are of bronze.[106] In addition to the Day of Atonement, described above, there were three times in the Israelite religious calendar when all

Israelite males were to appear at the temple: "Three times in the year shall all your males appear before the Lord God, the God of Israel." (Exodus 34:23. See also Exodus 23:17 and Deuteronomy 16:16.) It is important to remember that the Hebrew phrase "appear before the Lord" (Hebrew *lipne Yahweh*) refers to the temple. "In general, any cultic activity to which the biblical text applies the formula 'before the Lord' can be considered an indication of the existence of a temple at the site, because this expression stems from the basic conception of the temple as a divine dwelling-place and actually belongs to the temple's technical terminology."[107]

These three festivals are the pilgrimage festivals (Hebrew *hag*), which are national festivals of gathering to the holy sanctuary: the feasts of Unleavened Bread (the barley harvest—the first month, *Abib*—April—May), Weeks (the wheat harvest—seven weeks following the wave offering of first fruits from Unleavened Bread), and Booths (the produce of the fields and of the wine press are brought in at the end of harvest season in the Autumn) (Exodus 23:14–17). These are times of which the Prophet Isaiah speaks "you shall have a song in the night when the holy feast is kept; and gladness of heart, as when one sets out to the sound of the flute, to go to the mountain of the Lord, to the Rock of Israel" (Isaiah 30:29). The Hebrew word *hag* is used only of these three festivals in the Old Testament, and it is these three that "involve[s] a pilgrimage to the temple."[108]

The feast of Unleavened Bread is connected with the feast of Passover, celebrating the passage of Israel out of Egypt and the preservation of the Israelite firstborn at the time the firstborn of Pharaoh were destroyed (Exodus 12). Passover was to be celebrated from the first to the 14th days of the month of *Abib*, and on the 15th day of that month the festival of Unleavened Bread began, lasting seven days. It was a first fruits harvest, centering on the requirement to "bring the sheaf of the first fruits of your harvest to the priest; [i.e., an Aaronite] and he shall wave the sheaf before the Lord, that you may find acceptance; on the morrow after the Sabbath the priest shall wave it" (Leviticus 23:10–11). In addition to the wave offering, the Israelites were required to sacrifice a male lamb without blemish as a burnt offering, a cereal offering of fine flour mixed with oil, and a drink offering of wine (Leviticus 23:12–13).

The festival of Weeks took place seven weeks following the day after the Sabbath of the wave offering (Greek Pentecost). The offerings included a cereal offering of new grain, two loaves baked with leaven, seven one year old lambs without blemish, a young bull and two rams. These, along with the cereal offering and a drink offering were burnt in fire "an offering by fire, a pleasing odor to the Lord" (Leviticus 23:18). Further, a male goat was to be offered as a sin penance, and two male lambs a year old as peace offerings. These were waved "before the Lord" with the first fruit bread offerings" (Leviticus 23:15–21).

The Day of Atonement fell on the 10th day of the seventh month (September–October). Beginning on the 15th day of the same month, the festival of Booths lasted for seven days. After the produce of the fields and the vines had been gathered in, for seven days fire offerings were to be made to the Lord. "And you shall take on the first day the fruit of goodly trees, branches of palm trees, and boughs of leafy trees, and willows of the brook; and you shall rejoice before the Lord your God seven days (vs. 40). "You shall dwell in booths for seven days; all that are native in Israel shall dwell in booths, that your generations may know that I made the people Israel dwell in booths when I brought them out of the land of Egypt" (Leviticus 23:26–43).

The Temple of Solomon was finished in the eighth month, the month of *Bul*, October–November (1 Kings 6:38). The dedication was delayed for 11 months, until the seventh month following, the month of *Ethanim*, or *Tishri*, September–October (1 Kings 8:2), so that the dedication could take place during the New Year festivities. An important aspect of biblical criticism is founded in the prayer of dedication that Solomon gave at this time (1 Kings 8:23–61). The king dedicated the temple to the "name" of Yahweh (vss. 17, 18, 19, 20, 44, 48), rather than emphasizing that it was his "dwelling place," as was the case in more archaic Biblical passages, such as Psalms 74:2 ("Remember Mount Zion, where thou hast dwelt") and 76:2 ("His abode has been established in Salem, his dwelling place in Zion"), which are based more in the ancient Near Eastern views of temples. The "name" theology is seen as a more moderating influence, the reform movement of King Josiah, and thus the Deuteronomic revision of the Books of Samuel and Kings.[109]

For the dedication, King Solomon had a new altar constructed, one not heretofore mentioned in the Hebrew Bible, namely a bronze altar of burnt offerings, which was placed in the courtyard in front of the temple, in "the middle of the court that was before the house of the Lord" (1 Kings 8:64). The dimensions of this altar were "twenty cubits long, and twenty cubits wide, and ten cubits high" (2 Chronicles 4:1), in contrast to the regular altar of incense that stood in front of the temple, which was "five cubits long and five cubits broad…and its height shall be three cubits" (Exodus 27:1). The purpose of this altar was that "for there he offered the burnt offering and the cereal offering and the fat pieces of the peace offerings," and the reason for the larger size was "because the bronze altar that was before the Lord was too small to receive the burnt offerings and the cereal offering and the fat pieces of the peace offerings" (1 Kings 8:64), that is, because of the enormous size of the crowd assembled for the dedication, and the vast number of sacrifices required.[110]

The history of the Temple of Solomon for the duration of its existence, until its total destruction by the Babylonians in 587 B.C.E., is one of perennial looting, desecration, and a brief period of reform in the time of King Josiah. In the fifth year of Solomon's successor, Rehoboam,[111] Pharaoh Shoshenq I (Biblical Shishak) raided Jerusalem and "took away the treasures of the house of the Lord and the treasures of the king's house; he took away everything." (1 Kings 14:26). During the reign of Asa as king over the Kingdom of Judah (ca. 908–867 B.C.E.), the king "took all the silver and gold that were left in the treasures of the house of the Lord [i.e. all that were left after the depredations of Pharaoh Shoshenq] and gave them into the hands of his servants; and King Asa sent them to Ben-hadad the son of Tabrimmon, the son of Hezion, king of Syria, who dwelt in Damascus, saying, 'Let there be a league between me and you, as between my father and your father: behold, I am sending to you a present of silver and gold.'"[112] By the time of Jehoash, who reigned for 40 years as King of the Kingdom of Judah[113] (836–798 B.C.E.), the temple had obviously fallen into serious disrepair. The king attempted a policy of forced donations in order to accumulate enough resources to carry out the repairs. After having overcome corrupt priests, who were diverting the donations to themselves, he was able to fashion a workable program of repairs, employing "carpenters," "builders," "masons," and "stonecutters" for the work. However "there were not made for the house of the Lord basins of silver, snuffers, bowls, trumpets, or any vessels of gold, or of silver, from the money that was brought into the house of the Lord, for that was given to the workmen who were repairing the house of the Lord with it" (2 Kings 12:11–15). Later in the same reign, Hazael, King of Syria threatened Jerusalem, and Jehoash took all the remaining treasures of the temple and gave them to Hazael as a bribe not to attack (2 Kings 12:17–18).

During the reign of Amaziah[114] (798–769 B.C.E.), king of Judah, war broke out between him and Jehoash, king of the northern kingdom of Israel. Jehoash defeated Amaziah, took him hostage, and entered Jerusalem where "he seized all the gold and silver, and all the vessels that were found in the house of the Lord and in the treasuries of the king's house" (2 Kings 14:14).

The next king of Judah in whose reign there were significant events relating to the temple was Ahaz[115] (743–727 B.C.E.). The biblical record reports that Ahaz traveled to Damascus to meet with the Assyrian King Tiglath-pileser III, who had recently conquered the northern Kingdom of Israel, and had received a gift of vassalage from Ahaz of "silver and gold that found in the house of the Lord and in the treasures of the king's house" (2 Kings 16:8). While in Damascus Ahaz saw an altar, presumably a temple altar of a Syrian deity. He sent detailed plans of this altar to the priest Uriah, instructing him to build a similar altar in Jerusalem, and to install it in front of the temple, displacing the Solomonic bronze altar (that is, the larger altar of burnt offerings that Solomon had constructed for the temple dedication—1 Kings 8:64) to the north side of the new altar. Upon his return, Ahaz reviewed the new altar, found it to his liking, and "drew near to the altar, and went up on it, and burned his cereal offering, and poured his drink offering, and threw the blood of his peace offerings upon the altar" (2 Kings 16:13). Thus the king was acting as a priest.[116] Additionally, the king commanded the priest Uriah that "Upon this great altar burn the morning burnt offering, and the evening cereal offering and the king's burnt offering, and his cereal offering, with the burnt offering of all the people of the land, and their cereal offering, and their drink offering; and throw upon it all the blood of the burnt offering, and all the blood of the sacrifice; but the bronze altar shall be for me to inquire by" (2 Kings 16:15–16). Thus the king reserved the old Solomonic altar for his private consultation and worship (2 Kings 16:15). To increase his apostasy he then had the 10 bronze-wheeled laver stands that stood at the southern and northern corners of the temple (1 Kings 7:27–37) stripped of their lavers (basins), and had the bronze sea removed from its stand of twelve oxen, and placed on a stone base, "because of the king of Assyria."[117] The reign of Hezekiah[118] (715–687 B.C.E.) over the Kingdom of Judah was an exceptionally crucial and momentous time in the history of the Kingdom of Judah. The northern Kingdom of Israel had been destroyed in 721 B.C.E. by the Assyrian king Sargon II, and the inhabitants carried off into forced exile and dispersion (2 Kings 17). Hezekiah was likewise menaced by the Assyrian king Sennacherib, whose Annals record his invasion and siege of Jerusalem, and that he made Hezekiah "a prisoner in Jerusalem, his royal residence, like a bird in a cage."[119] The Bible reports that Hezekiah gave Sennacherib as tribute "all the silver that was found in the house of the Lord, and in the treasuries of the king's house. At that time Hezekiah stripped the gold from the doors of the temple of the Lord and from the doorposts which Hezekiah king of Judah had overlaid and gave it to the king of Assyria" (2 Kings 18:15–16). Sennacherib's Annals report that Hezekiah sent to the Assyrian capital at Nineveh "together with 30 talents of gold, 800 talents of silver, precious stones, antimony, large cuts of red stone, couches (inlaid) with ivory, *nimedu*-chairs (inlaid) with ivory, elephant hides, ebony-wood, boxwood (and) all kinds of valuable treasures, his (own) daughters, concubines, male and female musicians."[120] During the siege, Sennacherib had a threatening letter sent to Hezekiah, which the king "spread before the Lord," inside the *debir*, standing directly before the "Lord the God of Israel, who are enthroned above the cherubim....Incline thy ear" (2 Kings 19:15–16). This is the most dramatic evidence in the Hebrew Bible of the intense, intimate, full access that a king of Judah, obviously a nonpriest, had to the temple, including its innermost and holiest parts.[121] We saw above how David, Solomon, and Ahaz ministered at the altars in clearly priestly roles.

Hezekiah's son, Manasseh (ca. 697–642 B.C.E.), had probably the longest reign of any king of Judah, and is reckoned by the Deuteronomist as the most wicked king. To him are attributed all of the most horrific sins, including possibly infanticide, worshipping the gods of Canaan and other forms of apostasy, and practicing witchcraft and sorcery, introducing "houses of male cult prostitutes" into the temple courts (2 Kings 23:7), and placing altars to Canaanite sky gods in the temple courts. His most outlandish and corrupt move was that "the graven image of Asherah that he had made he set in the house of which the Lord said to David and to Solomon his son, 'In this house and in Jerusalem, which I have chosen out of all the tribes of Israel, I will put my name forever'" (2 Kings 21:7). Asherah was a Canaanite goddess, who is even in some recently discovered inscriptions described as the "consort" of Yahweh.[122] The obvious implication is that he had the Asherah placed in the *debir*, because that would be the only proper location for the statue of a deity in ancient Near Eastern temples.[123] Haran uses this evidence, along with other implications of Manasseh's actions, and subsequent history, to assume that it was at this time that the Ark was removed from the Holy of Holies, thus ending its role as the most renowned, auspicious, and charismatic sacred object in world history. Its actual presence is never again mentioned in the Hebrew Bible with respect to the Temple of Solomon, nor with any phase of the Second Temple. We will return to this absence, and to its profound implications and consequences, when we discuss the Second Temple in Chapter 3.

The Apocryphal Book of Maccabees states that Jeremiah "received an oracle" "that the tent and the ark should follow with him, and that he went out to the mountain where Moses had gone up [i.e., Mount Nebo, in the Transjordan] and had seen the inheritance of God. And Jeremiah came and found a cave, and he brought there the tent and the ark and the altar of incense, and he sealed up the entrance" (2 Maccabees 2:4–5). According to this same account, some followers of the prophet attempted to find the cave, and, when they could not, were rebuked by him, saying that the hiding place would not be revealed until God gathered his people together again (2 Maccabees 2:6–8). "For times when the temple was lost, Jewish tradition asserted that the vessels were not lost or destroyed, but were hidden away until God chose to provide another temple for them."[124] The Kingdom of Judah experienced one last recovery, one final moment of moral and spiritual greatness, before the tragic, violent, catastrophic end. This occurred during the reign of Josiah as king of Judah (ca. 648–609 B.C.E.). During a mandated cleaning and repair of the temple, the high priest, Hilkiah, found a scroll in the temple, possibly in a rubbish pile.[125] This scroll, a "Book of the Law," which in the opinion of most scholars was the Book of Deuteronomy, or some version of it[126] was brought to Josiah and read to him. He immediately "rent his clothes," in grief and shame, for "great is the wrath of the Lord that is kindled against us, because our fathers have not obeyed the words of this book, to do according to all that is written concerning us" (2 Kings 22:8–13). Josiah then brought all the people to the temple, where, standing in front of one of the bronze pillars in front of the temple, he read the Book of the Law, and covenanted the people that they would live according to the laws and precepts in the book.[127] He then instituted a massive reform, according to which the Canaanite altars and high places were destroyed, their priests were killed, the temple was cleansed of the depredations of Manasseh, sorcerers were destroyed, and other abominations were removed and destroyed (2 Kings 23:1–24). The ceremony of the covenant, in which the king stood before the bronze pillar, is a well-attested type of covenant ritual associated with ancient Near Eastern temples, and further serves to bring the Temple of Solomon into a more universal pattern of temple worship and ritual.[128]

The Babylonians defeated the Assyrians and Egyptians at the battle of Carchemish in 605 B.C.E., this opening up the Kingdom of Judah to direct invasion by the Babylonians. The first invasion came in 597 B.C.E., under Babylonian king Nebuchadnezzar, and Judahite king Jehoiachin. The number of Jews deported ranged between 3,000 and 10,000. "The king of Babylon [Nebuchadnezzar]…carried off all the treasures of the house of the Lord, and the treasures of the king's house, and cut in pieces all the vessels of gold in the temple of the Lord, which Solomon king of Israel had made, as the Lord had foretold" (2 Kings 24:12–13). Jehoiachin was one of these captives, and he was replaced by Zedekiah, an uncle of Jehoiachin who was installed by the Babylonian king (2 Kings 24). Zedekiah rebelled against Babylonian rule, and in 587/586 B.C.E. Nebuchadnezzar returned, and completely destroyed Jerusalem, carrying off all its inhabitants into Babylonian Exile. The temple was completely destroyed. The Hebrew Bible records the dismantling, breaking up, and carrying away into Babylon of the bronze artifacts of the temple, including the pillars, and of the gold and silver (2 Kings 25:13–17). The tragic end of Jerusalem and of the temple, the carrying off of its people, the sorrow, the desolation, the remorse, are all beautifully and poetically recorded in the Book of Lamentations: "The roads to Zion mourn, for none come to the appointed feasts. All her gates are desolate, her priests groan" (1:4); "The Lord has scorned his altar, disowned his sanctuary; he has delivered into the hand of the enemy the walls of her palaces; a clamor was raised in the house of the Lord as on the day of an appointed feast." (2:7).

CHAPTER 2

The World of the First Temple

The single most important fact regarding the Temple of Solomon is that there are no physical remains of the structure. There is not a single object or artifact that can be indubitably connected with the Temple of Solomon. In recent years a number of objects have surfaced in the Israel antiquities market, some of which were said to have had a connection with the Temple of Solomon. Most prominent among these was the ivory pomegranate inscribed in Hebrew with the phrase "Sacred donation for the priests in the House of Yahweh." This object, which entered the literature as an authentic remnant of the Temple of Solomon,[1] and was widely accepted and discussed, has now been stated by the Israel Antiquities Authority to be an ancient object but supplied with a modern, forged inscription.[2] It is highly unlikely, but of course not impossible, that authentic objects connected with the Temple of Solomon will appear in the future. In any case, if such objects continue to come forth in the antiquities trade, without archaeological provenance, it is improbable that they will be taken seriously or accepted within the body of evidence for the Temple of Solomon by scholars.

Given the nature of the present-day site, the *al-Haram al-Sharif,* the Noble Sanctuary of Islam, the third holiest site in Islam, the location of the Dome of the Rock and the al-Aqsa mosque, it is obvious that no archaeological excavation could take place today below the sacred platform, the *temenos*. Over the centuries, excavation and other forms of exploration have indeed taken place both below ground, on the western slope of the Kidron Valley, and on the southern edge of the Temple Mount, and we will discuss the results of these later in Chapter 3. But the fact remains that there is not a single piece of archaeological evidence of any kind that can be connected with the First Temple.

The chief, and indeed the only, methodology that has been employed by scholars over the past 150 years to attempt to understand the architectural and ritual nature of the Temple of Solomon has been the comparison of the remains of supposed temple structures unearthed in excavations in Syro-Palestinian sites with the information given in the biblical descriptions of the Temple of Solomon. This is an endeavor fraught with problems, and indeed has not yielded any universally agreed upon results. The same rather small number of temple plans from these sites is continually put forward as being comparable with the information given in the Bible.

As a matter of fact, from an archaeological point of view it is by no means certain that a given excavated structure, preserved only to the base of its original walls, often part of a lengthy chronological sequence of buildings at the same site, was actually a temple. This is a notoriously difficult problem within archaeology.[3] So we have the situation in which biblical information, often contradictory or unclear even within the Hebrew Bible, of a building for which no remains exist, is compared with poorly preserved remnants of buildings from excavations of sites thousands of years old, with only the bases of walls preserved, plus whatever artifacts may have been discovered within the excavated structure itself. Furthermore, within the Syro-Palestinian cultural sphere, it is most frequently the case that the excavated site yields no written records, or none that can be connected with the structure thought to have been a temple that bears some similarity with the biblical descriptions. In the biblical case, we only have written records, but these too are fraught with difficulties, due to the assumption that in many cases they were written down many centuries after the facts that they purport to describe (I am referring to the methodology of biblical criticism, which analyzes the Bible in terms of the Higher Criticism of the Bible, establishing a number of documents, the J, E, D, P, the Deuteronomist and the Chronicler, all of which represent much later compilations of events purported to have occurred at a much earlier time).

In the case of the Syro-Palestinian sites, we often have poorly preserved floor plans of buildings, with no related writings, or even of cult-related objects. Those items that exist are often far out of chronological sequence with the dates presumed for the Temple of Solomon, that is, either much earlier or much later. In the entire pre-Classical, ancient Near Eastern realm, there is not a single case of a fully preserved temple building (that is, with walls and roof intact) EXCEPT for Egypt, where we have relatively well-preserved, largely intact temples, making it possible to understand the interrelationship between architecture, ritual, and symbolism, with both reliefs, texts, and actual cult-related objects to assist us in understanding their purpose. As we will see, it is in this direction—Egypt—that our search will take us to find useful, illuminating parallels to what we think the Temple of Solomon looked like, how it was furnished, and how it functioned.

In order to study the architecture of ancient temples, we need first to clarify certain building types, and the terminology of these types within the literature. It is taken for granted that temples are formal architectural structures, not built in a haphazard way, but rather that they follow certain canonical, hieratic (that is, sacred) building methodologies, patterns, types, and traditions within a certain religious framework. Architecture follows religion (or theology), not the reverse, and incorporates ritual and the decorative program into the total design of the temple. The best example for this is ancient Egypt, where temple-building patterns persisted largely unchanged for several thousand years.[4] Traditions may be shared within a larger cultural sphere, such as the Syro-Palestinian area. Some of these traditions will carry greater weight of influence than others, due to the superior political, economic, religious, or imperial power and prestige of a dominant dynasty or civilization. Thus, for example, ancient Sumerian (located in southern Iraq) religion and architectural influences held wide sway far into Syria well into the second millennium B.C.E.[5] It is a given that ancient Israel in the time of David and Solomon was a small, regional power, without a strong, native, architectural tradition. The period of kingship in ancient Israel followed upon the village-based chiefdom of Joshua and Judges.[6] And that was preceded by the wilderness wanderings period. When it came time to be governed "like all the other nations" (1 Samuel 8:5), the Israelite kings had to look outside their own local cultural inheritance in order to find a suitable architectural model for the building of the king's palace and the temple on Mount Zion. The question is: to what neighboring culture did they look for this assistance? Did they look to neighboring Canaan, which had indeed been part of the international period of trade and diplomacy of the preceding Late Bronze Age Amarna Period? Did they look to the greater Syro-Phoenician cultural area, or to Egypt?

As a matter of fact, there are four potential cultures from whom the Israelites at the time of King Solomon could have drawn influence in the building of the temple: (1) the land of Canaan or Palestine itself, which, in the period immediately preceding the Israelite incursion into the land had been part of a dynamic, international network of trade, diplomacy, and military coalitions known as the Amarna Age. The international correspondence from this period, the Amarna Letters, include exchanges between the Egyptian king Akhenaten and his Palestinian/Canaanite vassals, such as Prince 'Abdu-Heba of Jerusalem.[7] Numerous fortified city-states existed in Canaan at that time, such as Jerusalem itself, Megiddo, Shechem, and Gezer; (2) Syria, one of the most ancient civilizations of the ancient Near East, mentioned above as a recipient of Sumerian influence. At the time of King David, David conquered Syria up to and including Damascus, where he installed a garrison and extracted tribute from the Aramean King Hadadezer (2 Samuel 8:3–80); (3) the Phoenician heartland on the coast of Lebanon, about which I have written in Chapter 1. Many of the raw materials for the building of the temple came from there, as well as the architectural and construction expertise. Additionally, there is the ritual importance of a newly victorious king making a campaign to the "Cedar Mountain" (i.e., the Lebanese coastal forests) to procure the highly desired cedar wood; (4) Finally, there is Egypt itself, which exercised a powerful cultural magnetism over the Israelites, originating in the tradition of their lengthy sojourn in Egypt. Furthermore, Solomon had an Egyptian wife, whom he took as part of a dynastic alliance with an unnamed Egyptian Pharaoh (1 Kings 3:1, 9:16, 24). It is a well-known fact of history that culturally high-placed wives often exercise a decisive influence on their husbands in religious matters, usually importing some aspect, possibly even a dominating aspect, of their native religion into their adopted kingdom.

As to the technical details of temple building, the dimensions given for the Temple of Solomon in the Hebrew Bible classify it as what scholars call a *langbau* building, that is rectangular or elongated, longer than it is wide. Furthermore, it is classified as tripartite, that is it consisted of three distinct architectural units: the *ulam* (porch), the *heikal* (shrine, nave, sanctuary), and the *debir* (the Holy of Holies). It is also categorized as being straight axis, rather than bent axis, which means that there was a straight line from the entryway to the innermost shrine, and that a potential worshipper would enter from the front, rather from the side, and would not be required to turn directions once he had entered, in order to face the innermost shrine. Theoretically, in a straight axis temple, a worshipper could stand at the entrance and look directly into the innermost shrine, even though, obviously, there are several doorways and thresholds to pass over before reaching the holy place, thus creating distance between the worshipper and the shrine. This arrangement also gives rise to the processional nature of the approach, and, when combined with the outer gates, and the concept of the ascent of the holy mountain, it is truly an overwhelming, awe-inspiring prospect to the pilgrim. A bent axis arrangement makes access more difficult, and gives a larger degree of privacy to the innermost shrine, much along the lines of a private house.

Finally, the three architectural units of the building are themselves categorized further. First, the porch is one of the most difficult and troubling units of the Temple of Solomon to understand as it must be understood in relationship to the two bronze pillars. Were the pillars freestanding, or were they structural elements built into the porch, that is engaged, bearing the weight of the walls of the porch as they extended outwards on either side of the entrance, in other words were the columns standing *in antis,* in the style of Classical buildings? There is a well-known type of architecture originating in the ancient Hittite cultural sphere, the so-called *bit-Hilani* porch, in which the columns stand *in antis*. Discussions of the Temple of Solomon attempt to resolve the question of whether the *ulam* was of this type, thus implying influence from more northerly directions, Syria and possibly even Turkey, the home of the ancient Hittite empire. The *bit-Hilani* house had a wide cultural dispersion into Syria and even into the Palestinian/Canaanite heartland.[8] Most of the attempted reconstructions of the Temple of Solomon represent the pillars as freestanding.[9] The *heikal* itself is a so-called *langraum* structure, that is a room longer than it is wide. And the *debir* is of course a perfect cube, constructed entirely of cedar. However, the status of the *debir* within the architectural plan is problematic, because it was a wooden room embedded within the massive stonework of the exterior walls. Since this room was separated from the *heikal* by a wooden door, therefore it would be very difficult to identify it as a separate room if it were to be excavated. This calls into question the supposed strict tripartite nature of the Temple of Solomon, transforming it rather into a building with an entryway porch or vestibule and a single *langraum,* which essentially has a wooden annex attached to, and embedded within, its rear,[10] in other words a bipartite structure. There are scholars who have viewed the *debir* as a piece of wooden furniture, analogous to items of wooden fixtures built for Egyptian temples,[11] in other words not an actual, separate, discreet room at all. At approximately 10 meters square however, it hardly seems accurate to see the *debir* as a piece of furniture.[12] In general then, in our search for parallels or prototypes to the Temple of Solomon, we will want to pay particular attention to temples of tripartite *langbau* type, straight axis, with a porch that has either freestanding or engaged columns, and with a shrine at the back of the building.

Let us then first go to the Palestinian/Canaanite cultural territory, the area the Israelites conquered and occupied, to see what the origins are of temples that could have been influential in the building of the Temple of Solomon. Floor plans of the primary excavated buildings that have continued to play the major roles in discussions can be conveniently studied in Keel,[13] and Wright.[14] We are discussing sites and buildings that are dated to the Middle Bronze Age, approximately 2000–1500 B.C.E., corresponding to the eleventh to seventeenth dynasties of the Egyptian Middle Kingdom and the Second Intermediate Period, the Late Bronze Age, approximately 1500–1200 B.C.E., corresponding roughly to the eighteenth and nineteenth dynasties of New Kingdom Egypt (1550–1196 B.C.E.), and to the Iron Age, with Iron Age I corresponding to 1200–1100 B.C.E., and Iron Age II corresponding to 1100–750 B.C.E. The Egyptian twentieth dynasty dates from 1196–1070 B.C.E.

In addition to the Canaanite city-states mentioned above as having functioned within the context of the Amarna Age, we want to briefly introduce and discuss the second major cultural force that the Israelites encountered once they crossed the Jordan river and entered the land of Canaan: the Philistines. The Philistines appear on the stage of history as one of a group of "Peoples of the Sea" (i.e., "Sea Peoples"), marauding bands who originated in the Aegean world, and who invaded the Delta of the Nile river during the reign of Ramesses III (1194–1163 B.C.E.). Ramesses's account of this event is found on the walls of his massive funerary temple, Medinet Habu, at Thebes. The Philistines, called *Peleshet* in the Egyptian texts, settled on the coastal areas of the territory that now bears their name: Palestine.[15] Numerous Philistine sites have been excavated in the coastal areas, and of course Israelite/Philistine confrontations are central to the books of 1 and 2 Samuel.

There are four Canaanite cities of the Late Bronze Age where temples have been excavated that could possibly have served as models, in whole or in part, for the Temple of Solomon. These cities are Shechem (modern Tell Balatah—located in the West Bank in north-central Israel [= Palestine] between the sacred mountains of Ebal and Gerizim); Megiddo (modern Tell el-Mutesellim—located in the Jezreel Valley, the Plain of Esdraelon); and Hazor (Tell el-Qedah—located north of the Sea of Galilee in the Upper Galilee). Of these, two (along with Gezer) are mentioned as playing prominent roles in Solomon's building efforts: "And this is the account of the forced labor which King Solomon levied to build the house of the Lord and his own house and the Millo and the wall of Jerusalem and Hazor and Megiddo and Gezer" (1 Kings 9:15).

Shechem plays a prominent role in the Books of Joshua and Judges. It was at Shechem, for example, where the Israelites were brought under covenant by Joshua at a shrine described as being "before God" (Joshua

24:1). Within this shrine there existed a sacred oak tree, and there Joshua set up a sacred stone, which served as a witness to the binding covenantal agreements the Israelites had entered into (Joshua 24:25–27). As a center of Canaanite religion, Shechem was home to a temple of the deity called Baal-berith, the "Baal of the covenant" (Judges 9:4). All of these cities are prominently mentioned in Late Bronze Age Egyptian texts, such as the Execration Texts and the Amarna Letters, as well as in New Kingdom Egyptian historical records. Hazor, famously mentioned in Joshua 11:10: "And Joshua turned back at that time, and took Hazor, and smote its king with the sword; for Hazor formerly was the head of all those kingdoms," was one of the largest and most important Canaanite cities of the second millennium B.C.E., and is mentioned in the Mari Letters of the 17th Century B.C.E.

A Middle Bronze Age/Late Bronze Age temple type that appears in the excavations of both Shechem and Megiddo is the so-called *migdal,* fortress-type temple, with massive stairway towers projecting our from either side in the front. The Shechem exemplar of this type is the Middle Bronze III, Late Bronze, Early Iron Age I structure, located in Field V, and identified by the excavators as potentially the temple of Baal-Berith mentioned in Judges 9:4, 46 (in v. 46 it is called "El-Berith"). A bronze figurine of Baal was discovered in a succeeding stratum in another area of the site, thus possibly reinforcing the identification of this structure as the temple of Baal-Berith.[16] The external measurement of the temple itself was 26.30 meters long by 21.30 meters wide, compared to the Temple of Solomon's 30 meters long by 10 meters wide. According to G. E. Wright, quoting R.B.Y. Scott, this measurement represents the first temple built in Palestine using the long or sacred cubit of Ezekiel.[17] According to Toombs it is possibly the earliest tripartite temple in Palestine.[18] This temple had massive, 5-meter thick foundation walls, implying an upper storey or storeys. The plan consisted of an antechamber, a narrow entryway, and a rectangular hall with a colonnade. A single stone column stood in the entryway in the Middle Bronze period. In the later phase, this column was removed and bases for *massebahs* (stone pillars), were installed on either side of the entryway. In the Late Bronze period, a podium accessed by a flight of steps stood at the wall of the inner sanctum, which is thought to have been a base for statues of the deities worshipped in the temple. There was a large altar in the forecourt.[19]

The city of Megiddo, which dominates the Jezreel Valley in the Plain of Esdraelon, was exceptionally rich and powerful in the Middle and Late Bronze periods. During the periods of Strata VIII and VII, dating from 1479–1150 B.C.E., thus Late Bronze Age to Iron Age I, a massive *migdal* or fortress-type of temple, very similar to that of Shechem, flourished in several phases. This temple, called Temple 2048 by the excavators, had three-meter-thick walls, and two projecting towers in the front. There was evidence of a colonnade in the entryway. A niche—a typical evidence of an inner sanctum—was cut into the back wall, opposite the entryway. Thus the tripartite definition of this temple is somewhat suspect, with the three rooms defined as the entryway, the main hall or cella, and the niche in the back wall. In the VII-B phase, a 1.1-meter altar replaced the niche along the back wall, while stone slabs and basins were found strewn around the floors. In the VII-A phase, the time of Pharaoh Ramesses III, whose cartouche was found on an ivory plaque, the temple was again changed. A niche was recut in the back wall, and a platform mounted by steps was built in front of the niche. Again, the tripartite nature of this temple series is determined as was the case at Shechem.[20]

One of the greatest finds in Near Eastern archaeology, and one that has extraordinary implications for the Temple of Solomon, was the ivory cache, found in Room 3100 of the palace of Phase VIII, which will be discussed later in this chapter.

Hazor is perhaps the most remarkable of these three great Middle and Late Bronze Canaanite cities. Given its strategic location in the Upper Galilee, it was a major city on the east-west trade routes, and is "the only Canaanite city mentioned (together with Laish-Dan) in the Mari documents of the eighteenth century B.C., which points to Hazor having been one of the major commercial centers in the Fertile Crescent."[21] In the Hazor lower city, at the northern tip, the excavators excavated and recognized a tripartite temple with a *breitraum* (broad room) cella or main hall, which had three major chronological levels and corresponding architectural developments. This temple, in Area H, was first constructed in Stratum 3, corresponding to the Middle Bronze Age II-B period, the seventeenth and sixteenth centuries B.C.E. This temple had a broad main hall, the cella, with a niche cut into the back (roughly northwest) end of this room. There were emplacements for two columns in the middle of this room. An entryway to this room was flanked by two massive towers. A raised podium stood within the entryway, approached by a flight of steps.

The Stratum 2 (fifteenth century B.C.E.) phase of this temple was basically the same, architecturally, with the addition of a large closed court in front, which held a *bamah*, high place, with a number of smaller altars around the court. A drainage channel led away from the *bamah*, presumably to hold the blood of sacrificed animals. Large numbers of presumed ritual vessels were found here. There were fragments of clay models of animal livers, used in divination, and one of these bore an Akkadian inscription. An extraordinary hammered bronze Egyptianizing statue of a robed priest, with his right hand help aloft in a priestly gesture, was found in this courtyard.[22]

The next phase of this temple, Stratum 1-b, dates to the fourteenth century (the Amarna period). The temple was essentially the same plan as the previous, but with a major addition: around the bottom of the walls (the dado) in the entryway vestibule and the cella were installed sculpted basalt orthostats, of which a lion, carved in relief, one of two that flanked the entryway, was found buried nearby. This is a feature prominently found in temple excavations in north Syria, in sites showing Aramean and Hittite influence, such as Alalakh, Carchemish, Tell Halaf, and 'Ain Dara'. The excavators found a basalt obelisk near the entrance.

The final phase of this temple, Stratum 1-a, is assigned by the excavator to the destruction of the site by the Israelites in the mid-thirteenth century B.C.E. (Joshua 11:10–11: "And Joshua turned back at that time, and took Hazor, and smote its king with the sword; for Hazor was formerly the head of all those kingdoms. And they put to the sword all who were in it, utterly destroying them; there was none left that breathed, and he burned Hazor with fire." In this phase of the temple there were "two round bases found in situ. Their location indicates that they had a cultic significance similar to that of the pillars 'Jachin and Boaz' in Solomon's Temple."[23] A number of highly significant cultic objects was found in the holy of holies of this phase of the temple, including a large, round basalt basin, which the excavator likened to the bronze "Sea" of the Solomonic Temple,[24] a number of libation tables, and an altar of basalt incised with a four-pointed star inside a circle (the symbol of the storm god), and two raised, rectangular strips below it.[25]

The Hazor Lower City Area H temple in its later phases is definitely the most closely related architecturally to the Temple of Solomon, in spite of the fact that, although it is a *langbau* temple in its overall design, the individual rooms within it are *breitbau*, that is, wider than they are deep, in contrast to the Solomonic *heikal*, which is a *langbau* room. We can agree with Wright in saying that the general layout of these temples, along with the distinct cultic objects found within them "make these temples on general appearances the Bronze Age forerunners of the Solomonic Temple at Jerusalem."[26]

There is one additional Palestinian temple that we must discuss, the so-called "Israelite" temple of Strata XI–VII[27] at Tel Arad, in the northern end of the Negev desert in Israel. The significance of this temple is not that it is supposed to have influenced the architecture of the Temple of Solomon, but that it evinces the existence of a "Yahwistic-Israelite sanctuary—the first uncovered in archaeological excavations."[28] The Arad temple consists of a broadroom cella or sanctuary, with a narrow holy of holies built into the western wall of this cella. Three or four steps led into the holy of holies, with two stone incense altars flanking the top of the staircase. Inside the holy of holies (which was oriented towards the east) there was a *bamah* or paved high place for offering, and a *massebah,* or stone stele, painted red. In the courtyard preceding the cella stood a massive altar for burnt offerings built of brick and rubble, of biblical construction technique and dimensions, but without horns.[29] Wright agrees that the temple is a Yahweh temple, but derives its design features from the Israelite four room house, not from the *langbau* tradition of the Temple of Solomon.[30] The implications of this temple for the Temple of Solomon are enormous, attesting as it does biblical prescriptions in an actual archaeological setting, and, for this reason, there is much controversy surrounding this site and the interpretation as a temple of Yahweh.[31] Furthermore, because the excavators assume that the destruction and/or abolition of this temple in Stratum VII is to be attributed to the cultic reforms of King Hezekiah,[32] this would give us our sole instance in archaeology where an excavated event within Palestine can be correlated with the Hebrew Bible.

Perhaps the single most important, noteworthy, and diagnostic design element in the Temple of Solomon, aside from features such as Jachin and Boaz, is the pomegranate ornamentation that was widely used. Pomegranates served as a decorative border on the two capitals atop the pillars, Jachin and Boaz, and were also embroidered in blue and purple fabric and linen on the hem of the blue ephod of the high priest, to be interchanged with a golden bell (Exodus 28:33–34, Exodus 39:24–26). Pomegranates were also attached to the chainwork that stretched from the *debir* to the tops of the columns, Jachin and Boaz (2 Chronicles 3:16). The pomegranate, *Punica granatum* Hebrew *rimmon,* was a very popular fruit in antiquity, named as one of the seven species of produce with which ancient Israel was blessed: "a land of wheat and barley, of vines and the fig trees and pomegranates, a land of olive trees and honey..." (Deuteronomy 9:8). The name *rimmon,* pomegranate, appears as the second element in a number of place names: Gath-rimmon, 'En-rimmon.[33]

There are two exceptionally outstanding and famous ancient Near Eastern artifacts, each of which has a sterling provenance, with pomegranate design: the tripod from Ras Shamra (ancient Ugarit, on the Syrian coast near Latakia), and the pomegranate vase from the Tomb of Tutankhamun (1333–1323 b.c.e.—no. 469 in the inventory of the tomb). The bronze stand from Ugarit (fifteenth to fourteenth century b.c.e.) has a pendant ring of pomegranates around the base, indicating "the manner in which a cultic implement could be decorated with pomegranates."[34]

The silver (or electrum) pomegranate vase from the Tomb of Tutankhamun is "the finest of Tutankhamun's metal vessels."[35] The pomegranate "was brought back to Egypt from Asia following the campaigns of Tuthmosis III [1479–1425 B.C.E.], perhaps [explaining] its popularity as a vessel form during the later years of the 18th Dynasty."[36]

The pomegranate carries symbols and implications of love and fertility, and of female beauty, most famously throughout the very erotic Song of Solomon, for example "I would lead you and bring you into the house of my mother, and into the chamber of her that conceived me. I would give you spiced wine to drink, the juice of pomegranates."[37]

All of this begs the question why pomegranates played such a prominent role in the design program of the Temple of Solomon, and in the high priest's garment? In antiquity the pomegranate is clearly related, not only to human fertility and sexuality, but to fertility goddesses, including the Great Goddess, Cybele and to Persephone, and is prominent within a ritual or temple framework, as we see above, at Ugarit.[38] The two pillars Jachin and Boaz are one of the most polyvalent structures in religious history. I have pointed out elsewhere, in addition to this chapter and Chapter 1, the wide range of symbols that the pillars represented:

> Pillars are known to have been associated with temples in Mesopotamia and Palestine since at least Chalcolithic times. It is probable that the practice of erecting bronze pillars, as in Jerusalem, developed from the practice of erecting wooden pillars that were sheathed with bronze. We have examples of this practice in the Gudea inscriptions and at Khorsabad. The bronze pillars thus represent the ubiquitous trees of life that flank temple entrances and that border scenes of temple ritual (Khorsabad in the former case, Mari in the latter). Like the *djed* pillar in Egyptian architecture, the pillar symbolizes strength, solidity, binding efficacy, endurance, continuity, cosmic order.[39]

One scholar has noted "the degree of freedom evidenced in reporting the appearance of ancient Near Eastern-Canaanite fertility symbolism in the ornamentation of the great bronze objects of the Jerusalem temple."[40] The pomegranate motif is thus a widespread, and expected symbol in the Temple of Solomon, and in temples elsewhere, part of a complex symbol described at length above, that is, relating to fertility, life in all its aspects, trees of life, waters of life, and sacred gardens.[41]

As we move further north into Syrian cultural territory, we find a somewhat different picture. There, over a period of roughly two thousand years, a strongly delineated bi- or tripartite *langbau* temple type flourished. One can view a dramatic schematization of nine such plans, along with the suggested plan for the Temple of Solomon (in Wood, 1988, p. 193). These temples include examples from the mid-third millennium B.C.E. site of Tell Chuera in the Syrian Jazirah,[42] the oldest example of this architectural type; Temple D on the citadel of Ebla, in northern Syria, dating to almost 1,000 years later than the temples of Tell Chuera mentioned above. Temple D, dedicated to Ishtar, had a clear tripartite structure, with a cult niche cut into the back wall. A podium stood in front of this niche. In front of the podium stood a *betyl,* or nonfigurative standing cult stone. There was a large basin in the cella, decorated with mythological motifs. Amiet writes that "This temple was, in plan, a remote ancestor of Solomon's temple."[43] The excavator of Ebla, Paolo Matthiae, wrote that this temple "may be considered a very old antecedent of Solomon's Temple in Jerusalem."[44]

From more recent excavations on the Great Bend of the Euphrates River in Syria, an extraordinary site, ancient Emar (modern Meskene) has been uncovered. Remains of four temples have been excavated on the citadel of the site, dating to the late Bronze Age (the city was destroyed in 1187 B.C.E.). Two temples are of particular interest: a double sanctuary, two temples dedicated to Baal and Astarte respectively. They both have entryway porches with two columns in the porch, then an elongated cella or cult room with benches along its back wall, on which benches the statue of the god presumably stood. Just in front of the benches, in both temples, stood a baked clay table of offerings, on which the priest would have stood while making offerings to the statues. Unusually, the large sacrificial altar serving both these temples stood behind them on the citadel.[45]

The next temple in the Syrian cultural realm that I want to discuss is the one that is most often put forward as perhaps the single most similar to the Temple of Solomon, even though it dates to the eighth century B.C.E., that is later than the Temple of Solomon. This is the temple of Ta'yinat (also spelled Tayinat and Tainat), located in the Plain of Antioch in Turkey. The temple is rectangular (11.75 by 25.35 meters), tripartite, and straight axis. The entryway has the two side walls *in antis,* the same as the Temple of Solomon, with two pillars standing in the entryway. The pillars stood on bases decorated with two crouching lions. This is followed by the elongated cella or main hall, and then the holy of holies, a distinct chapel, with two side walls extending out in to the room, meaning that a door of some type would have closed this opening, thus sealing the holy of holies off from the cella that preceded it.[46]

Another feature of Ta'yinat that bears comparison with the Temple of Solomon, is the fact that a massive palace complex stands immediately next to the temple, dwarfing it really, which is exactly the same situation with Solomon's palace, "the House of the Forest of Lebanon," with a "Hall of Pillars," a Hall of the Throne," along with his own quarters, next to the temple on the Temple Mount (1 Kings 7:1–12), massively larger than the temple.[47]

There has been much debate among scholars as to just how closely the temple of Ta'yinat should be compared to the Temple of Solomon, especially given the problems involved in interpreting excavated ruins, as stated above.[48] There is no doubt however about the general, elongated nature of the plan and its closeness to Solomon's Temple.

One final temple excavated in Syria during the 1980's has a very important architectural similarity to the Temple of Solomon, one not found elsewhere in the Syro-Palestinian cultural realm for the earlier period. This is the temple of 'Ain Dara', in the Afrin Valley, northwest of Aleppo. The temple is dated by the excavators to three phases of Level VII, approximately 1300–740 B.C.E.[49] The temple is tripartite, with an entryway,

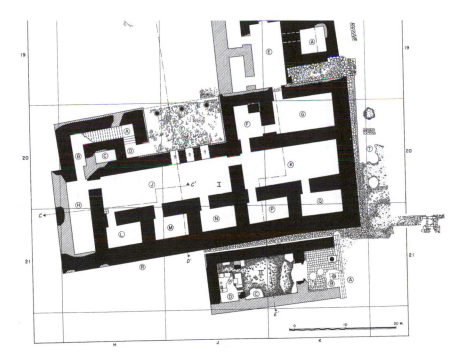

Tell Tayinat, Temple II and Palace I: 9th Century B.C.E. Richard C. Haines, *Excavations in the Plain of Antioch, II: The Structural Remains of the Later Phases: Chatal Huyuk, Tell Al-Judaidah, and Tell Tayinat.* Oriental Institute Publications, 95. Chicago: The University of Chicago Press, 1970, Plate 103. Courtesy of the Oriental Institute of the University of Chicago.

a vestibule, and the cella, looking very much in plan like Temple 2048 at Megiddo.[50] It is an orthostat temple, with the orthostats of the main façade and in the cella very much in the Hittite style of orthostat construction, such as Bogazkoy and Alaca Hoyuk.[51]

The feature of 'Ain Dara' that is so fascinating in comparison with the Temple of Solomon is the structure constructed around its three sides (excluding the front), which various authorities compare with the three-storey annex built around and offset from the walls of three sides of the Temple of Solomon.[52] This *Wandelgang* as the excavators call it (literally "foyer, lobby"), was fitted out with orthostats on its exterior and in the entryway, along with stelae along the sides of the corridor depicting an enthroned king, a palm tree, a standing god, and offerings.[53] The foundation of the corridor was not structurally connected with the foundation of the temple itself, making an interesting comparison with the annex attached to the Temple of Solomon by offsets in the wall "in order that the supporting beams should not be inserted into the walls of the house."[54] The excavators do not speculate whether or not the corridor was multi-storeyed, but it was definitely intimately connected with the worship in the temple.[55] Because at one point in the life of this corridor it was possible for one to enter through one doorway, walk through the corridor along three sides of the temple and exit through another,[56] it gives off the character of a circumambulatory passageway, an issue of great interest with respect to the Temple of Solomon, because such passageways are inevitably part of the temple worship, that is circumambulation, walking around the sacred space. Is it possible that the first level of the Solomonic annex, which was five cubits high, was a circumambulatory space? Such structures function in Egyptian temples for circumambulation, as well as to give commoners access to the sacred precincts, but outside the inner halls and chapels, as is the case at Kom Ombo, for example.[57] The Psalms of the Hebrew Bible make clear that circumambulation was part of the ritual of the worship of the temple: "Walk about Zion, go round about her, number her towers, consider well her ramparts, go through her citadels, that you may tell the next generation that this is God, our God for ever and ever. He will be our guide for ever" (Psalms 48:12–14).

One additional important feature of the temple of 'Ain Dara' is that its cella, or shrine, was very close to square in dimension, 16.70 by 16.80 meters.[58] The *debir* of the Temple of Solomon was approximately 11 meters square.

There is a fascinating typological comparison between the Temple of Solomon and the orthostat temples that we have discussed, particularly at Hazor and the 'Ain Dara' temple. With the more fully preserved orthostats at 'Ain Dara', we get a picture of how extensive and massive these sculpted

The Temple of 'Ain Dara', Syria. Level VII, Phase 2 (1000–900 B.C.E.). An overview of the temple from the south, looking from the entryway into the rear. Peter Grunwald

figures were, how they dominated and overpowered the design scheme of the temple. Two massive basalt sphinxes greeted worshipers at the entryway to the 'Ain Dara' temple.[59] Two colossal basalt lions flanked the entryway into the inner sanctuary. Colossal footprints (one meter long) were carved into the stone floors of the antecella, "marking the deity's procession into the cella."[60] The dado reliefs in the cella are .58 centimeter high, and consist of mountain gods and part human, part animal beings, all with their hands raised in the attitude of praise.[61] In other words, the walls of these temples, usually the bottoms of the walls (the dado), the entryways, the exterior walls, were covered with carved stone sphinxes, fabulous (mythical) beasts, and mountain deities. "Both [the Temple of Solomon and the temple at 'Ain Dara'] were built on the same tripartite plan, with columns flanking the entrance. At 'Ain Dara', immense lions and cherubs depicted with stylized palms guarded the entrances onto the temple platform and in the temple proper and cella. The deity inhabiting the temple was also of superhuman size."[62]

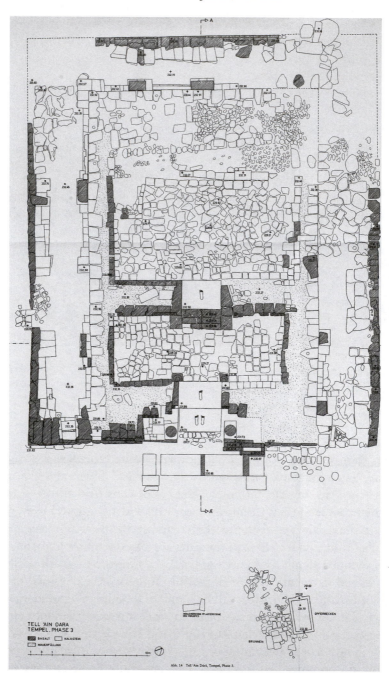

Tell 'Ain Dara', temple, Phase 2. Ali Abou Assaf, *Der Temple von Ain Dara*. Damaszener Forschungen, Bd. 3. Mainz am Rhein: P. V. Zabern, 1990. Abb. 14. Courtesy Renate Barcsay-Regner.

Likewise the Temple of Solomon was covered, on the interior wall surfaces, the doorways, or the veil (2 Chronicles 3:14), with worked, figured, or carved cherubim: "He carved all the walls of the house round about with carved figures of cherubim and palm trees and open flowers, in the inner and outer rooms" (1 Kings 6:29). "For the entrance to the inner sanctuary he made doors of olivewood; the lintel and the doorposts formed a pentagon. He covered the two doors of olivewood with carvings of cherubim, palm trees, and open flowers; he overlaid them with gold, and spread gold upon the cherubim and upon the palm trees" (1 Kings 6:31). "So also he made for the entrance to the nave doorposts of olivewood, in the form of a square, and two doors of cypress wood; the two leaves of the one door were folding, and the two leaves of the other door were folding. On them he carved cherubim and palm trees and open flowers" (1 Kings 6:33–35). Likewise the 10 stands upon which the lavers stood, had panels with carved "lions, oxen, and cherubim" (1 Kings 7:29), and on the supports and stays of the corners of the stands "he carved cherubim, lions, and palm trees, according to the space of each, with wreaths round about" (1 Kings 7:26). We have here the same tradition of representing mythical guardian beasts in the temple interior, on many if not all surfaces, as well as on ritual implements, the only difference being in the raw material of the decorative scheme, stone at 'Ain Dara' (that is of what is preserved from that temple) but wood and bronze in the Temple of Solomon.[63]

I want to continue here with the theme of the cherubim, treated in detail in Chapter 1 in relation to the cherubim that towered over the Ark of the Covenant in the *debir*. If we return momentarily to the site of Megiddo, we can introduce the evidence of the famous ivory hoard of Egypto-Phoencian ivories found in the palace of Stratum VII A, which dates to the time of Ramesses III, the twelfth century B.C.E.. The most famous of these is of course the plaque showing tribute carriers appearing before an enthroned king, shown lifting a cup to his lips, with his queen standing in front of him, and a harpist behind her. To the side of the king's throne stands a winged sphinx, with human head and lion paws, its wings sweeping up in the same line as the back of the throne.[64] We can see here the general *mileau* of the cherubim of Solomon's Temple, the gilded wooden giants that stood in the *debir* as well as those that were carved into all wall surfaces of the interior. It is the same *milieu* as that of the Hazor orthostat temple, and of 'Ain Dara'.

There are no excavated temple remains in the Phoenician homeland, within the date range of the Temple of Solomon, that are similar to or bear comparison with that temple. Likewise, there are no Philistine, or presumed Philistine, temples that fit into the bi-or tripartite, straight axis, *langbau*

Ivory Plaque, Megiddo, Late Bronze Age Period, 14th–12th Centuries B.C.E. IDAM 38.780. *Treasures of the Holy Land: Ancient Art from the Israel Museum.* New York: The Metropolitan Museum of Art, 1986, pp. 148–149. The Israel Museum, Jerusalem.

tradition.[65] However, there are numerous finds of Egypto-Phoenician ivories from this region, such as those described in the preceding paragraph. Another well-known product of Phoenicia are the model shrines, a number of which are illustrated and discussed in Keel.[66] Of particular importance are those that show cherubim or sphinx-like creatures filling the interior of the most holy place of the miniature shrine, as was the case in the *debir* of the Temple of Solomon. There two limestone *naoi* possibly from Sidon,[67] the latter of which, dating to the fifth century B.C.E., dramatically shows the winged creature, its wings completely filling the interior of the most holy place. Additional examples show the cherubim combined with the throne, as we saw above in the Megiddo plaque, and as was the case in the *debir* of the Temple of Solomon: "to bring up from there the ark of God, which is called by the name of the Lord of hosts, who sits enthroned on the cherubim" (2 Samuel 6:2). "Then the priests brought the ark of the covenant of the Lord to its place, in the inner sanctuary of the house, in the most holy place, underneath the wings of the cherubim" (1 Kings 8:4).

We now come to Egypt. There has now been a strong Egyptian-Canaanite historical/archaeological/religious connection established through the excavations at the eastern Nile River Delta site of Tell ed-Dab'a, excavated since 1966 by an Austrian team under the direction of Manfred Bietak. It is now established that Tell ed-Dab'a is the site of Avaris, the capital of the foreign, Canaanite Hyksos Dynasty of Egypt, who reigned during the Second Intermediate Period, Dynasties 14–17 (1750–1550 B.C.E.). With their ouster by Ahmose, first Pharaoh of the 18th Dynasty, in about 1530 B.C.E., and the reestablishment of native Egyptian rule in Thebes, the site became the Delta residence of Ramesses II, Piramesse. Some scholars believe this is the same as the site of biblical Raamses, one of the two store cities the Israelites were forced to build for the Pharaoh (Exodus 1:11— Ramesses II is widely believed to have been the Pharaoh of the Exodus).

Whether or not the site of Tell ed-Dab'a/Avaris/Piramesse is actually the same as mentioned in the Hebrew Bible, is not germane to this book.[68] What is important is that the excavators have discovered the remains of a Middle Bronze Age *migdal* or fortress-like temple (my phrase) similar to that of Hazor Lower City Area H temple sequence that began in the Middle Bronze Age. The Tell ed-Dab'a temple, called Temple III "is one of the largest sanctuaries known from the Middle Bronze Age world, being about 30 m. long."[69] The walls were 4 meters thick on the sides, and 5 meters thick at the back. Its plan, placed side-by-side with that of the Hazor temple, from Stratum II, looks remarkably similar to it. The Tell ed-Dab'a temple is tripartite, straight axis, with a *breitraum* porch, a *breitraum* vestibule or "pro-cella" (i.e., antecella) in Bietak's phrase, and the main cella or sanctuary. A niche, that is, the most holy place, 8 meters wide, was extended out from the back wall of the cella. Bietak speculates that a door probably closed off this niche from the cella.[70] The temple was painted blue, "thus it was probably dedicated to a cosmic god."[71] About 15 meters in front of the temple, in the midst of the sacred area of which this temple, other temples and mortuary temples were situated, was a mud brick altar, a *bamah,* "covered, or rather filled, with ashes and charred bones. In its direct vicinity were deep pits, filled with more charred bones, mainly of cattle and a few sheep, but not a single pig bone was found, although there is much evidence of the pig in the food-offerings of the tombs. It looks as if, for offerings to the gods, pigs were already considered as taboo."[72]

The ultimate prototype of the classic Egyptian straight axis temple, which is the same floor plan as the Solomonic except that it is much more elaborately developed, with many more rooms, halls, courtyards, and side rooms can be seen on an ivory plaque excavated by Flinders Petrie in the royal cemetery at Abydos in Middle Egypt, and published in 1901.[73] This plaque, ascribed to Dynasty One king Aha (c. 2850 B.C.E.), shows, on the top line, "a shrine and temenos of [Egyptian goddess] Neith."[74] On the sacred platform or *temenos* itself, which we should read from left to right, horizontally, moving from the entrance to the chapel at the rear, we see first, on the left, the two flag poles, facing each other, which are found in classic Egyptian temples installed on either side of the entryway pylons, and yield the Egyptian hieroglyphic sign for "god" (*ntr*). This is extremely important for our consideration of the bronze pillars Jachin and Boaz that stood in front of the Temple of Solomon. Jachin and Boaz certainly played the same role as these two "primeval" symbols of the Egyptian temple, symbols of the presence of divinity, in that most holy, sacred place on earth where divinity can be found and approached. We have the same phenomenon in ancient Sumer, and there, in the earliest depictions of the temple, we have the Euphrates Valley marsh land reed hut, fronted by the two emblems of the goddess Inanna, the "gatepost-with- streamer" pillars, which stand in front of the sacred reed shrine, and play an analogous role as the flagpoles of Egyptian temples, and Jachin and Boaz of the Temple of Solomon. The most famous example of this motif in Sumerian art is the Uruk Vase.[75] Thus the twin bronze pillars Jachin and Boaz are to be situated within the primordial Near Eastern tradition by which the presence of a deity in his/her temple is signaled with a pillar or flagpole at the entryway.[76]

Returning to the ivory plaque from Abydos, reading from left to right, we next see the symbol of the goddess Neith, crossed arrows and a shield, and finally come to the reed shrine itself, the classic shape of the primitive Egyptian shrine, which is seen as the determinative hieroglyphic sign in, for example, the Egyptian word *Pr-wr*, "Great House," "name of the

Ivory Plaque, Striding Sphinx, Samaria, Israelite Period, 9th–8th Centuries B.C.E. IDAM 33-2572. *Treasures of the Holy Land: Ancient Art from the Israel Museum.* New York: The Metropolitan Museum of Art, 1986, pp. 166–168. The Israel Museum, Jerusalem.

pre-dynastic national shrine of Upper Egypt at Hierankonpolis (*Nhn*)."[77]
It is this shrine which is later "installed" in the classic Egyptian temple, in
the back, the innermost shrine or most holy place, but now rendered in
stone: "the stone masons still set out to imitate the designs and patterns
which, for centuries, they had employed in the reed and brick structures."[78]
Even as late as late as the Ptolemaic period, Egyptian temples continued
to be viewed as the archaic tent shrine, though they were built entirely in
stone.[79] The stone *naos* in the most holy shrine of the Edfu temple consists of a stone base representing the primeval tent shrine, topped by the
pyramidion.[80] This can be further illustrated in the Temple of Sethos I at
Abydos, where the king is shown unlatching the doorway into the most
holy place, where a statue of the deity is placed. The chapel wherein the
statue of the deity stands in these scenes is the same hieroglyphic shape
as described above for the primitive shrine.[81] Here we can see the concept
that the most sacred chapel is, as it were, "placed inside of," or "set down
inside" the walls of the temple. This is the concept that we can see with the
debir in the Temple Solomon, and why some scholars go so far as to view
it as a piece of furniture, something fabricated on the outside and installed.
But here too, analogous to Egypt, the *debir* originates as a primordial or
primitive shrine, the tent shrine of the desert wanderings.

The Temple of Solomon was the first solid "house" built for Yahweh:
"Thus says the Lord: Would you build me a house to dwell in? I have
not dwelt in a house since the day I brought up the people of Israel from
Egypt to this day, but I have been moving about in a tent for my dwelling" (2 Samuel 7:6). At Mount Sinai, during the Wilderness Wanderings

Ivory Plaque, Abydos, Egypt, Tablets of Kings Narmer and Men. 2850 B.C.E.
W. M. Flinders Petrie, *The Royal Tombs of the Earliest Dynasties,* with a Chapter by
F. Ll. Griffith. Twenty-First Memoir of the Egypt Exploration Fund. Part 2. London:
The Offices of the Egypt Exploration Fund and Kegan Paul, Trench, Trubner &
Co., 1901. Plate X, 2. Asian and Middle Eastern Division, The New York Public
Library, Astor, Lenox and Tilden Foundations.

period, when Israel was a nomadic people, the Lord revealed to them the plan of a sanctuary typical of a nomadic people, a tent shrine, something that is well known and well documented among modern nomads of the Middle East.[82] This is the primordial shrine of the People of Israel, their counterpart to the archaic reed shrines of Sumer and Egypt. The Ark of the Covenant was brought from Kirjath-jearim, where it had been stored, and installed in the Temple of Solomon as the final act of its construction: "And they brought up the ark of the Lord, the tent of meeting (*ohel moed*), and all the holy vessels that were in the tent ('*ohel*)" (1 Kings 8:4). "Then the priests brought the ark of the covenant of the Lord to its place, in the inner sanctuary of the house, in the most holy place, underneath the wings of the cherubim" (1 Kings 8:6).

The primordial chapel, either reed hut or tent, is "installed" inside the stone-built temple, itself transformed into a more sophisticated material (in this case cedar), but the symbolism of its original form is never lost, that is the tent. Yahweh is always represented as living in a tent upon the holy mountain. "Let me dwell in thy tent forever! Oh to be safe under the shelter of thy wings!" (Psalms 61:4). The simple nomad/village peasant way of life was transformed through the transition to urbanism, the tent transformed into a massive, luxurious, stone building.[83] At its center is the innermost holy place. In Egyptian building, the temple was built from the inward out, from the innermost chapels to the outer halls, courts, and so on. The entire meaning and purpose of the temple was the inner sanctuary, where the god dwelt in darkness. The courts, the halls, and the thresholds, all pointed towards this place. This was the true center, the goal of pilgrimage, the goal of the magnificent processionals.

We come finally to that most renowned cult object in human history, the Ark of the Covenant. If we wish to look for prototypes, influences, or predecessors, we can only look in one place, Egypt. Assuming, with Haran[84] that the Wilderness ark was not the fabulously luxurious ark of the Temple of Solomon, but was rather a simple tent shrine, closer to those of modern-day Arab Bedouin described by Morgenstern,[85] then we may assume the same transformation for the ark as we did for the pillars Jachin and Boaz (above, and Chapter 1), namely that an archaic or primeval cultic object was transformed from its nomadic or pastoral origins, as a reed or tent shrine, into the glorious object that sat in the *debir* of the Temple of Solomon, underneath the outstretched wings of the cherubim.

A gilded wood shrine, to Anubis, with a statue of Anubis seated on top, and with attached carrying poles, was discovered in the Tomb of Tutankhamun in the room designated the Treasury.[86] The shrine itself, of gessoed and gilded wood, has the shape of a pylon, with a cavetto cornice roof.[87] The shrine has five inner compartments, holding materials and objects of which Carter surmised that they "seem to signify the perpetuation of, or belong to, the ritual of mummification."[88] Anubis is the guardian of the burial chamber. One of the compartments contained "eight large pectoral" (neck) ornaments. Carter speculated that these might have been either "the god's jewelry," or "perhaps they were worn by his eight priests who carried him in procession to the tomb?"[89]

Shrine no. 261 measures 95 centimeters long, by 54.3 centimeters high, by 37 centimeters wide.[90] To compare this with the Ark of the Covenant, the Ark is approximately 52.5 inches long, by 31.5 inches wide, by 31.5 inches tall. The Tutankhamun shrine is approximately 37 inches long by 13.5 inches wide by 54.3 inches tall. The Tutankhamun shrine is not strictly analogous to the Ark of the Covenant, only that it is an ark-like object, of gilded wood, within a sacred, in this case burial environment, actually "guarding" the Treasury, that it contains compartments wherein sacred objects are stored, and that it was carried, by its *permanently attached poles* (1 Kings 8:8), by eight priests in the funerary procession to the Tomb of Tutankhamun. Several of these sentences also apply to the Ark of the Covenant, its fabrication, its role, and the procession by which the Ark of the Covenant was carried to the Temple Mount and installed in the Temple of Solomon (1 Kings 8:3–6). It is to Egypt that, in any case, we may, and indeed must, look in order to find a possible *Sitz im Leben* for the Ark of the Covenant.

The other great "ark-like" ritual object from Egypt that bears interesting similarities to the descriptions of the Ark of the Covenant in the Hebrew Bible is the sacred bark (or barque) and the bark shrine, the shrine that carried the statue or image of the deity in processions from temple to temple, borne on the shoulders of priests by means of the poles,[91] and that was stored in the holy of holies of the Egyptian temple, or, in some cases, in a chapel, upon a stand, immediately behind the holy of the holies, as at Edfu.[92]

There are vivid and extremely beautiful painted reliefs of these barks in many Egyptian temples, perhaps most notably in the Temple of Sethos I at Abydos. Two examples can be given: (1) the sacred bark of Osiris in the Osiris chapel at Abydos;[93] and (2) the sacred bark of Amen-Re, in the chapel of Amen-Re, at Abydos.[94] In each case the bark—the boat—is carrying the archaic shrine-shaped *naos* of the god, which is actually seen in the bark shrine of the temple, because the king himself is seen censing the shrine. Plate 11, the bark shrine of Amen-Re, is directly analogous to the Ark of the Covenant sitting in the *debir* of the Temple of Solomon, because the scene that we are viewing is of the shrine ensconced within its

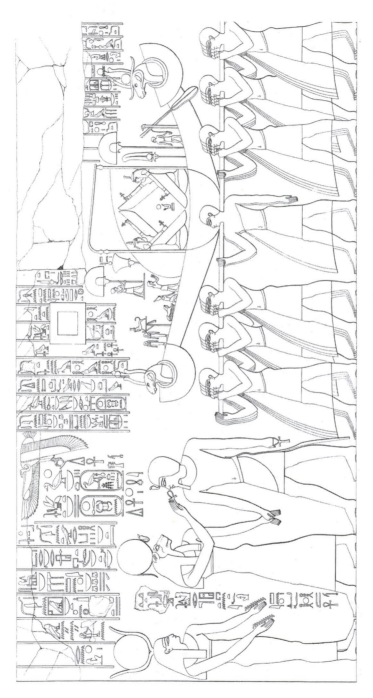

The Barque (Bark) of Amun being carried in procession by Egyptian priests, with winged figures of the Egyptian goddess Ma'at depicted inside the shrine. The Temple of Karnak, Egypt, Third Pylon, South. Richard Lepsius, *Denkmaeler aus Aegypten und Aethiopien: nach Zeichnungen der von Seiner Majestat dem Koenige von Preussen Friedrich Wilhelm IV nach diesen landern gesendeten und in den Jahren 1842–45 ausgefuhrten wissenschaftlichen Expedition…*. Berlin: Nicolaische Buchhandlung (1849–56). Twelve volumes. Abtheilung III, Blatt 14. Asian and Middle Eastern Division, The New York Public Library, Astor, Lenox and Tilden Foundations.

Sethos Opens the Door for Osiris. The Temple of Sethos I at Abydos, Egypt. Sir Alan Henderson Gardiner. *The Temple of King Sethos I at Abydos.* Copied by Amice M. Calverley with the Assistance of Myrtle F. Broome, and edited by Alan H. Gardiner. London: The Egypt Exploration Society, Chicago: The University of Chicago Press, 1933–58. Four volumes. Vol. I, Plate I, Frontispiece. Courtesy of the Oriental Institute of the University of Chicago and the Egypt Exploration Society. Asian and Middle Eastern Division, The New York Public Library, Astor, Lenox and Tilden Foundations.

shrine in back of the temple, within the sacred chapel, *with its carrying poles in place,* again, exactly as was the case with the Ark of the Covenant. The Hebrew Bible is emphatic that the carrying poles were not to be removed as the Ark sat in the *debir* (1 Kings 8:7–8). The poles are a fascinating, highly authentic diagnostic feature, and yet they have hardly been noticed in the literature. Busink seems to support the view that the poles were permanently attached to the Ark.[95] His suggested reconstruction of the Ark within the *debir* shows the Ark sitting with its long side showing, the poles in place.[96]

In the Abydos scenes, the king is approaching, censing the chapel, and, in the case of the Osiris chapel, censing and libating, just as we noted in Chapter 1 that several early kings, most notably David, Solomon, and Hezekiah approached, and presumably went inside of, the *debir,* functioning, for all intents and purposes, as priests.[97] There is one other feature in the Abydos reliefs that is of exceptional interest in relationship to the Temple of Solomon: the scenes that show the king unlocking the door of the temple shrine, the holy of holies, within which stands the statue of the deity.[98] I am not aware of any other visual evidence from the ancient Near East that shows this process or scene so vividly. Keel states that the *debir* was provided with "a double door and bolt," referring to 1 Kings 6:31–32, although the Hebrew text of verse 31 is extremely difficult and is interpreted in a wide range of ways by different authorities, not necessarily supporting the idea of a "bolt."[99] In any case, because there was doubtless a bolt on the door of the *debir,* it seems reasonable to employ the Abydos reliefs to throw light on these structural features of the Temple of Solomon, in this case actually showing the process of unlocking the bolt of an innermost shrine of a temple.

We have thus surveyed an extensive amount of archaeological, textual, art-historical, and religious evidence from ancient Palestine, Syria, Phoenicia, and Egypt, in order to attempt to throw light on what the physical appearance of the Temple of Solomon may have been, what its ritual objects may have looked like, how they may have been constructed, what the ritual processes in the Temple may have involved, in addition to the biblical evidence, what influences may have played a role in the building of the Temple of Solomon, and where these influences may have come from. I began this chapter with the statement that there is no single piece of archaeological evidence that can be certainly connected with the Temple of Solomon, and yet, as I hope the evidence presented in this chapter shows, the Temple was, and is today, within the purview of the evidence that we have available to us, an actual, real, dynamic, *believable,* and within certain limits, reconstructable, sanctuary that rightly maintains its position as one of the most fabled and influential sacred structures in world history.

CHAPTER 3

The Second Temple

The Temple of Zerubbabel

The rebuilding of the Temple of Jerusalem following the long period of ruin and abandonment after 586 B.C.E. occurred through the magnanimity and initiative of one of the greatest, most enlightened kings of antiquity, Cyrus I, King of Persia (ruled 539–530 B.C.E.). Cyrus entered Babylon peacefully in 539 B.C.E., having defeated the last Babylonian king, Nabonidus (ruled 559–539 B.C.E.). The famous Cyrus Cylinder gives us one of the most remarkable pictures of a merciful, visionary, tolerant ruler, entering the city of Babylon in peace, sparing the inhabitants and the sanctuaries, and, most crucially

> I returned to these sacred cities on the other side of the Tigris, the sanctuaries of which have been in ruins for a long time, the images which used to live therein and established for them permanent sanctuaries. I also gathered all their former inhabitants and returned to them their habitations. Furthermore, I resettled upon the command of Marduk, the great lord, all the gods of Sumer and Akkad whom Nabonidus has brought into Babylon to the anger of the lord of the gods, unharmed, in their former chapels, the places which make them happy.[1]

It is this generous spirit, just quoted, that has a direct echo in the first chapter of the Book of Ezra:

> In the first year of Cyrus king of Persia [i.e. 539 B.C.E.], that the word of the Lord by the mouth of Jeremiah might be accomplished, the Lord stirred up the spirit of Cyrus king of Persia so that he made a proclamation throughout all his kingdom and also put it in writing: 'Thus says Cyrus king of Persia: The Lord, the God of heaven, has given me all the kingdoms of the earth, and he has charged me to build him a house in Jerusalem, which is in Judah. Whoever is among you of all his people, may his God be with him, and let him go up to Jerusalem, which is in Judah, and rebuild the house of the Lord, the God of Israel—he is the God who is in Jerusalem; and let each survivor, in whatever place he sojourns, be assisted by the men of his place with silver and gold, with goods and with beasts, besides freewill offerings for the house of God which is in Jerusalem." (Ezra 1:1–4)

Furthermore, a few verses later we read that

> Cyrus the king also brought out the vessels of the house of the Lord which Nebuchandnezzar had carried away from Jerusalem and place in the house of his gods. Cyrus king of Persia brought these out in charge of Mithredath the treasurer, who counted them out to Sheshbazzar the prince of Judah. And this was the number of them: a thousand basins of gold, a thousand basins of silver, twenty-nine censers, thirty bowls of gold, two thousand four hundred and ten bowls of silver, and a thousand other vessels; all the vessels of gold and silver were five thousand four hundred and sixty nine. All these did Sheshbazzar bring up, when the exiles were brought up from Babylonia to Jerusalem. (Ezra 1:7–11)

Thus, although the Jewish exiles are not actually mentioned in the Cyrus Cylinder, it is obvious that the Cyrus decree, as quoted in the Book of Ezra, is of the same spirit, and can be confidently viewed as an authentic reflection, from the Jewish point of view, of a state document of the Persian state archives.[2] Just as the Cyrus Cylinder states that it was the Babylonian state god Marduk who commanded Cyrus to return the captured gods to their home temples,[3] so here the decree in Ezra states that "the Lord stirred up the spirit of Cyrus king of Persia so that he made a proclamation" (Ezra 1:1).[4]

The accounts of the rebuilding of the temple as found in Ezra are notoriously complicated, subject to varying interpretations by scholars, and difficult to understand or sort out chronologically. The author of the books

Ezra and Nehemiah is presumed to have been the Chronicler, who compiled these books as a kind of supplement to the Books of Chronicles, bringing the history of Israel, from the point of view of the Chronicler, down to about 424 B.C.E. Since the book of 2 Chronicles ends with the disaster of the destruction of the Temple of Solomon and the carrying off into Babylonian exile of the Jewish people, with the prophecy that their exile should last seventy years, the Books of Ezra and Nehemiah serve to lay out the history of how the exiles were returned to their land, and were enabled to rebuild the temple, all in the fulfillment of prophecy. Part of the Cyrus decree contained in Ezra (1:1–3a) ends the book of 2 Chronicles. I am adopting a sequence here that is reasonable and defensible.

The returning Jewish exiles immediately set about to rebuild the temple under the leadership of Sheshbazzar (this is the Babylonian name of a Jewish official—Ezra 1:5–11; Ezra 5:13–16). Zerubbabel (of Davidic descent) and the priest Jeshua (of Zadokite descent—see Ezekiel 40:46) are pictured as taking leading roles in the return, and soon replace Sheshbazzar, whose name disappears from the record. However, the laying of the foundations of the temple is attributed to the influence and work of Sheshbazzar (Ezra 5:16). A census of the Jewish people was taken, presumably for the purpose of identifying true Israelites, in distinction to the local peoples, including Samaritans.[5] Some claiming the priesthood were excluded as being unclean (Ezra 2). In the "seventh month" (Ezra 3:1–536 B.C.E.), "the altar of the God of Israel" was constructed in the ruins of the Temple of Solomon under the direction of Zerubbabel, and Jeshua (Ezra 3:2). The Feast of Booths was observed, and numerous burnt offerings and freewill offerings were celebrated. Since "the foundation of the temple of the Lord was not yet laid" (Ezra 3:6), and in accordance with established building practices from the time of the building of the Temple of Solomon, the Jewish leaders enlisted the aid of Phoenician/Tyrian masons and carpenters, and solicited the shipment of cedar logs via a sea route from Lebanon to Joppa (Ezra 3:7). Priests and Levites oversaw the work.

There is considerable disagreement among scholars as to the chronology of these events, and the date that should be assigned to "the seventh month" of Ezra 3:1. The editors of *The New Oxford Annotated Bible with the Apocrypha* assign the seventh month to 520 B.C.E., in the reign of Darius (p. 576), in whose reign we know that the temple was completed. They reconstruct two periods of return from exile, the first under Sheshbazzar upon the Cyrus decree, the second under Zerubbabel and Jeshua around 520 B.C.E. (p. 573). Jacob Meyers assigns the "seventh month" to 536 B.C.E., on the basis of Ezra 3:12: "But many of the priests and Levites and heads of fathers' houses, old men who had seen the first house, wept with a loud voice when they saw the foundation of this house being laid, though many shouted aloud for joy." His reasoning is simply that by 520 B.C.E., there would not have been, and could not have been such a group still alive, that had "seen the first house," or that it would have been exceptionally small, and thus would not have merited such a prominent mention as we have here.[6] There is another problem with the text as far as assigning the Zerubbabel group to the later (Darius) date: Ezra 5:16 states that "Shesh-bazzar came and laid the foundations of the house of God which is in Jerusalem." Ezra 3 gives as the sequence of rebuilding under Zerubbabel and Jeshua that first the altar was rebuilt, burnt offerings and the Feast of Booths celebrated, after which the foundations of the temple were laid, with the assistance of the Tyrian masons and carpenters and cedar trees from Lebanon. In other words, the Book of Ezra associates both Shesh-bazzar and Zerubbabel and Jeshua with the laying of the foundations of the temple. Meyers suggests that Sheshbazzar may have been an old man at that time, and was replaced by Zerubbabel, who may have been his assistant.[7] As soon as the foundations were laid, the priests donned their sacred vestments, the trumpets were sounded and songs and shouts of joy were raised. The rejoicing was overheard by the inhabitants of the land, those who had stayed behind at the beginning of the exile, Samaritans, and others. They at first offered to assist in the building, but, when the Jews rebuffed them, the enemies proceeded to interfere with the work, placing numerous impediments in their way. The work was thus stopped, and this state of affairs persisted through the remaining years of the reign of Cyrus, and into the second year of the reign of his successor, Darius (ruled 522–486 B.C.E.; Ezra 4:1–5; 24).

"In the second year of Darius the king, in the sixth month, the word of the Lord came by Haggai the prophet to Zerubbabel the son of Shealtiel, governor of Judah, and to Joshua the son of Jehozadak, the high priest, 'Thus says the Lord of hosts: This people say the time has not yet come to rebuild the house of the Lord.'...Thus says the Lord of hosts: 'Consider how you have fared. Go up to the hills and bring wood and build the house, that I may take pleasure in it and that I may appear in my glory,' says the Lord" (Haggai 1:1–2, 7–8).

Thus, with the thundering prophetic oracles of Haggai and Zechariah (Haggai 2:1–4; Zechariah 4:9; 6:15) to encourage them, Zerubbabel and Joshua (i.e., Jeshua) resumed work on the temple in the second year of Darius, 520 B.C.E. At that time, Tattenai, the governor of the larger province of Beyond the River (Hebrew *Abr Nahrain*) enquired as to their authorization to engage in the building, asking "Who gave you a decree to build this house and to finish this structure?" (Ezra 5:3). The Jewish leaders replied that they had been given permission by Cyrus to return to their ancestral lands and to rebuild the house of their God. Darius inquired into the Persian royal archives at Ecbatana, and discovered the original Cyrus decree. The decree is then again inserted into the text of Ezra, this time in Aramaic language (Ezra 6:1–5). However, there are several remarkable statements in the Aramaic decree of Ezra 6 that are not contained in the Ezra 1 version: (1) the dimensions of the temple as well as building instructions are specified: it should be 60 cubits high and 60 cubits wide (the Temple of Solomon was 60 cubits long, 20 wide, and 30 high—1 Kings 6:2), with three courses of stone and one course of timber; (2) the cost of the construction should be paid from the royal treasury. Darius then issued a decree to the governor, Tattenai, stating that the construction should be resumed and not impeded. The Jewish people and their leaders should carry out the project, and the costs will be paid from the royal treasuries, "from royal revenue, the tribute of the province from Beyond the River." (Ezra 6:8). Whatever the Jews would need for daily sacrifices, whether animals, grains, oils, wine, or salt, will be provided to them "that they may offer pleasing sacrifices to the God of heaven, and pray for the life of the king and his sons" (Ezra 6:9–10).

The construction of the temple was completed "the third day of Adar, in the sixth year of the reign of Darius the king" (Ezra 6:15 = March–April [the twelfth month] 516 B.C.E.). From the perspective of the Hebrew Bible, this date is significant as fulfilling, and completing, the prophecies of a seventy year exile, for example in Jeremiah 25:11–12 and Jeremiah 29:10. The seventy years are calculated from 586 B.C.E., the destruction of the Temple of Solomon by Nebuchadnezzar, to 516 B.C.E.[8]

An enormous festival of dedication was held, and the Priests and Levites were placed in readiness for their service in the temple. In the following month therefore, on the 14th day of the first month, Abib, the Passover was observed, followed by the Feast of Unleavened Bread (Ezra 7:16–22).

This, in essence, is all that we know from the Hebrew Bible of the building and ritual details of the Zerubbabel phase of the Second Temple. The account of Josephus (*Jewish Antiquities* XI) does not add any significant detail relating to the building itself. It seems obvious that the returning exiles would have paid close attention to the building plans of the first temple, that they would have built upon the ruins of the foundations of the earlier structure, and the accounts in Ezra give much emphasis to the vast numbers of gold and silver temple vessels which had been installed by Nebuchadnezzar in "the temple of Babylon" (Ezra 5:14). This latter fact by the way is of enormous importance as a historical detail that dovetails with the claims of the Cyrus Cylinder, that the king "resettled upon the command of Marduk, the great lord, all the gods of Sumer and Akkad whom Nabonidus has brought into Babylon to the anger of the lord of the gods, unharmed, in their former chapels, the places which make them happy."[9] Obviously, Nebuchadnezzar, King of Babylon before Nabonidus, had installed the "gods" of the Jewish temple in the temple of Marduk in Babylon, making them unhappy. Cyrus was now undoing this wrong.

The prophets Haggai and Zechariah, who supported the building of the temple with prophetic oracles and admonitions, give us deep insight into some of what I call the "temple typology,"[10] that is, the theological, symbolic, and "cosmic" ideas behind temple building in general. For example Haggai attributes lack of rainfall and the subsequent drought to the failure to build the temple (Haggai 1:10–11). Later in the book, the prophet states adamantly that "before a stone was placed upon a stone in the temple of the Lord, how did you fare?" The answer: "When one came to a heap of twenty measures, there were but ten; when one came to the wine vat to draw fifty measures, there were but twenty. I smote you and all the products of your toil with blight and mildew and hail" (Haggai 2:15–17). However, from the day of the laying of the foundation stone of the temple: "Is the seed yet in the barn? Do the vine, the fig tree, the pomegranate, and the olive tree still yield nothing? From this day on I will bless you" (Haggai 2:19). This is a universal idea among temple-building peoples, and relates to my observation that "The temple is associated with abundance and prosperity, indeed is perceived as the giver of these."[11]

Zechariah evokes the idea of the temple as cosmic mountain (Zechariah 8:3), and presents a visionary reprise of the golden lamp stand of the Tabernacle (Zechariah 4:1–2; Exodus 25:31–40), and, as the vision continues, introduces two olive trees (symbols of sacred trees—trees of life—that are always associated with temples—Ezekiel 47:12) on either side of the lamp stand (also images of prophetic/priestly/messianic authority with which the temple is always associated), then the symbol of the sacred mountain, then the symbol of the "top stone," and the image of laying the foundation of the temple (Zechariah 4:3–14).[12]

From this we can conclude that the Temple of Jerusalem, from its beginnings, is embedded within, represents, and evokes a symbolism that permeates all aspects of biblical teaching and doctrine, both within the Hebrew Bible, within the New Testament, within the Dead Sea/Qumran community, and within the vast Apocryphal and Pseudepigraphical scriptural literature. The temple is at the center of the teachings of this tradition. Temple symbolism informs and illuminates doctrinal presentations in Scripture. The community of God exists within the shade of the temple, underneath the protective shadow of the holy mountain. All aspects of their lives and being are illuminated by that which emanates from the holy mountain, and this illumination projects out into the world. This is the meaning of the idea of "the center."

Having come this far, however, we must now confront certain crucial aspects of the Second Temple that are absent for the duration of the Second Temple's existence, up to 70 C.E. That which is of utmost importance to the Temple of Solomon, without which we, and on the evidence of the Hebrew Bible itself, cannot imagine that it could be a truly authentic edifice, functioning in its divinely intended purposes, namely the Ark of the Covenant, the Mercy Seat, and the Cherubim, these are totally absent in the Second Temple, and are in fact never mentioned henceforth in the Hebrew Bible, in Josephus, or in the Apocryphal literature. The reason for their absence is obvious, namely that they were destroyed at some point during the existence of the Temple of Solomon. But given their centrality to the ritual of the temple, to the ritual year of the ancient Jewish people, to the very act of purgation of sin on the Day of Atonement, their absence is astonishing and cannot simply be forgotten or ignored. It is sobering indeed to realize, given what we know of the grandeur and magnificence of the Temple of Solomon, that, during the entire duration of the Second Temple, every time the High Priest entered the *debir* on the Day of Atonement, that the sacred chapel was empty.

When we deal with temples, we often forget exact language, and speak of "the temple." But the central feature of the temple is the holy of holies, the central, innermost chapel, where the statue of the deity resides, where the most sacred rituals connected with the temple are carried out, the rituals upon which the connection between heaven and earth is based, the rituals that cement the solidity and stability of society, and their connection to and relationship with deity. The holy of holies is viewed as the primary place of the creation of the earth, the place so sacred that it may only be entered by the high priest, in the case of the Temple Jerusalem once a year, or by the king on certain other occasions. The holy of holies is viewed as the earthly counterpart of the throne of god in heaven. So we must recognize this gaping void in the Second Temple, and see what implications this may have as we proceed.

There is another primary feature of the Second Temple that is lacking, namely the two bronze pillars, Jachin and Boaz, which stood in the front of the building, and symbolized the cosmic relationships that connected the earth with the heavens. Why were these pillars not rebuilt? There was obviously only *one* Ark of the Covenant. It obviously could not simply be "rebuilt" or "replaced." Its destruction was unimaginably catastrophic. But in the case of the pillars, one would expect that they would be rebuilt. One possible answer, the one that comes most readily to mind for the Zerubbabel phase of the Second Temple, is that reflected in Haggai 2:3: "Who is left among you that saw this house in its former glory? How do you see it now? Is it not in your sight as nothing?" This implies that the Zerubbabel temple was simply a poorer version of the Temple of Solomon, which makes sense in the light of the historical details of its rebuilding by the returning exiles. Although in this same chapter of Haggai the Lord states that He will cause untold treasures to come into the land, gold and silver, so that "The latter splendor of this house shall be greater than the former," (Haggai 2:9) this points towards the future, in all probability towards the Messianic Age, to which we will turn in a later chapter.

There is one more important feature missing in the Second Temple, that was a fundamental feature of the Temple of Solomon. That is that the temple existed within the context of a political state, an independent polity, with a royal dynasty that was legitimized by its connection with the cosmic temple, identifying the kingship with heavenly authority and legitimacy.[13] Post-Exilic Judah was a tributary province, first of the Persian Empire, "lacking full political autonomy."[14] At the time of Solomon, a magnificent and costly royal palace dwarfed the temple on the Temple Mount (1 Kings 7:1–12). There was no such palatial structure on the Temple Mount to accompany the Temple of Zerubbabel, nor was there ever such in the history of the Second Temple.[15] From Second Temple times on, the focus is no longer on the king, but rather on the priesthood, and particularly the person of the High Priest.

From post-biblical times, the clearest picture we get of the Zerubbabel Temple comes from the Apocryphal books of Maccabees, particularly 1 and 2 Maccabees. Set in the time of the Ptolemaic and Seleucid empires, which ruled in Egypt and Syria, respectively, Maccabees outlines the history of the Hasmonean dynasty, a family of priestly, but non-Aaronite/Zadokite Jews who originated in the village of Modein, northwest of Jerusalem. The centerpiece of the history takes place in the time of Antiochus IV, Epiphanes (ruled 175–164 B.C.E.), a descendant of Seleucus, the general of Alexander the Great who took over the Syrian conquests of Alexander following the latter's death in 323 B.C.E. Judea in the time of Antiochus was caught up in a frenzy of Hellenization, according to which many Jews took on Greek style of dress, built a gymnasium where they exercised in the nude, according to Greek styles, and in other ways forsook the laws of Torah (1 Maccabees 1:11–15).

Antiochus returned to Judea from Egypt in 168 B.C.E., following a failed military campaign against Ptolemaic dynasty there. In Jerusalem, "he arrogantly entered the sanctuary and took the golden altar, the lampstand for the light, and all its utensils. He took also the table for the bread of the Presence, the cups for drink offerings, the bowls, the golden censers, the curtain, the crowns, and the gold decoration on the front of the temple; he stripped it all off. He took the silver and the gold, and the costly vessels; he took also the hidden treasures which he found. Taking them all, he departed to his own land" (1 Maccabees 1:21–24). Two years later, he sent a large military force to Jerusalem, which sacked the city and set up a garrison in the City of David. The king commanded that all people in his kingdom "should be one people, and that each should give up his customs" (1 Maccabees 1:41). Many Jews accepted this decree, "and adopted his religion" (1 Maccabees 1:43). This involved numerous acts that defiled the sanctuary and the priesthood, such as forbidding burnt offerings, building shrines to other gods, and sacrificing swine, which refusing to do carried the penalty of death (1 Maccabees 1:44–50). All of these are acts that defile the priesthood and the Temple and constitute gross acts of rebellion against Torah. The final degradation came on the 15th of Chislev (December) 167 B.C.E., when "they erected a desolating sacrilege upon the altar of burnt offering" (1 Maccabees 1:54). This incident is described in 2 Maccabees: "Not long after this, the king sent an Athenian senator to compel the Jews to forsake the laws of their fathers and cease to live by the laws of God, and also to pollute the temple in Jerusalem and call it the temple of Olympian Zeus" (6:1–2).

The main pious response to these depradations came from a family from the village of Modein, a man named Mattathias, of priestly lineage. He had five sons, John, Simon, Judas, called Maccabeus, Eleazar, and Jonathan. Mattathias instigated a revolt against the Seleucids and against the corruption of Jewish life and worship. Upon the death of Mattathias, Judas Maccabeus took over leadership of the revolt. Antiochus IV raised a large army under the leadership of one Lysias, in order to invade Judea and destroy it once and for all. Judas Maccabeus led the Jewish forces against this army, defeated them twice in successive years, and recaptured the citadel of Zion, where the temple stood. Upon entering into the temple precincts, "they saw the sanctuary desolate, the altar profaned, and the gates burned. In the courts they saw bushes sprung up as in a thicket, or as one of the mountains. They saw also the chambers of the priests in ruins" (1 Maccabees 4:38). Priests were chosen to cleanse the sacred area. The altar of burnt offering had been profaned by the "desolating sacrilege" sacrificed upon it by Antiochus IV (1 Maccabees 1:54). This altar was therefore torn down, and the stones

Stored…in a convenient place on the temple hill until there should come a prophet to tell what to do with them. They took unhewn stones, as the law directs, and built a new altar like the former one. They also rebuilt the sanctuary and the interior of the temple, and consecrated the courts. They made new holy vessels, and brought the lampstand, the altar of incense, and the table into the temple. Then they burned incense on the altar and lighted lamps on the lampstand, and these gave light in the temple. They placed the bread on the table and hung up the curtains. Thus they finished all the work they had undertaken. (1 Maccabees 4:46–51)

The temple was rededicated on the 25th of the month Chislev (December), 164 B.C.E. "So they celebrated the dedication of the altar for eight days, and offered burnt offerings with gladness; they offered a sacrifice of deliverance and praise. They decorated the front of the temple with golden crowns and small shields; they restored the gates and the chambers for the priests, and furnished them with doors" (1 Maccabees 4:56–57). This feast, the Festival of Hanukkah, was then decreed as a permanent Jewish festival by Judas and his brothers, to be celebrated for eight days every year starting on the 25th of the month Chislev (1 Maccabees 4:59).

This was a momentous stage in the history of ancient Judaism, and it raises Judas Maccabeus into the ranks of the great Israelite temple builders and restorers, such as Solomon, Josiah, and Zerubbabel.[16] However there is also great irony here, because Judas was neither a king (nor of Davidic lineage), nor of high priestly lineage, nor was there prophetic support such as was the case in the time of Solomon, Josiah (Huldah, the prophetess), and Zerubbabel (Haggai and Zechariah). In fact, the temple traditions of ancient Israel were always based on the three pillars of Davidic lineage and/or kingship, Aaronite/Zadokite high priesthood, and prophecy, that is until this time that we are presently discussing. There are two passages in 1 Maccabees that explicitly state the absence of prophetic authority at that time: 1 Maccabees 4:46: "And stored the stones in a convenient place on the temple hill until there should come a prophet to tell what to do with them;" and 1 Maccabees 14:41; "And the Jews and their priests decided that Simon should be their leader and high priest forever, until a trustworthy prophet should arise."[17] In fact, the traditional end of "official" biblical prophecy is the ministry of Malachi, around 500–450 B.C.E.

The successor to Judas Maccabeus, his brother Jonathan, usurped the high priesthood at the hands of the Seleucid king Alexander I Epiphanes, Alexander Balas! We read "And so we have appointed you today to be the high priest of your nation; you are to be called the king's friend" (and he sent him a purple robe and a golden crown). "So Jonathan put on the holy garments in the seventh month of the one hundred sixtieth year [152 B.C.E.], at the feast of the tabernacles..." (1 Maccabees 10:20–21).

The high priesthood then became hereditary in the Hasmonean family, with Simon, then his son John Hyrcanus holding the office. Ironically, the book of 1 Maccabees ends with the cryptic phrase "The rest of the acts of John [Hyrcanus]...behold, they are written in the chronicles of his high priesthood [a lost work], from the time that he became high priest after his father" (1 Maccabees 16:23–24). The son of Hyrcanus, Aristobulus, took the title of "king," which continued in the family, along with the high priesthood, down to the time of Antigonus II, who was replaced as king of Judah and Jerusalem by Herod, by the Roman overseers in 37 B.C.E. (Josephus, *Antiquities,* XIII-XIV).[18]

A number of non-biblical texts that were composed in this period of time, and that contain interesting and valuable comments relating to the Zerubbabel Temple, have come down to us. These include the writings of Hecataeus of Abdera, a Greek philosopher who live around the time of Alexander the Great, and whose work is contained within the *Contra Apionem* of Josephus, the *Letter of Aristeas,* a Pseudepigraphical work written by an Alexandrian Jew during the reign of the Egyptian king Ptolemy II Philadelphus (ruled 285–247 B.C.E.), and the *Wisdom of Jesus Ben Sira,* in both Hebrew (around 175 B.C.E.) and Greek (approximately 135–104 B.C.E.), an Apocryphal scripture. The temple-related segments of these writings have been conveniently collected by Hayward (1996).

According to Hayward, "If Hecataeus was truly the author of the writings which Josephus reproduces, we have before us one of the oldest surviving descriptions (outside the Bible) of the Jewish Temple and its Service, most unusually written by a non-Jew. For these reasons alone, such information should occupy a special place in any account of the Temple and its rites."[19]

Hecataeus of Abdera stated that Jerusalem was a city of 120,000 men (which Hayward thinks is an exaggeration), and that its circumference was about 50 stades (a stade was about 1/10th of a mile, or a furlong, therefore six miles), and that there were 15 hundred priests "who receive the tithe of the revenue and administer the affairs of the community." In *Contra Apionem* II, 108, Josephus gave the number of priests as 20,000, that is the four priestly clans who returned with Zerubbabel (Ezra 2:36) at 5,000 each: "these officiate by rotation for a fixed period of days; when the term of one party ends, others come to offer the sacrifices in their place, and assembling at midday in the temple, take over from the outgoing ministers the keys of the building and all its vessels, duly numbered" (*Contra Apionem* II, 108).

Josephus gave the circumference as 35 stades.[20] He (Hecataeus) claimed that the temple was nearly in the middle of the city (*kata meson malista teis poleos*), and he described a *temenos* of five plethora long and a hundred cubits wide (500 feet by 150 feet), enclosed within a stone wall entered through double gates. He must be describing the inner court, or the "court of the priests" described by Josephus in *Contra Apionem* II, 104, accessible only to "the priests robed in their priestly vestments," comparable in the Temple of Solomon to the "court of the priests" described in 2 Chronicles 4:9: "He made the court of the priests, and the great court, and doors for the court, and overlaid their doors with bronze."

Hecataeus is here describing this court, its doors or double gates, and then "a square altar composed of unhewn, undressed stones collected together. Each side is twenty cubits, and its height ten cubits."[21] This would be the (bronze) altar of burnt offering that is mentioned for the first time with its dimensions in 2 Chronicles 4:1, an altar that King Solomon had constructed for the burnt offerings in the middle of the court in front of the temple, for the temple dedication, "because the bronze altar [i.e., the smaller stone, bronze covered four-horned altar of burnt offerings that stood in front of the temple—Exodus 27:1] was too small to receive the burnt offering and the cereal offering and the fat pieces of the peace offerings" (1 Kings 8:64). This latter altar is the one that King Ahaz removed from its place in order to replace it with the altar he had seen in Damascus, and had replicated to be placed for his use in front of the temple in the inner court (2 Kings 16:14).[22]

Hecataeus then describes the temple itself, calling it a "building," (Greek *oikema*), namely "a large building where there is an altar and a lampstand; both are golden, and their weight two talents."[23] The altar is the altar of incense, standing in the *heikal* (Exodus 30:1–4) and the lampstand is the seven-branched candlestick (Exodus 25:31–40). According to Exodus 25:29, the weight of the lampstand was one talent, and the altar of incense was overlaid with gold (Exodus 30:3–4).[24] Here Hecataeus gives as two talents the combined weight of both. A talent was about 75 pounds.

The *Letter of Aristeas,* ostensibly dating to about a generation after Hecataeus, although its date is quite disputed,[25] derives its greatest fame and importance from the fact that it is the only ancient text that documents the process by which the Hebrew Bible was translated into Greek, giving us the Septuagint. The background is that the king wanted his librarian to assemble all of the books in the world for the library at Alexandria. The librarian, Demetrius of Phalerum, wanted to include a copy of the Jewish law, and commissioned a letter to be written to the high priest at Jerusalem, asking him to assign six members of each of the 12 tribes as translators. Embedded within this narrative is a description of Jerusalem and the Temple, by Aristeas himself, encompassing verses 83–120.[26] There are many historical and literary anachronisms in *Aristeas*, such as for example that the author assumes the existence of and quotes from the Septuagint before it has supposedly come into existence. This points towards a later date than the text itself claims,[27] and may cast doubt on the work as an eyewitness account.

Aristeas' description of Jerusalem and the temple begins with his account of how the city itself stood out from the surrounding countryside on such a high mountain (verse 83), and that the temple stood out prominently even above height of the city in general, "towering above all."[28] He describes "three enclosing walls over seventy cubits [i.e. about one hundred twenty three feet] in size [i.e. high]"[29] "...everything was built with a magnificence and expense which excelled in every respect" (verse 84).[30] Hayward comments on this last statement in the light of what we have see earlier in Haggai 2:3, regarding the inferior appearance of the Zerubbabel Temple in comparison with the Solomonic, and asks whether this is mere hyperbole, or pro-Jewish propaganda, or whether the temple had actually been improved during the Hasmonean period.[31]

Beginning in verse 87, and continuing to verse 99, *Aristeas* gives an extraordinary description of the altar of burnt offering, the orientation of the temple, the water, cistern, and reservoir supply, the manner of the service of the priests, including the actual way in which the priests hoist joints of sacrificial animals up onto the altar, and, incredibly a complete description of the actual priestly dress of the high priest Eleazar, whom he sees exiting the temple in full priestly regalia.

To begin with the altar, in verse 87, he makes the unusual comment regarding the necessity for a ramp on the altar, rather than a staircase, in order to protect the modesty of the ministrants as they mount the ramp, so that their nakedness would not be revealed, as Exodus 20:26 requires.

Verses 88 through 91 deal with, and enumerate the "endless supply of water, as if indeed a strongly flowing natural spring were issuing forth from within [the Temple]; and In addition there exist marvelous and indescribable reservoirs underground—as they showed me—for five stades around the foundation of the Temple; and each of them has numberless channels such that the streams join up together with each other from different sides."[32] This emphasis on the overabundant reservoirs and water sources has two implications, one theoretical and one quite practical. First, the theoretical. It relates to the cosmic aspect of the temple, the waters of creation, the abysses, the deep underground waters that represent the primeval beginnings of the temple, and that are ever-present in the temple's history, providing constant access to the "waters of life," as in the famous passage from Ezekiel relating to the Messianic temple of the future:

> Then he brought me back to the door of the temple; and behold, water was issuing from below the threshold of the temple toward the east (for the temple faced east); and the water was flowing down from below the south end of the threshold of the temple, south of the altar. Then he brought me out by way of the north gate, and led me round on the outside to the outer gate, that faces toward the east; and the water was coming out on the south side. (Ezekiel 47:1–2)

The way I phrased this aspect of the cosmic symbolism of the temple is

> The temple is often associated with the waters of life which flow forth from a spring within the building itself-or rather the temple is viewed as incorporating within itself or as having been built upon such a spring. The reason such springs exist in temples is that they are perceived as the primeval waters of creation, Nun in Egypt, Abzu in Mesopotamia. The temple is thus founded on and stands in contact with the primeval waters.[33]

At verse 89 of the *Letter of Aristeas* we read that "there is an endless supply of water, as if indeed a strongly flowing natural spring were issuing forth from within [the Temple]; and in addition there exist marvelous and indescribable reservoirs underground—as they showed me."

Hayward points out that *Aristeas* uses the Greek work *katabole* for "foundation," as in the phrase "for five stades around the foundation of the Temple" (Verse 89). This same word appears several times in the New Testament, as in Matthew 13:35, 25:34; Luke 11:50; John 17:24; Ephesians 1:4. The characteristic phrase is "since the foundation of the world," "from the foundation of the world," and "before the foundation of the world." Thus, according to Hayward, was the author of *Aristeas* referring to "the abysses, in which the foundations of the world were fixed, the Temple forming an essential link between them, the earth, and heaven?"[34]

The practical aspect of the emphasis on water sources underneath the temple relates to the enormity of the animal sacrifices (in verse 88 it is claimed that "many tens of thousands of beasts are brought for sacrifice on the days of the festivals"), and the amounts of water, and of water channels, necessary for the outflow both of the blood of the sacrificed animals, and of the water needed to wash the blood away. He states that the reservoirs and water channels were leaded and plastered, and that there were numerous openings at the base of the altar of burnt offerings, not apparent except to those doing the sacrificing, "so that all the blood of the sacrifices, which is collected in huge amounts, is cleansed by the downward momentum of the slope" (verse 90).

Continuing, the writer of the *Letter of Aristeas* gives us yet more fascinating detail on the actual operation of the sacrificial process, detail of a kind that is not found in the Hebrew Bible. In verse 93, he describes in vivid detail the manner in which an officiating priest hoists the legs of a sacrificial calf up onto the altar:

> For with both hands they take up the legs of the calf, each of which for the most part are more than two talents' [i.e. about one hundred fifty pounds] weight, and in a wonderful manner throw them with each hand to the correct height [for the altar] and do not miss in their aim. Likewise the portions of the lambs and of the goats are also wonderful in weight and fatness. For those whose duty it is always choose those which are without blemish and which excel in fatness.[35]

In other words, what is being described here is an athletic move, in which the priests lift up animal's joints, with one movement, as would a weight lifter the "weight," and hoist them in one move onto the proper place on the altar. Thus these verses give color and interest and invaluable information to illuminate the interminable chapters of the Hebrew Bible where these processes are described.

At this point in the *Aristeas* narrative, the author goes on to describe in glowing terms the "high priest," one Eleazar, namely the one to whom a letter by King Ptolemy II was written requesting that he choose the six members of each tribe for the translation of the Torah from Hebrew into Greek. This Eleazar is otherwise unknown as a high priest, though a "scribe" of the same name appears in 2 Maccabees 6:18–20. The author of *Aristeas* describes Eleazar in his priestly role, magnificently attired in the priestly dress, along with the turban with the name of deity inscribed in gold letters on the crown (verses 96–98; Exodus 28). His description of the robe focuses intently on the magnificence and splendor of the cloth, and its beautiful colors. He mentions the golden bells, with the pomegranate-shaped cloth (in blue, purple, and scarlet—Exodus 28:34) on either side of each bell, on the bottom fringe of the robe of the ephod, "which possessed a marvelous color" (verse 96). The bells "gave out a particular sound of musical note" (verse 96).

Aristeas describes the 12 stones that the high priest wore on the breastplate of judgment, each inscribed with the name of one of the tribes of Israel (verse 97—Exodus 28:15–30), as well as the turban, with the divine name inscribed in golden letters on the forehead (verse 98—Exodus 28:36–38). Everywhere the author speaks in tones of ineffability, mystery, almost incomprehensible beauty, awe, an unearthly aura: "The overall appearance of these things created awe and confusion, so as to make one think that he has come close to another man from outside the world." (verse 99).[36] Or, in the translation of Andrew: "Their appearance created such awe and confusion of mind as to make one feel that one had come into the presence of a man who belonged to a different world."[37]

The author of *Aristeas* gives extensive emphasis to the idea that the Temple cult was carried out in absolute silence: "The Service of the priests is in every respect unsurpassed in the physical strength (required of them) and in its orderly and silent arrangement" (verse 92).[38] In a subsequent verse he states that "And a complete silence reigns, with the result that one might suppose that there was not a single person present in the place, even though there are around seven hundred ministering priests present and a great number of men bringing up the sacrifices; but everything is discharged with awe and in a manner worthy of the great Godhead" (verse 95).[39]

There a school of thought among biblical scholars that asserts the complete, total, and absolute silence of the Temple service "within the priestly realm of the Temple."[40] That means, there was total silence, as indicated by the writer of *Aristeas*, inside the Court of the Priests. There is no evidence within the Hebrew Bible to support this idea, and Hayward himself discusses it at length, in his commentary to these verses, showing that such an idea contradicts the Mishnah, as well as common sense, because both the biblical record and the Mishnah evidence for the specifics of the Temple cult give us a picture of vast numbers of priests, extensive and complex movements and activities, large numbers of animals being slaughtered, and of prayers and incantations being offered. That the service was conducted with a sense of awe[41] ("…but everything is discharged with awe and in a manner worthy of the great Godhead"—*Aristeas*, verse 95), does not contravene the probable fact of noise, hubbub, and even of tumult.

How did the author of *Aristeas* actually observe all that is described of Jerusalem and the priestly activities and dress that are described here? The author claims to have personally observed these matters from atop a citadel (Greek *akra*), which gave the viewer an untrammeled view of events transpiring the temple courts. This *akra* would be the Akra, or Acra, the citadel built on the Temple Mount by Antiochus IV Epiphanes: "Then they [i.e., the followers of Antiochus] fortified the city of David with a great strong wall and strong towers, and it became their citadel. And they stationed there a sinful people, lawless men. These strengthened their position; they stored up arms and food, and collecting the spoils of Jerusalem they stored them there, and became a great snare" (1 Maccabees 1:33–35). Of the many proposed reconstructions of the place and architecture of this citadel, that of Ben-Dov seems the most convincing, based on his excavations in the foot of the Temple Mount.[42] He places it directly up against the southern perimeter wall of the Temple Mount, in a position that would allow someone standing on its ramparts to view activities within the temple precincts below. The writer of *Aristeas* states

> But in order that we might gain complete information, we ascended to the summit of the neighboring citadel and looked around us. It is situated in a very lofty spot, and is fortified with many towers, which have been built up to the very top of immense stones, with the object, as we were informed, of guarding the temple precincts, so that if there were an attack, or an insurrection or an onslaught of the enemy, no one would be able to force an entrance within the walls that surround the temple....They [the guards] were very reluctant to admit us—though we were but two unarmed men—to view the offering of the sacrifices....The citadel was the special protection of the temple. (verses 100–104)[43]

Thus, in the *Letter to Aristeas* we have, despite the controversies and differences of scholarly opinion on its authorship, date, and purpose, a record that provides us with the strong possibility of an invaluable first-person, eyewitness account of important temple and temple-related architecture, ritual, and priestly functions and appearance from a time late in the history of the Zerubbabel Temple.

We now come to an Apocryphal text, *Ecclesiasticus*, or the *Wisdom of Jesus the Son of Sirach*, or the *Wisdom of Jesus Ben Sira in Hebrew*,[44] hereafter *Sirach*. This Apocryphal scripture, "the only book in the Apocrypha of which the name of the author is known" (*The New Oxford Annotated Bible with the Apocrypha, Revised Standard Version, The Apocrypha of The Old Testament, Revised Standard Version*, p. 128), is also firmly dated to around 175 B.C.E.[45] Chapter 50 of this scripture is devoted to a poetic (the entire book is written in traditional Hebrew poetry) eulogy of the Zadokite high priest Simon (Simeon) II (high priest 219–196 B.C.E.), who served during the time that the Seleucids wrested control of Judea from the Ptolemies. Antiochus III the Great had defeated a Ptolemaic army at Paneas in 198 B.C.E., and thus came into control of Palestine. It was in the generation following that of Simon II that the Hellenization described in 1 Maccabees 1 began to infiltrate Judea, causing so much consternation to Orthodox Jews.

Sirach's poetry is transcendently beautiful, and his praise for Simon in chapter 50 reaches poetic heights placing it high in the ranks of great

Hebrew poetry. Given the fact that the background of the poem is the service of the high priest in the temple, including possibly in the *debir* on the Day of Atonement, it becomes one of the most important and unique documents relating to the Temple of Zerubbabel. "How glorious he was when the people gathered around him as he came out of the inner sanctuary" (verse 5—literally, "the house of the veil," i.e., the *debir*). There is much debate as to whether this verse describes the high priest exiting the *debir*, in which case it could only have been on the Day of Atonement because that is the one day in the year when the high priest, and he alone, may enter that holy chapel (Leviticus 16), or whether it describes him exiting the *heikal* into the courtyard where the altar of burnt offerings stands. The "veil," (Hebrew *paroket)* stood before the holy of holies, the *debir* (2 Chronicles 3:14). The Hebrew Bible makes it quite clear that the purpose of the veil is that it shall "separate the holy place (i.e., *heikal*) from the most holy (i.e., *debir*)" (Exodus 26:33).

It seems that the poem of *Sirach,* chapter 50, is an almost perfect account of one who actually witnessed the high priest exiting the *debir* on the Day of Atonement. The sixteenth chapter of Leviticus, in which we have the sole description of the rituals of this day in the Hebrew Bible, gives the following sequence of events after the high priest has exited the *debir,* following the atoning sacrifices he has completed there (Leviticus 16:1–22): Upon exiting, he takes off the simple linen garments "which he put on when he went into the holy place, and shall leave them there" (Leviticus 16:23). He then washed "and put on his garments, and come forth, and offer his burnt offering of the people, and make atonement for himself and for the people" (Leviticus 16:24).

The verses in *Sirach* that seem to correspond exactly to this moment state that, after he has come out from the "house of the veil" (*Sirach* 50:5), "he covered himself with the garments of glory and clothed himself in garments of beauty. When he went up to the altar there was majesty: He made honorable the court of the sanctuary" (*Sirach* 50:11).[46] In other words, he exited the *debir,* removed the simple linen garments that he wore in the most holy place, washed, and put on a new set of garments, presumably the "garments of glory... garments of beauty" of Sirach 50:11. At this exact point, in Leviticus 16: "And the fat of the sin offering he shall burn upon the altar" (Leviticus 16:25). At the corresponding moment in *Sirach* we read: "When he received the portions from the hand of his brothers, and he himself stood up over the arranged pieces.... Until he finished ministering at the altar and set in order the arranged pieces of the Most High" (*Sirach* 50:12, 14). So, in both Leviticus and in *Sirach* the high priest clothes himself in new garments, and then proceeds to minister at the altar of burnt offerings.

Leviticus 16 ends with a review of the Day of Atonement requirements and an admonition to celebrate this Day forever. *Sirach,* chapter 50, ends with the sound of trumpets, singing, rejoicing, and with a benediction on the assembled congregation invoking the divine name. The commentators to *The New Oxford Annotated Bible With The Apocrypha,* Expanded Edition, in their commentary to *Sirach* 50:20: "Then Simon came down, and lifted up his hands over the whole congregation of the sons of Israel, to pronounce the blessing of the Lord with his lips, and to glory in his name" (*Sirach* 50:20), state that: "*His name,* only the high priest (and only once a year, on the Day of Atonement), could utter the ineffable name 'Yahweh.'" It thus seems justified in claiming for this Apocryphon an extraordinary eyewitness account of the workings of the high priest on the Day of Atonement in the days of the Zerubbabel Temple.[47]

Throughout this book, it is my purpose to relate all evidence that I survey to the actual Temple of Jerusalem itself, in one of its manifestations, during its actual existence, or, once it no longer existed, to its afterlife as a symbol, its echo, its reverberations in the Judaic, Christian, and Muslim traditions of early antiquity up to the Middle Ages. Furthermore, I want to examine non-biblical scriptural and secular sources that echo or reflect the Temple of Jerusalem, either as an ideal, as a theory, or in its "heavenly," mystical traditions as part of the secret tradition of late antiquity, but not necessarily in any direct or actual contact with the First or Second Temple in Jerusalem itself. With that in mind, I want to now examine the evidence from the Dead Sea Scrolls and the Pseudepigraphical literature. I have chosen to include the discussion of this material in the section on the Zerubbabel Temple, even though the dates of such literature range from approximately the third to second centuries B.C.E. up to the early Middle Ages.

The Temple in the Dead Sea Scrolls

It is widely assumed that the Dead Sea or Qumran people belonged to the Jewish party of the Essenes, and flourished in Palestine between approximately the third century B.C.E. to 70 C.E., when their remnants were destroyed by the Romans at the time of the destruction of the Temple of Herod. The classic ancient definitions of the various sects within Judaism in Second Temple times are those of Philo, Josephus, and Pliny. There were three sects: Pharisees, Sadducees, and Essenes. In addition to definitions given in the authors mentioned, it is possible to gain a self-definition of the Qumran community from their own writings, particularly the *Damascus Document* (designated CD in the corpus of Qumran scrolls), the *Manual of Discipline* or *Community Rule* (1QS), and such other documents as the War

Scroll (1QM). The Essenes/Qumran community were separatist, that is they rejected the priestly establishment in Jerusalem and the sacrificial and ritual calendar of the Temple of Jerusalem; they were Messianic, awaiting the coming of the Messiah to free them from their enemies in a last, apocalyptic battle of light versus darkness, good versus evil. They were a "righteous remnant," led by a Messianic leader known as the "Teacher of Righteousness," who left Jerusalem to live in the desolate area around the Dead Sea to practice their austere rites and to compose their scriptures, both those of the Hebrew Bible, with every book of the Hebrew Bible represented in the Qumran scrolls with the exception of Ruth and Jonah; biblical commentaries on books such as Isaiah, Hosea, Nahum, and Habakkuk; fragments of books of the Apocrypha and Pseudepigrapha, particularly apocalyptic works such as the Enoch literature and Jubilees; and their own scriptural creations and community histories (that is, books not known in any canon heretofore, chief among these many apocalyptic works). Of this latter category of Qumran scrolls, none is more important, sensational, or challenging to our received notions of biblical history, doctrine, and ritual than the *Temple Scroll* (11QT). The story of how this scroll came to light in the dark underworld of illicit excavation and antiquities dealers, to be translated and commented upon in a magisterial publication by Yigael Yadin (1983), and to reside in the Shrine of the Book in Jerusalem's Israel Museum, is beyond the scope of this book.[48] Its importance to the study of the Temple of Jerusalem, and thus to this book is, however, of the highest level.

The central issue of the *Temple Scroll* for this book is the following: is its description of the temple actually based on the temple that existed in the time of its composition, that is the Temple of Zerubbabel. If it is, then it is of inestimable value in expanding our understanding of the architectural structure and the ritual processes of that temple. Or is it primarily a vision of a Messianic temple of the Messianic age, which would put it more in the category of Ezekiel's vision, or of that of the Book of Revelation. However, even in this latter case, if we look more closely at Ezekiel's vision, we will recall that (1) Ezekiel was a priest; and (2) that he actually lived in the time of the Temple of Solomon, and actually experienced its destruction. This means, therefore, that even though his vision is a Messianic one, that elements of his vision would naturally be based on a temple reality that he actually knew. That means that we can learn details of the architecture and ritual of the Temple of Solomon from the vision of Ezekiel, as I have pointed out in Chapter 1. The third category of temple description of ancient times is that of the vision of the heavenly temple, one that is essentially disconnected from the earthly temple, but that gives us a clear picture of the *symbols upon which the earthly temple is based*. This latter case is what we see in the Pseudepigraphical scriptures, to be discussed shortly. Yigael Yadin answers this question strongly in favor of a modified version of option one, above, that is, that it was a plan, from the point of view of the Qumran sectaries, of an actual temple that was to have been built by the group, upon the instructions given by the deity to Moses on Mount Sinai, when they entered the promised land. It had, therefore, no actual connection to the Temple of Zerubbabel (although we will see some interesting similarities with the Temple of Herod), which they in any case rejected, nor can it be used by us to assist in reconstructing that temple. It is a visionary temple,[49] based on direct revelation from God to Moses, as seen through the prism of the Qumran sect's prophetic traditions.[50] It is generally thought that the Qumran sect viewed the *Temple Scroll* as a direct revelation from God.[51] This raises the question, who was the Qumran prophet to whom this scripture was revealed? The probable answer: the Teacher of Righteousness of the *Damascus Document* and the *Commentary on Habakkuk* (1QPHab).[52] The sect may have viewed him as the new Moses, prophesied in Deuteronomy 18:15: "The Lord your God will raise up for you a prophet like me from among your own people."[53]

The Temple of the *Temple Scroll* is a composite temple: "the square court is Ezekiel's design, but in other respects it is not Ezekiel's temple at all. The temple building itself is Solomonic; most of the other installations are not. So it is a composite, with many original elements."[54] The original elements are both architectural and ritual. First, the architecture prescribes new structures not known in the biblical descriptions of either of the two temples. Chief among these are a "House of the Staircase," a massive tower to be built on the northwest corner of the temple, with a walkway allowing access to the sanctuary from its top. This building was to have walls four cubits square, a 12-cubit interior measurement, with a four-cubit square column on the inside. The staircase was to wind around this column. The rooftop access was to be to the *heikal*, which means the nave or sanctuary, not directly to the Holy of Holies. The text states that "through the gate on…to the entrance of [the roof(?) of the] *heikal*, through which one may enter unto the upper chamber of the *heikal*."[55] All surfaces of this structure, inside and out, were to be overlaid with gold. A "winding staircase" is described in 1 Kings 6:8, on either the south or the north side of the "House" (Hebrew *beit*), which gave access from the bottom of the three-annex storeys to the upper two.[56]

Another unique structure described in the *Temple Scroll* is a "House of the Laver," to be situated at the southeast corner of the main temple. It was to be 21 cubits square, and be located 50 cubits from the Altar of the Burnt Offerings. It was here that the priests washed themselves before and after performing their priestly duties, and it was here that they were to store the clothes they wore to the temple. A drain was to be constructed around this house to receive the water runoff from the washing.[57] The *Temple Scroll* places maximum emphasis on holiness, and includes admonitions that no priest enter the sacred precincts "...and he is not clothed with the [the holy] gar[ments with wh]ich(?) he was ordained to minister, they, too, shall be put to death."[58] Elsewhere the *Temple Scroll*, reflecting Ezekiel 44:18–19, states that the priests should not leave the sacred precincts, that is the inner court, while wearing their priestly clothes (Ezekiel 44:18: "They shall have linen turbans upon their heads, and linen breeches upon their loins; they shall not gird themselves with anything that causes sweat" that is, the priests were not to enter the inner court while wearing wool. The inner court was for linen, thus the House of the Laver would be the place where they would wash, store their "street" clothes, and don the priestly, linen, apparel). The phrase appears in Column XXXIII, line 7: "they shall(?) [not] communicate holiness to my people with the holy garments." This reflects Ezekiel 44:19: "And when they go out into the outer court to the people, they shall put off the garments in which they have been ministering, and lay them in the holy chambers; and they shall put on their other garments, lest they communicate holiness to the people with their garments." In other words, everyday clothing is not allowed in the inner court, and priestly clothing is not allowed in the outer courts.[59] The House of the Laver facilitates this process, as illustrated in the "holy chambers" of Ezekiel 44:19.

The remaining structures, unique to the *Temple Scroll* include the House of the Utensils, the same size as the House of the Laver, located seven cubits from the House of the Laver. The purpose of this house was for storage of the temple utensils used for sacrifice on the altar.[60] Immediately following the description of the House of the Utensils comes a description of slaughterhouse, a 12-columned building on the northwest corner of the inner courtyard. Chains and rings hung from the ceiling, to which animals were attached. Descriptions are given for the elaborate slaughtering procedures, including dismemberment, flaying of the skins, washing, salting, and all preparations for sacrifice on the Altar of Burnt Offerings. This is extremely valuable information because no such structure nor the detailed methodology of slaughter for sacrifice is given in the Hebrew Bible.[61] A similar structure is described in the Talmud, Tractate *Middoth* for the Temple of Herod.[62]

The final unique structure described in the *Temple Scroll* is a Stoa or colonnade, on the west side of the temple (that is, the back). It was to this place that the he-goats for the sin offerings and the rams for the guilt offerings were to be brought, and tethered to the columns, and where they were to be strictly separated into those for the priests and those for the people. There is a reflection of this installation in the Hebrew Bible, both in Ezekiel (46:19–20), and in 1 Chronicles (26:18), where we meet the unknown word *parbar* (which Yadin amends to *paror*, "a stoa of columns").[63] On the basis of the *Temple Scroll* description of the Stoa, Yadin connects these passages with the description of the Stoa and its role in keeping the sacrificial animals separate:[64] "and there I saw a place at the extreme western end of them [that is, on the back—western—end of the Temple]. And he said to me, 'This is the place where the priests shall boil the guilt offering and the sin offering, and where they shall bake the cereal offering, in order not to bring them out into the outer court and so communicate holiness to the people'" (Ezekiel 46:19–20).

There are six annual festivals prescribed for the temple in the *Temple Scroll* that are not found in the Hebrew Bible: an eight day priestly consecration (this was a one-time event in the Hebrew Bible—Exodus 29; Leviticus 8); a festival of new barley, of new wheat, of new wine, of new oil, and a wood festival. The New Wheat festival was the day on which the Qumran sectaries renewed their covenants, in ceremonies that are described in the *Manual of Discipline* 1:16–2:25.[65]

As is true for the temple described in Ezekiel's visions, and that of the Book of Revelation, so also the temple described in the *Temple Scroll* envisions the entire city of Jerusalem as a holy, temple-based city, where, for example, the cleanliness laws of the Hebrew Bible, along with even more stringent laws that are unique to the *Temple Scroll*, would be enforced throughout the holy city.

The Temple in the Pseudepigrapha

The Pseudepigraphical scriptures of the Old Testament are a vast body of purported scriptures, most of which have the name of a prominent biblical figure attached to them as author, thus the designation Pseudepigrapha. They range in date from approximately the third century B.C.E. to the Middle Ages, and are preserved in a wide range of languages and versions. They reflect both Jewish and Christian backgrounds and influences.[66] Their content is exceptionally wide, including works that expand upon the Old Testament, in its various versions, legendary material, prayers and psalms, and a large number of apocalypses and testaments. As is to be expected, the temple is a major theme in this literature. The aspect of the temple theme in the Pseudepigrapha, which I want to emphasize here, is that which is found primarily in the visionary, apocalyptic works.

The concrete, historical temple, as we know and understand it, does not play a dominant role in the Pseudepigrapha. What appears in these works are what I call the primordial symbols that underlie and precede the temple: the sacred mountain, the tree of life, the waters of life, the heavenly temple, and the throne of God in heaven. In other words the Pseudepigrapha give us a THEORY of the temple, a "temple ideology" as I have called it elsewhere.[67]

The temple is a concrete earthly representation of these visionary symbols, which underlie and provide a foundation for the earthly temple. They provide a "theory" for the temple, and for our understanding of it. The keynote of the Pseudepigrapha is *primordiality*, not the actual temple itself, that is the temple that existed in the days of the writings of these works, either the Zerubbabel or Herodian versions of the Second Temple, which the writers of these scriptures viewed as corrupt. Their interest lay in those cosmic phenomena that the built temple incorporated into itself, as (virtual) symbols. That is, NOT the earthly representation of heaven (which is the primary meaning of the earthly temple), but heaven itself, not the throne of God present in the most holy place in the temple, but the actual throne of God in heaven, not the "Mountain of the Lord's House," but the mountain itself, not the image of God in the most holy place, but the very face of God in the tenth heaven!

The earthly temple is the image of the universe, the cosmos, the heavenly realms, and gives humans access on earth to the heavenly realms. It is "heaven on earth," the "meeting place of heaven and earth."[68] Its architecture, ritual, and symbolism all reflect this connection. In turn, scriptural teachings reflect and are based on the temple symbolism. The entire mission and theology of Jesus, as it is presented in the New Testament, is based on temple symbols and theology, and is interpreted in the light of these.[69] Once the actual earthly temple ceases to exist, or has become corrupt and is therefore unacceptable to a community of believers (as we see in the Qumran community), the eyes of the prophet or the visionary turn to the REAL temple, the one in heaven, and this becomes the focal point of the revelation. It is in this light that we are to understand most of the temple-related discourses in the Pseudepigrapha. A representative case can be made using the Apocalypses of Enoch, the Enoch literature.

We begin with the 1 Enoch, the Ethiopic Apocalypse of Enoch (second century B.C.E.—first century C.E.).[70] We are immediately introduced to the origin of the vision: "This is a holy vision from the heavens which the angels showed me" (1:2). "The God of the universe, the Holy Great One, will come forth from his dwelling. And from there he will march upon Mount Sinai and appear in his camp emerging from heaven with a mighty power" (1:3–4). Enoch is shown a vision of the earth by the angels, of the vastness of time and history, and taken on a journey of the cosmos. At one point he is taken to an area of seven mountains made of precious stones, surrounded by fragrant trees. Michael, the chief of the angels is accompanying him and asks Enoch why he is so inquisitive about the fragrance of the tree. Enoch responds that he is desirous of knowing everything. Then Michael explains that

> This tall mountain which you saw whose summit resembles the throne of God is (indeed) his throne, on which the Holy and Great Lord of Glory, the Eternal King, will sit when he descends to visit the earth with goodness. And as for this fragrant tree, not a single human being has the authority to touch it until the great judgment....And the elect will be presented with its fruit for life. He will plant it in the direction of the northeast, upon the holy place—in the direction of the house of the Lord. (24:1–6; 25:1–5)

In the next chapter Enoch travels to the center of the earth where he sees a "blessed place." There is a holy mountain, shaded by branches, underneath which "there was a stream which was flowing in the direction of the north" (26:1–3; cf. Ezekiel 47:1–12). Over the next several chapters he observes mountains with trees with fragrant spices and fruit, the paradise scenes that are always so much a part of temple complexes, what I have called the "primordial landscape,"[71] the landscape of creation, of what the ancient Egyptians called the "landscape of the first time."[72] In the Book of Jubilees we read that "He [= Noah] knew that the garden of Eden was the holy of holies and the dwelling place of the Lord" (8:19).[73] Enoch eventually is led to the gates of heaven (33:1–3), and later to the "heaven of heavens" (60:1), then an angel shows him "the hidden things: what is first and last in heaven, above it, beneath the earth, in the depth, in the extreme ends of heaven, the extent of heaven" (60:11–12).

The angel Uriel then shows Enoch the tablets of heaven. It is by means of these tablets that he is able to understand "all the deeds of humanity and all the children of the flesh upon the earth for all the generations of the world" (81:1–3). The tablets of heaven, or the tablets of destiny, as they are also known, play a major role in temple symbolism and ritual. The Urim and Thummim, the oracle of the high priest, as well as the tablets of the law that were contained within the Ark of the Covenant, are central to this idea. "The tablets of destiny ('tablets of the decrees') are consulted both in the cosmic sense by the gods, and yearly in a special chamber, in the Eninnu temple of Gudea's time. It is by this means that the will of the deity is communicated to the people through the king or the prophet for a given year."[74] The heavenly tablets are thus a primary point of communication between the heaven and earth within the temple economy, the means by which the will of heaven is revealed to human beings. And this communication must occur within the temple, and furthermore within the Holy of Holies of the temple. "As in heaven, so on earth."

The heavenly tablets play a major role in another important Pseudepigraphon, Jubilees (second century B.C.E.). In 3:31 we read that "Therefore it is commanded in the heavenly tablets to all who will know the judgment of the law." In 4:32: "Therefore it is ordained in the heavenly tablets." In 6:29: "And they set them upon the heavenly tablets [= "the feasts of remembrance forever" of Noah]. In 16:28–29: "And we eternally blessed him and his seed who are after him [= Abraham] in every generation of the earth because he observed this feast in its (appointed) time according to the testimony of the heavenly tablets. Therefore it is ordained in the heavenly tablets concerning Israel that they will be observers of the feast of booths seven days with joy in the seventh month." In 32:15: "And the whole tithe of oxen and sheep is holy to the Lord and it will belong to the priests who will eat it before him year after year because it is so ordered and engraved on the heavenly tablets concerning the tithe."[75] In other words, the very temple ritual itself, the Law, the ordinances, come down to earth from heaven, from the heavenly tablets, where everything regarding the temple is engraved.[76]

In the 2 (Slavonic Apocalypse of) Enoch (Late First Century CE), we are introduced to Enoch as he is brought to the third heaven, where he sees paradise, with trees in full flower, giving every kind of fruit and pleasant spice, in the midst of which was the tree of life "at that place where the Lord takes a rest when he goes into paradise" (8)[77] We saw that in Jubilees "And he knew that the garden of Eden was the holy of holies and the dwelling place of the Lord" (8:19). The Garden of Eden, paradise, the trees and waters of life:

> The temple is often associated with the waters of life which flow forth from a spring within the building itself—or rather the temple is viewed as incorporating within itself or as having been built upon such a spring. The reason such springs exist in temples is that they are perceived as the primeval waters of creation, Nun in Egypt, Abzu in Mesopotamia. The temple is thus founded on and stands in contact with the primeval waters.[78]

The holy of holies of the temple incorporates all of the above-delineated ideas: it is the place where the tablets of destiny are stored and from which they are read at the New Year by the king or the prophet. It is the place that represents the Garden of Eden, the place of primeval creation, the place of the creative waters and vegetation that the primeval creation represents.

Continuing on in 2 Enoch, he reaches the tenth heaven where "I saw the view of the face of the Lord, like iron made burning hot in a fire.... Thus even I saw the face of the Lord...and the Lord's throne, supremely great and not made not by hands." (2 Enoch 22).[79] Here, again, we would be in the most holy place of the earthly temple. Enoch is experiencing these visions in "real time," firsthand, at the *fons et origo*, in heaven.

Later on in this same chapter, we see Enoch being anointed and clothed "into the clothes of my glory." He looked at himself and thought "I had become like one of his glorious ones."[80] Washing, anointing, and clothing in the garments of the holy priesthood (Exodus 28–29; Leviticus 16; Ezekiel 44:17–19) are central and essential to the temple ritual. By means of this process, the initiate "become[s] like one of his glorious ones." This is the equivalent of the temple ritual, most vividly attested in Egyptian temple ritual, to the initiate being admitted into the presence of the deity, into the holy assembly, into paradise. It is the "presentation before the deity" motif, the introduction into the presence of the deity, attested, to give just one example of the many that can be given, in the Tomb of Sethos 1 (1294–1279 B.C.E.) in the Valley of the Kings.[81]

In the 3 (Hebrew Apocalypse of) Enoch (Fifth-Sixth Century C.E.), we see the visions of the heavenly temple most vividly portrayed. Enoch ascends into the heavens, to view the vision of the chariot, and he ascends up to the door of the seventh palace, where he prays before the Holy One (2 Enoch 1:1–2).[82] He enters the seventh palace and is "led to the camp of the Shekinah and presented...before the throne of glory" (2 Enoch 1:6). The translator notes that this phrase "is used as a designation of the inner court and the holy place in the Temple" in the Rabbinic literature.[83] The angel Metatron reveals that "All the mysteries of the world and all the orders of nature stand revealed before me as they stand revealed before the Creator. From that time onward I looked and beheld deep secrets and wonderful mysteries" (3 Enoch 11:1–2).

Over and over again in these visions, the seer is shown variations of scenes that we would place in the most holy place of the temple, the innermost sanctum of heaven, in the highest heaven. Metatron, the angel of 3 Enoch (Metatron is Enoch) who is enlightening Rabbi Ishmael, gives Rabbi Ishmael numerous visions of the throne of God, the various beings who surround it, the Cherubim and the Seraphim.

> The angels of mercy stand on his right, the angels of peace stand on his left, and the angels of destruction stand facing him. A scribe stands below him and a scribe stands above him. Glorious seraphim surround the throne on its four sides with walls of lightning, and the ophanim surround them like

torches, round the throne of glory, and clouds of fire and clouds of flame are round about them. (3 Enoch 33:1–3)

3 Enoch finally gives us the account of a phenomenal vision that reaches to the heart of the temple ideology: a vision of the heavenly throne with the veil. "R. Ishmael said: Metatron said to me: 'Come and I will show you the curtain (Hebrew *pargod*, cognate with Persian *pardag*) of the Omnipresent One, which is spread before the Holy One, blessed be he, and on which are printed all the generations of the world and all their deeds" (3 Enoch 45:1).[84] This tells us that the most holy place of the earthly temple, with its veil, has its archetype and prototype and "type" in heaven, where God, sitting on his throne, is veiled off from the rest of the heavenly host. "It shields the angels from the destructive glare of the divine glory."[85] Analogous to the tablets of heaven, "the whole course of human history is already worked out 'in blueprint' in the heavenly realm," and inscribed upon the veil.[86]

The Book of Jubilees (second century B.C.E.) gives us a clear view of the writer's concept of the temple and its ritual as both primordial, that is existent since the creation, and of heavenly origin, with the earthly paralleling the heavenly. The descendants of Levi are to "minister before the Lord always just as we [= the heavenly angels who minister before the Lord in heaven] do" (Jubilees 30:18).[87] In the Blessing of Levi, as accounted in Jubilees, "A spirit of prophecy came down upon his [= Isaac's] mouth. And he turned to Levi first to Levi and he began to bless him first, and he said to him…'May he draw you and your seed near to him from all flesh to serve in the sanctuary as the angels of the presence and the holy ones'" (Jubilees 31:12, 14). Thus the angels serve God at his throne in heaven as a model and example for the priests serving in the earthly temple. "As in heaven, so on earth."

"According to Jubilees, aspects of the Temple Service and the order of the festivals were known from the time of Adam and his descendants, and were carefully carried out before the days of Moses."[88] In Jubilees 8:19 "He [= Noah] knew that the garden of Eden was the holy of holies and the dwelling of the Lord." Hayward writes that "Both ben Sira and Jubilees, in their different ways, bring Adam into direct association with the Temple understood as Eden. According to Jubilees, the first ritual act of worship was offered by Adam immediately after his expulsion from the garden."[89] The passage in question is Jubilees 3:26–27: "And he made for them garments of skin and dressed them and sent them from the garden of Eden. And on that day when Adam went out from the garden of Eden, he offered a sweet-smelling sacrifice—frankincense, galbanum, stacte, and spices—in the morning of the rising of the sun from the day he covered his shame." "Adam is thereby constituted the first priest in a succession which will lead to Levi, and then to Aaron and his sons."[90]

The Festival of Passover was celebrated by Abraham, in honor of the sparing of his son, "according to the seven days during which he went and returned in peace. And thus it is ordained and written in the heavenly tablets concerning Israel and his seed to observe this festival seven days with festal joy" (Jubilees 18:17–19). "The heavenly reality which this represents on earth is constantly emphasized with reference to the heavenly tablets."[91]

There is yet another extraordinary text from Qumran, the so-called "Songs of the Sabbath Sacrifice,"[92] or "Songs for the Holocaust of the Sabbath."[93] These texts, 4Q400–407, 11Q17, and Masada 1039–200, date to the first century B.C.E., except for the Masada fragments, which date to 73/74 C.E., the date of the fall of the Jewish fortress on the heights of Masada to the Roman army following the defeat of the Zealot revolt of 66–74 C.E. The hymns, based on a cycle of 13 Sabbath sacrifices, are a kind of esoteric temple mysticism, a prophetic means of ritual ascent to the heavenly temple, making it possible for one to join the heavenly angels who surround the throne of God in the highest heaven.[94] They are also related to the Jewish *Hekhaloth* (heavenly palaces or shrines) and *Merkabah* (heavenly chariot) literature.[95] Because the Qumran sectaries viewed the Temple in Jerusalem as corrupt "they seem to have turned their attention to developing a cult of the celestial Temple."[96]

The "Songs of the Sabbath Sacrifice" (known as "The Angelic Liturgy" by its first editor, John Strugnell)[97] are transcendently beautiful and poetic, riveting in their exultation at the prospect of ascending to the heavenly temple. The language is among the most profoundly ecstatic of any that we possess in canonical or Pseudepigraphical texts. Carol Newsom describes the texts as "a quasi-mystical liturgy designed to evoke a sense of being present in the heavenly temple…. In addition to references to esoteric knowledge and the revealing of secrets, the strong influence of Ezekiel 1, 10, and 40–48, and the number of parallels between the Shirot [The "Songs of the Sabbath Sacrifice"] and contemporary apocalypses suggest a relation to visionary traditions."[98]

Throughout, one can discern references to and reminiscences of the actual earthly Temple, projected into the highest heaven:

A voice of blessing issues forth from the princes of His innermost sanctuary…and the voice of blessing is glorious in the hearing of the divine beings and those who establish…the blessing. All the crafted furnishings of the innermost sanctum shall hasten to take part in the wondrous psalms of the innermost sanctum...of wonder, sanctum to sanctum with the sound of thronging holy ones.... The chariots of His innermost sanctum shall offer praise as one, and their Cherubim and wheel-beings shall marvelously bless...the chiefs of the divine building. They shall praise Him in his holy innermost sanctum.[99]

Heaven, seven wondrous realms set out by the precepts governing His temples...the temples of the realm of the sevenfold priesthood, in the wondrous temple belonging to the seven holy councils...the High priest of the inner sanctum...the exaltation coming from their tongues...seven mysteries of knowledge in the wondrous mystery attached to the seven utterly holy realms.[100]

The likeness of living divine beings is carved on the walls of the vestibules by which the King enters, luminous spiritual figures [in the innermost sanctums of the K]ing, figures of glorious li[ght] wondrous spirits. [In] the midst of the glorious spirits stand wondrous embroidered works, figures of living divine beings.[101]

"All around are what appear to be streams of fire, resembling electrum, and [sh]ining handiwork comprising wonderful colors embroidered together, pure and glorious."[102]

Their holy places. At their wondrous stations are spirits, clothed with embroidery, a sort of woven handiwork, engraved with splendid figures. In the midst of what looks like scarlet and colors of utterly holy spiritual light, the spirits take up their holy stand in the presence of the [K]ing—[splendidly] colored spirits surrounded by the appearance of whiteness. This latter glorious spiritual substance is like golden handiwork, shimmering in [the lig]ht. All their crafted garments are splendidly purified, crafted by the weaver's art. These spirits are the leaders of those who are wondrously clothed for service, the leaders of each and every holy kingdom belonging to the holy King, who serve in all the exalted temples of his glorious realm.[103]

Corbin, drawing upon John Strugnell, writes that

He [Strugnell] made it perfectly clear that what is at issue is not an angelic liturgy at which a visionary happens to be present, but an earthly liturgy to which the Angels are summoned and at which they are present—a liturgy in which the celestial Temple is contemplated as the archetype of the earthly Temple. There is synchronicity—interpenetration—between the liturgy celebrated in the celestial Temple and that celebrated in the earthly Temple.[104]

"It is clear that the last five Sabbath songs describe the heavenly temple and angelic worship in a progressive fashion. The account begins with the outer temple, its vestibules and nave…then moves to a description of the…veil which separates the outer area from the debir.… The next section…appears to contain a description of the debir, concluding with an account of multiple chariot thrones.… In the twelfth Sabbath song there is an extended description of the merkabah which bears the Glory, followed by a description of the praise of the angels who process in and out of the heavenly temple."[105]

Thus, with the Qumran scrolls, particularly the *Temple Scroll,* and the Pseudepigrapha of the Old Testament, we get an extraordinary insight into views of the temple, and of temple ideology, theory, and practice during Second Temple times. It helps us to fill out our knowledge of this period in the history of the Temple of Jerusalem, to combine information on the actual building with biblical and non-biblical speculation. From these sources we learn that the temple and its ritual are two-fold: (1) they are preordained in heaven, with the ordinances inscribed on the heavenly tablets, and originate with the heavenly prototype (throne, veil, cherubim, etc)[106]; (2) they are primordial, in existence since the creation, originally revealed to Adam, and preserved through his posterity down to the time of Moses and Solomon and beyond.

The Temple of Herod

Our main sources for the Temple of Herod are found in Josephus, a Jewish priest who observed and recorded the Jewish revolt against the Romans, culminating in the destruction of the temple in 70 C.E., whose main works are *Jewish Antiquities,* the *Jewish War,* and *Against Apion;* and the Babylonian Talmud Tractate *Middoth* (Measurements), first set down in writing approximately the third to sixth centuries C.E. Additional sources are the writings of Philo of Alexandria, a Jew who lived in the first century C.E., and the New Testament itself. Josephus was an eyewitness observer of the temple, whereas the writer of *Middoth* worked from secondhand accounts perhaps in the second century C.E.[107]

Herod (73–4 B.C.E.) was an Idumean (Edomite), a son of an Idumean noble, Antipator (100–43 B.C.E.). This family had converted to Judaism, and was deeply involved in the Hasmonean dynastic problems of the second century B.C.E. Herod's mother was from a Nabatean royal family. Antipator was involved in the Hasmonean governance of Judea during the reign of Alexandra, the widow of Aristobulus, the son of John Hyrcanus I. Antipator supported Hyrcanus II, against his brother Aristobulus II, both sons of Alexandra. Pompey the Great intervened in Hasmonean affairs as a result of the civil war between the two brothers, and in 63 B.C.E. Pompey captured Jerusalem. Hyrcanus II was made high priest and ethnarch by Pompey. With the death of Hyrcanus II in 40 B.C.E., Antigonus II became ruler of Judea, supported by Rome's greatest enemy, the Iranian Parthians. At the same time, Herod had become appointed king of Judea, and he returned to Judea, and, with Roman help, captured Jerusalem in 37 B.C.E.

Herod's building campaigns and achievements rank him as one of the greatest builders of ancient times. He built entire cities, such as Caesarea Maritima and Sebaste, a magnificent palace at Masada, a summer palace in Jericho, the fortress palace Herodium, and of course the Temple of Jerusalem.[108] The Herodian rebuilding and expansion of the Temple of Jerusalem began in 20 B.C.E., and was not complete at his death in 4 B.C.E., nor, for that matter, by the time of its total destruction in 70 C.E.[109] The actual Temple was completed within about 18 months (*Jewish Antiquities* XV, 421). *Jewish Antiquities* XX, 219, states that "Just now, too, the temple had been completed," which was in the time of the Procurator Albinus (62–64 C.E.). This no doubt referred to the entire temple precincts, the courtyards, and other areas. We read in the Gospel of John 2:20 that "The Jews then said 'It has taken forty six years to build this temple, and will you raise it up in three days?'" This would indicate a date of around 28–30 C.E. for either the completion of the building, or that the building process was still underway.[110] Herod had grandiose ambitions and plans, wanting to please his entire constituency, which included traditional Jews, for whom the restoration of the sacred building would be their premier wish, more cosmopolitan Hellenistic Jews, many of whom lived in the great cities of that time such as Corinth, Antioch, and Rome, and who would want to see Jerusalem fitted out with a magnificent temple that would be the equal of the great temples of the Greek and Roman world, and his Roman patrons.[111] In the eighteenth year of his reign (20 B.C.E.) Herod made a stirring speech to the assembled Jews of Jerusalem (*Jewish Antiquities* XV, 380–387), and then set about carrying out his plans for a total expansion of the Temple Mount, and a complete renovation and rebuilding of the temple.

The greatest fear of the Jewish citizens of Jerusalem was that he would tear down the existing temple, and then not have the resources or the will to carry out the rebuilding. To allay these fears, Herod promised that he would not tear down the existing structure without first preparing all building materials necessary for the rebuilding. He then "prepared a thousand wagons to carry the stones, selected ten thousand of the most skilled workmen, purchased priestly (or "workmen's") robes for a thousand priests, and trained some as masons, others as carpenters, and began the construction only after all these preparations had diligently been made by him" (*Jewish Antiquities* XV, 388–390).

First, we shall discuss the platform itself, the nature of the expansion of the Temple Mount made under Herod's project. Josephus addresses the issue of the nature of the Temple Mount in the time of Solomon, and attributes various building techniques and structures of the *temenos* to King Solomon. Josephus proceeds to describe the temple citadel wall constructed by Solomon, how he sunk enormous ashlars into the ravine running around the Temple Mount, joined with iron clamps to ensure that the stones would remain bonded, after which he leveled off the summit, creating a smooth surface (*Jewish Antiquities* XV, 398–400). Josephus at this point gives the measurements of the Solomonic Temple Mount, namely one stade for each side, or a circumference of four stades (*Jewish Antiquities* XV, 400). A stade is approximately 585–600 feet. The Mishnah Tractate *Middoth* gives as the circumference of the Solomonic Temple Mount as 500 cubits by 500: "its largest [open] space was to the south, the next largest to the east, the third largest to the north, and its smallest [open space] was to the west" (*Middoth* 2, 1. All translations from the Mishnah are from Danby, 1933). Based on work done at the Temple Mount some years ago, Leen Ritmeyer was able to confirm the Middoth measurement of 500 square cubits, based on the royal cubit of 20.67.[112]

F. J. Hollis, in *The Archaeology of Herod's Temple: With a Commentary on the Tractate Middoth* (London, 1934), gave as the measurements of the current Temple Mount the following: on the south 929 feet; on the north 1,041 feet; on the east 1,556 feet; and on the west 1,596 feet.[113] Schwartz gives virtually the same measurements as Hollis, with an extent of 30 acres, and adding the height above sea level: 2,420 feet.[114] Ben-Dov gives the population of Jerusalem around 70 CE at about 150,000.[115] Thus, we have a vivid image of by how much the Herodian Temple Mount was expanded over the Solomonic (plus Hasmonean extensions), for example 1,556 feet on the east side in the Herodian Temple Mount, compared with 861 feet (by Ritmeyer's measurements) for the Solomonic. Thus almost 700 feet longer since the time of Solomon.

Meyers gives the area as 172,000 square yards.[116] In any case, the platform was enormous, "making it the largest site of its kind in the ancient world. The entire holy area was twice as large as the monumental Forum Romanum built by Trajan, and three and a half times more extensive than the combined temples of Jupiter and Astarte-Venus at Baalbek."[117] Gibson and Jacobson give the area as 144,00 square meters, or 36 acres, comparing it with the Acropolis at Athens at 30,000 square meters.[118] The Marduk Temple complex at Babylon in the Neo-Babylonian period was about 36 acres, which would make it comparable to the Temple Mount in Jerusalem in the time of Herod, which calls into question the claim of Meyers, above.

> The retaining walls themselves towered more than 80 feet above the roadways going around its perimeter and reached over 50 feet below street level in their foundations courses. The stones used to build these walls were gigantic. On the Western Wall (the "Wailing Wall" in Jewish tradition), the largest stones are about 40 feet long; an even larger one in the S. wall weighs over 100 tons.[119]

One of the most interesting and important issues relating to the architecture and the dating of the Herodian Temple Mount is the so-called "straight joint," or "seam," a line in the masonry located in the east wall approximately 100 feet north of the southeastern corner of the current wall. To the right of this line is a type of ashlar masonry of a rougher type of finish than that of the Herodian, showing a more pronounced "boss," or projecting central area, roughly finished in the middle. To the left of this line is the classic Herodian masonry, smoothly finished, with a central boss that barely protrudes and is smooth.[120] It is widely assumed that the section to the right of the seam is related to the building activity of Zerubbabel, or, alternately, is Hasmonean, and has been associated with the work of Simon Maccabeus, who "strengthened the fortifications of the Temple Mount by the side of the Akra...." (1 Maccabees 13:52). Leen Ritmeyer has confirmed this relationship by measuring the Hasmonean masonry north of the straight joint on the east wall, and has concluded that it begins exactly at the point, 861 feet from the northeast corner, where the Solomonic wall ends.[121]

Having established the dimensions of the platform itself, I am now going to begin describing the structures on the Temple Mount, beginning on the outer edges, and moving in, towards the Temple. Josephus states that "The temple was built of hard, white stones, each of which was about twenty-five cubits in length, eight in height and twelve in width" (*Jewish Antiquities*, XV, 392). He is referring of course to the limestone ashlars that can still be seen today. The dimensions that he gives here correspond to an ashlar measuring about 43 feet long, 13 feet high, and 20 feet wide.

All four sides of the Temple Mount wall were built up with porticoes or stoa, which were double sided on the north, east, and west sides, and triple on the southern, the so-call Royal Portico. The Royal Portico extended the entire length of the southern wall, from east to west. It consisted of three aisles made up of 162 27-foot high, highly polished white columns,

Second Temple Model. Photo Copyright Holyland Tourism 1992, Ltd., by Garo Nalbaldian.

in the Corinthian order.[122] The middle aisle was one and one half times as wide, and twice as high, as the other two aisles, thus towering over them. The ceilings of the aisles were ornamented with cedar wood carvings.[123] Of this portico Josephus described the Royal Portico in exuberant and enthusiastic phrases: "And it was a structure more noteworthy than any under the sun" "…which caused amazement by the magnificence of its whole effect," "…so that these structures seemed incredible to those who had not seen them, and were beheld with amazement by those who set eyes on them."[124]

The Sanhedrin, the 71-member supreme tribunal of Jewish law, associated with the temple, met in the Royal Portico following their expulsion from the Chamber of Hewn Stone (which was located in the inner court of the Temple—*Middoth* 5, 4). That part of the Royal Portico where they met was called *Hanuyot*, which means "shops" in Hebrew. The Apostle Paul's teacher, Gamaliel (Acts 22:3), taught in the *Hanuyot* section of the Royal Portico. It is assumed that one of the towers of the Royal Portico, either the eastern or the western, was the "pinnacle" of Matthew 4:5; "Then the devil took him to the holy city, and set him on the pinnacle of the temple, and said to him, 'If you are the Son of God, thrown yourself down" and Luke 4:9.[125] Jesus also upset the tables of the moneychangers inside the

Royal Portico, as recorded in Matthew 21:12–13, Mark 11:11, 15–19; Luke 19:45–48, and John 2:13–17. John 2:13–17 reads:

> The Passover of the Jews was at hand, and Jesus went up to Jerusalem. In the temple he found those who were selling oxen and sheep and pigeons, and the money-changers at their business. And making a whip of cords, he drove them all out of the temple; and he poured out the coins of the money-changers and overturned their tables. And he told those who sold the pigeons, Take these things away; you shall not make my Father's house a house of trade.

Moneychangers were operating in the Temple precincts because Jews came to the Temple from all over the Roman Empire, and were required to pay the Temple tax, which paid for the *Tamid,* or daily offerings. They brought foreign currency with them, and this required a currency changing operation.[126]

Josephus makes a statement regarding the southwest height from the Royal Portico that relates to these New Testament passages regarding one of the temptations of Jesus. The Temple Mount stands on a ridge that rises above two ravines, the Kidron Valley on the east, and the Tyropoeon Valley on the west. Given the height of the wall itself,[127] and then to build the Royal Portico above this, creates a truly awe-inspiring and frightening height. Josephus' words are:

> For while the depth of the ravine was great [i.e. the southwest corner], and no none who bent over to look into it from above could bear to look down to the bottom, the height of the portico standing over it was so very great that if anyone looked down form its rooftop, combining the two elevations, he would become dizzy and his vision would be unable to reach the end of so measureless a depth (*Jewish Antiquities* XV, 412).

It was also from the southwest corner, from atop the Royal Portico tower, that "a priest would blow a horn to announce the beginning and end of the Sabbath."[128]

Mishnah Tractate *Middoth*, 1, 3, states that there were five gates giving access onto the Temple Mount: the Huldah gates on the south, the gate of Kiponus on the west, the gate of Tadi on the north, and the eastern gate: "Through this gate the High Priest that burned the [Red] Heifer [Numbers 19], and the heifer, and all that aided him went forth to the Mount of Olives."

Along the base of the southern wall were built two monumental gates, the Huldah gates, approached by a 215 feet wide monumental staircase.

There was a double gate on the west, and a triple gate on the east. It was these gates through which Jesus entered the Temple, before mounting to the Royal Portico, where he threw over the tables of the moneychangers. These gates were referred to in the Talmud as the "stairs at the Temple Mount." Crowds of pilgrims would gather on the plaza in front of the stairs ascending to these gates.[129] A passage in the Talmud (*Tosefta, Sanhedrin* 2, 2, refers to Rabbi "Gamaliel and the Elders who stood at the top of the stairs of the Temple Mount." This is the Gamaliel who was the teacher of the Apostle Paul of Acts 5:34–39.[130] The depths of the stairs varied, first 12 inches, then 35 inches, then again 12 inches, the purpose of which being that the pilgrim would ascend in a way "that required each worshipper to approach the Temple slowly and with some deliberation."[131] Once inside the double gate gateway, a vestibule and entrance tunnel led gradually upwards—the tunnel still existing directly underneath the al-Aqsa Mosque—to the level of the esplanade, and into the Royal Portico.[132] This, in other words, was the primary entrance onto the Temple Mount in antiquity.[133] Fragments of magnificently decorated stucco masonry from the cupolas of the entryway vestibule were found in debris along the southern wall during excavations. Additionally, four original domes from this entryway are still intact, along with their design motifs, inside the double entryway passage.[134]

The design motifs, a dazzling array of stamped square lozenges, in various geometric patterns (pyramid, labyrinth, rosette, interlaced half-moon), with meandering vine leaves curling through the design, reflect the Oriental/Hellenistic syncretism of that time, and point also to the Nabatean origins of Herod's family.[135]

The Temple was approached from the west, from the ancient Upper City, by means of two stairway/overpasses, allowing for access over the Tyropoeon Valley and onto the Temple Mount, and two gates. Josephus indicates that there were four gates in the western wall (*Jewish Antiquities* XV, 410). One of these, at the southwestern corner, now known as Robinson's Arch, consisted of a stairway rising to the north, then turning at a right angle to form the platform that led into the Royal Portico. This would be the gate Josephus describes as "the last [which] led to the other part of the city, from which it was separate my many steps going down to the ravine and from here up again to the hill."[136]

The next gate on the western wall is now known as Wilson's Arch, after its main discoverer, and was a viaduct that also led across the Tyropoeon Valley directly onto the Temple Mount esplanade, in this case onto the western portico. The Kiponus (or Kiphonos—named after the Roman Procurator Coponius, 609 C.E.) Gate, named in *Middoth* 1, 3, is now known as Barclay's

Gate, and is the gate that can still be partly seen in the section reserved for women on the southern end of the Western (formerly Wailing) Wall.[137] The Kiponus Gate, which was reserved for non-Jews,[138] led into an underground vestibule and via a staircase onto the esplanade courts.[139] It was located just north of Robinson's Arch. The fourth gate mentioned by Josephus is thought by some to be of unknown location, but by others is identified with Warren's Gate, north of Wilson's Arch on the western wall.[140]

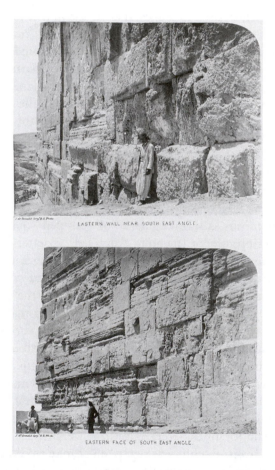

EASTERN WALL NEAR SOUTH EAST ANGLE.

EASTERN FACE OF SOUTH EAST ANGLE.

Exterior of the Haram-ash-Sharif: a. eastern wall near south east angle; b. eastern face of south east angle. James McDonald, Photographer. *Ordnance Survey of Jerusalem, made with the sanction of the Earl de Grey and Ripon, Secretary of State for War, under the direction of Col. Sir Henry James. 1865.* Plate 11. Albumen prints. 17 × 21.5 cm.; 16.5 × 21 cm. Humanities and Social Sciences Library, Photography Collection, Miriam and Ira D. Wallach Division of Art, Prints, and Photographs. The New York Public Library, Astor, Lenox and Tilden Foundations.

A street ran along the western wall, at its base, with shops located in niches in the walls along its length, just as we can see, for example, in the remains of one of the great Roman cities, Jerash, in Jordan.[141] The locations of the gates mentioned in *Middoth* 1, 3 for the northern and eastern walls are not known with certainty. Of the northern gate, that is Tadi, the Mishnah states that it "was not used [by the public] at all" (*Middoth* 1, 3). The Golden Gate, located 1,023 feet north of the southeastern corner, is of Byzantine or Umayyad date, while the location of the eastern gate mentioned in *Middoth* 1, 3, known as the Susa Gate, has not been located.[142] Our understanding of ancient Near Eastern temples built in the general style of the Temple of Jerusalem virtually requires that there would have been a gateway on the east in direct line with, and on the same axis as, the Holy of Holies. The Golden Gate is not on the same line as the Holy of Holies, if we accept the present-day Dome of the Rock as standing on the same place as the Temple. This is an issue that remains unresolved. However, the researches of Asher S. Kaufman, and his proposal to move the location of the Temple some 100 yards further north on the Temple Mount, with the present-day Muslim Dome of the Spirits or Dome of the Tablets said in this theory to cover what would have been the Rock of Foundation within the *debir* of the Temple, resolves this problem, as this orientation is directly in line with the Golden Gate.[143] Th. A. Busink accepts the traditional siting of the Temple, that is as having been located where the Dome of the Rock now stands.[144]

The remaining prominent structure from Herodian times embedded within the Temple Mount is the series of chambers underneath the surface of the esplanade on the southeastern corner known as the "Solomon's Stables." These vaulted halls were used as storehouses for the Temple in this period. They were modified and rebuilt during the Umayyad period, then during the Crusades, and again in recent times. The bases of the columns used in the Crusader work in this area of the Temple Mount that transformed the halls into stables, are Herodian.[145] Once a visitor or pilgrim had arrived on the main plaza he or she, Jew or non-Jew could move around the vast outer courts without restriction. It was in these courts, the so-called Courts of the Gentiles, that mass gatherings were held, but there were also various storage facilities for the Temple in these areas.[146]

As one approached the center of the esplanade, one would draw near to a stone balustrade, the *Soreg* (*Middoth* 2, 3), a latticed balustrade or railing "ten handbreadths high" (*Middoth* 2, 3) (*Jewish War* states that it was "three cubits high and of exquisite workmanship" which bore the inscription, sometimes in Greek and Latin "prohibiting the entrance of a foreigner under threat of the penalty of death" (*Jewish Antiquities* XV, 418; *Jewish War* V, 193–194). A complete Greek language inscription of this prohibition has been found, which reads: "No foreigner is to enter within the balus-trade and embankment around the sanctuary. Whoever is caught will have himself to blame for his death which follows."[147] The Apostle Paul was accused of bringing "Greeks into the temple, and he has defiled this holy place" (Acts 21:26–28). A crowd of aroused Jews "seized Paul and dragged him out of the temple, and at once the gates were shut. And as they were trying to kill him, word came to the tribune that all Jerusalem was in con-fusion" (Acts 21:30–31).

From here, that is from the *Soreg,* one would mount a flight of 14 steps (*Middoth* 2, 3 says there were 12 steps), to enter the massive fortification wall which ran around the inner, most sacred and off-limits courts. Jose-phus refers to the precincts within this wall as *hieron hagion,* that is, "holy place" (*Jewish War* V,194). This wall was quadrangular, and surrounded the Court of Women. A ten cubit wide terrace, called the *Hel* (*Middoth* 2, 3; *Jewish War* V, 196), surrounded the entire sacred precincts. Then another five steps led up to the gates, four on each side, north and south, of the sacred precinct. Each gate formed a kind of gate house rising above it, 40 cubits high (66 feet), and 14 cubits wide (23 feet) (*Jewish War* V, 203). The entryway structures give very much the sense and feel of an Egyptian

Fragment of a Parapet from the Temple enclosure, Hebrew Inscription: "To the Place of Trumpeting…." Jerusalem, 1st Century C.E. *Treasures of the Holy Land: Ancient Art from the Israel Museum.* New York: Metropolitan Museum of Art, 1986, pp. 210–211. The Israel Museum, Jerusalem.

temple pylon. It is important to reiterate here the ascension theme in the architecture and theology of the Temple of Jerusalem. The theme of ascent is most beautifully portrayed in the "Ascent" Psalms, 120–134, which focused on the 15 steps rising before the Nicanor Gate.[148] The pilgrim is ascending to the "Mountain of the house of the Lord" (Isaiah 2:2–3), and, in addition to the dramatic ascent that one had already made by reaching the esplanade itself from the lower city, one would now continue that ascent, rising at each new threshold, exactly as is the case in ancient Egyptian temples. "Who shall ascend to hill of the Lord? And who shall stand in his holy place?" (Psalms 24:3). As I have written elsewhere regarding the section plan through the temple of Dendera in Egypt: "This section [view] through the temple of Dendera, Egypt, clearly illustrates the worshipper's progress from the outside world through increasing degrees of sacredness to the holy of holies."[149]

The section plan of the upper courtyards of the Temple of Herod, which we can see in Mazar, Cornfeld, and Freedman (1975, p. 116), is virtually identical to that of Dendera, with the threshold gradually rising as one would approach the innermost sanctuary of the Temple. As a matter of fact, the entire inner courts were surrounded on their outer walls by treasury chambers. There were colonnades associated with these treasuries just inside three faces of the perimeter wall, the north, south, and east, creating a kind of ambulatory around the three sides of the perimeter of the sacred precincts, and these colonnades were created by "exceedingly beautiful and lofty columns" (*Jewish War* V, 200). The complete statement in Josephus is "The porticoes between the gates, on the inner side of the wall in front of the treasury chambers, were supported by exceedingly beautiful and lofty columns; these porticoes were single, but, except in point of size, in no way inferior to those in the lower court" (*Jewish War* V, 200). Thus the Temple of Herod replicated, *after a certain fashion* the effect of the Egyptian hypostyle hall or colonnaded courtyard, the hall preceding the holy of holies. All of the reproductions of the Temple of Herod vividly display this similarity.[150] The construction of the Temple of Edfu, to give one example, was only completed in 67 B.C.E.[151]

One ascended the 14 steps, then reached a level space of 10 cubits, the *Hel,* then ascended a second flight of five steps to the actual gates into the sacred precincts. We have now reached the point where we introduce and discuss the inner courts of the Temple, the most sacred precincts, beyond which no non-Jew could pass. According to Josephus:

It had four surrounding courts, each with its special statutory restrictions. The outer court was open to all, foreigners included; women during their impurity were alone refused admission. To the second court all Jews were admitted and, when uncontaminated by any defilement, their wives; to the third male Jews, if clean and purified; to the fourth the priests in their priestly vestments (*Contra Apionem* II, 103–104).

We have discussed the outer court, the first in Josephus' list, above. The next court was the Court of Women. This court was 135 cubits (222 feet) square. Each of the four corners of the Court of Women had a square chamber, open-roofed, the southeastern one for the Nazirites to boil their peace offerings and shave and burn their hair (Numbers 6:18); the northeastern chamber was a wood chamber where priests with physical deformities separated out wormy wood as unfit for the altar; the northwestern chamber was for lepers to purify themselves before receiving the blood of the offering on their thumb; and the southwestern for the storage of oil. The Court of the Women had a balcony surrounding it "so that the women should behold from above and the men from below and that they should not mingle together" (*Middoth 2*, 5). Josephus also states that this was court was entered through a gate on the east "through which those of us who were ritually clean used to pass with our wives" (*Jewish Antiquities* XV, 418). Josephus further states that in the Court of Women "a special place was walled off for the women, rendering a second gate requisite" (*Jewish War* V, 199). Additionally, Josephus tells us that the special gate through women alone must enter the Court of Women was the gate on the east, the one opposite the Nicanor Gate. It is obvious therefore that Jewish men were allowed in the Court of Women, and that there were special quarters within that Court for women to worship separately, as stated both in *Middoth* and in Josephus. The Court of Women was therefore not so named because it was exclusive to and for women, but because it was the only court to which (Jewish) women had access.

At this point we need to discuss the gates that either surrounded or were enclosed within the sacred precincts. There were 10 such gates, four each on the northern and southern sides, and two on the east side. Josephus emphasizes that the back of the Temple, the west end, did not have a gate (*Jewish War* V, 200). Of these gates, all except one were completely overlaid with gold and silver, along with their door posts and lintels. Each gateway had two doors, 30 cubits high and 15 cubits wide. There was an exception to these measurements, the gateway entering into the Court of Women, on the east side of the sacred precincts, the gate opposite the sanctuary itself, and thus the gateway into the Temple proper. This gate was 50 cubits high (86 feet), with doors 40 cubits high, truly a monumental

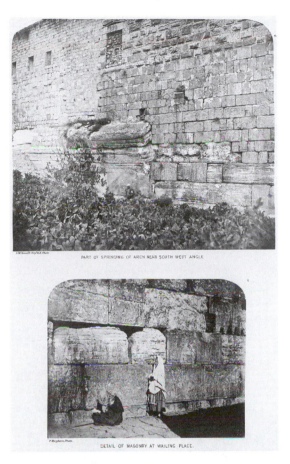

PART OF SPRINGING OF ARCH NEAR SOUTH WEST ANGLE

DETAIL OF MASONRY AT WAILING PLACE.

Exterior of the Haram-al-Sharif: a. part of springing arch near south west angle; b. detail of masonry at Wailing Place. P. Bergheim and James McDonald, Photographers. *Ordnance Survey of Jerusalem, made with the sanction of the Earl de Grey and Ripon, Secretary of State for War, under the direction of Col. Sir Henry James.* 1865. Plate 14. Albumen prints. 24 × 27.5 cm; 16.5 × 21 cm. Photography Collection, Miriam and Ira D. Wallach Division of Art, Prints and Photographs, The New York Public Library, Astor, Lenox and Tilden Foundations.

entrance. This is the so-called "Beautiful Gate" of Acts 3:1–2: "Now Peter and John were going up to the temple at the hour of prayer, the ninth hour. And a man lame from birth was being carried, whom they laid daily at that gate of the temple which is called Beautiful to ask alms of those who entered the temple."[152] Busink believed this gate was the East gate of the Temple Mount or Esplanade, rather than the East gate to the actual Temple precincts.[153] The whole issue of the East gate of the Temple Mount is by no means resolved, and great confusion reigns in the literature regarding the location and terminology of this gate in the scriptures, as we see here. It seems more and more likely that we should look to a predecessor, lower level gate on the same line as the Golden Gate, but that this gate should be on the same line as the Temple itself, thus reinforcing the value of the proposals of Asher S. Kaufman.

The tenth gate, the Nicanor Gate, divided the Court of Women from the next innermost court, the Court of Israel, and this gate was overlaid with Corinthian bronze, making it even more valuable than the gates overlaid with gold and silver (*Jewish War* V, 198–206). A stairway of fifteen steps

Golden Gate, Temple Mount, Jerusalem. Felix Bonfils, Photographer, *Views of Egypt, Palestine, and Syria.* Thirty two Photographic Prints. [Created 1867?–1871]. Plate 360. Albumen print. 30 × 23 cm. Photography Collection, Miriam and Ira D. Wallach Division of Art, Prints, and Photographs. The New York Public Library, Astor, Lenox and Tilden Foundations.

led from the Court of Women to the Nicanor Gate (*Jewish War* V, 206). This stairway is described in *Middoth* as having been "not four-square, but rounded like the half of a round threshing floor" (2, 5), which is reflected in all the reproductions of the Temple of Herod.[154] The 15 steps are further related in *Middoth* (2, 5) to the ascent Psalms (120–134) of the Hebrew Bible, which the Levites chanted on the steps of the Nicanor Gate.

It was on the 15 steps of the Nicanor Gate that the ritual of the "water of bitterness" was carried out (Numbers 5:18–28), by which a woman suspected of adultery would undergo an ordeal in which she would be "set...before the Lord" (Numbers 5:16), her hair unbound (Numbers 5:18), forced to take an oath of innocence, and forced to drink "the water of bitterness," which would cause her body to swell if she were guilty. The episode of the woman accused of adultery in John 8:1–7 should be understood to have taken place in the Court of Women on the steps of the Nicanor Gate. We read that Jesus "came again to the temple; all the people came to him, and he sat down and taught them. The scribes and the Pharisees brought a woman who had been caught in adultery, and placing her in the midst they said to him, 'Teacher, this woman has been caught in the act of adultery.'"[155]

The Court of Women had a colonnade running around it, and along the walls of this colonnade were placed 13 horns or trumpets for the deposit of the temple offerings, both required and voluntary. It is to these receptacles that the New Testament refers as "the treasury," for example John 8:20: "These words he spoke in the treasury, as he taught in the temple." The famous passage regarding a "poor widow" is also set within the Court of Women, and the offering receptacles; "He looked up and saw the rich putting their gifts into the treasury; and he saw a poor widow put in two copper coins. And he said, 'Truly I tell you, this poor widow has put in more than all of them.'"[156]

Having ascended the 15 steps and passed through the Nicanor Gate, the individual would now enter into what *Middoth* calls *Azarah* (Danby, "Temple Court" *Middoth* 1, 4; 5, 1,3,4) the innermost courts or the Temple Courts. The *Azarah* was also surrounded by its own wall, and measured 187 cubits long by 135 cubits wide (approximately 322 feet by 232 feet; *Middoth 2, 6*). The first of these was the Court of Israel, into which women could not enter. The Court of Israel measured one hundred thirty five cubits across the breadth of the court, from north to south, by eleven cubits east to west. Thus it was an extremely narrow area, and was separated from the next most sacred court, the Inner Court or Court of the Priests, by a low wall of stones, or flagstones (*Middoth 2, 6*). At this court, great throngs of pilgrims would gather for the holidays and Passover. There were so many

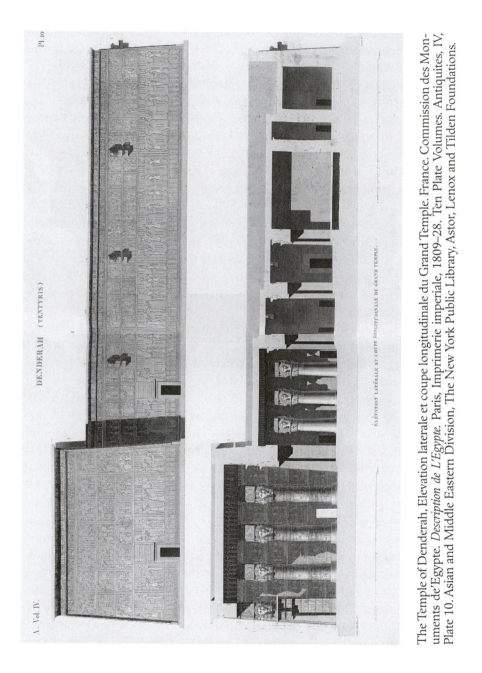

The Temple of Denderah, Elevation laterale et coupe longitudinale du Grand Temple. France. Commission des Monuments de l'Egypte. *Description de L'Egypte.* Paris, Imprimerie imperiale, 1809–28. Ten Plate Volumes. Antiquites, IV, Plate 10. Asian and Middle Eastern Division, The New York Public Library, Astor, Lenox and Tilden Foundations.

people that there had to be three Passover sessions held to accommodate the crowd.[157] In one of the most convincing and satisfying points of correlation between the Hebrew Bible and the architecture of the Temple of Herod, as we understand it, it was precisely this place, the wide, narrow Court of Israel, to which Jewish men were commanded to assemble three times every year: "Three times in the year shall all your males appear before the Lord God, the God of Israel" (Exodus 34:23).

There was a podium in the Court of Israel, raised a one-cubit step above the floor level of the court, and this podium itself had three steps of one-half cubit each. Thus the Court of the Priests was raised two and one half cubits above the Court of Israel (*Middoth 2*, 6). "And there were chambers beneath the Court of Israelites which opened into the Court of Women, and there the Levites played upon harps and lyres and the cymbals and all instruments of music" (*Middoth* 2, 6). Furthermore, there was a Chamber of the Hearth at the northeast corner of the inner courts, the *Azarah*, where priests of the night watch spent the night. At the opposite, southern, corner of the Court of Israel was a Chamber of Hewn Stone, where the Great Sanhedrin of Israel sat and judged to approximately 30 C.E.[158] It was in the Chamber of Hewn Stone that the four daily lots were taken to decide which priests should perform the duties of cleansing the altar and preparing the fires for the burnt offerings, which should offer the sacrifice, along with his assistants, which should offer the incense offerings within the *heikal*, and which should actually burn the sacrificial pieces on the altar.[159] Also located on the southeastern corner of the Court of Israel was the Golah Chamber where there was a fixed cistern (the Golah cistern—said to have been built by the returned exiles—Mishnah *Erubin* 10, 14) with a wheel over it, and from there water was provided for all the *Azarah* (*Middoth* 5, 4). The *Letter of Aristeas*, of approximately the second century B.C.E., has a lengthy discourse on the water supplies for the Temple:

And there is an endless supply of water, as if indeed a strongly flowing natural spring were issuing forth from within [the Temple]; and in addition there exist marvelous and indescribable reservoirs underground—as they showed me—for five stades around the foundation of the Temple; and each of them has numberless channels such that the streams join up together with each other from different sides. And all these down to the bottom were leaded, and over the walls of these a vast quantity of plaster had been spread; everything had been done effectively. There were also very many openings at the base (of the altar) which were invisible to all except to those who have the duty of carrying out the Service, so that all the blood of the sacrifices, which is collected in huge amounts, is cleansed by the downward momentum and slope.[160]

Mazar, Cornfeld, and Freedman provide a diagram that shows the extensive network of reservoirs underneath the Temple Mount.[161] More recently, Gibson and Jacobson have devoted a substantial volume to documenting "the cisterns, subterranean chambers and conduits on the *Haram al-Sharif*."[162]

We have now reached the actual Temple precincts, within which is located the fourth of Josephus' courts, the Court of the Priests. *Middoth* gives the dimensions of the Court of the Priests as the same as those of the Court of Israel, a narrow area of 135 cubits long by 11 cubits in breadth. It is further stated that there was "a row of stones [which] separated the Court of Israel from the Court of the Priests" (*Middoth* 2, 6). Josephus describes this row of stones somewhat differently: "Surrounding both the sanctuary and the altar was a low stone parapet, fair and graceful, about a cubit high, which separated the laity outside from the priests" (*Jewish War* V, 226).

The Temple itself was built in eighteen months (*Jewish Antiquities* XV, 421). The old foundations were removed, and new ones laid upon the same ground plan (*Jewish Antiquities* XV, 391). The Temple of Herod was built upon the same floor plan as the Temple of Solomon, with the same tripartite division, and the same dimensions of the floor plan.[163] Upon its completion, Herod himself sacrificed 300 oxen (Herod did not enter into the courts that were surrounded by the *Hel* [*Jewish Antiquities* XV, 420]), and the Jewish people sacrificed untold numbers of additional sacrifices (*Jewish Antiquities* XV, 421–423).

The Temple itself was approached by a stairway of 12 steps. The façade or porch (*ulam*) was the same height and width (100 cubits) or approximately a 17-storey building. The structure behind the façade was 40 cubits narrower, "for in front it had as it were shoulders extending twenty cubits on either side" (*Jewish War* V, 207). The famous phrase in *Middoth* which summarizes this features is: "...as a lion is narrow behind and wide in front, so the Sanctuary was narrow behind and wide in front" (4, 7). The gateway into the *ulam* was 70 cubits high and 25 wide, without doors, "displaying unexcluded the void expanse of heaven: (*Jewish War* V, 207–208). The façade of this gate was covered with gold, and allowed an unalloyed view into the *heikal*. "From the Court of Israel where the throngs of worshipers would gather, it was possible to see right through it to the interior of the entrance hall."[164] The gateway of the *ulam* had five courses of cedar (Danby: "oak") beams serving as the lintel, each course extending wider than the previous one (*Middoth* 3, 7).

The *heikal* was 40 cubits long, and 20 wide (the 20 being the width of the actual ritual space because the additional 40 cubits of its width, as stated by Josephus, are taken up by the annex, about which we will learn more shortly). The *heikal* had golden doors 55 cubits high and 16 cubits wide. It also had golden vines wound around pillars, and grape clusters "as tall as a man" (*Jewish War* V, 210–211; *Middoth* 3, 8). Before it hung a "Babylonian" tapestry, or veil, of the same size, embroidered in linen of blue, purple, and scarlet. Josephus ascribed mystical meaning to this tapestry:

> the scarlet seemed emblematical of fire, the fine linen of the earth, the blue of the air, and the purple of the sea; the comparison in two cases being suggested by their color, and in that of the fine linen and purple by their origin, as the one is produced by the earth and other by the sea. On this tapestry was portrayed a panorama of the heavens, the signs of the Zodiac excepted. (*Jewish War* V, 213)

In modern terms, we would say that the temple is a microcosm of the universe, the meeting place of heaven and earth, that it is a cosmic place. In the words of Floyd Filson, "the panorama of the heavens…was embroidered on the curtain before the Holy Place," which "appears to suggest that here was worshiped the one God of earth and heaven."[165]

The *heikal*

> contained within it three most wonderful works of art, universally renowned: a lampstand, a table, and an altar of incense. The seven lamps (such being the number of the branches from the lampstand) represented the planets; the loaves on the table, twelve in number, the circle of the Zodiac and the year; while the altar of incense, by the thirteen fragrant spices from sea and from land, both desert and inhabited, with which it was replenished, signified all things are of God and for God. (*Jewish War* V, 216–218)

The Holy of Holies, the *debir,* a 20-cubit (34 feet) square, was empty: "In this stood nothing whatever: unapproachable, inviolable, invisible to all, it was called the Holy of Holy" (*Jewish War* V, 219). The *debir* was approached by a ramp or flight of stairs. According to Rabbinical tradition two veils (*parokket*) were used to cover access to the Holy of Holies. A one cubit space was left between the two veils. The outer veil was connected to the northern wall, the inner to the southern wall. On the Day of Atonement, when the High Priest entered the Holy of Holies, he entered from the southern veil, moved slightly to the north in the one cubit space, and then actually entered the holy place through the corner of the northern veil, presumably so that there would never be the danger of a full-view sight line into the Most Holy Place.[166] The Qumran Temple Scroll prescribes a golden veil here.[167]

The three-storey annex that surrounded the Temple of Solomon was also reconstructed in the Temple of Herod. The gateways in the northern and southern walls, directly opposite the Temple, offered access directly into these precincts for priests (*Jewish War* V, 221). *Middoth* states that there were 38 cells comprising the annex, 15 on the northern and southern sides, and eight on the west (back) side (4, 3). These were interconnecting, and were used for storage of vessels and treasures, as well as for priestly functions related to the ritual of the Temple.[168] The outside of the Temple was overlaid with plates of gold, thus,

> the sun was no sooner up than it radiated so fiery a flash that persons straining to look at it were compelled to avert their eyes, as from the solar rays. To approaching strangers it appeared from a distance like a snow-clad mountain; for all that was not overlaid with gold was of purest white [that is, from the pure white limestone ashlars]. (*Jewish War* V, 222–223)

Golden spikes were laid onto the roof "to prevent birds from settling upon and polluting" it (*Jewish War* V, 224). Josephus gives as dimensions for the building stones of the Temple the stupendous sizes of 44 cubits long by five cubits high by six cubits wide (75 feet by eight and one half feet by ten feet) (*Jewish War* V, 224). Elsewhere he gives the dimensions as 25 cubits long by eight cubits high by 12 cubits wide (43 long by fourteen wide by 20½ wide; *Jewish Antiquities* XV, 392).

In front of the Temple stood the altar of burnt offerings, given differing dimensions in Josephus and *Middoth*, but nevertheless enormous. A sloping ramp let up to it, and a line in red was drawn around its middle, indicating the area to which the blood of sacrificial animals was to be sprinkled: above the line was for sacrifices that were to be eaten, below for sacrifices that were to be wholly consumed in the fire.[169] No iron was used in the construction of the altar, according to biblical injunctions, because, according to *Middoth* "...for iron was created to shorten man's days, while the Altar was created to prolong man's days...." (3, 4). The altar was whitewashed every Friday to remove blood stains (*Middoth* 3, 4).

Just to the south of the altar was the enormous bronze laver, of biblical dimensions (Exodus 30:18–21), standing on 12 massive lions. The basin was drained and refilled every evening and morning. It allowed space for 12 priests to wash at the same time.[170] There was a slaughtering shed north of the altar of burnt offerings consisting of eight small pillars with cedar blocks attached. Hooks of iron were affixed to these on which carcasses were hung. Marble tables that stood between the pillars were used for flaying the skin of the animals (*Middoth* 3, 5). This structure bears interesting comparison with a similar one in the Qumran Temple Scroll.[171] It fits in well with the instructions in Leviticus and Deuteronomy, but of course no such installation is described for the Temple of Solomon, although it must have existed. Some scholars think that the blocks of cedar wood mentioned in *Middoth* 3, 5, were actually a cedar roof covering the installation.[172] The various reproductions show it as open, without a roof.[173]

Middoth (4, 5) describes a fascinating roof passage that bears comparison with the "House of the Winding Stairhouse" of the Qumran Temple Scroll.[174] In the Temple of Herod, the winding staircase went from the northeast corner to the northwest corner, that is from the base of the passageways in the northeast corner, to the roof, thence to the northwest corner. One would walk along this rooftop passageway on the northern wall, then turn to the south and walk along the western wall, then turn to the east and walk along the southern wall (of the Temple), until one reached

the entrance to the upper chamber, for the entrance to the upper chamber opened towards the south. And at the entrance to the upper chamber were two cedar posts by which they could mount to the roof of the upper chamber. And in the upper chamber the ends of the flagstones marked where was the division between the Sanctuary and the Holy of Holies. And in the upper story there were openings into the Holy of Holies by which they used to let down the workmen in boxes, so that they should not feast their eyes on the Holy of Holies. (*Middoth* 4, 5)

Yadin interestingly refers the reader to 1 Chronicles 28:11: "Then David gave Solomon his son the plan of the vestibule of the temple, and of its houses, its treasuries, its upper rooms, and its inner chambers, and of the room for the mercy seat."[175]

The revolt against Roman rule led by Simon Bar Kochba between 132–135 C.E. led to the minting of coins by the rebels bearing the inscription "Year 1," and "Year 2." According to many, but not all, authorities, these coins bear a representation of the façade of the Second Temple, thus offering us our only such visual evidence of what it might actually have looked like from such an early date. Mosaics in the floor of the sixth century C.E. Theotokos Chapel on Mt. Nebo give a representation of the façade of the Second Temple, which bears strong similarity to that of the Bar Kochba coins. This mosaic is in the floor just behind what was once a chancel screen, and in front of the altar.[176]

M. Avi-Yonah has given a convincing interpretation of the meaning of the façade on the obverse of these tetradrachms. He starts with the assumption that "architecture on coins always represents an actual building,"[177] and that there could only be one building, the Temple of Herod, that a Jewish ruler (Bar Kochba and his army controlled Jerusalem for three years) would have represented on a coin commemorating his rule.[178] By comparing the façade on the Bar Kochba coin with the façade of a temple from Palmyra, and with the representation of a similar façade on a fresco over the Torah shrine at the Dura Europos synagogue, from eastern Syria of the early third century C.E., Avi-Yonah arrived at an understanding of the façade as representing the four-columned façade of the Temple of Herod, with the central "door" on the coin representing the doorway into the Sanctuary or *heikal* of the Temple. Avi-Yonah's reconstruction can now be seen as reflected in the model of Herod's Temple at the Holyland Hotel in Jerusalem (see, for example http://www.ebibleteacher.com/images/templef.jpg).[179] Other authorities interpret the railing running below the façade on the coin as a chancel screen, or, more specifically for the Second Temple, the *soreg*, the railing atop the Temple Mount that divided off the area beyond which non-Jews were not allowed to enter.[180]

Stevenson presents the opinion that the view represented by the façade on the coins "present the view of the high priest as he stands on the Mount of Olives and looks into the Herodian Temple through Solomon's Porch [the portico or stoa along the eastern wall] while sacrificing the Red Heifer."[181] Also to be considered here in the inventory of the depictions of Temple facades in post-70 C.E. synagogue construction is the mosaic floor in the Beth-Shean synagogue, which shows the four-columned Temple façade, combining elements that we see on the Bar Kochba coins and at Dura-Europos, although in Beth-Shean the central door is covered by the *paroket* or veil.[182]

The core of the Temple ritual, aside from the great festivals that we have discussed before, was the daily service, the *Tamid*, the delineation of which constitutes the content of a tractate of the Mishnah by the same name. Through the detail of the *Tamid* performances, we get a much broader and deeper insight into the dazzling, bustling, even chaotic activity that took place on the Temple Mount each day, but especially within the Temple Courts themselves, as people of both sexes, of all social and economic classes of Jews, of all manners of illness, despair, bereavement, and dispossession, of spiritual or physical need, came to the Temple, purchased the animal or fowl offering appropriate to their state and their sacrificial need, and their financial condition, and brought it to the to the Court of Israel to be given to the priests for immolation and for sprinkling of the blood at the appropriate place on the altar, to smell the incense, and to hear the singing, chanting, and musical instruments. A description of the details and particulars of the *Tamid* helps to breathe life into the architectural structures and ritual prescriptions and performances about which we read in Josephus, in *Middoth,* and in other Mishnaic tractates. An excellent, concise summary of the *Tamid* and the other sacrifices in the Temple can be found in Mazar, Cornfeld, and Freedman.[183]

Both Josephus and fellow Jewish writer of that period, Philo of Alexandria, were extensively fascinated by the High Priestly vestment, and Philo, in particular, wrote about it in the allegorizing manner that we saw with Josephus on the colors and fabric of the veil. Josephus reiterates the descriptions of the priestly vestments as contained in Exodus (*Jewish War* V, 231–237). Philo, in his *De Vita Mosis,* expounds in a much more grandiose way, in the manner of Hellenizing allegory, than does Josephus, who essentially repeats the biblical prescriptions. For Philo, the garments "have a meaning which must not be passed over in silence. For the whole is in fact a representation and copy of the cosmos, and the parts are the representations of its several portions."[184] He then goes on to explain, in great detail, the various meanings of each item of the clothing, the fabric and the colors, with their cosmic, astronomical, philosophical, and moralistic symbolism, afterwards going on to the breastplate, the tiara, and the Urim and Thummim.[185]

Representative examples from Philo are "the tunic is completely violet, a model of the air.... The embroidered flowers are a symbol of the earth.... The pomegranates are a symbol of water, appropriately so called because of their flowing juice."[186] "Reason represents the ephod as a symbol of heaven.... Also six names had to be engraved on each of the stones, because each of the hemispheres also splits the zodiac into two and takes over six zodiacal signs."[187] Philo is deeply imprinted with the influence of Greek philosophy, but for him,

> Jewish tradition...is never far away: even the cosmic and universal explanations of the Temple Service, so congenial to educated non-Jews, have their place in the writings of his Jewish predecessors such as Jesus ben Sira and the writer of *Aristeas.* Likewise, the union of earth and heaven in the worship of the Temple often adduced by Philo, was a matter of moment for the Jews of Qumran.[188]

Bar-Kokhba Coin, Tetradrachm. *Treasures of the Holy Land: Ancient Art from the Israel Museum*. New York: The Metropolitan Museum of Art, 1986, pp. 225–227. The Israel Museum, Jerusalem.

The cosmic interpretation of the temple is one that we meet wherever we go, that is that it represents a manifestation of the heavenly sphere brought down to earth, in which every detail of the earthly practice is based on a heavenly "type," the *Tabnit* that we have seen so deeply imprinted within the Hebrew Bible, the pattern of the Temple that is in, and that in fact is, or constitutes, heaven.[189] This means that we cannot simply dismiss the interpretations and allegorizations of a Josephus or a Philo, because they are in the mainstream of temple theory, or of Temple Ideology as I call it, a process of interpretation that has come down to us from antiquity.

An additional detail of great importance that Josephus describes is that of the incense to be offered on the altar of incense in the *heikal*. He states that there are "thirteen fragrant spices from sea and from land, both desert and inhabited, with which it was replenished, signified that all things are of God and for God" (*Jewish War* V, 218). The injunctions of the Hebrew Bible stipulate four spices: stacte (oil of myrrh), onycha (an extract from a Red Sea mollusk), galbanum (an aromatic resin), and frankincense

(Exodus 30:34 with commentary from *The New Oxford Annotated Bible with the Apocrypha, Revised Standard Version*). The Rabbinical tradition added nine additional spices: myrrh, cassia, spikenard, saffron, costus, mace, cinnamon, salt, and an herb that made the smoke rise (Thackeray, *Jewish War*, pp. 68–69). Jubilees 16:24 lists seven spices. Philo gives an allegoristic interpretation to the four spices of Exodus 30:

> And I believe that these four, of which the incense are made up, are symbols of the elements out of which the whole universe was completed. For he [Moses] compares stacte with water, and cloves with earth, and galbanum with air, and clear frankincense with fire. For stacte is like water because of its drops; cloves are dry like earth; 'sweet' is added to galbanum to refer to the air, for there is a sweet smell in air; and 'clear' is added to frankincense to demonstrate light.[190]

The Jewish Revolt of 66–70 C.E. was primarily the work of a fourth Jewish party, one not mentioned heretofore, the Zealots, called by the Romans *Sicarii,* that is, "dagger men."[191] It was in 40 C.E. that the Roman Emperor Caligula tried to have an image of himself installed in the Temple, setting off riots amongst the Jewish population. In 66 C.E., the Roman Procurator Gessius Florus attempted to loot the Temple treasuries, setting off intense riots.[192] Jewish forces, as enthusiastic as they were to throw off the oppressive Roman yoke, were no match for the Roman legions, under Titus, the son of the Emperor, Vespasian. Titus took over command of the Roman army in Judea upon the elevation of his father, Vespasian, to the Emperorship. The Roman forces numbered about 78,000, comprising four legions plus auxiliaries, while the Zealot forces under John of Gishhala and Simeon Bar Giora, numbered about 20,000. The Romans carried extensive siege equipment, including battering rams and siege towers. Following a five-month siege, the city was captured, the Temple Mount utterly devastated. A vivid account is given by Josephus in *Jewish War* III. It is said that Titus hesitated to destroy the Temple, but that a Roman legionary threw a burning piece of wood into the Temple Courts, thus setting off the final blaze. The very luxury of the Temple Mount, the extensive wood, for example, made for even greater and hotter fires of destruction. The Jewish defenders used the Temple Courts for their defensive positions, thus guaranteeing their total destruction. There was widespread slaughter in the city following the defeat, and Jews were banned from Jerusalem for several centuries thereafter.[193] Everything was either destroyed or carried off, including the seven-branched candelabrum, which is depicted on the victory Arch of Titus, in Rome.[194] The traditional date of the destruction of both the First and Second Temples is the ninth of

Ab, in the Jewish calendar, and this is also the date on which, according to Jewish tradition, the Messiah will be born.[195] A vivid photograph reproduced by Mazar shows debris from the destruction of 70 c.e. that had spilled down the slope, and had lain there until the excavations of the 1970s.[196]

> The Temple as the Stone of Foundation, as the center of responsibility, is essential for the maintenance of the cosmos.[197]
>
> And so you find that all the time the service of the Temple was performed there was blessing in the world...and the crop was plentiful, and the wine was plentiful and man ate and was satisfied, and the beast ate and was satisfied.... When the Temple was ruined, the blessing departed from the world.[198]

In these passages, the terms "the world stands," and "the world rests" [Mishnah *Aboth* 1:2] should be understood within the context of their full mythic import. The Temple and its ritual serve as the cosmic pillars or "sacred pole" supporting the world. If its service is interrupted or broken, if an error is made, then the world, the blessing, the fertility, indeed all of creation which flows from the Center, will likewise be disrupted.[199]

The Meaning of the Temple of Jerusalem in the Jewish Community Following 70 C.E.

The key point in the history of Judaism before the Holocaust is the destruction of the Second Temple in 70 C.E. Before that momentous event, Judaism was Temple-centered, and Temple-sacrifice centered, with the ritual year revolving around the three mandatory feasts (Exodus 23:14–17). Furthermore, Judaism in the time of the Temple was largely in the control of the party of the Sadducees, who were associated with the Temple, and controlled its service. Even though the Synagogue had come into being during the existence of the Second Temple, as the center of Jewish communal life, and even though the party of the Pharisees existed and had effective control over Jewish communal life in the synagogues, still, the Temple was at the religious, ritual, and indeed cosmic center of Jewish life.

The famous passage in Josephus's *Antiquities* XVIII, 11–22, names and defines the three main Jewish parties that we are familiar with from the Hebrew Bible, the New Testament, the Qumran Scrolls, and other sources. Here Josephus names the three main parties as the Pharisees, the Sadducees, and the Essenes. The main distinction between the Pharisees and the Sadducees is that the former accept both the written and the oral Torah, whereas the latter accept only the written. The Pharisees live simple lives, and enjoy the attention and the devotion of the masses. They believe in an afterlife, and are "extremely influential among the townsfolk; and all prayers and sacred rites of divine worship are performed according to their exposition. This is the great tribute that the inhabitants of the cities, by practicing the highest ideals both in their way of living and in their discourse, have paid to the excellence of the Pharisees."[1]

The Sadducees did not believe in a life after death, and accepted only the authority of the written Torah. They indulge in luxury, are an upper-class party, and do not enjoy the support of the masses. Thus they "submit...to the formulas of the Pharisees, since otherwise the masses would not tolerate them."[2]

The differences between the two parties were further summarized by Josephus in the following manner:

> For the present I wish merely to explain that the Pharisees had passed on to the people certain regulations handed down by former generations and not recorded in the Laws of Moses, for which reason they are rejected by the Sadducaean group, who hold that only those regulations should be considered valid which were written down (in Scripture), and that those which had been handed down by former generations need not be observed. And concerning these matters the two parties came to have controversies and serious differences, the Sadducees having the confidence of the wealthy alone but no following among the populace, while the Pharisees have the support of the masses.[3]

With the destruction of the Temple, the Pharisees "took the position, naturally and almost immediately, of sole and undisputed leaders of such Jewish life as survived."[4] For all intents and purposes, even though the evidence is not completely clear, "We may conclude that in all likelihood there was some close connection between the post-70 rabbis and the pre-70 Pharisees."[5] This event, the destruction of the Temple, "marked...the extinction of the priesthood and the Temple worship which until then had been the centre of Jewish national and religious life."[6]

There is a famous legend regarding Rabbi Johanan ben Zakkai, that demonstrates the transition from Temple to Rabbinic Judaism, at the time of the destruction of the Second Temple. According to this legend, Yohanan ben Zakkai, when he realized that all was lost, that the Temple would be destroyed and the Zealots and thousands of other Jews destroyed, had himself secreted out of the city in a coffin, and brought to the Roman general, Vespasian. He accurately predicted that Vespasian would soon be emperor, and was granted a wish by the new emperor. He is reported to have said: "Give me Yavneh and its sages."[7] Johanan ben Zakkai therewith reestablished the Rabbinical court, the Sanhedrin, in Yavneh (Greek Jamnia; also spelled Jabneh), on the Mediterranean coast, south of present-day Haifa (Jaffa). The primary source for this incident, the *Avot of Rabbi Nathan*, is dramatic enough that it bears quotation in full:

> Now, after Rabban Johanan ben Zakkai had spoken to them one day, two and three days, and they still would not listen to him, he sent for his disciples, for Rabbi Eliezer and Rabbi Joshua. 'My Sons,' he said to them, 'arise and take me out of here. Make a coffin for me that I might lie in it.' Rabbi Eliezer took hold of the head end of it, Rabbi Joshua took hold of the foot; and they began carrying him as the sun set, until they reached the gates of Jerusalem. 'Who is this?' the gatekeepers demanded. 'It's a dead man,' they replied. 'Do you not know that a dead man may not be held overnight in Jerusalem?' 'If it's a dead man,' the gatekeepers said to them, 'take him out.' So they took him out and continued carrying him until they reached Vespasian. They opened the coffin and Rabban Johanan stood up before him. 'Are you Rabban Johanan ben Zakkai?' Vespasian inquired; 'tell me, what may I give you?' 'I ask nothing of you,' Rabban Johanan replied, 'save Jabne [Jamnia], where I might go and teach my disciples and there establish a prayer[house] and perform all the commandments.' 'Go,' Vespasian said to him, 'and do as you wish.'[8]

According to the Mishnah Tractate *Aboth*, the chain of authority in Jewish law begins with Moses receiving the Law (*Torah*) on Mount Sinai. Moses then gave this authority (that is, the Law) to Joshua, and Joshua gave it to the elders (Joshua 24:31), who gave it (the Law) to the Prophets (Jeremiah 7:25). The Prophets gave the Law to the men of the Great Synagogue, who returned from Exile with Ezra. These men gave it to Simeon the Just, who gave it to Antigonus of Soko, after which it was given in turn to five "pairs," Jose ben Joezer and Jose ben Johanan, Joshua ben Perahyah and Nittai the Arbelite, Judan ben Tabbai and Simeon ben Shetah, Shemaiah and Abtalion, and Hillel and Shammai. The dates of Hillel and Shammai are ca. 30 B.C.E. to 10 C.E.[9] Rabbi Johanan ben Zakkai (died ca. 80 C.E.) received the Law from Hillel and Shammai (*Aboth* 2:8).

The record of the Oral Torah that was compiled in the approximately two centuries following the destruction of the Temple is the Mishnah. The Mishnah is based on three principles that are stated in Tractate *Aboth*, 1:1: "Be deliberate in judgment, raise up many disciples, and make a fence around the Law." The "making a fence around the Law" implies the Oral Torah is at the basis of Pharisaic Judaism. "Making a fence around the law means giving supplementary rulings that hinder a man or woman from even coming close to breaking a scriptural command. These supplementary rulings have no direct biblical foundation, but are meant to prevent one from getting into a situation in which one might break a biblical command."[10]

The Mishnah was compiled by Rabbi Judah the Patriarch, usually known simply as "Rabbi," who was born in 135 c.e.[11] The Mishnaic tractates are a compilation of the "traditions of the Elders," the Oral Torah, the collections of extra-biblical traditional laws or *Halakoth* (singular *Halakah*) from which Rabbi Judah the Patriarch compiled the Mishnah that had come down to us. The generation of scribes whose teachings are represented in the Mishnah are known at *Tannaim* ("repeaters"), as compared with the generation of the *Amoraim*, the later generation of Talmud compilers. The Talmud (Jerusalem Talmud was compiled around the end of the fourth or beginning of fifth centuries c.e.; the Babylonian Talmud was compiled around one century later) consists of an elaborate commentary on the Mishnah, in which the Mishnaic text is given, followed by the *Gemara* ("completion") of the *Amoraic* commentator.[12]

> Much of Rabbi's material may go back to a time before or not long after the destruction of the Temple. Thus the tractates *Middoth* and *Yoma* which deal with the structure and cultus of the Temple are, according to a reliable source, derived (as far as their anonymous contents are concerned) respectively from Eliezer ben Jacob and Simeon of Mizpah, both of whom lived at a time when the Temple was still standing. Another tractate, *Tamid* ("The Daily Whole Offering"), seems to have been drawn upon by Simeon of Mizpah or to have been derived from him; and portions of the tractate *Shekalim* also bear indications of a pre-Destruction origin.[13]

Thus "approximately the half of the Mishnah has no longer any practical bearing on the present practice of Judaism, not had it any practical bearing even when it was compiled."[14] However, this in no way detracted then, nor has it detracted since that time, from the devoted study and attention that Jews have given to this work, the sacredness of which places it second only to the Hebrew Bible in the Jewish consciousness. Danby quotes from Samuel Krauss, whose book *Die Mischna (Volksschriften uber die judische Religion)*, was written in 1914: "That [the Mishnah] was the final great act of Palestine in the service of Judaism; the old mother did not forsake her hated and hunted children without inner strength; she did not let them go without the hope that they would find the way back to her."[15]

It is obvious therefore how very important those tractates of the Mishnah are to us today that describe the Temple, its architecture, plan, and layout, its daily service, and the manner in which the great festivals were performed. Without this invaluable source, our knowledge of the Second Temple would be immeasurably poorer, because, as was pointed out above, these tractates derive from the time when the Temple still stood. It is clear from Chapter Three, The Second Temple, how important tractate *Middoth* ("Measurements") is to our understanding of the layout of the Temple Mount and the architecture of the Temple and its courts. Without this source, we would be unable to fully relate the Temple layout to the ritual prescriptions that are given in the Hebrew Bible, or to the numerous references in the New Testament to events that occurred on the Temple Mount, its entrances, or somewhere within the Temple or its courtyards. The Mishnah, to a large extent, is either explicitly based upon Temple ritual, prescriptions, architecture, layout, or else implies the background, the presence of the Temple, or reflects the communal memory of the Temple, from that time when it no longer existed.

It is widely stated among Christian scholars of Judaism in the time of the destruction of the Second Temple that the destruction had a paralyzing impact upon Judaism, that it knocked the very center and foundation of Judaism out from under it. The famous book by S.G.F. Brandon stands at the center of this contention: "[The destruction] had a paralyzing affect on the life of the Jewish people, and from it they only slowly recovered and settled to an essentially maimed existence, with their cherished religion bereft of much of its *raison d'etre*."[16]

Neusner points out, which a reader of the Mishnah can determine for himself, that the Mishnah does not in any way reflect paralysis or a "maimed existence." It is a dynamic, almost matter-of-fact depiction of the world of the Temple, as though that world still exists and is vital. It is not "a time of decay and dissolution, but a remarkable age of reconstruction and creativity in the history of Judaism."[17] Neusner calls the Mishnah a "map without a territory." That is, "a map for a fictitious territory. It describes, with remarkable precision and concrete detail, a perfect fantasy."[18] We need to recall that at the time of the compilation of the Mishnah by Rabbi Judah the Patriarch, the Jews had no Temple, no city of Jerusalem, and no access to the Temple site.[19] And yet, the Mishnah allows for only one Temple, that of Jerusalem.[20] It is not advocating the building of a new Temple somewhere else, where the Priestly laws and rules of the Temple cult will be reinstated. It is not a work of eschatology, looking forward to the Messianic Age, and the new Temple, as in the Book of Ezekiel or the Qumran Temple Scroll. And yet, according to Neusner, the extreme concreteness of the Mishnaic reproduction of the details of the Temple cult "must mean they wanted the Temple rebuilt and the cult restored."[21] Be that as it may, in this time of greatest crisis, there was a "circling of the wagons," a "canonization" of the details of the Temple cult, in the hands, of, and by means of, the Sages. " [A]ll know what priests know. But in this society all know it in the form and language given by sages, accessible only among their circles. To put matters simply: In the world of disaster and cataclysmic change, Mishnah stands as a statement of how the old is to be retained. It defines and effects the conditions of permanence amid change."[22]

The Synagogue

The Temple was central, and could be only One, the One central sanctuary, which required the removal of all others, both Jewish and pagan, including high places and any forms of ritual worship to any god that could be labeled as "cosmic," that is partook of the old ancient Near Eastern royal ideology that required a central temple to unite heaven and earth along with the ruling dynasty in the primary city of the empire. Where did this leave ordinary worshipers? Obviously, every state system and its accompanying religion in the ancient Near East had forms of local worship, or better popular worship, as compared with the official worship of the state temple. It is estimated that the Jewish population in the Roman Empire was about seven percent, or 5–7 million.[23] This population, spread over the entire Empire, needed formal, officially recognized places of worship apart from the Temple, which this entire population could not regularly, or in many cases ever, visit, where they could pray and "perform all the commandments" (see the quotation from Johanan ben Zakkai, above). There are many vivid and authentic accounts of synagogue methods of worship in the New Testament, and indeed, in the Apostle Paul's travels around the Roman Empire to preach the Gospel, he constantly availed himself of synagogues to preach.

> Now Paul and his company set sail from Paphos, and came to Perga in Pamphylia. And John left them and returned to Jerusalem; but they passed on from Perga and came to Antioch of Pisidia. And on the Sabbath day they went into the synagogue and sat down. After the reading of the law and the prophets, the rulers of the synagogue sent to them, saying, 'Brethren, if you have any word of exhortation for the people say it.' So Paul stood up, and motioning with his hand said: 'Men of Israel....' (Acts 13:13–16)

"Now at Iconium they entered together into the Jewish synagogue, and so spoke that a great company believed" (Acts 14:1). "Now when they had passed through Amphipolis and Apollonia, they came to Thessalonica, where there was a synagogue of the Jews. And Paul went in, as was his custom, and for three weeks he argued with them from the scriptures" (Acts 17:1–2).

In this sense, the following quotation from Skarsaune is inaccurate: "The most concrete expression of this unconscious preparation for the post-70 situation was the establishment of the synagogue."[24] The synagogue was not established in order to provide a replacement when the Temple was no longer there, because this institution was founded well before the destruction of 70 C.E. (as early as the Babylonian Exile—although the earliest concrete evidence for synagogues dates to the third century B.C.E.[25]), and secondly because the purpose for which the synagogue arose as an institution within Judaism was to provide a place for more ordinary forms of worship outside of the Temple, and because, in any case the synagogue could not replace the Temple—they are incommensurate institutions within ancient Israel. Cohen gives as the purposes for which the synagogue arose within Judaism as the provision for a house of prayer, a study hall or school, and a community center.[26] So, in other words, this speaks against the idea of "an unconscious preparation for the post-70 situation."

The synagogue was thus "a house of prayer," an assembly hall where there was a cycle of scripture read during the year (the reading cycle included the Torah and accompanying and commensurate passages from the Prophets) a place of preachment where any male could "exhort" the congregation (Acts 13:15, above), and a communal center for the congregation.[27] The cycle of scripture reading is vividly brought out in the incident of Jesus in the synagogue in Nazareth:

> And he came to Nazareth, where he had been brought up; and he went to the synagogue, as his custom was, on the Sabbath day. And he stood up to read; and there was given to him the book of the prophet Isaiah. He opened the book and found the place where it was written….And he closed the book, and gave it back to the attendant, and sat down; and the eyes of all in the synagogue were fixed on him. (Luke 4:16–21)

That the Temple and the synagogue were incommensurate is clearly laid out by Shaye J. D. Cohen: they differed in three aspects: place, cult, and personnel. As to place, the Temple was the one central, cosmic Temple, the meeting place of heaven and earth, the replication on earth of the heavenly Temple; the synagogue was many (it is widely estimated, based on Rabbinical sources, that there were either 394 or 480 synagogues in Jerusalem alone[28]). As to cult, the cult of the Temple consisted in the sacrifices, "the slaughter, roasting, and eating of animals. It was a very bloody affair; as the

Rabbis state, 'It is a glory for the sons of Aaron that they walk in blood up to their ankles'" (Babylonian Talmud *Pesahim* 65b). There was obviously no blood sacrifice in the synagogue. As to personnel, the Temple personnel was the priesthood, the Aaronites. "Lay Israelites were not allowed even to enter the sacred precincts, let alone to minister before the Lord....The synagogue, in contrast, was a lay institution *par excellence*. Torah study and prayer were virtues to be cultivated by every Israelite (i.e., every male Israel ite)....'Teachers' and 'heads of synagogues' were titles and professions open to all (including women)."[29]

This is not to say that the *concept* of the sacrifices did not play a central role in the synagogue: they were, after all, central to Torah. However, they become *spiritualized* in the liturgy of the synagogue. Once, Rabbi Joshua followed behind Rabbi Johanan ben Zakkai as they viewed the ruins of the Temple. "Woe unto us," Rabbi Joshua cried, "that this, the place where the iniquities of Israel were atoned, is laid waste!" "My son," Rabban Johanan said to him, "be not grieved; we have another atonement as effective as this." "And what is it?" "Acts of loving kindness. As it is said, 'for I desire mercy and not sacrifice.'"[30]

Within the synagogue liturgy, prayer and Torah study were viewed not as replacing sacrifice, but as being their equivalent, even though the Rabbis "hoped and expected that the sacrificial cult would be restored."[31] In the Tannaitic *Siphre* on Deuteronomy we read in the commentary to Deuteronomy 11:13, "*To love the lord your God and to serve Him,* that "This is Torah study....Just as the sacrificial cult is called 'service' (*Abodah*), so too is Torah study called 'service' (*Abodah*). Another opinion: 'to serve Him' is prayer....Just as the sacrificial cult is called 'service' (*Abodah*), so too prayer is called 'service' (*Abodah*)."[32]

> This is why the synagogue was not a replacement for the temple. It could substitute for many of the *practical* elements of temple worship, but it could not substitute for the *symbolic* significance of the temple. The synagogue was not constitutive of Jewish identity in the way the temple was. It did not reflect association with Sinai and the covenant, was not connected to Zion and the Davidic monarchy, did not represent the unique election of the Jewish people and God's presence in their midst, and did not possess comparable nationalistic significance. Although there were areas of ritual and ideological overlap, the synagogue and temple were completely different institutions *symbolically.*[33]

The Rabbis, according to Cohen, "speak of a heavenly temple, a heavenly Jerusalem, a heavenly court, and a heavenly Sanhedrin. To this list they add a heavenly altar, a heavenly academy, and a heavenly school. But nowhere, neither in their mystical speculations nor in their musings about the end of days nor in the apocalyptic texts of the sixth and seventh centuries, do the Rabbis refer to a heavenly synagogue."[34]

At the same time, in the centuries following the destruction of the Temple in 70 c.e., the synagogue more and more took on features and characteristics that were associated with the Temple, "a number of customs perpetuating the memory of the Jerusalem Temple."[35] "[T]he synagogue became increasingly associated with the Jerusalem Temple…a miniature or small sanctuary."[36] These included the orientation of the ritual or liturgical wall of the building towards Jerusalem, the reading of Numbers 28–29, the Order of Sacrifices that were prescribed for the Temple, and the recitation of the Yom Kippur ritual, among others.[37] The architecture of synagogues in the centuries following 70 c.e. shows a wide range of influences, including Greek, Roman, and Hellenistic. Some Jewish communities were more conservative, some more Hellenized. Mosaic designs in the floors emphasized religious themes and symbols, "such as the menorah, the Torah ark, shofar, lulav and ethrog, or biblical figures and scenes such as the binding of Isaac."[38] The Ark of the Law, with the Torah scroll, located on the Jerusalem-side wall, replaced the Holy of Holies of the Temple, for all intents and purposes.[39]

In the centuries following the destruction of the Temple of Herod, as the synagogue came to incorporate more and more Temple symbolism, ritual, and imagery, these trends evoked "Christian discomfort about the relationship between synagogue and Temple paraphernalia."[40] The early Christian Father, John Chrysostom, wrote disparagingly about Jewish presumptions regarding the Ark and the priesthood, and mocked Jews, whose synagogues had "no tables of the law, no holy of holies, no veil, no high priest, no incense, no holocaust, no sacrifice, none of the other things that made the ark of old solemn and august."[41] Christians both envied the majestic power and authority of the Temple, while at the same time denying any "residual" Temple sanctity to synagogues.

The Synagogue of Dura-Europos

The site of Dura-Europos is located on the Euphrates River in Syria, near the modern Syrian village of as-Salihiyeh, about 57 miles southeast of the Syrian border town, Deir ez-Zor, on Syria's border with Iraq. Following its discovery as an ancient city in the 1920s, the site was excavated first under the auspices of the French Academy of Inscriptions and Letters in Damascus, and subsequently, for 10 seasons (between 1928 and 1937) in a joint excavation between the French Academy and Yale University. Dura-Europos (this was the ancient name of the city) was a caravan city connecting eastern cities such as Seleucis/Ctesiphon, with Damascus and Palmyra to the west. Control of the city went back and forth between Seleucid (the city was established about 300 B.C.E. by Seleucus I Nicator), Parthian/Iranian (from 114 B.C.E.), the Romans under Trajan (116–118 C.E.), Parthian, and then again Roman (under Lucius Verus from 168 C.E.). The city came under attack by the Sasanian/Iranian kingdom under Ardashir in 239 C.E., and was besieged until it fell by the Sasanian king Shapur between 253–256 C.E.[42]

The key archaeological sites for our purposes were built up inside the embankment along the western wall, to the north and south of the city gate, the Palmyra Gate. The famous Christian Building ("the earliest clearly identifiable church building from the Roman world"[43]) was excavated south of the gate, and the synagogue to the north of the gate. The synagogue is one of the earliest recovered synagogue sites from the Diaspora.[44] The synagogue was originally built in its location along the western embankment in the period before 244–245 C.E., at which time it was renovated and expanded. It was then destroyed in the Sasanian assault on the city.[45]

The Dura-Europos synagogue consisted of a series of rooms built around a central courtyard, with the assembly hall up against the city wall. All four walls of the assembly hall were painted in a professional manner with scenes that "reflect a high degree of familiarity with stories that appear in rabbinic literature and a clear stylistic continuity with the pagan and Christian wall paintings at Dura."[46] There were benches built into and along the bases of all four walls in the assembly hall. We are most interested in the West wall, the wall that was aligned towards Jerusalem, and the one that contained the paintings of Temple-related scenes that are so famous, and can be seen reinstalled in the national Museum of Syria in Damascus.

The West wall is painted with a number of Bible-based, Temple-related scenes, including those above the arch in the Torah niche, and, in the central panel or Register B of Kraeling's plan. These include, from the left, the Tabernacle with Moses at the Well, then, the Tabernacle with Aaron and his attendants. From the right side of the West wall in Register B, there is, first, the destroyed Philistine temple with the Ark of the Covenant in the wagon, and then the controversial "Closed Temple" of Goodenough's designation, generally accepted as depicting the Temple of Solomon.[47] The painting above the niche in the central Torah Shrine depicts, on the right, the Sacrifice of Isaac by Abraham, and on the left the seven-branched candlestick with a *lulab* and an *ethrog,* and, in the middle, the façade of the Second Temple, analogous to that on the Bar Kochba coin,[48] which we discussed at length in Chapter 3.

Kraeling makes an important distinction in the comparison of the Temple façade on the Bar Kochba coins with the Temple façade in the Torah shrine at Dura-Europos: "In this case the design on the coins should be a schematic representation of the Temple, showing the Ark of the Covenant within, and the design on the Dura Synagogue's Torah Shrine should show the Temple itself with the Ark become the door of the Temple."[49] The association of the Sacrifice of Isaac with Mount Moriah, which then became the site of the Temple of Solomon (II Chronicles 3:1), also further confirms the Temple façade here as that of the Temple of Jerusalem (albeit in its Herodian manifestation).[50] And, of the decorations and paintings of the West wall, we are most interested in the central niche or aedicula, mounted by stairs, which housed the Torah shrine, and the painting of the Temple of Jerusalem, above and to the right of the niche.

The Torah Shrine protruded from the middle of the West wall, opposite the central door, "as in the pagan naoi."[51] and consists of three steps, which would lead one to the platform (*bema*) in and on which the Torah scroll would be placed. There are two columns on either side, painted in blue with a veining technique. There are five painted panels on the back wall of the *bema,* painted to imitate marble wainscoting. Their design motifs are triangles, "eyes," wavy lines, and a central veined black diamond. As is almost always the case with the Torah Shrine, a conch shell fills the top of the niche. The purpose of the Torah Shrine is to hold the Scroll Chest, also called the ark. It takes the place of the Holy of Holies in the Jerusalem Temple, with the Scroll Chest replacing the Ark of the Covenant. We can see the Holy of Holies relationship in the mosaic floor from the Beth-Shean synagogue, where the opening to the Holy of Holies (of the Torah Shrine) is covered by the *paroket* or veil.[52] The Torah Shrine is sometimes referred to as the "ark,"[53] or as a "sacred niche," which "served as the resting place of the ark."[54] "We suggest that the basis of the relationship is the conscious effort of later Judaism to model significant elements after the supposed or schematized forms of more ancient Jewish *sacra,* particularly those of the Temple."[55] One can see an artist's conception of an ancient Torah Shrine in use in Fine and Meyers.[56]

The Hekhalot Literature

All ancient religions assume the existence of heaven, and have some conceptions of such a place, however varied the traditions of the different ancient religions might be. Furthermore, the idea of a heavenly temple, that is of a perfect "prototype," THE temple, which is either a part of or the entirety of heaven, is equally widespread. I have dealt with this theme at great length in this book, in a variety of contexts. Elsewhere I have written that:

The basic idea is that there exists in the sky a perfect place, the 'city' of the gods. The goal of human life is both to establish contact with this place, and to return to it after death, thus to share in the life of the gods. The primary way by which the gods share with humans the knowledge of this place, and information on how one gets there is through the temple. The earthly temple is an exact replica of a heavenly temple.

The god reveals to a king, prophet or shaman the architectural plan for the earthly temple, which is a replica of the heavenly temple. Exodus chapters 19 and 25 give us the classic pattern: the prophet ascends the mountain. There, the prophet is given a 'pattern' to examine. That 'pattern' is the temple (or here, tabernacle, the prototype of the Israelite temple in Jerusalem) which exists in heaven: 'According to all that I show you concerning the pattern of the tabernacle and of all its furniture, shall you make it' (Exodus 25:9).

Likewise Ezekiel was 'brought…in the visions of God into the land of Israel, and [set] down upon a very high mountain, on which was a structure like a city opposite me' (Ezekiel 40:2). Here the prophet was taken in visions in order to measure the Temple of Solomon in Jerusalem. A heavenly messenger guiding him held 'a measuring reed in his hand' (Ezekiel 40:3). We find a similar motif in the Book of Revelation, where the Apostle John was visited by an angel and 'In the Spirit…carried…away to a great, high mountain' (Revelation 21:10). The angel 'had a measuring rod of gold to measure the city and its gates and walls' (Revelation 21:15). John had been transported to the mountain in order to view the Heavenly city of Jerusalem, which in the context of the Book of Revelation was one vast temple.

We see in both the Old and New Testament passages an important pattern, according to which the prophet is given a shaman-like vision on a mountain both prior to building the temple (where he views the heavenly model in order to transfer its architecture to the earth), and (as in the cases of Ezekiel and John), where he views either the temple or the heavenly temple-city prior to their restoration to the earth at the end of time.

The theme of the heavenly temple-city of Jerusalem, which at the end of time would be lowered down to earth, making of the entire earth one vast temple, persists throughout the Middle Ages, as can be seen in one of the illuminations to an early Spanish Beatus Apocalypse. There we see the plan view of the heavenly city, with John and the angel in the center, the angel holding the golden measuring rod while John holds the book in which the revelations are recorded.[57]

In her recent, excellent article on the Jewish *Hekhalot* Apocalyptic literature, Rachel Elior speculates on what might have caused the development of this vast, phantasmagorical, mystical literature of ascents to heavenly temples, the transference of the earthly Temple ritual, and symbolism to the heavens:

> The most plausible explanation for the emergence of this new esotericism is apparently a visionary eruption which, drawing on a sanctified ritual tradition, refused to accept a cruel, arbitrary reality in which the cultic center, the focus of religious worship, no longer existed. Denying the historical reality of destruction and annihilation, this eruption created a new spiritual world that rested on a mystical-ritual fulcrum, a surrogate for the no longer extant Temple.[58]

Similarly April D. De Conick, writing in 1999, states that "Refusing to accept the end of their religious worship in the wake of the destruction of their cult center, they focused on the notion of a spiritual world whose cultic practices now operated on a mystical-ritual praxis. The structure of the earthly Temple was projected into the heavens as a series of three or seven *hekhalot* or shrines, *markavot* or chariots, *devirim* or Holy of Holies."[59]

Although it may seem hypercritical to object to these two stated views, these conceptions are nevertheless not accurate, in the strict sense. The concept of the Heavenly Temple was part and parcel of many pre-modern religious systems from earliest times, as I indicated above in the lengthy quote from my *The Temple: Meeting Place of Heaven and Earth*. I have dealt with this question at length in several other places:

> Just as the mountain gives the temple architecture its external, directly visible appearance, and the cave, along with the labyrinth or maze give the temple its ritual processes, so heaven supplies the earthly temple with its floor plan. Because the earthly temple is a projection onto the surface of the earth of the heavenly temple, there must be continual contact and communication maintained between the two spheres....The temple, with its celestial decorative motifs, gives us the topography of the heavenly realms. The heavenly prototype is transferred to earth.[60]

In other words, it was not necessary for the Jews, following the destruction of the Temple in 70 C.E., to find "a surrogate for the no longer extant Temple,"[61] or to project "the earthly Temple...into the heavens as a series of three...shrines...or chariots...or Holy of Holies."[62] The Heavenly Temple was always part of the worldview of ancient peoples, as we see from the visions of Ezekiel, for example, or from the Qumran *Songs of the Sabbath Sacrifice*.[63] Concepts of ascent into and descent from the heavenly realms are deeply embedded within the mythical and scriptural traditions of ancient people, are an independent part of the common ancient Near Eastern religious heritage, and are not dependent upon nor are they caused by the destruction of the Temple. Margaret Barker expresses this same idea in the following way:

> The entire epistle [Letter to the Hebrews] is set in the temple, which was believed to be a microcosm of the creation, its liturgy and rituals mirroring those of heaven. To say *mirroring* is a concession to our ways of thinking and the limitations of our language, because the temple was believed to be heaven itself and its priests the angels. This was the world view of the ancient priests of Israel and owes nothing to Platonism.[64]

The heavenly Temple was always there, and came to the fore or was emphasized more strongly in the absence of (following the destructions of the two Temples) or the corruption of (in the view of the Qumran Community) the earthly Temple, or some combination of these two. The Pseudepigrapha that we have discussed so extensively in this book all arose in the wake of the destruction or corruption of either the First or the Second Temples of Jerusalem, where the everpresent reality of the Heavenly Temple, which was indeed present already in the Hebrew Bible, reasserted itself in a perfectly human and understandable manner, in the yearnings for that perfect place, Heaven, and its Temple.[65]

There is most definitely an esoteric Temple tradition embedded within the Hebrew Bible. The central feature of this tradition is the vision of any, or all, aspects of the Heavenly Temple, or in other words, the interplay or interaction of Heavenly angels, choirs, and messengers with mortal prophets. This tradition is not fully exposed within the Hebrew Bible, primarily because the esoteric tradition is always a secret tradition, not revealed except within the close boundaries of a group of initiated individuals.[66] Elements of the esoteric tradition can be seen in Isaiah 6:1: "In the year that King Uzziah died I saw the Lord sitting upon a throne, high and lifted up; and his train filled the temple. Above him stood the seraphim; each had six wings; with two he covered his face, and with two he covered his feet, and with two he flew." Here the Prophet Isaiah is observing a vision of the Heavenly Temple, with the Lord of Hosts seated therein on

His throne. Ezekiel (Chapter 1) likewise was vouchsafed a vision of the Heavens, and of the beings who dwell there. It is from this vision that the mysticism of the Throne of Glory and the chariot that bears it (*Merkabah*) so essential to Jewish mysticism, comes. "The mysteries of the world of the Throne, together with those of the Divine Glory which is revealed there, are the parallels in Jewish esoteric tradition to the revelations on the realm of the divine in Gnosticism."[67] Within the Pseudepigraphal literature, we see visions of the Heavenly Temple in, among others, the Testament of Levi, I Enoch, 2 Enoch, the Apocalypse of Abraham, and the Ascension of Isaiah.[68]

> The vision of the Chariot, the Merkavah, revealed to the exiled priest Ezekiel shortly after the destruction of the First Temple, is seen by the authors of the Hekhalot [*hekhalot* = heavenly palaces or shrines, from Hebrew *heikal*—the main Sanctuary in the Temple [69]] literature as a framework for their mystical world-view after the destruction of the Second Temple. Ezekiel, torn from the proper venue of his priestly duties, who 'saw the visions of God' in 'the fifth year of the exile of King Jehoiachin' [Ezekiel 1:1–2], transformed the cultic Temple vessels into visionary entities in the celestial shrine and the golden 'pattern of the chariot—the cherubs' from the Holy of Holies [1 Chronicles 28:18] into the sublime heavenly Chariot/Merkavah of the Cherubim and the holy Hayyot. The writers of Hekhalot literature, for their part, grappling with the chaotic reality of loss and desolation after the destruction of the Second Temple, also endeavored to recreate the ruined Temple in their mind's eye, to perpetuate in their vision the numinous aspects of the Levitical and priestly service....With Ezekiel's vision to inspire them as a conceptual prototype, they replaced the ruined earthly Temple with the eternal supernal shrines. In their minds, moreover, the visionary entities originally associated with the cult of the terrestrial Temple became the functionaries of the cult in the heavenly shrine.[70]

We have already seen that the visionary idea of the Heavenly Temple was deeply embedded within the Qumran Community, as expressed in the *Songs of the Sabbath Sacrifice*. Carol Newsom refers to "the imaging of heaven as a temple."[71] She writes, further, that "The Sabbath Shirot differ from many of the contemporary texts which refer to the heavenly temple in that they devote much more attention to the details of the structure of the heavenly sanctuary, its priesthood, holy vestments, etc."[72] There is no separation between the earthly community and the actual heavenly temple: "Through these calls to praise and the descriptions of heavenly worship the earthly community evokes that sense of being present in the heavenly

temple."[73] Drawing upon the work of Johann Maier, Newsom concludes that "the idea ["of the notion of a liturgical communion with the angels at Qumran"] derives from a traditional view of the temple as the place of intersection between the earthly and heavenly realms, so that service in the earthly temple is at the same time service in the heavenly presence of God and of God's ministering angels."[74]

We learn from the Mishnah that there was an esoteric tradition in the Tannaitic period:

> The forbidden degrees [Leviticus 18:6ff.] may not be expounded before three persons, nor the Story of Creation before two, nor [the chapter of] the Chariot [Ezekiel 1] before one alone, unless he is a Sage that understands of his own knowledge. Whosoever gives his mind to four things it were better for him if he had not come into the world—what is above? What is beneath? What was beforetime? and what will be hereafter?[75]

Parsing these verses, Scholem writes that "Evidence concerning the involvement of Johanan b. Zakkai and his disciples in this sort of exposition proves that this esotericism could grow in the very center of a developing rabbinic Judaism, and that consequently this Judaism had a particular esoteric aspect from its very beginning."[76]

Elior notes the direct, one-to-one correspondence between the (seeming) fantastic expositions of the *Hekhalot* literature and the descriptions that we find in the Hebrew Bible: "The Merkavah beings are described in terms deriving from Temple worship in general."[77] She calls our attention to II Chronicles 5:11–13:

> When the priests came out of the sanctuary—all the priests present had sanctified themselves...—all the Levite singers...dressed in fine linen, holding cymbals, harps, and lyres, were standing to the east of the altar, and with them were 120 priests who blew trumpets. The trumpeters and the singers joined in unison to praise and extol the Lord; and as the sound of the trumpets, cymbals, and other musical instruments, and the praise of the Lord...grew stronger.

She then compares this passage with several, including one from the *Hekhalot Rabbati:*

> The holy Hayyot likewise devote themselves, sanctify and purify themselves more than them

And each and every one bears one thousand thousand crowns of various
  luminaries on his head
And they clothe themselves in garments of fire
And wrap themselves in raiment of flame
And cover their faces in lightning
Why do they the holy Hayyot and glorious Ofannim and majestic
  Cherubim
Purify and sanctify and clothe and wrap themselves…?
Because the Merkavah is before them
And they all stand in terror and fear, in purity and sanctity
And utter song, praise, hymn, rejoicing and extolling in unison,
In one utterance, in one mind and one melody.

And another from the *Ma'aseh Merkavah:*

Said R. Ishmael: YHWH, YHWH, a God compassionate and gracious,
  God of Israel
Of the Ofannim and the Hayyot and on the wheels of the Chariot and on
  the Seraphim
All standing in one mystery, of one mind, in unison
And the Ofannim and the holy Hayyot and the majestic Ofannim and the
  enflamed Seraphim and the wheels of the Chariot
Speak with a loud voice, with a great rushing sound, mighty and strong
With a great rushing sound, they say:
Blessed be the name of the glory of His Kingdom to all eternity

From the place of the house of his Presence.[78]

There is a unity, and an influence, connecting the *Merkabah,* the *Hek-halot* literatures, and Kabbalah. The key scriptural figure that stands at the center of these traditions is Enoch: "When Enoch had lived sixty-five years, he became the father of Methuselah. Enoch walked with God after the birth of Methuselah three hundred years, and had other sons and daughters. Thus all the days of Enoch were three hundred and sixty-five years. Enoch walked with God; and he was not, for God took him" (Genesis 5:21–24). The vast Enoch literature is a literature of esotericism, an esotericism based upon the Temple, namely the Heavenly Temple, the Heavenly Throne, and ascent to the Heavenly Throne.[79]

The Qumran Community "possessed the original Book of Enoch, both in Hebrew and Aramaic, although it is quite likely that it was composed in the period preceding the split between the Pharisees and the members of the Qumran sect."[80] Scholem further writes that "We should not dismiss the possibility of a continuous flow of specific ideas from the Qumran sect to the Merkabah mystics and rabbinic circles in the case of the *Shi'ur Komah* [that is, the "measure of the body"—a mysticism developed from Ezekiel 1:26: "and seated above the likeness of a throne was a likeness as it were of a human form."]."[81]

Enoch becomes transformed into the "Prince of the Divine Presence" of the 3 (Hebrew Apocalypse of) Enoch, that is, Metatron, the archetypal figure of the *Hekhalot* apocalyptic literature and the later Kabbalah. Particularly telling are the passages in 3 Enoch 11:

> The Holy One, blessed be he, revealed to me from that time onward, all the mysteries of wisdom, all the depths of the perfect Torah and all the thoughts of men's hearts. All the mysteries of the world and all the orders of nature stand revealed before me as they stand revealed before the Creator. From that time onward I looked the beheld the deep secrets and wonderful mysteries. Before a man thinks in secret, I see his thoughts; before he acts, I see his act. There is nothing in heaven above or deep within the earth concealed from me.[82]

Kabbalah

The latest phase of Jewish esoteric scripture developed out of the *Hekhalot* and the *Merkabah* traditions is Kabbalah. Kabbalah was developed in Provence, that is southern France and Spain from approximately the mid-twelfth century on. Underlying it was the *Sefer Yezirah,* the "Book of Creation," a mystical work based on the earlier esoteric tradition of *ma'aseh bereshit* (Account of Creation).[83] The *Sefir Yezirah* could have been written as early as the third to sixth centuries c.e., and was in existence, in a shorter (six chapters) and longer version, by the tenth century c.e.[84]

Kabbalah continues the tradition of ascent mysticism such as we have seen in *Merkabah* esotericism:

> In the Second Temple period of Jewish history…what is now known as Kabbalah was called the Work of the Chariot [*ma'aseh Merkabah*]. The name comes from the prophetic vision of Ezekiel, whose writings form the basis of much Jewish mystical experience and thought. Chapter 1 of Ezekiel expresses, in the metaphysical language of the time, the hierarchy of Worlds: the World of Action, on earth; the World of the Chariot, or Formation; the World of the Throne, or Creation; and the Divine World of Emanation, shown as Adam, the likeness of the Glory of God.[85]

The *Sefir Yezirah* is founded on language mysticism, or "linguistic esotericism,"[86] according to which "The world-process is essentially a linguistic one, based on the unlimited combinations of the letters."[87] The "thirty two secret paths of wisdom" by which the world came into being, consist of the 22 letters of the Hebrew alphabet, and the "ten Sefirot of nothingness [that is "closed," "closed within itself," or "without actuality, ideal"[88]]."[89] The term *sefirot* as used in the *Sefer Yezirah* refers only partly to the theory of emanation so well known in the scripture of Kabbalah, the *Zohar.*

The *Sefer ha-Zohar* ("The Book of Splendor"), was authored by Moses de Leon, a Spanish Kabbalist, in a highly Hebraicized Aramaic, in the years between 1280–1286 C.E.[90] The central theological concept of the *Zohar* is *Ein-Sof,* Infinite, without end:[91] "the absolute perfection in which there are no distinctions and no differentiations....It does not reveal itself in a way that makes knowledge of its nature possible, and it is not accessible even to the innermost thought...of the contemplative."[92] The Infinite manifests Himself through a sequence or series of ten emanations, the *Sefirot.* "Since all created things come into being through the agency of the *Sefirot,* the latter contain the root of all change, although they emanate from the one principle, *Ein-Sof,* 'outside of which there is nothing.'"[93]

The ten *Sefirot* are arranged in a tree-like image, a kind of Tree of Life, with three triangles, going from top to bottom, *Keter* (Crown), *Hokhmah* (Wisdom), and *Binah* (Intelligence or Understanding), then *Hesed* (Mercy, Greatness, Love), *Gevurah* (Power, or Strength), and *Tiferet* (Beauty), then *Nezah* (Endurance, Victory), *Hod* (Majesty, Glory), and *Yesod Olam* (Foundation of the World), and finally *Malkhut* (kingdom).[94] The sequence of numbers given here also represents the sequence of emanation.[95]

The *Sefirot* of the *Zohar* are related to the Temple of Jerusalem in a number of ways, always keeping in mind that we are dealing, in Kabbalah, with an extreme form of "spiritualization," an "interiorization," of the scriptures in general, of ritual processes, and of the concept of the Temple of Jerusalem. In the section of the *Zohar* which deals with the Book of Genesis (Scholem calls these sections "basically a Kabbalistic Midrash [that is, an interpretative commentary] on the Torah"),[96] it is stated that, in commentary to Genesis 1:26:

Rabbi Simeon [ben Yohai, a *Tanna,* of the generation that produced the Mishnah] then rose and spoke: 'In meditating, I have perceived that when God was about to create man, then above and below all creatures commenced to tremble. The course of the sixth day was unfolding when at last the divine decision was made. Then there blazed forth the source of all lights and opened up the gate of the East, from where light flows. The light which had been bestowed on it at the beginning, the South gave forth in full glory, and the South took hold upon the East. The East took hold on the North, and the North awakened and, opening forth, called loud to the West that he should come to him. Then the West traveled up into the North and came together with it, and after that the South took hold on the West, and the North and the South surrounded the Garden [of Eden] , being its fences. Then the East drew near to the West, and the West was gladdened and it said, 'Let us make man in our image, after our likeness,' to embrace like us the four quarters and the higher and the lower. Thereupon were East and West united, [that is, as the Omphalos, the Center of the Cosmos] and produced man. Therefore have our sages said that man arose out from the site of the Temple."[97]

The Rock of Foundation that underlies the Temple of Jerusalem on the Temple Mount is known in Hebrew as the *Eben Shetiyyah*, and it is this Stone that was

the first solid thing created, and was placed by God amidst the as yet boundless fluid of the primeval waters. Legend has it that just as the body of an embryo is built up in its mother's womb from its navel, so God built up the earth concentrically around this Stone, the Navel of the Earth. And just as the body of the embryo receives its nourishment from the navel, so the whole earth too receives the waters that nourish it from this Navel. The waters of the Deep crouch underneath the *Shetiyyah* stone at a depth of a thousand cubits, and down to them reach the *shitin*, the shafts, also created according to legend in the days of creation. Thus when the libations flowed down from the bowls on the altar into the shafts, they finally reached the waters of the Deep and could so fulfill their mission. They raised the levels of the Deep, a task in which, as we have seen, they were assisted by the singing of the fifteen Songs of Ascents [Psalms 120–134]."[98]

I have written on this phenomenon that

The temple is often associated with the waters of life which flow forth from a spring within the building itself—or rather the temple is viewed as incorporating within itself or as having been built upon such a spring. The reason that such springs exist in temple is that they are perceived as the primeval waters of creation, *Nun* in Egypt, *abzu* in Mesopotamia, *tehom* in Israel. The temple is thus founded upon and stands in contact with the waters of creation. These waters carry the dual symbolism of the chaotic waters that were organized during the creation and of the life-giving, saving nature of the waters of life.[99]

The passage from the Zohar quoted above emphasizes that, in the sixth day of Creation, just before the creation of humans, as the cosmos, in the form of the four cardinal directions, was gathering in to the Temple Mount, where "man arose," was gathering in, "Then there blazed forth the source of all lights and opened up the gate of the East, from where light flows."[100] The Rock of Foundation, upon which the Temple was built, is the source of the waters of creation and of the creation of humans, and also of that other most important element of nature and of life, light.

> It was from the spot on which later the Temple was erected that the first ray of light issued and illuminated the world. This light continued to emanate from the spot after the Temple was built upon it. Its source was the Holy of Holies in which the Holy Ark stood, and it lit up the Temple itself and shone forth through the windows. These windows were built not to let the light in from the outside…but to let out the light from within. In accordance with this reversed function the form of the windows was also reversed. They were narrow on their inner side and widened towards their outer side.[101]

One of the most interesting and important aspects of Kabbalah as it relates to the Temple is in its preoccupation with and interpretation of Jacob's dream (Genesis 28:10–17), which is itself perhaps the supreme archetype within the Temple-based scriptures of the Temple, its origins, its sanctity as a place, and its relationship with heaven.

> Jacob left Beersheba, and went toward Haran. And he came to a certain place, and stayed there that night, because the sun had set. Taking one of the stones of the place, he put it under his head and lay down in that place to sleep. And he dreamed that there was a ladder set up on the earth, and the top of it reached to heaven; and behold, the angels of God were ascending and descending on it! And behold, the Lord stood above it, and said, 'I am the Lord, the God of Abraham your father and the God of Isaac; the land on which you lie I will give to you and to your descendants; and your descendants shall be like the dust of the earth, and you shall spread abroad to the west and to the east and to the north and to the south; and by you and your descendants shall all the families of the earth bless themselves. Behold, I am with you and will keep you wherever you go, and will bring you back to this land; for I will not leave you until I have done that of which I have spoken to you.' Then Jacob awoke from his sleep and said, 'Surely the Lord is in this place; and I did not know it.' And he was afraid, and said, 'How awesome is this place! This is none other than the house of God, and this is the gate of heaven.'

We see here that the Temple is located in that place where the revelation of the Divine occurs. Within the biblical tradition, this place is Mt. Moriah, later the threshing floor of Araunah, which is discussed in Chapter 1. It is THE *Place*, par excellence, within the Temple traditions of the world.

> In rabbinic thought, Temple-building is equated with 'world-building,' or creation. As is recorded in the Talmud, 'Rav Judah said in the name of Rav: Betsalel [Bezalel, the architect and craftsman of the Tabernacle—Exodus 31:1–11] knew how to combine the letters by which the heavens and earth were created' (Talmud, *Berakhot* 55a). Just as God creates through His mastery over the letters, so Betsalel is qualified to build the sacred microcosm on account of his wisdom in relation to the same letters. Betsalel duly builds the prototypical Jewish Temple, the *Mishkan*. Moreover, the place of Jacob's dream is construed as the 'navel' of the world, the place from which the creation of the world began. There is a deeper allusion in the term 'place,' for throughout rabbinic literature, the term 'Place' refers to God. God is considered to be the 'Place of the world.' At the same time, the work 'place' (*makom*) and the name 'Jacob' are deemed to be equivalent by a complex gematria (the value of *ya'kov* [Jacob] is 182; add to this 4, representing the four letters of the sacred Name, and you have a total of 186, which is the gematria of *makom* [place]).[102]

There is a seeming discrepancy in the Genesis account of Jacob's dream, in that in Genesis 28:11, it states that "Taking one of the *stones* of the place, he put it under his head and lay down in that place to sleep." Later, in Genesis 28:18, we read "So Jacob rose early in the morning, and he took the *stone* which he had put under his head and set it up for a pillar and poured oil on the top of it."

The *Zohar* interprets these passages in the following manner:

> These are the twelve holy stones, and they were all made into one stone, as it is written, 'And this stone which I have set up as a pillar' (Genesis 28:22). He called them 'stone.' What is the reason? Because all twelve stones are included in one holy supernal stone that is above them [the *Shekhinah*], for it is written, 'And this stone which I have set up as a pillar shall become the House of God [i.e. the Temple], where the *Shekhinah* dwells'....On account of all this, all is in the secret of the twelve: the supernal twelve, concealed above, sealed in the holy supernal mystery. They are the secret of the Torah, and they emerge from one small voice....There are twelve others hidden below, corresponding to them, and they emerge from within another voice of that very stone, as it is written, 'From there is the shepherd, the very stone

of Israel' (Genesis 49:24....This is the *Shekhinah*, who is called 'a tried stone' (Isaiah 28:16), the stone of Israel.[103]

The *Shekhinah* is "the personified Presence or Glory of God,"[104] or "the presence of God Himself in the world."[105] Later, however, the *Shekhinah* "becomes a hypostasis distinguished from God," as in the Midrash to Proverbs: "the *Shekhinah* stood before the Holy One, blessed be He, and said to him."[106]

The *Shekhinah* also came to represent the *Keneset Yisrael*, the community of Israel. She is also the *Matrona*, the mother or bride or the daughter, the consort of the "king," "the receptive aspect of 'the holy nuptial.' "[107] In this latter form we enter the erotic world of the *Zohar* and of Jewish legendary material in general. At work here is the idea of the Holy of Holies of the Jerusalem Temple as the Nuptial Chamber, where the sacred marriage of God and his holy consort, the Matrona, that is the community of Israel, is carried out.[108] In Kabbalistic thinking, there is a three-fold relationship, consisting of the *Sefirot Tiferet,Malkhut,* and *Yesod.* According to this theory, *Malkhut* ("Kingdom") is "the centre, the Temple, which raises them all," "the place of the Holy Temple, the place *par excellence* where 'above' and 'below' are unified."[109] Rabbinic theory postulated that the *Shekhinah* withdrew herself gradually "from the intimate relationship She had enjoyed both with the higher dimension of God and with the Jewish people," that is, through the instrumentality of the Temple.[110]

Raphael Patai gives a long quotation, remarkable for the vividness of its eroticism, from the *Zohar Hadash,* the "New Light."[111] The *Zohar Hadash* is "a collection of sayings and texts found in the manuscripts of the Safed Kabbalists after the printing of the bulk of the Zohar and assembled by Abraham b. Eliezer ha-Levi Berukhim."[112] According to Patai,

...since the destruction of the Temple the Matrona descends night after night to the place of the Temple, enters the place of the Holy of Holies, sees that her dwelling-house and her couch are ruined and soiled, and she wails and laments, wanders up and down, she looks at the place of the Cherubs and weeps bitterly, and she lifts up her voice and says: 'My couch, my couch, my dwelling place...place of precious stones...in these came unto me the Lord of the World, my husband, and he would lie in my arms and all that I wished for he would give me. At this hour he used to come unto me, he left his dwelling-place and played betwixt my breasts. My couch, my couch, dost thou not remember how I came to thee rejoicing and happy, and those youths (the Cherubs) came forth to meet me, beating their wings in welcome...how came to be forgotten the Ark of the Covenant which stood here. From here went forth nourishment unto all the world and light and blessings to all! I seek for my husband but he is not here, I seek in every place. At this hour my husband used to come unto me and round about him many pious youths, and all the maidens were ready to welcome him. And I would hear from afar the sound of the twin-bells tinkling between his feet that I might hear him even before he came unto me. All my maidens would praise and laud the Holy One blessed be he, then retire each to her place, and we remained in solitude embracing in kisses and love. My husband, my husband, whereto hast thou turned?…Dost thou not remember how thou heldst thy left arm beneath my head and thy right arm about me…and thou didst swear that thou wouldst never cease to love me, saying "If I forget thee O Jerusalem, let my right hand forget…"[113]

But there are even more explicit expressions of the "union between God and Zion" in the Zohar. Patai quotes the following passage from Zohar III:296a–b:

The male member is the completion of the entire body [of God the King] and it is called *Yesod* (Foundation), and this is the feature that delights the Female, and all the desire of the Male for the Female which is in this Yesod penetrates the Female at the place called Zion, for there is the covered place of the Female, like unto the womb in a woman. This is why the Lord of Hosts is called *Yesod.* It is written: 'For the Lord hath chosen Zion, He hath desired it for His habitation' [Psalms 132:13]—when the Matronit separated from Him. And she unites with the King face to face on the Sabbath eve, and both become one body. Then the Holy One, blessed be He, seats himself on His throne, and all cry, His Name is complete, the Holy Name, blessed is His Name forever and ever!…When the Matronit unites with the King all the worlds become blessed and all are in a state of great joy…and the Matronit becomes intoxicated with joy and blessed in the place that is called the Holy of Holies here below, as it is written, 'For there the Lord commanded the blessing.' [Psalms 133:3].[114]

Patai interprets this passage as indicating that "Here Mount Zion appears as the *mons veneris* of the Matronit into which the generative organ of God the King, driven by a mighty desire, penetrates. In the mystical scheme of the universe created by the Kabbalists, Zion thus became the focal point, the spot in which the actual union of God and the Matronit (who here is not merely the female aspect of the deity but also symbolic of Israel, the people, and Israel, the land) takes place, and from which, consequently, blessings emanate into the entire world."[115]

CHAPTER 5

The Idea of the Temple within Christianity

The Temple is everywhere in the New Testament, both as a physical presence, as we have seen in a number of examples in Chapter 3, and as a theological presence, in the sense that the atoning sacrifice of Jesus is understood totally within the context of the sacrificial system of the Temple as it is outlined in the Hebrew Bible.[1] One vivid example of its physical presence is found in a remarkable story setting in the beginning of the Gospel of Luke that shows us an Aaronite priest actually at work within the Temple. The priest's name was Zechariah, and he is the father of John the Baptist. He was an Aaronite "of the division of Abijah" (1 Chronicles 24:10), and was on duty serving within the *heikal,* carrying out the daily process of burning incense at the altar of incense (Exodus 30:1, 6–8). He received this assignment through the system of four lots, which were taken in the Chamber of Hewn Stone, located at the southern corner of the Court of Israel, in order to choose priests to cleanse the altar of burnt offerings and prepare its fires, to carry out the burnt offerings for the day, to offer incense for the morning service, and to place the pieces of the slaughtered animal upon the altar.[2] The large group of Israelite men who had gathered at the Court of Israel waited in anticipation for the priest who offered the incense to pronounce the prescribed prayers: "And the whole multitude of the people were praying outside at the hour of incense" (Luke 1:10). But as Zechariah had experienced a vision inside the Temple, he was delayed in making his exit, was unable to speak when he came out, and was reduced to making hand signs to the crowd (Luke 1:5–23).[3]

The most vivid and memorable impression of the Temple that is experienced within Christianity relates to the atoning sacrifice of Jesus, which forms the basis of the extended simile of Jesus as the unblemished firstborn son who is sacrificed, once and for all, to atone for the sins of his people. This theology finds its clearest, most extensive expression in the Letter to the Hebrews, traditionally attributed to Paul's authorship, particularly chapters 7–10.

To begin with, Jesus is assigned to the High Priesthood, specifically as THE High Priest, "the surety of a better covenant," (Letter to the Hebrews 7:22), "a high priest forever, after the order of Melchizedek" (Letter to the Hebrews 7:17). From the point of view of Christianity, the "law," that is the Mosaic law, Torah, is a "shadow of good things to come instead of the true form of these realities" (Letter to the Hebrews 10:1), and is therefore superceded by a New Covenant, a new Torah ("He abolishes the first in order to establish the second"—Letter to the Hebrews 10:9), based on the sacrifice of Jesus, just as the Old Covenant had been based on the daily, yearly sacrifices in the Temple carried out by the priests, particularly by the High Priest on the Day of Atonement. "But when Christ had offered for all time a single sacrifice for sins, he sat down at the right hand of God, then to wait until his enemies should be made a stool for his feet" (Letter to the Hebrews 10:12). And the symbolism continues, drawing upon each and every architectural and design and ritual feature of the actual temple: "Therefore, brethren, since we have confidence to enter the sanctuary by the blood of Jesus, by the new and living way that he opened for us through the curtain, that is, through his flesh, and since we have a great priest over the house of God" (Letter to the Hebrews 10:19–21).

The author of the Letter to the Hebrews emphasizes the four central aspects of the Temple sacrifices of the Hebrew Bible, and relates each of these to Jesus. These are the nature of the animal sacrifices themselves, with the emphasis on the blood that was shed ("without the shedding of blood there is no forgiveness of sins"—Letter to the Hebrews 9:22), the authority of the priesthood by which these sacrifices were carried out, the relationship of such sacrifices to sin and to the atonement (removal of the consequences) of sin, and finally to the actual architectural structure of the Temple itself and the sequence of the sacrifices as they relate to the architecture, particularly to the Holy of Holies.

All of these aspects just mentioned come together within the context of the simile that Jesus was the unblemished first-born son of the Father, analogous to the first-born male of Passover of Exodus 12, who was sacrificed and his blood was brought within the holy place (that is, not the *debir* of the earthly temple, but in its actual heavenly counterpart—see Revelation 11:19: "Then God's temple in heaven was opened, and the ark of his covenant was seen within his temple"), once and for all, functioning as the great High Priest of the New Covenant, thus atoning for the sins of humankind once and for all, so that such sacrifices will no longer be necessary.

> But when Christ appeared as a high priest of the good things that have come, then through the greater and more perfect tent (not made with hands, that is, not of this creation) he entered once and for all into the Holy Place, taking, not the blood of goats and calves but his own blood, thus securing an eternal redemption. For if the sprinkling of defiled persons with the blood of goats and bulls and with the ashes of a heifer sanctifies for the purification of the flesh, how much more shall the blood of Christ, who through the eternal Spirit offered himself without blemish to God, purify your conscience from dead works to serve the living God. Therefore he is the mediator of a new covenant. (Letter to the Hebrews 9:11–15)

An examination of the theology of Jesus' death as stated in the Letter to the Hebrews, and elsewhere in the New Testament, will confirm that the death of Jesus is interpreted and based upon two aspects of the theology of the Hebrew Bible, both of which are Temple-centered. These two are (1) the Passover, as presented in Exodus 12, which becomes the Feast of Unleavened Bread, one of the three festivals to which all Jewish males are commanded to celebrate at the Temple every year (Exodus 23:14–17), and which is both a Temple-centered and a family-centered ritual.[4] Jesus' death occurred during the week of the Passover festival. He was the Paschal Lamb, the unblemished, first-born male (Exodus 12:5; Matthew 27–28; 1 Peter 1:19–20). In this sense, Christ was the victim, the sacrificial offering. (2) the Day of Atonement, in which Christ served as High Priest, entering the Most Holy Place one last time, once and for all, taking with him his own blood, offering himself:

> For Christ has entered, not into a sanctuary made with hands, a copy of the true one, but into heaven itself, now to appear in the presence of God on our behalf. Nor was it to offer himself repeatedly, as the high priest enters the Holy Place yearly with blood not his own; for then he would have had

to suffer repeatedly since the foundation of the world. But as it is, he has appeared once for all at the end of the age to put away sin by the sacrifice of himself. (Letter to the Hebrews 9:24–26)

Thus Jesus was both the Paschal Victim, and the Great High Priest, who entered the Most Holy Place (that is, the One in Heaven, through His death), "once and for all."[5]

By the logic of Jesus' mission as it is explained in the Letter to the Hebrews, and elsewhere in the New Testament, we can conclude that the destruction of the Temple was not a particularly traumatic event within early Christianity. In fact, Jesus himself foretold its destruction, as recorded with the Gospels: "And as he came out of the temple, one of his disciples said to him, 'Look, Teacher, what wonderful stones and what wonderful buildings!' And Jesus said to him, 'Do you see these great buildings? There will not be left here one stone upon another, that will not be thrown down'" (Mark 13:1–2). In fact, the early Church saw in the destruction of the Temple both the fulfillment of prophecy, and the passing away of the Old Covenant. We shall see that the image of the Temple could not be dismissed so readily, and that its shadow loomed over the Church well into the Middle Ages, and informed and inspired the building of the great Gothic cathedrals, instilling the Christian Middle Ages with a sense of loss, of yearning, of nostalgia for something that, as we have seen, was conceived in heaven itself, and indeed continues to exist in heaven, giving us a model and an image of perfection itself, of the world with which we long to be reconciled:

Now the point in what we are saying is this: we have such a high priest, one who is seated at the right hand of the throne of the Majesty in heaven, a minister in the sanctuary and the true tent which is set up not by man but by the Lord. For every high priest is appointed to offer gifts and sacrifices; hence it is necessary for this priest also to have something to offer. Now if he were on earth, he would not be a priest at all, since there are priests who offer gifts according to the law. They serve a copy and shadow of the heavenly sanctuary; for when Moses was about to erect the tent, he was instructed by God, saying 'See that you make everything according to the pattern which was shown you on the mountain.' (Letter to the Hebrews 8:1–5)[6]

The Temple continues to play a role during the narratives of the Book of Acts. For example when it is reported that "Peter and John were going up to the temple at the hour of prayer, the ninth hour. And a man lame from birth was being carried, whom they laid daily at the gate of the temple which is called Beautiful [the Eastern gateway to the actual Temple precincts atop the Temple Mount][7] to ask alms of those who entered the temple" (Acts 3:1–2). With the opening up of the Gospel of Christ to non-Jews—that is the Gentiles (Acts 10–11)—and the shifting focus of the geographical settings of the main books of the post-Gospels New Testament outside the Holy Land, the strictly Jewish aspects of Christianity, those that dominate its beginnings, play a lesser role,[8] and in that sense the Temple plays a lesser role, aside from the heavy theological emphasis already described.

In the aftermath of the destruction of the Temple by Titus, Jews were forbidden by imperial decree from entering the city.[9] Roman soldiers encamped within the city made abundant use of Temple debris—pillars, building stones, and so on—in order to fabricate milestones. Two of these were discovered in Temple Mount excavations.[10]

In the time of Roman Emperor Hadrian, the Romans attempted to impose Roman religion and culture on the peoples of the East, partly as a defensive mechanism against the Iranian Parthians who were threatening Rome from the East. At the same time, Jews had continued to visit the Temple Mount, and had ardent hopes that they would be able to rebuild the Temple.[11] Jews reacted against this policy with great ferocity, the result of which was yet another rebellion, this time under the leadership of Simon Bar Kosiva, nicknamed Bar Kochba. The rebels were able to retake Jerusalem in 132 C.E., establish an independent state, and even issued coins, some of which bore an impression of the façade of the Temple of Jerusalem.[12] The representation of the Temple on these coins is probably "the earliest representations of the Temple...."[13] The revolt was put down by the Romans in 135 C.E., after which Jerusalem was renamed Aelia Capitolina, and a Roman temple to Jupiter Capitolinus was constructed on the ruins of the Temple of Herod.[14]

A Byzantine era Christian work, the *Chronicon Pashcale*, gives us important information on the Hadrianic temple upon the Temple Mount. It states that Hadrian "pulled down the temple (*naos*) of the Jews at Jerusalem and built the two *demosia* (public baths), the theatre, the *Trikameron* (the Temple of Jupiter, divided into three parts with statues of Jupiter, Juno, and Minerva), the *Tetranymphon* (one of the public baths), the *Dodekapylon* (the colonnade)...formerly known as the *Anabathmoi* (the 'Steps') and the *Kodra* (the square podium of the Temple Mount); and he divided the city into seven quarters."[15] This implies that the Zealot rebels under Bar Kochba had possibly partially rebuilt the Temple of Jerusalem, and that it was this temple referred to here as having been torn down by Hadrian.[16]

The next, and most important phase of post-Temple Jerusalem came in the reign of Emperor Constantine, during which Christianity was designated as the official religion of the Roman Empire (312 c.e.—the result of a vision he received prior to the battle with rival Maxentius). Immediately following the convening of the Council of Nicea by Constantine in 325 c.e., the Temple of Jupiter, which Hadrian had built upon the Temple Mount, was demolished, under the orders of Constantine himself, by Macarius, the Bishop of Jerusalem.[17] Constantine's pious mother, Helena, having identified the places of the crucifixion and burial of Jesus (Golgotha—"the place of the skull" of John 19:17), initiated the effort to build a splendid basilica at this site, the Church of the Holy Sepulchre, located near the site of the Roman Forum in northwestern Jerusalem, "built within a mere four hundred meters of the Temple Mount."[18]

The idea was that the Church of the Holy Sepulchre would draw to itself all the symbolism, the cosmic symbolism, of the Temple itself, including the idea that the Temple was the Navel of the World,[19] thus reestablishing Jerusalem as the pivot and center of the world, and distinctly downgrading the importance of the Temple Mount itself.[20] Constantine was hailed by Church writers of that time as a new Solomon: "It is our most peaceful Solomon who built this temple…, and the latter glory of this House is greater than the former."[21] The early pilgrim Egeria (late fourth century) "equates the consecration of the Holy Sepulchre, the new temple for the Christians, with 'the day when the holy ruler Solomon stood and prayed before the altar of God in the newly completed house of God which had had built.'"[22] "In effect, the Holy Sepulchre became the New Temple."[23] Numerous elements of the liturgy of the Holy Sepulchre are reflections of those of the Temple:

> For example, the timing of the Morning Whole-Offering at the Temple is paralleled in the Weekday Morning Hymns at the Holy Sepulchre. Both began at cockcrow with the opening of the doors; morning prayers or hymns were begun at daylight. Subsequently, in the Temple service, the High Priest and other priests entered the Temple and prostrated themselves; whereas at the Holy Sepulchre, the Bishop and clergy entered the Tomb Aedicula [the Holy of Holies] for prayers and blessings.[24]

The fourth-century writer Eusebius is the earliest Christian writer to make allusions to the architecture and layout of the Temple of Solomon as the basis of Christian churches from his own time. He associates the builder of the basilica church at Tyre, Paulinus "with important predecessors from the Hebrew Bible, calling him the new Bezalel [the builder of the Tabernacle in the Wilderness], Solomon, and Zerubbabel, all builders of sanctuaries to God."[25] Eusebius described two levels of increasing sanctity in the Tyre church, analogous to the progression of sacrality as one would move towards the inner precincts of the Temple of Solomon: "Having thus completed the temple…he [the bishop] placed in the midst the holy of holies…the altar, and again surrounded this part also, that the multitude might not tread thereon, with a fence of wooden lattice-work" [analogous to the *soreg* of the Second Temple].[26]

Chancel screens were introduced in these early churches to separate areas of increasing sanctity as one entered the church and proceeded towards the sanctuary area, the "holy of holies" in Medieval Christian churches.[27] These features, along with much more elaborate Rood screens, have continued to characterize and differentiate zones of sacredness in Christian churches to the present day. Furthermore, "the Early Fathers of the Church considered the temple in Jerusalem with its sacrifices and ritual as symbols and types of the Christian place of worship with its altar and sacrifice."[28] Syrian churches viewed the interior arrangements as reproducing the arrangements of the Temple of Solomon, where "the nave

Chapel of St. Helena—Crypt of the Holy Sepulchre. David Roberts, Artist, Louis Haghe, Lithographer. George Croly, *The Holy Land, Syria, Idumea, Arabia, Egypt and Nubia: From Drawings Made on the Spot*. By David Roberts…With Historical Descriptions by the Reverend George Croly…Lithographed by Louis Haghe. Six Volumes in Four. London: F. G. Moon, 1842–49. Vol. 1, Plate 19. The Dorot Jewish Division, The New York Public Library, Astor, Lenox and Tilden Foundations.

symbolizes earth and the space enclosed by the chancel walls, Heaven. The altar represents the throne of God, a sacred role once played by the Ark of the Covenant in the first Jerusalem Temple. The bishop's seat, altar, and other hieratic structures are, significantly, located behind the chancel."[29]

The Temple Mount itself lay empty, largely neglected and ignored, up to the time of the Muslim conquest of Jerusalem in 628 C.E., and the building of the *Qubbat es-Sakhra*, the Dome of the Rock, finished in 691 C.E., and the al-Aqsa Mosque, built between 709–715 C.E. An early traveler, the Bordeaux Pilgrim (333 C.E.) visited the site and referred to the rock formation, *es-Sakhra* as *lapis pertusus*, that is "perforated rock." This same pilgrim observed that Jews came to this place once a year, on the ninth of the month of Ab (late July), the day of the final destruction of both temples, to anoint the stone and to mourn the destruction of the Temple.[30]

Christians had allowed the site to lay abandoned due to Jesus' prophecies.[31] Furthermore, as a result of Constantine's massive building program, and the enthusiasm of his followers, particularly Pope Leo 1 (440–461 C.E.), there was an attempt made to make Rome supplant Jerusalem as the "holy among cities."[32] At this time the sacredness and centrality of Jerusalem was taken over by Rome, the place of the Temple of Jerusalem with its mysteries, priesthood, and ordinances, assumed by St. Peter's tomb.[33] At the same time however Jerusalem entered upon a phase of great building activity during the reigns of Theodosius II (401–450 C.E.) and Justinian (483–565 C.E.), during which time it became a magnet drawing Christians, particularly wealthy Christians, from all over the empire. Extensive remains of Byzantine buildings, including a monastery, have been excavated on the southern side of the Temple Mount.[34]

A massive church, the Nea, was dedicated in 543 C.E., built on the hill in the Jewish Quarter opposite the Temple Mount on the southwest. It was intended to take the place of the Temple of Jerusalem, and the Emperor Justinian even had an expedition go to Carthage in North Africa to retrieve temple treasures that had been taken there as plunder by Roman soldiers, to be placed within the Nea Church. However, this was totally unacceptable to the Jews, an unwelcome Christian usurpation of the Temple Mount, and the church was eventually destroyed.[35] The Madeba mosaic map, located in a church in Madeba, Jordan, and dating to the time of Justinian, locates Jerusalem at the center of Palestine, and the Church of the Holy Sepulchre at the center of Jerusalem.[36]

In addition to the Madeba Map, there were numerous other attempts during the Medieval period to illustrate the Temple of Solomon. Although Medieval scholars could read the actual dimensions of the Temple of Solomon in the Bible itself, still, in the total absence of architectural guides from the Temple Mount, their illustrations mostly took the forms of early Christian, Byzantine, and Medieval church buildings, which in turn drew upon Classical, primarily Roman, but also on Asian and early Middle Eastern sacred building models.[37] A number of illustrators based their understanding of the Temple of Solomon on the Dome of the Rock.[38] Two fifteenth-century artists explicitly labeled their illustrations of the Dome of the Rock as "Templum Salamonis."[39] An eleventh-century Spanish Bible, the Bible of San Pedro de Roda, is a rare attempt to illustrate the Temple of Solomon based on the biblical descriptions. "The artist showed the series of walled enclosures and the sanctuary containing seraphim, a veil, and an altar, and a nearby sacrifice altar, following the biblical text" [in the right portion].[40] The Temple here, shown as a tripartite vertical structure in the left portion, shows Solomon "sending a message to Hiram" in the upper register. The middle register shows Hiram on his journey, and in the lower one Hiram is sending out his men.[41]

A seventh-century codex, the Codex Amiatinus "contains an illumination of the earliest *plan* of the Tabernacle."[42] Of Northumbrian origin, this illumination is remarkably accurate in its plan of the Tabernacle, showing it as a rectangular structure, with "cloth-like draperies hung between columns, suggesting the possibility of a tent."[43] The tent stands within a broad, rectangular, columned courtyard. The tent itself has two clear chambers. Within the first of these chambers are the various Temple ritual objects, the golden table for the showbread, the menorah, and the incense altar. The second of the two chambers is labeled *SCA SCORUM* (the Most Holy Place), and it holds the Ark of the Covenant, "a golden box-like object on short legs…and upon this box are winged figures, also in gold, the cherubim."[44] The Altar of Burnt Offerings is seen in the forecourt of the Temple, along with "a large amphora, LABRUM."[45] Finally, one of the most distinctive maps of Jerusalem preserved from the Middle Ages, the Flemish Map of Jerusalem, shows Jerusalem as a circular city divided into four quarters or quadrants. The circular Dome of the Rock, in the upper quadrant, is labeled *Templum Domini,* and the basilica-like al-Aqsa Mosque, to its right in the upper quadrant, is labeled *Templum Salomonis.* Below this latter structure is a group of houses labeled *Claustrum Templi Salomonis,* or "Cloister of the Temple of Solomon." On the upper-right edge of the city is the *Porta Aurea,* the Golden Gate, through which it was believed Christ entered Jerusalem.[46] The seeming confusion as to which of the two Muslim buildings should be identified as the Temple of Solomon might be explained with reference to the biblical idea of two or more Temples, including the Temple at Bethel, (*Templum Domini*), and the Temple of Solomon (*Templum Salomonis*), or even signifying the dualism on the biblical Temple Mount between the Temple and Palace of Solomon. There is also the significance on the map of a domed and a basilical structure, which reflects the reality of the two Muslim sanctuaries, as well as the typical Medieval conjoining of the domed and basilical structure in a Cathedral complex.[47]

On July 17, 1099, the Christian Crusader army under Raymond of Toulouse and Godfrey of Bouillon, along with other knights, soldiers, and camp followers, entered the captured city of Jerusalem and celebrated a mass of victory at the Church of the Holy Sepulchre. They had massacred all inhabitants of the city.[48] On December 25, 1119, Hugh de Payens and eight other knights were sworn to oaths of a new order of poverty, chastity, and obedience by the Patriarch of Jerusalem in the Church of the Holy Sepulchre.[49] They were assigned to serve in the church, called *Templum Domini,* built over the ruins of the Temple of Jerusalem, that is over the Dome of the Rock, which was equipped with a cross, and in other ways structurally modified. The new order was called, variously, *Paupers commilitione Christi templique Salomoniaci,* "The Poor Fellow Soldiers of Jesus Christ and the Temple of Solomon," "The Knights of the Temple of Solomon," "The Knights of the Temple," "the Templars," or "The Temple." Their primary role was to protect pilgrims coming to the Holy Land.[50]

The Knights Templar are viewed, in a number of documents from the eighteenth century, as the recipients and heirs of an ancient, Essene secret tradition of secret initiations that goes back to the Second Temple. According to these traditions, Hugh de Payens and the other knights were initiated into these secret traditions at the time they were given their church over the ruins of the Temple of Jerusalem.[51] Central to these documents was a "longing for the Temple," a desire to rebuild the ancient Temple, and to install a new order of esoteric Christianity, with a new Temple, outside the range of the corrupt exoteric Church that existed at that time.[52] There is a distinctive reminiscence here of the Essenes of ancient times, as embodied in the Qumran sect, and in fact the legend of the Essenes and of their mysteries persisted throughout the Middle Ages, to be re-embodied in the Templar order.

> Here, again, we observe that the Templars had been formed as such because they had been entrusted with an exalted transcendental science, transmitted from sage to sage since earliest times. The theme of a secret and superior authority, hidden behind the Order, which is manifested in history, leads on to the idea of the knight-priests....The link between the knights of the Temple and the canons of the Temple was effective from then on. The latter

had inherited the esoteric sciences of the Essenes through the intermediary of seven hermits, descendants, across the vicissitudes of successive transmissions, of the primitive Essene community. Their hermits were the first people met by Hugh de Payens and his comrades. They preserved the tradition of a prophecy announcing that eternal Wisdom, *Sophia aeterna,* would manifest herself once more 'in the ancient sanctuary of Jerusalem, when the knights clothed in white come from beyond the seas to defend the Holy City.'[53]

According to these same traditions, the Knights Templar obtained various treasures underneath the Dome of the Rock, including the seven-branched gold candlestick and texts relating the secrets of the ancient Temple.[54] It is true that the Knights Templar excavated underneath the rock formation upon which the *debir,* the Holy of Holies, of the Temple of Solomon is thought to have stood, and which is today enclosed by the Dome of the Rock. According to Ritmeyer they carried out various quarrying operations, including cutting "a broad staircase from the bedrock leading up to *es-Sakhra* on the west, so that the High Altar, which stood on top of *es-Sakhra* could be reached more easily. At this time the entire rock mass was covered with marble slabs."[55] One can see a late-nineteenth-century drawing of this staircase and the Muslim shrine built at its bottom, by C. W. Wilson, in Gibson and Jacobson.[56]

The Templar tradition ended on March 19, 1314, with the execution of Jacques de Molay, the last Grand Master of the order. Traditions from that time onward claim that the Templar legacy, authority, Temple treasures, and secret initiation rituals were dispersed, primarily to Scotland, giving rise to the Scottish Rite of Freemasonry.[57] Thus the Freemasons become the heirs of Templar traditions, to which are added the legend of the Holy Grail, the cup that received the blood of Christ on the cross.[58]

It is doubtless true that any human entity from the Judeo-Christian tradition that encountered the Temple Mount in the Middle Ages, following several hundred years of Muslim occupation of Jerusalem, would be deeply inspired by having direct access to what was thought to have been the actual building site of the Temple of Jerusalem, and indeed to its very Holy of Holies. It was also at the time of the beginnings of the Templar movement that the magnificent building project of the Gothic cathedral was set in motion. The choir of Canterbury Cathedral was dedicated in 1130 C.E., 11 years after the founding of the Knights Templar order, as "more splendid than any other of its kind 'since the dedication of the Temple of Solomon'.... The assembly chanted 'Awesome is this place. Truly, this is the house of God and the gate of Heaven, and it will be called the court of the Lord.'"[59]

Many scholars suggest that the Templars dug up ancient Essene documents underneath the Dome of the Rock, thus the former *debir* of the ancient Temple, and that they thereby became heirs to a secret initiatic Temple tradition emanating from the Temple of Jerusalem itself. This tradition was said to have been carried into Scotland, where it resides, most spectacularly, at Rosslyn Chapel, which is itself purported to have incorporated replicas or variations of some aspects of the Temple of Solomon into its structure.[60] The ancient, Templar-discovered secret documents are said to be within a crypt in the Chapel; however, we are unable to make a judgment as to their authenticity. In any case, we have to go no further than to the aforementioned Gothic Cathedral building project to see the full flowering of a Temple of Jerusalem-inspired tradition of sacred architecture. And the tradition of Gothic Cathedrals began to flower in the same era as the Crusader conquest of Jerusalem, with for example the choir of the Cathedral of Canterbury dedicated in 1130, the choir of the Cathedral of St.-Denis dedicated in 1144, Sens Cathedral, begun in 1130. The Templars' true legacy is therefore the retransmission of the Temple concept to Western Europe on the watershed between monastic Romanesque and knightly Gothic forms of architecture and symbolism.[61] This legacy includes the increasing contact of Western Europe with Islam, and with Islamic building forms, which in their turn had a dramatic impact on the development of Gothic architecture.[62] There was one individual, Bernard of Clairvaux, who was associated with the Knights Templar,[63] with the Crusades,[64] and with the growth and development of the Gothic Cathedral.[65]

Henry Corbin is a persuasive and highly authoritative advocate of the view that there was a Templar secret initiatic tradition going back to the Temple of Solomon. In other words, Corbin believes that the Templars discovered and restored this Temple-based initiatic tradition, and that it resides today in Scotland. "In both directions, the filiation is established through the conjunction of the initiatic idea with the idea of spiritual knighthood, claims to descent from the primitive Judaeo-Christian community of Jerusalem, and through this from the community of the Essenes."[66] Corbin speaks of "Temple knighthood—of the Order of the Temple," which "remains indissolubly linked to the concept of initiatic knighthood,"[67] and further that "...initiatic knighthood...is perpetuated from century to century, unknown to the majority of men."[68] "The aspirations of Christian esotericism were polarized in the historical Order of the Knights of the Temple, conceived as having been the seat of this esotericism....For this ancestry was always traced back to the Temple of Solomon through the Esssene community and other related communities."[69] "What Templar tradition claims is precisely the heritage of the Essenes and, through them, of the Judaeo-Christian gnosis of the Church of James."[70]

Corbin then proceeds to outline the various historical trajectories through which the Essene-initiatic-revelatory discoveries of the Knights Templar were transmitted into various European countries and kingdoms, from the time of Hugh De Payens, and following the execution of Jacques de Molay, Grand Master of the Order of the Temple, in 1314.[71] Some of these trajectories are supposed to have derived from the early Essene community itself, and from the early Christian sect of the Ebionites, founded by James the brother of Jesus. It was their descendants who resurfaced at the time of the capture of Jerusalem during the First Crusade, and intended to assist the Crusaders in building the Third Temple. These descendants actually possessed the "mystical measurements of the first Temple."[72]

What is the meaning of "initiatic knighthood...perpetuated from century to century?"[73] Corbin states that such a tradition is not historical in the strict sense, that is "cannot leave any trace in any archive."[74] It is, rather, "subtle history," "parahistory," or "hierology," "always traced back to the Temple of Solomon through the Essene community and other related communities."[75] "There was no need to restore in a material sense the historic Order of the Temple, as many wished to do. What was needed

Interior of Rosslyn Chapel, Scotland. The Crypt, with the Stairs leading down. Completed 1486. Jack N. H. Lundquist.

Rosslyn Chapel, interior. Apprentice Pillar (background), and Journeyman Pillar (foreground). Jack N. H. Lundquist.

was to affirm one's spiritual descent by taking one's place in the tradition that the Order had made its own in the course of two centuries."[76] Secret knowledge is temple knowledge. An "initiatic tradition,"[77] can only be based on Temple ritual. This is what the Templars would have discovered in the vault underneath the Rock of the Temple Mount. The Templars were representatives and inheritors of a Primordial Tradition, which means the combination of revelation and authoritative initiatic transmission from the Center.[78]

It can be stated with some confidence that the Knights Templar and their successor associations did indeed possess an initiatic tradition, based for example on ritual initiation into ever higher degrees of the order, secret passwords and handgrips, penalty signs, and the wearing (and changing) of ritual clothing. One of the most informative, persuasive, and authoritative authors on these traditions is Francis King (*Sexuality, Magic and Perversion*, 2002 (1971), and *The Secret Rituals of the O.T.O,* 1973). King calls such initiatic traditions "ceremonial," or "ritual magic,"[79] and he gives a much abbreviated version of the history of the same Templar tradition as Corbin, but with a much more skeptical eye.[80] King brings that history up to the twentieth century with the figures of Aleister Crowley, Madame Blavatsky, and Rudolf Steiner.[81]

At the same time, King gives one of the most thorough and informative accounts of Templar/Masonic/Ordo Templi Orientis rituals. A representative sample of such a ritual follows:

First Point (Consecration)

The place is open in the first degree.

S. (Saladin): Brother-soldiers…is now a candidate to be consecrated a Magician; we must first give proofs of his worthiness to acquire virtue. I shall therefore put the necessary questions. (E—Emir brings C—Candidate to face throne)

S. Where were you first prepared for your initiation?

C. In heart, verily.

S. Where next?

C. In a convenient place, hard by a spring.

S. How long did you remain there?

C. For nine moons.

S. Where were you initiated?

C. In an oasis.

S. At what hour?

C. Dawn.

S. The sun is risen. Do you pledge your honor as a Man, and your fidelity as a Brother, that you will steadily persevere through the ceremony of being consecrated a magician?

C. I do.

S. I warn you that a severe test of your sincerity will be required. Unless you are prepared to jeopardize your social position, and possibly your liberty, or your life, it will be better for you to withdraw on the instant. I wish to further impress firmly upon you that this Order is a serious body of men, courageous, earnest, and faithful, and that these remarks are not the make believe terrors of orders instituted for the amusement of grown-up children. (Pause).

S. (Loudly). Candidate, do you persist in your Will to be consecrated a Magician?

C. I do.

S. Do you likewise pledge yourself, under penalty of your obligation, that you will conceal what I shall now import to you with the same strict caution as our other secrets?

C. I do.

S. Then I will entrust to you the Pass Grip and Pass Word leading to the degree to which you seek admission. The Pass Grip is given by joining hands as you have been taught, and twisting the wrist sharply to the right. The Pass Word is Thelema, which means WILL in the Greek language. Look frankly and fearlessly into my eyes, and say with me: The Word of the Law is THELEMA. You will now retire from the Camp to a prepared place, there to undergo the necessary preparations for your consecration.

(E. takes C. out)

Second Point (The Oath)

The C. is prepared by baring the right arm to the shoulder the sleeve of his robe being securely pinned back. The Camp is opened in the Second Degree. E. goes out, prepares C., and knocks twice. W. (Wazir) opens the door.

W. Whom have you there?

E. A Man and a Brother who wills to be consecrated a Magician.

W. Halt! (W. applies Disk to Breast of C.)

S. Do you vouch that he is properly prepared?

W. I do.

S. Admit him in due form. (C. is led to throne by E.).

S. (Gives Grip). What is this?

C. The Grip or Token of a Man and a Brother.

S. What does it demand?

C. A Word.

S. Give me that Word.

C. At my initiation I was taught to be cautious; I will letter it with you.

S. I agree; begin (Done). What is its import?

C. The Lord.

S. (Gives the Pass Grip). What is this?

C. The Pass Grip, leading from the First to the Second Degree.

S. What does it demand?

C. A Pass Word.

S. Give me that Word.

C. Thelema.

S. What is its import?

C. Will.

S. Pass, Thelema (E. takes C. to centre).

S. You now stand at the centre of our Camp, the place of the Balance. Hear first the Book of the Balance (Orator, who may be any member of the Oasis, and is selected for the excellence of his delivery, read Liber Librae—published in Equinox I).

S. Another and more serious obligation will now be required of you. Are you willing to take it?

C. I am.

S. Officers, do your duty (They go to Altar, W. directs C. to place right hand on the Open Book. He places Dagger on C.'s heart, while E. presses Disk upon his head).

S. Repeat your name at length, and say after me: I,... in the Presence of the Powers of Life visible and invisible, and of this Camp of Magicians, do hereby and hereon most solemnly promise and swear:
Never to reveal
What I learn beneath the seal
Within the guarded border
Of this Most Holy order
Unless it be to a true brother
And not another....

S. Besides the oath of Secrecy, there are certain obligations designed to make your more efficient in your Way as in ours. Are you willing to take these?

C. I am.

S. Say after me: I solemnly pledge myself to know, to will, to dare, to keep silence. These several points I solemnly swear to observe, under no less a penalty that that of having my Breast cut across, my Heart torn therefrom, and thrown to the fowls of the air, that they may devour it....

S. Sign (C. signs. W. takes papers).

S. In the Name of the Secret master, (Puts book to the brow). In the name of the O.T.O. [Ordo Templi Orientis] (Puts Dagger to throat). By the authority of the Grand master Baphomet (Puts Disk to heart).

S. I consecrate you a Magician (O.T.O applause). I now gird you with this sacred sword; for you will have need of it. I appoint you sentinel of this Camp, while we enjoy the siesta of noon (E. leads C. to door, and bids him guard it, with his face outwards).[82]

From "The Book of the Unveiling of the Sangraal," "Being the Secret Instruction of the Ninth Degree" (of the O.T.O.), comes the following statement:

He [God] revealed unto the wise men of old time, the Way of this Attainment. The Gnostics and Manichees preserved it in their most secret assemblies as they had received it from the greatest of the magi of Egypt; nor were the Ophites ignorant of this mystery, nor the men that did worship unto Mithras, and the secret is hidden in the fable of Samson; Our Lord

Jesus Christ established it through the mouth of the Beloved Disciple. This was the inmost secret of the Knights of the Temple, and the Brethren of the Rose Crosse concealed it in their College of the Holy Ghost. From them and from their successors the hermetic Brothers of Light have we received it directly, and here declare it openly to you.[83]

There can be no doubt that this statement gives us a correct lineage for the secrets, rites, and mysteries of the Knights Templar and their successors.

Whatever the truth of the matter [the accusations brought against the Knights Templar that led to their suppression in the early fourteenth century], it is undeniable that the accusations against the Order of the Temple led to its suppression, after which it was almost forgotten for over four hundred years. It was the explosive eighteenth century growth of European speculative free-masonry that led to a revival of interest in the Knights Templar.... Within a few years the Europeans, particularly the French, were founding their own Lodges, taking their rituals, their mystic words...and their secret signs and steps from the English Lodges whom they were imitating.[84]

It is beyond the scope of this book to trace in detail and to fill in the various links in the chain of esotericism from antiquity to the Knights Templar to the Freemasons. But this connection can be made. To give just a few examples: The Egyptian Book of the Dead, and Egyptian funerary rites in general, are the probable ultimate parent of this kind of esotericism. Spell 144 of the Book of the Dead, titled "The Keepers of the Gates," and Spell 146, titled "For entering by the mysterious portals of the House of Osiris in the Field of Rushes," introduce us to the concept of the gate keepers in the underworld, those who bar the way to the unrighteous. The deceased must have the secret knowledge of the names of the various gate keepers, and must be able to recite them in order to be allowed to pass to the next gate. At each gate the formula is repeated: "What is to be said by N [the candidate] when arriving at the...portal: Make way for me, for I know you, I know your name, and I know who is with you."[85]

These ritual practices were taken over into the various Greek mysteries, many of whose adepts were initiated into the Egyptian mysteries. The concepts of hand grips, secret formulas, passwords, ritual clothing, and penalties warning one not to reveal what one has experienced, abound in these ancient rituals.[86] In the *Golden Ass* of Apuleius, the account of the initiation of Lucius into the mysteries of Isis and Osiris, Lucius speaks of donning "a new linen gown," after which "the priest grasped my hand

and conducted me into the Holy of Holies." As to how much he is willing to reveal of the details of the initiation itself, he tells us that "I would tell you if it were permitted to tell. But both the ears that heard such things and the tongue that told them would reap a heavy penalty for such rashness."[87]

A fourth-century Coptic Gnostic codex, that forms chapter 52 of the Coptic Gnostic Second Book of Jeu, is a spell for "ascending through the heavens." The spell is fascinating and merits quotation in full:

> When you come out of the body and you reach the first of the aeons, and the archons of that aeon arrive before you, seal yourselves with this seal [illustration of the seal given in the ancient text]
> This is its name: Zozeze
> Say it one time only.
> Grasp this pebble with both your hands: 1119, eleven hundred nineteen.
> When you have finished sealing yourselves with this seal, and you recite its name one time only, say these protective spells also: "Retreat Prote(th), Persomphon, Chous, archons of the first aeon, for I invoke Eaza Zeozaz Zozeoz."
> Whenever the archons of the first aeon hear these names, they will be very afraid, withdraw to themselves, and flee leftward to the west, while you journey on up.
> When you reach the second of the aeons, Chouncheoch will arrive before you. Seal yourselves with this seal: [given in text]
> This is its name; say it one time only: Thozoaz
> Grasp this pebble with both your hands: 2219, twenty two hundred nineteen.
> When you have finished sealing yourselves with this seal, and you recite its name one time only, say these protective spells also: "Retreat Chouncheoch, archon of the second of the aeons, for I invoke Ezaoz Zoeza Zoozaz."
> Yet again the archons of the second aeon will withdraw to themselves and flee westward to the left, while you journey on up.
> When you reach the third of the aeons, Yaldabaoth and Choucho will be arriving before you. Seal yourselves with this seal: [given in the text]
> This is its name: Zozeaz.
> Say it one time only.
> Grasp this pebble with your hands: 3349, thirty three hundred forty nine.
> When you have finished sealing yourselves with this seal, and have recited its name one time only, say these protective spells also: "Retreat Yaldabaoth and Choucho, archons of the third of the aeons, for I invoke Zozezaz Zaozoz Chozoz.

Yet again the archons of the third of the aeons will withdraw to themselves and flee westward to the left, while you journey on up.[88]

Handclasps and hand grips played a major role in most antique mystery traditions, and were carried on into Medieval Christianity. As in the Ordo Templi Orientis ritual detailed above, whenever we are dealing with initiation into a succession of higher orders, including into the various heavenly degrees, handclasps and hand grips play two roles: (1) as a secret sign known only to members of the mystery tradition and used as a means of identification; and (2) as a symbol of welcome into the new, higher order. Todd M. Compton has studied this phenomenon at length. He relates this practice as "any token serving as proof of identity," functioning within the "recognition drama."[89] A painting from a second-century c.e. tomb of participants in the Sabazian mysteries shows a messenger leading the deceased into the sacred realms in an *inductio* ceremony, symbolizing "eschatological reunion," "to the banquet of the blessed," into the afterlife.[90] The fifth–sixth century Apocryphal Acts of Pilate, also known as the Gospel of Nicodemus, features Jesus' descent into Hell, bringing salvation to those who had languished there. As Jesus ascends into Heaven, bringing the saints with him, He brought Adam up from Hell, "holding the right hand of Adam" (8 [24]:1); "holding the right hand of Adam, ascended from the underworld, and all the saints followed him" (8[24]:2). "Then the Lord, holding the hand of Adam, delivered him to the archangel Michael, and all the saints followed the archangel Michael, and he brought them all into the glorious grace of paradise" (9[25]:1).[91] The right hand is operative here as the ritual right hand, the gesture, the hand grip, used to introduce the initiated into higher grades of initiation, or into paradise.[92]

There can be no doubt that it is from these ancient sources that Templarism ritual originated. This is the source of what Corbin calls "initiatic knighthood." Of course, there were numerous other ancient and Medieval esoteric movements that fed into European mystery traditions. In addition to those named above (ancient Egyptian ritual, the ritual traditions of Isis and Osiris, Gnosticism, Sabazianism) there were Druidism, the Mithraic rituals, Scandinavian mystery traditions, the Eleusinian mysteries, the Orphic mysteries, and the mysteries of Dionysus, Jewish traditions, particularly Kabbalah, and alchemy.[93] All of these fed into European culture from late Antiquity on into the Middle Ages.[94]

A centerpiece of the Renaissance and Early Modern interest in ancient Egypt was Isis, the foremost Egyptian goddess, the sister-spouse of Osiris in the mythology. Evidence of her cult has been unearthed all over Europe, and she, in her role as the heavenly nursing mother of pharaohs and the nursing mother of her son, Horus, played an enormous role in the development of Mariology in the early Christian centuries. In fact, many aspects of Egyptian religion influenced early Christian theology and eschatology.

Earlier in the sixteenth century an extraordinary ancient tablet in bronze with gold and silver inlay had been discovered in Rome. The tablet contained Egyptian hieroglyphic inscriptions, figures of Isis, Egyptian deities, and ritual scenes. The tablet was a product of the early Roman period, was itself an Egyptianizing piece form the reign of Claudius, and reflected late Roman understandings and misunderstandings of Pharaonic culture as it was known at that time. It presumably came from a temple to Isis, and in its present form represents a barbaric attempt to reproduce Egyptian religious figures. The hieroglyphs on the tablet were used as mere ornament, not to represent an actual linguistic text. The first edition of an engraving of this tablet was published in 1559 by the man who invented the science of numismatics, Enea Vico de Parma. This work *Vetustissimae hoc est sacris quem ex Torquati edidit nunc Tabulae Aeneae Aegyptiorum Literis Bembi Musaeo an M.D.LIX aeneas* was published later in an engraving, in 1600 by G. Franco. These publications of the tablet, which was owned by Cardinal Bembo, were the first in a long series of publications and explications of the *Mensa Isiaca,* the "Tablet of Isis." From that time to the present the *Mensa Isiaca* has served as a rich source of Egyptianizing design motifs and for mystical speculation on subjects ranging from the Kabbala to Rosicrucianism, and was until the nineteenth century a primary reference tool for the study of ancient Egypt.[95]

All of this means that Templar, and subsequently Masonic, ritual need not be attributed to the discovery by the Knights of secret Essene documents and authentic relics from the Temple of Solomon underneath the Dome of the Rock (for which there is no believable evidence). It further means that it is not necessary to be able to trace Masonic initiation directly back to the Temple of Solomon, which is in any case impossible. However there is a definite historic link connecting various ancient mystery traditions with the Templar/Masonic/Rosicrucian movements of Early Modern Europe.

Initiation into ever-higher degrees or the successive revelation of ever higher mysteries requires, by definition—because of the secret nature of esoteric knowledge—the use of passwords, sacred hand grips, secret names, ritual ablutions and changes of clothing, and penalties for revealing the secrets. Although there is little or no evidence for mystery traditions in the Temple of Jerusalem in the Hebrew Bible or the New Testament, we must assume that the ritual of the Temple of Jerusalem included an esoteric foundation. The Temple of Jerusalem was an integral part of its ancient religious environment, and we have seen how harmonious it was in its architecture and its symbolism with temples of its cultural milieu. We have seen in Chapter 4 what was the nature of the evidence for an esoteric tradition within the Temple of Jerusalem. The very concept of "Ascent," as in the Psalms of Ascent (Psalms 120–134), which were sung by the Levites in the Second Temple as they ascended the 15 steps from the Court of the Women to the Gate of Nicanor, and into the Court of the Israelites, implies Ascent symbolism such as we see in the Apocrypha and Pseudepigrapha. There is certainly a (secret) "Name" theology in the Hebrew Bible, as we see in connection with the Day of Atonement (Exodus 20:7; Exodus 29; Leviticus 16; Sirach 50:20; Mishnah *Yoma* 3:8, 6:2; Mishnah *Tamid* 3:8).[96] The High Priest wore the divine name on his forehead when he wore the turban and entered the *debir* on the Day of Atonement.[97] According to Elior the role of the Sacred Name on the Day of Atonement "hints at the

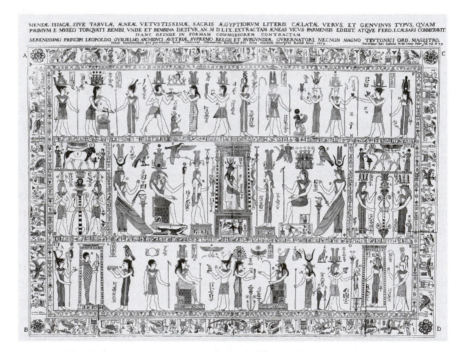

Isiac Tablet (*Mensae Isiacae*). Athanasius Kircher…*Oedipus aegytpiacus, hoc est universalis hieroglyphicae veterum doctrinae temporum iniuria abolitae instauratio, opus ex omni orientalium, doctrina & sapientia conditum, nec non viginti diuersarium linguarum authoritate satbilitum.*…Romae: Ex typographia V. Mascardi, 1952–54. Three volumes in four. Volume 3, between pp. 78–79. Asian and Middle Eastern Division, The New York Public Library, Astor, Lenox and Tilden Foundations.

existence of an esoteric tradition of enunciating the Sacred Names, related to the ritual tradition of the Temple, to which the priests were privy."[98] This esoteric Name mysticism plays a major role in the post-70 c.e. Jewish *Hekhalot* literature.[99] There are ritual ablutions and changes of clothing mandated in the Hebrew Bible (Exodus 19:10, 14; Leviticus 16:4, 23–24, 32). In the Pseudepigraphical Testament of Levi and the 2 Enoch the heroes are "washed, anointed, clothed in the priestly garments" after they have arrived at the "uppermost heaven the Holy of Holies in which the great Glory is enthroned."[100] Within early Christian Valentinian Gnostic traditions initiates were invested with a sacred Name (i.e., Christ) and advised that "the Name which is hidden…from every deity, dominion, and power, which Jesus the Nazarene donned in the spheres of light."[101] "The Christians who have been invested with this Name, know the Name but do not speak it."[102]

The early Christian Church Father, Origen (185–255 c.e.), in his *Contra Celsum,* writing on the Gnostic "sect of the Ophians," explains that

> An important part of the Ophian teaching was concerned with the ascent of the soul to heaven after death.…To reach its goal in the realm of the Father and the Son the soul had to pass through a "Barrier of Evil," which is defined as "the gates of the archons which are shut for ever." There are seven archons controlling the gates…; To persuade the archons to let him pass, the soul must address them by name, recite the correct formula, and show to each of them a "symbol." [103]

The foundations for the Temple-based mystery tradition that are elaborated so massively in the Apocrypha and Pseudepigrapha of both the Old and New Testaments are found in the Hebrew Bible, in the Temple itself.[104] It is from these traditions that Medieval and Early Modern esotericism and mystery ritual developed.

Before taking up the theme of the Gothic Cathedral, we need to say something more about the Freemasons, who will be referred to hereafter as Masons. Masons claim to be a secret society that originated at the time of the building of the Temple of Solomon, their order taking its secrets and mysteries related to sacred building from Hiram Abif, the "skilled man" sent to Solomon by King Hiram of Tyre to supervise the building of the Temple (2 Chronicles 2:13–14). This Hiram was "trained to work in gold, silver, bronze, iron, stone, and wood, and in purple, blue, and crimson fabrics and fine linen, and to do all sorts of engraving and execute any design that may be assigned him, with your craftsmen, the craftsmen of my lord, David, your father" (2 Chronicles 2:14). In Masonic lore and history, Hiram

Abif was responsible for the origin of Operative Masonry, that aspect of Masonry which actually builds buildings, the "secrets" thereof consisting of knowledge of the inner workings of the Temple of Solomon, and its various rituals. According to Masonic historians, Hiram Abif divided Masons into three craft groups: Entered Apprentices, Fellow-Craftsmen, and Master Masons.[105]

From approximately the eighteenth century on, the Masons have been at the forefront of the "chain of occult sciences," purportedly in the line of authority that preserves and perpetuates the esoteric, Temple-based initiations of antiquity into the modern world. In this regard, there are various attempts to tie the Masons in with the Templars, the Rosicrucians, and yet other groups to maintain an unbroken line of the occult knowledge: "The Gnostic sects, the Arabs, Alchemists, Templars, Rosicrucians, and lastly the Freemasons, form the Western chain in the transmission of occult science."[106]

Beginning in the Medieval period, Masons came to be called "Free Masons," due to the fact that they were not bound to the traditional town-based craft guilds, but could travel freely, and could and did work across Europe.[107] The "secrets" of the Medieval Freemasons consisted in their knowledge of building lore, and these secrets, along with oaths that were administered to them, such as secret handshakes, were intended to maintain the knowledge of the building trades within the group. A large group of Masons, from many European polities, met in Regensburg, Germany, in 1459, and entered into a unified guild organization. Their document of incorporation states the essence of their secret: "Also no workman, nor master, nor parlier, nor journeyman shall teach anyone, whatever he may be called, not being one of our handicraft and never having done mason work, how to take the elevation from the ground plan."[108] "A secret never to be revealed enchanted the minds of these poetical scholars. Their intention was to have the secret of the masons remain a secret forever."[109] Von Simson gives a slightly fuller description of the nature of the Masonic secret:

> With but a single dimension given, the Gothic architect developed all other magnitudes of his ground plan and elevation by strictly geometrical means, using as modules certain regular polygons, above all the square. The knowledge of this way of determining architectural proportions was considered so essential that it was kept a professional secret by the medieval lodges. Only toward the end of the fifteenth century—and of the cathedral age—was it made public by Matthew Roriczer, the builder of Regensburg Cathedral. He teaches "how to take the elevation from the ground plan" by means of a single square.[110]

It is the romantic view of the beauty of secrecy, particularly a secrecy based in sacred architecture, ultimately the architecture of the Temple of Solomon, that gave rise to the second aspect of Masonry, that of Speculative (non-Operative—we would say "theoretical," non-craft based) Masonry, which is the kind we are most familiar with today, with its passwords, hand-shakes, and "secret" initiations. "All Freemasonary in existence today can ultimately be traced to the Grand Lodge of England constituted in 1717."[111]

In a somewhat later period, Speculative Masonic theory and ritual was developed to a great extent by a Jewish convert to Catholicism, Martinez de Pasqually (b. 1727?), and, following him, by Lyonnais silk merchant, Jean Baptist Wilermoz, founder of the Rectified Scottish Rite in Lyons. Their theology is based on a Gnostic conception of the universe as an emanation from the Godhead in a descending four-tiered structure based on the four-tiered Temple of Solomon: "the Divine Immensity above Temple, the Supercelestial Immensity (the Sanctuary), the Celestial Immensity (the Interior Temple) and the Terrestrial Universe (the Porch)."[112] The three levels of the Temple are related to the three parts of the human being, body, soul, and spirit. These three become the first three Grades of initiation. The Grades of Masonic initiation are "intended to 're-build' this cosmic Temple of Solomon which has been dis-integrated and dis-jointed by the Fall. As the adept ascends through the degrees, he is gradually restored to the original role of the first man, Adam, whose purpose was to unite and govern the cosmic Temple....Initiation marks the passage of the novice from the outer porch to the inner sanctuary."[113]

> More commonly this divine union is symbolized by the traditional Masonic images such as the pillars Joachim and Boas and the Seal of Solomon. The two pillars which stand outside the Temple, called by the biblical names of Joachim and Boas, symbolize the two divine principles of sun and moon, male and female. Secondly, this is symbolized by the union of the Compass and the Square, whose two interlocking triangles form the Seal of Solomon and represent the perfect union of heaven and earth, spirit and flesh, rejoining of the world of creation with its Eternal Creator....Ultimately, by rebuilding the Great Cosmic Temple of Jerusalem, by reintegrating the cosmic hierarchy, the initiate can ascend to the highest stage of gnosis and union with the Deity.[114]

Gothic Cathedral architecture is suffused with ideas that originate in the ancient temple building cultures, including Egypt, Mesopotamia, and the Temples of Jerusalem. These include the idea that the cathedral is an earthly replication of a heavenly model, and thus that God is the ultimate architect. From this, it is believed that the cathedral is heaven on earth, that the architectural plan of the cathedral is revealed to the architect, that the prototype of the cathedral was the Temple of Solomon, and that the community of believers represent the body of Christ on earth, with His temple at their cosmic center.

Medieval builders derived their primary inspiration from the biblical accounts of the Temple of Solomon and Ezekiel, and, along with the Book of Revelation, viewed the earthly cathedral as the incarnation of the Heavenly City. An early twelfth-century miniature from the *Liber Floridus* illustrates the *Jherusalem Celestis* in the image of a medieval cathedral, and places this image in direct juxtaposition with the passages from 2 Chronicles 2 that relate the building of the Temple of Solomon. "The twofold relationship makes it quite clear that the church was conceived as an image of the Celestial Jerusalem, but that the Celestial Jerusalem in turn was thought to have been prefigured in the Solomon Temple."[115]

The image of the Celestial City that is described in the Book of Revelation is always related directly to the cathedral in the dedication ceremony.[116] One scholar has attempted to demonstrate that "all important elements of Gothic architecture [are] almost literal representations of features of the Heavenly Jerusalem as described by St. John."[117] "Nearly every Gothic church built after that date [1144—St.-Denis] aspired to be the image of the New Jerusalem of St. John's Revelation, whose walls had foundations that were studded with precious stones."[118] Abbot Suger of St.-Denis inquired urgently of pilgrims returning from Jerusalem of their impressions, and held two architectural prototypes before him as models for St.-Denis: the Hagia Sophia in Constantinople, and the Temple of Solomon.[119] "We have seen…how cosmological as well as mystical speculations prompted many a medieval builder to consider Solomon's Temple a kind of ideal prototype for his own work."[120]

"Virtually all consecration rites [of churches] of the period [10th century]" used Revelation 21:2–5 for the main lesson in the service: "And I saw the holy city, new Jerusalem, coming down out of heaven from God" (Revelation 21:20).[121] "Thus the emphasis upon the Heavenly Jerusalem and its relationship to the consecration of an earthly church is apparent in the tenth century."[122] The imagery of the heavenly temple is preserved in the liturgies of both the Roman Mass and the Eucharistic celebrations of the Greek Orthodox church. "During the Roman Mass and the Greek eucharist, the congregation is supposed to lift up their hearts to heaven and sing with the angels before God's throne as Isaiah heard during his throne vision (Isa. 6:3), 'Holy, Holy, Holy is the Lord God.'"[123] According to Gilles Quispel "the idea that the faithful make a heavenly journey during the Eucharist is not just simply a metaphor, but must be taken quite literally."[124]

The main portal of the Gothic Cathedral, the *porta caeli*, the Gate of Heaven, was intended to usher the pilgrim/initiate into heaven itself, into the Heavenly City. It is to Abbot Suger and his design for St.-Denis that we owe the first attempt to represent the portal in this manner, "the idea that the sanctuary is, in the words of the liturgy, the gate of heaven."[125] "The very motif of the *porta caeli* was to be understood as a threshold leading from the life in this world to the eternity that lies beyond." "The visitor to Suger's sanctuary—itself the mystical image of heaven—was reminded by him that he must leave behind the experience of his senses."[126]

The dedicatory liturgy of a Gothic Cathedral, such as was the case at St.-Denis, was a hymn extolling the new sanctuary as the equivalent of the Heavenly Jerusalem:

> Blessed city of Jerusalem, known as vision of peace
> > Built in Heaven of living stones,
> > Decorated with angels, like a noble bride.
> > Once more thou descendest from Heaven,
> > Prepared for the bridal covenant with the Lord,
> > Thy walls and roofs are of pure gold.
> > Thy doors stand open, shining with pearls
> > And the brightness of virtues; they permit entry to all those
> > Who, for Christ's Name's sake, have suffered oppression
> > Polished smooth by affliction,
> > The stones are now ready, and are inserted
> > Into the sacred building by the craftsmen's skilled hand.[127]

The essence of the Gothic Cathedral was light, the light of Heaven, the brilliant light, representing the precious stones alluded to in the hymn, which were supplied by the stained glass of the Rose windows. This symbolism in turn originated with the image of the Heavenly Jerusalem in the Revelation of John. "And night shall be no more; they need no light of lamp or sun, for the Lord God will be their light, and they shall reign for ever and ever" (Revelation 22:5). The key to the Heavenly Jerusalem is that the entire city is a Temple, as we also see in the Qumran Temple Scroll. "And I saw no temple in the city, for its temple is the Lord God the Almighty and the Lamb" (Revelation 21:22). "And...he showed me the holy city of Jerusalem...having the glory of God, its radiance like a most rare jewel, like a jasper, clear as crystal" (Revelation 21:10–11).

> The wall was built of jasper, while the city was pure gold, clear as glass. The foundations of the wall of the city were adorned with every jewel; the first

West Façade of Notre Dame Cathedral, Paris. Ca. 1200–1250. Margaret Lundquist.

was jasper, the second sapphire, the third agate, the fourth emerald, the fifth onyx, the sixth carnelian, the seventh chrysolite, the eight beryl, the ninth topaz, the tenth chrysoprase, the eleventh jacinth, the twelfth amethyst. And the twelve gates were twelve pearls, each of the gates made of a single pearl, and the street was of pure gold, transparent as glass. (Revelation 21:18–21)

Herein we have the theological foundation of the architecture of the Gothic Cathedral. As Abbot Suger said: "the entire sanctuary is thus pervaded by a wonderful and continuous light entering through the most sacred windows."[128] Gothic architecture is "luminosity and concordance of parts."[129] Suger himself gives us the direct counterpoint to the Heavenly City of the Revelation of John:

Often, out of a pure love for our Holy Mother the Church, I regard the various new and old adornments. When I behold how the wonderful cross of St. Eloysius, along with smaller crosses and some incomparable jewelry, stand on the golden altar, I way from the bottom of my heart: 'Every precious stone is Thy garment, the sardonyx, the topaz, the jasper, the chrysolith, the onyx, the beryl, the sapphire, the carbuncle, and the emerald....' Those who know the properties of precious stones realize to their great astonishment that no single one of them is lacking here, except the carbuncle, and that nearly all of them are richly present.

When, in my joy over the beauty of the House of God through the love-liness of the many-colored jewels, I am withdrawn from outward cares and a worthy meditation leads me, through transposition of the material into the spiritual, to perceive the various holy virtues, it seems to me as if I dwelt in a strange part of the universe, such as exists neither in the mire of the earth nor in the purity of Heaven, and then, with God's grace, it may happen that in anagogical manner, I am raised up from this lower to that higher world.[130]

The spiritual unity of the inner space, covered by a canopy of stone, is ensured by the fact that the outside walls, although transparent, do not have holes in them: the luminous curtain of stained glass protects the interior space from the profane outside world. The church must not appear as if illuminated from without, but as if its walls, like the Heavenly Jerusalem, were fashioned out of self-luminous precious stones. The Romanesque church building is earth in its lower reaches, Heaven in its heights. Around the space in a Gothic church, Heaven descends like a mantle of crystalline light.[131]

One of the most astonishing representations of the connection between heaven and earth in sacred architecture was built into Chartres Cathe-dral. On the Royal Portal, the Cathedral's west front, the three tympanums above the doors themselves represent the Savior in the three aspects of his mission: on the right-hand entrance as he first descended to earth, on the left-hand side as he ascended to heaven, and in the middle as he sits in full glory as the triumphant Savior. Thus the doors represent him as the Alpha and Omega, the only doorway to salvation.

The seven planets are symbolized on the right-hand tympanum in the guise of the Seven Liberal Arts that are sculpted around the archivolt that surrounds Jesus seated on his mother's lap as an infant. The signs of the zodiac are carved around the archivolt on the left-hand tympa-num, except for Pisces and Gemini (which are found on the right-hand door). "These belong to the unchanging heaven of the fixed stars and thus represent the kingdom of the Divine Spirit, to whom this door, with its representation of the ascension of Christ, is dedicated. The seven planets, on the other hand, govern according to the ancient viewpoint, the world of the soul."[132]

Paradoxically, whereas the birth of Christ is represented on the south side of the Cathedral's main axis (which ordinarily would indeed be the

Eight-cornered tower with Baroque Dome, St. Nicolaas (H. Nicolaas within the Ramparts), Amsterdam. Roman Catholic Church, built 1884–1887 by A. C. Bleijs. Lila Emily Lundquist.

New Testament side), his ascension is found on the north side (the Old Testament side). The solution to this seeming paradox is to be found in the solar alignment of the doors. They apparently relate to the ancient idea of the "two doors of heaven,"—*januae coeli*—namely, the two solstices. Through the first door, the "door of winter," the newly returning sun enters into our world, and through the second, the "door of summer," this same light leaves the world. "The location of the winter solstice, which occurs during the Christmas season, is in the southern heavens, and the location of the summer solstice in the northern; it would seem that the representational order in the west door of Chartres Cathedral is a direct reference to this: through the southern door the Divine Light descends into the world; through the northern it returns into the invisible. Between the two gates of Heaven stands the immutable axis of the world; to this the central door corresponds."[133]

Another extraordinary temple-related feature of Gothic Cathedrals are the labyrinths laid into the pavements along the central nave in front of the altar. The traversal of these was seen as a substitute for the pilgrimage to

Jerusalem. The centers of these mazes were referred to as "'*ciel*—[Heaven], or Jerusalem.'"[134] These places therefore constituted the "Holy Land" within the sanctuary, the "center of the world."[135] Some Medieval traditions tell of an image of the Cretan Minotaur that was laid into the center of the labyrinth. It is said that the image in the center of the labyrinth at Chartres Cathedral could be seen up to the time of the French Revolution, when it was removed and used to make cannon balls."[136]

We have reviewed the dramatic history of the idea of the Temple of Jerusalem in Christianity from its beginnings through the Middle Ages. It is a history fraught with ambivalence, in the sense that early Christianity viewed the Temple as having been superceded by the sacrifice of Jesus Christ that "the temple made with hands" was no longer necessary. The Old had given way to the New, and the Temple was part of the Old that no longer existed. The Temple Mount was a "dung heap," a garbage dump, when Caliph Omar entered Jerusalem in 638, causing him much astonishment.[137] And yet, its image, its symbolism, and its history as outlined in the Hebrew Bible, haunted Christianity in the early centuries, and could never be overcome, eradicated, or removed from Christian sensibility. It is this continuity of the idea of the Temple, as the basis for the theology of the mission of Christ, as the chief inspiration for the architecture of Christian churches and ritual, and as a presence ever hovering over the Christian community, that I have attempted to outline here.

CHAPTER 6

The Idea of the Temple within Islam

For centuries before the lifetime of the Prophet Muhammad (570–632 c.e.), Jewish and Christian communities had flourished in the Arabian Peninsula, and indeed in all parts of the Syro-Palestinian heartland and in other parts of the Middle East. The fame and renown of the narratives of the biblical prophets and kings, such as Abraham, Moses, David, and Solomon, as well as the renown of the Temple of Jerusalem, had doubtless penetrated these areas. Indeed, the Temple of Jerusalem played a role in early Islamic post-Qura'nic sources, and these sources show knowledge of its presence in Jerusalem and of its history, and to some extent the fame and sanctity of the Temple overshadowed and influenced the pre-Islamic peoples of the Arabian Peninsula just as it did other peoples of the Syro-Palestinian world.[1] One scholar describes early Islamic descriptions of the Temple of Solomon as "part of the cultural *koine* of early Islam."[2] A particularly large role is played by the Temple Mount itself, the *Haram al-Sharif*, the "Noble Sanctuary," the site of the third-holiest building within Islam, the Dome of the Rock, which sits on the Temple Mount in the same location as the Temple of Jerusalem had stood. The "history of the Temple was considered to be part of the past of Islam, since Islam was heir to the biblical tradition."[3]

Neither the Temple of Jerusalem nor Jerusalem itself occur undisputedly within the Qur'an by name,[4] even though (Islamicized) transformations of Old and New Testament narratives make up a significantly large part of the Qur'an's content. There are Byzantine-era inscriptions that give the name of the city as IEROUSALAIM, and the Muslims eventually settled on the name *Madinat bayt al-Maqdis*, "City of the Temple."[5] At an early point in the Muslim period, *Madinat bayt al-Maqdis* was restricted to the Temple Mount, whereas the remainder of the city was called *Iliya*, reflecting the Roman name given the city following the destruction of 70 C.E.: *Aelia Capitolina*. Then, eventually, the Temple Mount came to be known by Muslims as *al-Haram al-Sharif*, "The Noble Sanctuary," and the rest of the city *Bayt al-Maqdis*.[6] This latter term translates Hebrew *Beit ha-Miqdash*. "Based on relevant passages in the Qur'an, Muslim tradition created an image of Jerusalem that combined Jewish and Christian elements with specifically Islamic ones."[7] The Temple itself is mentioned in a number of cases in the Qur'an, as in 17:7: "If ye [the Children of Israel] did well, ye did it for yourselves; if ye did evil, (Ye did it) against yourselves. So when the second of the warnings came to pass, (We permitted your enemies) To disfigure your faces, and to enter your Temple [*as-masjid*] As they had entered it before; And to visit with destruction all that fell into their power." This is thus a reference to the two destructions of the Temple of Jerusalem.[8]

Within Islam, it is both Mecca and the Ka'ba itself that play the role similar to that of Jerusalem and the Temple of Jerusalem within the Judeo-Christian tradition, that is, the primordial, cosmic city and temple, the navel of the earth, the meeting place of heaven and earth, the heavenly sanctuary brought down to earth, the place of initial creation, and the home of Adam and Eve.[9] After the Adamic Ka'ba had been destroyed in the Flood, Abraham and his chosen son Ishmael rebuilt the house at the command of God (Qur'an 2:125–127). To a large extent the body of cosmic symbols detailed here were taken over by the Muslims and applied to Mecca and the Ka'ba on the pattern of the Temple of Jerusalem, the history, legends, and symbolism of which were well known in the centuries leading up to the time of the Prophet Muhammad.[10]

It has moreover been proven that Islam adopted almost all the early, originally Jewish legends of the Rock and subsequently transferred them to Mecca: Mecca was created before everything else in the world; it is there that Adam was created; light from heaven radiates upon Mecca; the tombs of the prophets are there; the Celestial Temple is situated over Mecca.[11]

According to a Muslim compiler of *fada'il* (religious merits) literature, Bakr al-Wasiti, who lived before 1019 C.E., Mount Moriah (the rock outcropping, *as-Sakhra*) was the second place created on earth, following Mecca. Mount Moriah was the place from where God ascended to Heaven following the Creation, where the Prophets David and Solomon performed many miracles, where Solomon built *Bayt Muqaddas* (the Temple of Solomon), and the place where the Prophet Muhammad led the other Prophets, Abraham, Moses, and Jesus in prayer as soon as he arrived in Jerusalem during the Night Journey.[12]

Jerusalem and the Temple Mount play two important roles within the Qur'an, although not by name. Although some Muslim commentators interpret these verses as referring to places other than Jerusalem, there is widespread unanimity that Jerusalem is indeed the proper referent for these accounts. These two events are the change of the direction of prayer, the *qiblah* from Jerusalem to the Ka'ba in Mecca,[13] and the Prophet's Night Journey (*isra'*) *to* Jerusalem and subsequent Ascension into heaven (*mi'raj*).[14]

The mention of the Prophet's *mi'raj* (Ascension) brings us to that aspect of the topography of Jerusalem that plays a central and perennial role within Islam, the rock massif that underlies the Dome of the Rock, and is presumed to have underlain the Holy of Holies of the Temple of Jerusalem. The key passage in the Qur'an is the following: "Glory to (Allah) who did take His Servant for a journey by night from the sacred mosque (*al-masjid al-haram*) *to* the farthest mosque (*al-masjid al-aqsa*)" (Qur'an 17:1). According to the earliest biographer of the Prophet, Ibn Ishaq, "the archangel Gabriel woke him during the night, and mounted him on Buraq, an animal 'whose stride carried it as far as the eye could reach.' Accompanied by Gabriel, the Apostle reached the temple in Jerusalem, where he found Abraham, Moses and Jesus awaiting him. They all prayed there together."[15]

> Tradition relates that from Jerusalem the Apostle mounted up to the seven heavens, where he met Adam, Noah, Moses, Abraham and Jesus. Passing beyond all these until even the Archangel Gabriel dared go no further, he found himself in the presence of God. He also was allowed a glimpse of Paradise and a glance into the infernal regions. On this occasion also, he received detailed orders regarding the ritual prayers already described. Thence, remounting Buraq, he returned in a few minutes to Mecca.[16]

It is from the rock outcrop, *as-Sakhra*, that the Prophet Muhammad is thought to have ascended to heaven. According to traditions, his footprints

"The Mi'raj or Night Ride of the Prophet Muhammad. The Prophet's human-headed mount, Buraq, has a larger round object tied to its saddle from which gold rays emanate—an unusual, if not unique, symbol for Muhammad. The angel Jibra'il (Gabriel), is represented as a giant, large and half-hidden by buildings of Jerusalem, holds a rope that encircles Buraq's neck. Eight angels. Heavens with bands of gold and silver and tumultuous clouds colored gold, cherry red, pale green and yellow." *Yusuf va Zulaykha* by Jami, Nur al-Din 'Abd al-Rahman (d. 898/1492). Copied ca. 1143–1148/1730–1735, probably in Kashmir. Barbara Schmitz, *Islamic Manuscripts in the New York Public Library*. With Contributions by Latif Khayyat, Svat Soucek, Massoud Pourfarrokh. New York, Oxford: Oxford University Press and The New York Public Library, 1992, pp. 193–194. Folio 9v. Spencer Collection, The New York Public Library, Astor, Lenox and Tilden Foundations.

can be seen on the rock surface.[17] It was said that the cave located directly below the Rock was created at this time, when the Rock rose up to meet the Prophet. Some traditions have the Prophet praying in the cave, and others that marks on the rocks of the cave come from his turban, made while he was praying in the cave.[18] There are two *mihrabs* (prayer niches) at the base of the stairs, one on either side, that lead down into the cave.[19] A major early Jewish tradition, taken over in early Islam, was that the earthly Temple stood directly beneath the Celestial Temple, and that even though the earthly Temple had been destroyed, the Celestial Temple still remained. Thus the Prophet was brought to *as-Sakhra* for the ascent to heaven via the *mi'raj* (ladder) because of this perception that the ancient earthly Temple had stood immediately below the Heavenly Temple, and provided direct access into heaven.[20]

The ascension traditions of the 3 (Hebrew Apocalypse of) Enoch, which date to around the fifth–sixth centuries c.e., were known in the Arabian Peninsula, and were the source of inspiration, speculation, and expectations of prophetic experience. There were ancient traditions, both inside and outside the Bible, that the prophetic calling is "sealed," confirmed, or verified by a bona fide ascent to the uppermost heaven, in which the prophet is vouchsafed a direct interview with God, is shown the mysteries and secrets of the highest heavens, and is indeed given a book, based upon the Heavenly Tablets. This book is sealed and brought back to earth by the prophet as proof, in the mind of his disciples, of his heavenly visitation and of his calling.

> It goes without saying that the Apostle of God, Muhammad, received *this* Heavenly Book, which is identical with the Book handed over to the earlier Apostles. When it is said in a revelation to him: 'And thus we have sent down the Book to thee, and those to whom we have given the Book believe in it.' [Qur'an 29:47]. Then it is quite obvious that the Book communicated to Muhammad is the same as that given to the Apostles before him, for his Kur'an actually is that very Heavenly Book. That much is perfectly clear from the fact that what Muhammad preached is 'a glorious Kur'an" to be found on the 'preserved tablet' [Qur'an 85:21–22] or is written in "a treasured Book" [Qur'an 56:77]. The Kur'an presented by Muhammad is the terrestrial edition of this heavenly Scripture, for we read in an important passage: 'By the Book that maketh clear! We made it an Arabic Kur'an that perhaps ye may understand. And behold, it is in the Mother of the Book with us, truly lofty and wise.' [Qur'an 43:1–3][21]

Jerusalem was conquered in 638 c.e. by the second Caliph, Umar ibn al-Khattab (634–644 c.e.). According to tradition, he first asked to be

The Cave under the Great Rock on Mount Moriah. Harry Fenn, Artist, J. John-stone, Wood-Engraver. Sir Charles William Wilson, Editor. *Picturesque Palestine, Sinai and Egypt*. Assisted by the Most Eminent Palestine Explorers, etc., with numerous engravings on steel and wood from original drawings by Harry Fenn and J. D. Woodward. New York: D. Appleton, 1881–84, Vol. I, p. 60. The Dorot Jewish Division, The New York Public Library, Astor, Lenox and Tilden Foundations.

escorted (presumably by the Patriarch of Jerusalem, Sophronius) to "the glorious Temple that Solomon had built."[22] There, he was shocked to discover that the Temple Mount was a garbage dump, "an area covered with refuse and architectural debris—columns, piers, cut and carved stones, fragments of arches and architraves—and possibly some standing remains from the Roman temple and the old Herodian Temple."[23] According to tradition, Umar ibn al-Khattab immediately began clearing the debris, after which he prayed alone.[24] According to the early Muslim historian al-Tabari (838–923 C.E.), a Jewish convert to Islam, Ka'b al-Ahbar, pressured Umar to build an Islamic place of worship on the north side of the Rock, so that both *qiblahs*—the original one of Jerusalem and now-prescribed one of Mecca—would be incorporated. Umar rebuked Ka'b for this suggestion, accusing Ka'b of attempting to introduce Judaizing tendencies, and he prayed to the south of the Rock.[25] Islamic traditions also indicate that by this time, 638 c.e. (the Prophet had died only eight years prior to this), knowledge and memories of the Night Journey and the Ascension were vivid within the Islamic community. Additionally, it is believed that Umar brought such recollections with him to Jerusalem and had indeed brought details of the topography of the sacred areas with him that originated in the Prophet's accounts of his visionary experiences.

> ...it is reasonable that a very important aspect of the Prophet's Revelation—his real and physical or spiritual and mystical journey to cosmic boundaries—was a major part of the collective memory carried by the faithful. Anticipating the later names of gates to the Haram, many stories relate that the caliph Umar entered the sacred precinct through the southern *Bab al-Nabi* or "Gate of the Prophet," [one of the Huldah Gates. Other authorities view the Golden Gate as the one which is the setting of the Prophet's entry into Jerusalem as part of his vision][26] which would have been the gate through which the Prophet came on his mystical journey. [27]

Caliph Umar was the first Muslim ruler to erect a mosque on the Temple Mount, namely the earliest version of what would become known as the Al-Aqsa mosque, located on the south side of the original Temple Mount. Umar was succeeded as Caliph by Uthmann and then by Ali, the son-in-law of the Prophet. Ali was assassinated in 661 c.e. by Muawiyya, a distant cousin of the Prophet, and the founder of the Umayyad Dynasty, which ruled from Damascus (661–750 c.e.). Muawiyya crowned himself Caliph in Jerusalem, and ruled between 661–680 c.e.[28] During this time, a Christian pilgrim, the Gallic Bishop Arculf, visited the Temple Mount and recorded that "in that renowned place...placed in the neighborhood of the wall from the East, the Saracens now prepared a quadrangular place of prayer which they have built rudely constructed by setting beams on some remains of ruins."[29] Arculf wrote that the mosque was constructed to hold 3,000 worshippers.[30] The Al-Aqsa mosque thus stands on the southern edge of the original Herodian esplanade. This mosque, which has undergone numerous rebuildings, renovations, and repairs over the centuries, as recently as the 1990s, was completed in its original magnificent form during the reign of the fifth Umayyad Caliph, al-Walid (705–715 c.e.).

> It had originally been built in basilical shape, consisting of a central nave with seven parallel aisles flanking it on each side. At the head of the central nave and against the south wall is a *mihrab* (prayer niche) oriented to Mecca. In front of the latter and above rose the dome of the mosque. Underneath the whole length of the central nave runs a wide underground passage

called the *Aqsa-el-Qadima* (the Ancient). In Herodian times and later, in Ommayad days, this passage began at the entrance to the Double Hulda Gate...it proceeds as far as the front entrance to the mosque.[31]

Grabar sees the construction of the Al-Aqsa as beginning around 660, when, "a large area of the Jewish Temple had been cleared, a rude mosque had been built on its southern end, one or more teams of laborers were available to build and repair, and several new groups of people had come to settle in the city."[32]

"The Dome of the Rock is the earliest work of Islamic architecture still standing in more or less its original shape and with much of its original decoration."[33] Grabar further states that "the Dome of the Rock was the first monument sponsored by a Muslim ruler that was conceived as a work of art, a monument deliberately transcending its function by the quality of its forms and expression."[34] The Dome of the Rock (Arabic *Qubbat es-Sakhra*) was completed in 692 c.e., during the rule of Umayyad Caliph

Jerusalem: Mosquee el-Aksa, interieur. Felix Bonfils, Photographer. *Palestine and Egypt, March 1894*. Plate 18. Albumen print. 22 × 28.5. Photography Collection, Miriam and Ira D. Wallach Division of Art, Prints, and Photographs, The New York Public Library, Astor, Lenox and Tilden Foundations.

'Abd al-Malik (685–705 c.e.). The primary purpose of the building was to cover, to stand over, "primarily to shield the holy rock…which is identified with the Foundation Rock of Jewish tradition."[35] It was the third major building to stand upon this site, after the First and Second Temples (omitting from discussion here the Temple of Jupiter raised by the Romans), and it was to be the last, because it is still standing today. The building of a structure to enclose the Rock cannot be separated from its closely related purpose—that is to absorb, unify, and merge into itself and bring to finality all the traditions of the awesome power, beauty, and majesty attributed to the Temple of Solomon.[36] Additionally, as we have seen, the Dome of the Rock commemorates, in some way not fully understood from the point of view of the structure itself, the Night Journey and Ascension of the Prophet Mohammad. Finally, there is a purpose that most authorities attribute to 'Abd al-Malik, namely to construct for Muslims a magnificent building that would compete with, and draw their attention away from, the spectacular churches in Jerusalem, chief among them the Church of the Holy Sepulchre.

Most authorities quote the statement from the early Muslim geographer, Jerusalem-born al-Muqaddasi (d. ca. 991 c.e.), to the effect that the Dome of the Rock was built to compete with the Christian churches of Jerusalem:

Now one day I was speaking with my father's brother: 'O my uncle, verily it was not well of the caliph al-Walid…to expend so much of the wealth of the Muslims on the Mosque of Damascus. Had he expended the same on making roads, or in caravanserais, or in the restoration of the frontier fortresses, it would have been more fitting and more excellent of him.' But my uncle said to me in answer: 'O my little son, you have no understanding. Verily al-Walid was right and he was prompted to a worthy work. For he beheld Syria to be a country that had long been occupied by the Christians, and he noted there the beautiful churches still belonging to them, so enchantingly fair and so renowned for their splendor.…So he sought to build for the Muslims a mosque that should prevent their gazing at these and that should be unique and a wonder to the world. And in this manner is it not evident how the caliph Abd al-Malik, noting the greatness of the dome of Qumamah [the Church of the Holy Sepulchre] and its magnificence, was moved, lest it should dazzle the minds of the Muslims, and hence erected above the Rock the Dome which is seen there.'[37]

"It became the visual rival of the Holy Sepulchre and the Nea church. It is seen immediately as one leaves the Holy Sepulchre, signaling the rebirth,

Church of the Holy Sepulchre. Luigi Mayer, Artist. *Views in the Ottoman Dominions, in Europe, in Asia and some of the Mediterranean islands.* From the original drawings taken for Sir Robert Ainslie, by Luigi Mayer. 1810. Plate 64. Humanities and Social Sciences Library, Photography Collection, Miriam and Ira D. Wallach Division of Art, Prints, and Photographs, The New York Public Library, Astor, Lenox and Tilden Foundations.

under a new Muslim guise, of the old Jewish Temple area, and it is taller than the Christian sanctuary, even though the hill on which it stands is slightly lower than Golgotha."[38] The Dome of the Rock

is a deceptively simple building located on the high platform that was erected at some indeterminate time on the large esplanade in the southeastern corner of the city. Its wooden gilt dome is slightly over twenty meters in diameter and rises like a tall cylinder to a height of some thirty meters over the surrounding stone-paved platform. It is supported by a circular arcade of four piers and twelve columns. An octagon of two ambulatories on eight piers and sixteen columns holds the cylinder tightly, as in a ring. [the outer ambulatory, directly inside the building, is octagonal, while the inner ambulatory, which surrounds the Rock, is circular]. The ambulatory is fourteen meters deep, thus giving to the while building a diameter of forty eight meters,; it rises to only eleven meters inside and thirteen outside, thus strengthening the impact of the cupola, especially from afar. There are four doors, one at each of the cardinal points corresponding only approximately to the main axes of the Haram al-Sharif....An extensive decoration of mosaics, painted wood, marble, multi-colored tiles, carpets, and carved stone covers most of the building, inside and outside. This decoration comes from many different periods and has often been repaired with varying success, as the ravages of time and changes in taste affected the maintenance of the building. [39]

Within the context of this competition between the newly ascendant Muslims and the defeated Christians, "the Jews were left without any monumental building of their own."[40] The Christians had the Church of the Holy Sepulchre, along with many other magnificent churches (the Christians had rejected the Temple Mount in favor of the Church of the Holy Sepulchre, which was built over the tomb of Christ and the rock of Calvary),[41] and the Muslims now had the Dome of the Rock. "All they [the Jews] had left was access to the remains of the tremendous retaining walls of the Temple Mount, and more particularly the Western Wall."[42]

It is assumed that the octagonal shape of the Dome of the Rock was inspired by the octagonal shape of the Church of the Holy Sepulchre.[43] The rotunda form of the Dome of the Rock, encompassing the Dome itself, was foreign to Islamic architecture, and originated in Roman Empire structures, which are reflected all over the Late Empire, such as at Ravenna. "All the forms [that is, of the architecture and the decoration] belong to the language of Late Antique art in the Mediterranean area. In all aspects of planning, design, and even construction...the Dome of the Rock could have been a work of seventh century Byzantine, Italian, possibly even western European architecture."[44] But according to Grabar, the Dome of the Rock is unique in comparison to these other structures because "it has a dome that is more important as a sign to be seen from afar than as a visible focus of an interior architectural composition." Its focus is not on a straight-axis processional, as is often the case in Medieval sacred architecture, but rather "only one around which one may process. The whole geometry of the building's construction creates a visually magnetic shell for something sacred or holy, but does not make the liturgical usage clear...."[45] "This may mean that the building was planned in such a way that the specificity of the holy object—a rock to be touched or perhaps only seen—was replaced by the general evocation of something holy but almost invisible...an invisible presence consciously designed into the building."[46]

The mosaic design itself, particularly that on the pillars and arches of the outer ambulatory, is rich in "trees having multi-colored trunks, luxuriant blossoms and clusters of fruit, predominantly grapes."[47] The trunks

285 Vue generale de l'emplacement du temple de Salomon—General view of the site of Salomon's Temple. Felix Bonfils, Photographer. *Palestine and Egypt, March 1894*. Plate 16. Albumen print. 28 × 36 cm. Photography Collection, Miriam and Ira D. Wallach Division of Art, Prints, and Photographs, The New York Public Library, Astor, Lenox and Tilden Foundations.

of some trees are inlaid with jewels, some trees bear various fruits while growing up out of roots of jewels, and with tops of gold.[48] Some wall surfaces bear designs of various jewels, including pearls. The use of mother of pearl fragments along with the mosaic stones highlights the jewel-like effect.[49] All of this evokes the paradisiacal, Garden of Eden-like appearance of the design scheme of the Temple of Solomon, and it is this aspect of the Temple that plays such a large role in early Islamic traditions of the Temple of Solomon, including references to golden trees, luxuriant vegetation, jeweled walls, heavily laden vines, and riches of fruits.[50]

There is a 240-meter-long inscription in Arabic high on either side of the octagonal ambulatory, just below the cornice. This inscription gives key information as to the purpose of the building because it is contemporary with the structure. To begin, there is no reference to either the Night Journey or to the Ascension of the Prophet Muhammad. The primary themes of the inscription are the Oneness of God, that God has no partner, that God does not beget, that Jesus was the son of Mary, not the Son of

God, that God does not beget nor is He begotten, and that Muhammad is the Prophet of God, to whom all the faithful should look.[51] Thus the inscription can be seen in large part as an anti-Christian polemic, denying the divine sonship of Jesus, asserting the earthly-only parentage of Jesus, emphasizing over and over that God does not beget, has no partner, that there is no "Three" (i.e., the Trinity).

> The inscriptions decorating the interior clearly display a spirit of polemic against Christianity, while stressing at the same time the koranic doctrine that Jesus Christ was a true prophet. The formula *la sharika lahu* 'God has no companion' is repeated five times, the verses from Sura 19:34–37, which strongly deny Jesus sonship to God, are quoted together with the remarkable prayer: *allahumma salli…'ala rasulika wa'abdika'Isa b. Maryam* "Pray for your Prophet and Servant [not Son, of course] Jesus.[52]

There are many direct quotations of Qur'anic passages in this inscription, making them the earliest known versions of the Qur'an to have appeared, and which "precede by over two centuries any other dated or datable quotations of any length from the Holy Book including pages from manuscripts."[53]

The ritual carried out in the Dome of the Rock was simple but at the same time carried overtones that we would understand from the service in the Temple of Jerusalem. Forty servants, designated as Palestinians, were assigned to the Dome of the Rock. They would be assigned shifts to their service, and would stay inside the Dome of the Rock the entire time of their shift. A special service would be held every Tuesday and Thursday. To carry out this service, they would eat, bathe themselves, and don special clothes, consisting of a silk brocade garment, with a gold embellished girdle around their waists. They would then rub the Rock, the *Sakhra,* with a perfume, then place incense inside censers of gold and silver, which contained an odiferous Indian wood that was rubbed with musk. They then closed the curtains that surrounded the circular, inner ambulatory, the one that surrounded the *Sakhra,* and would let the space become filled with the incense. Once this had been achieved, they would open the curtains and give the invitation to all who wanted to circumambulate the *Sakhra.* It was said that of everyone to whom the scent clung would be known to have been inside the *Sakhra* on that day. The Rock would then be cleaned and dried and the curtains again closed.[54]

This service has many of the hallmarks of the service in the Temple of Jerusalem, including the role of a specially appointed "priesthood," the rituals of bathing and donning special clothing in order to carry out the ritual, the "Holy of Holies"-like quality of the innermost chamber of the *Sakhra,* which is closed with a "veil" during the ceremony, and the opening up of the Holy Place to general believers following the ritual prescriptions.

Kaplony emphasizes the concentric nature of the Dome of the Rock, which points us in the direction of ancient Temple architecture, with its regular combinations of circle and square, representing the cosmos,[55] and the necessity of ritual circumambulation.[56] The Dome of the Rock is a Muslim Temple, representing the restoration of the Temple of Solomon.

> Both the former and the eschatological Temples of Christian and Jewish tradition have in their centres the Holy of Holies, the place where God himself resides, surrounded by concentric courtyards, the world around the Temple—the city of Jerusalem, the Holy Land and the regions of the Gentiles—being a prolongation of this system of concentric circles. Architecture thereby declares the area the Temple, the Dome of the Rock by its mosaics a part of Heaven, and the Rock the place where God himself resides. This fits with the column of brilliant light hovering over the Rock recalling the fire column leading Israel through the desert and the tradition which declares the Rock the Nearest Throne of God.[57]

It is characteristic of the Judeo-Christian tradition that it looks upon the Temple Mount as "empty," that is, as bereft of the Temple that gave it its glory and renown, that gave such a sense of security and well-being and prestige to both communities in antiquity. The Judeo-Christian tradition obviously cannot accept any other building as filling the role of the Temple, or of replacing it. The "non-existence" of the Temple of Jerusalem for two millennia now makes it extremely difficult to fully understand just what it was, how it functioned, and most importantly what it looked like. And yet, upon closer examination of the Dome of the Rock, as I have demonstrated here, we must agree that it is a Temple, according to the features and characteristics that define a shrine as a temple, in the strictest sense.[58] It is a lapse on the part of the Judeo-Christian community that it cannot accept this fact, and that it must always yearn for the restoration of the ancient Temple. The "restoration" occurred in 692 C.E. Thus the Temple Mount is not "empty," and has not been since the construction of the Dome of the Rock. The Dome of the Rock is a cosmic Temple of transcendent beauty and spiritual power, and is a worthy successor of the primordial tradition upon which the Temple Mount is built. We can indeed say that Islam, as the heir to the biblical traditions, as, in its own view, the final stage in the prophetic tradition, the last and final revelation, can be said to have realized this tradition in its fullness because the Temple, founded on the basis of Prophetic revelation, "the Meeting Place of Heaven and Earth," is at the center of the Judeo-Christian, biblical tradition, and is indeed, the Millennial Temple.[59]

From both the Muslim (through the writings of Wasiti) and Jewish points of view of the first century of Muslim control of Jerusalem, the building of the Dome of the Rock was seen as the rebuilding of the Temple of Solomon, and 'Abd al-Malik was seen as the latter-day Solomon. The Arabic *Bayt al-Maqdis* (The Temple) is a direct translation of Hebrew *Beit ha-Miqdash*. Wasiti refers to the building as *haykal*, the Arabic equivalent of Hebrew *heikal*, the Sanctuary or Temple. There are Jewish apocalypses from the eighth century that extol the "Ishmaelite" (Arab), conquest of Jerusalem and the building of the Dome of the Rock as the rebuilding of the Temple of Solomon, and as a presage for the full redemption of the Jews. The true Third Temple, the Temple of the Messianic age, could and would only be built by the Messiah, but this Temple, the *Bayt al-Maqdis*, represented God's employment of a foreign ruler to assist in rebuilding the Temple, just as He had called Cyrus to assist in the rebuilding of the Temple of Solomon in the time of Zerubbabel. "There is no question from the context and the natural flow of the tradition that the source [the *fada'il*—"Praises of Jerusalem" traditions of Wasiti] regards the Dome of the Rock as the direct heir of Solomon's Temple."[60]

CHAPTER 7

The Meaning of the Temple in Our Times

The modern history of Jerusalem and of the Temple Mount begins in the early years of the Ottoman Empire. The Turkish Ottoman sultan Mehmed II (the Conqueror), defeated Constaninople on May 30, 1453, thus ending the Byzantine control of the city that had begun when the Roman Emperor Constantine founded the city in a village named Byzantium in 330 c.e.[1] The Ottoman sultans envisioned a vast Islamic empire, one that would rival the first great Muslim empire, the Umayyad, which ruled the Islamic world from Damascus (661–750 c.e.).

During the reign of the third Ottoman sultan, Selim I (the Grim— 1512–1520 c.e.) Syria, Palestine, and Egypt came under Ottoman control. The Turks defeated the Mamluk Empire in Syria, Palestine, and Egypt in 1517, and thus controlled all the pilgrimage holy sites, including Jerusalem, which was a particular interest and goal of the Ottomans.[2]

During the reign of Suleiman I (the Magnificent—1520–1566 c.e.), who considered himself to be the "second Solomon,"[3] major renovations and new construction were undertaken in Jerusalem. The driving force behind Suleiman's achievements was his architect, Sinan, one of the most important figures in world architectural history. Sinan designed the Suleimaniye mosque complex in Istanbul.[4] But, most importantly for our purposes, he oversaw restoration work on the Dome of the Rock, particularly the installation of the new ceramic Iznik tiles on the exterior of the building.[5] The rebuilding of the city walls of Jerusalem, "the most complete and finest city wall built anywhere in the sixteenth century" (1539–1542 C.E.),[6] gave the city the form that it still retains to this day.

During the time of the sultan Bayezid II (1492–1512 C.E.), the sultan had encouraged Jews, such as those fleeing from the Spanish Inquisition, to settle in the Ottoman lands. Later, his grandson Suleiman, encouraged both Jews and Muslims from Ottoman territory to settle in Jerusalem, and allowed Jews to settle near the Western Wall.[7] The religious/ethnic makeup of the city that has characterized the city since the time of Suleiman consists of four quarters within the rebuilt Ottoman walls: the Jewish Quarter immediately to the southwest of the Temple Mount, the Armenian Quarter directly west of the Jewish Quarter, the Christian Quarter directly north of the Armenian (with its most notable holy site, the Church of the Holy Sepulchre), and the Muslim Quarter bordering the Temple Mount on the west and north.[8] The Turkish empire was divided into provinces (*vilayets*) and *sanjaqs* (districts). Syria and Palestine were divided into two *vilayets*, with Jerusalem governed as a *sanjaq* under the *vilayet* of Damascus. During the latter part of the seventeenth and early part of the eighteenth centuries, conditions in the *sanjaq* deteriorated considerably, due largely to the growing impotence of the court in Istanbul. Local families, both Arab and Circassian, usurped power. Among these was one family in particular, that of a Circassian officer, whose son, Muhammad ibn Farukh, was appointed as *Amir el-Hajj* (Protector of the Pilgrimage), by the sultan. Families such as this, exercising considerable power in Jerusalem, carried out considerable persecution of the Jews, many of whom left the city.[9]

With the onset of the nineteenth century, European interest in the Middle East grew considerably, partly in response to the disintegration of the Ottoman Empire, now disparagingly nicknamed "the sick man of Europe." The population of Jerusalem in the early nineteenth century was approximately 12,000, including people of all three major faiths.[10] Early in the nineteenth century, an Albanian Ottoman military officer, Mohammed Ali, seized control of the area, and established his son, Ibrahim Pasha, as ruler of Syria and Palestine, governing from Damascus. Ibrahim Pasha gave the Jews of Jerusalem great latitude within the Jewish Quarter, and a number of synagogues were built for the first time with official permission. With the resumption of Turkish rule after 1840, Jerusalem continued to attract international attention, with European residents of the city gaining more and more independence over their affairs within the city.[11]

The Napoleonic campaign into Egypt, beginning in 1798, which had as one of its main purposes the French desire to outflank and upstage British commercial and territorial interests in the Middle East, led Napoleon to mount a campaign into Palestine, where his army was thrown back at Acre. Nevertheless, Napoleon championed the interests of the Jews in the Middle East, and in May of 1799 "published a manifesto calling upon the Jews of Asia and Africa to join him in rebuilding Jerusalem and restoring it to its former glory."[12]

As the European powers united to protect "the sick man of Europe" from Russian threats, the Crimean War broke out. The peace treaty that resulted in the end of this war, signed in 1856, gave additional special privileges to non-Muslim groups in the city, and this in turn led to renewed building by these groups, and additional migration to the city.[13] During the latter part of the nineteenth century there were several attempts by Jews to gain control of the Western Wall, with its adjacent courts, from the Muslim *waqf* (the Muslim religious foundation that controls the Temple Mount) through the exchange of other properties, but these attempts all failed.[14] From the point of view of the modern examination of the Temple Mount and its associated remains, the most important event was the founding of the Palestine Exploration Fund (PEF) in 1865, "which was established…as a society devoted to the scientific exploration of Palestine."[15] The PEF scientists and explorers had close ties to British military, and indeed enjoyed the benefit of protection by British military units, many of whose officers spoke Arabic. It was during this period that extensive mapping of Jerusalem and of the Temple Mount was carried out. Chief among the PEF explorers were Major-General Sir Charles W. Wilson, who carried out extensive surveys of Jerusalem and of the Temple Mount, resulting in accurate surveys of the underground cisterns, published in 1866.[16] General Sir Charles Warren, who explored in Jerusalem between 1867 and 1870, who continued the work of Wilson, and conducted excavations on the retaining walls of the Temple Mount, published in 1876, 1880, and 1884.[17] Conrad Schick, an architect and model maker, and archaeologist, "was the first to recognize the significance of the Siloam inscription. Carved into the rock, this ancient Hebrew inscription commemorates the completion of King Hezekiah's water conduit which brought water from the Gihon Spring outside the Israelite city walls to the Pool of Siloam, which was constructed inside the town."[18] Schick was commissioned to make a model of the Temple Mount for the Turkish display at the Great Exhibition in Vienna, in 1873. He later made additional models of the cisterns underneath the Temple Mount. His 1896 monograph on the Temple and the Tabernacle was primarily based on his models.[19]

Colonel Claude Reignier Condor commanded the Survey of Western Palestine from 1872 to 1876, which was completed by Lieutenant Herbert H. Kitchener in 1878. Condor carried out extensive survey of the Temple Mount, and of the cisterns underneath the Mount, although his work is characterized by Gibson and Jacobson as "almost entirely a synthesis of the descriptions of Wilson and Warren."[20] The population of Jerusalem grew rapidly during this period, especially outside the city walls. Numerous important buildings were constructed by the European sponsors of the various Christian and Jewish denominations that were established within the city.[21] The population of Jerusalem thus grew substantially during the nineteenth century. In 1844 the population was about 15,000, with 7,000 Jews, 5,000 Muslims, and 3,000 Christians. By 1905 the population had grown to 60,000, with 40,000 Jews, 13,000 Christians, and 7,000 Muslims.[22]

This brings us to World War I, and the first stages during the twentieth century of the momentous role that Palestine would play up to and including our own times. In 1916, during the fighting of World War I, the Western powers secretly drew up a plan that would parcel out the Middle Eastern parts of the soon-to-be morbid Ottoman Empire's territory to Britain and France, and other international arrangements. This agreement, the Sykes-Picot Treaty, decreed that certain areas would be under the control of either Britain or France, or under various Arab states under the influence of one or the other of the great powers. "Palestine would be ruled by an international condominium, whose character would be established in consultation with Russia and the other allies and with the agreement of Sharif Husein of Mecca."[23]

During this time, Zionism had begun and was rapidly growing as a religious, cultural, and political movement, based on the idea of the reestablishment of a Jewish home in Palestine. The views of Bible-influenced Jewish politicians such as Herbert Samuel played a major role in British actions. On November 2, 1917, a declaration by the British Foreign Secretary, Lord Arthur James Balfour, was issued. This was later approved by the British government, formally known as the Balfour Declaration. In the declaration the establishment of a Jewish National Home in Palestine is declared to be the official policy of the British government. The government of Britain formally petitioned the Sykes-Picot partners to be allowed to exercise protectorate status over the areas designated for the Jewish homeland. Around May of 1917, the Prime Minister of England, David Lloyd George, told General Edmund Allenby, who was in charge of the Egyptian Expeditionary Forces, "that he expected him to take 'Jerusalem before Christmas.'"[24] On December 11, 1917, General Allenby entered

Jerusalem on foot, through the Jaffa Gate, "401 years after the Ottoman sultan, Selim the Grim, had entered the gates of the city," and "730 years" following the Crusader expulsion from Jerusalem by Saladin.[25]

Palestine came under the authority of Britain, the so-called British Mandate government, and (now) Sir Herbert Samuel was appointed the first High Commissioner of Palestine in 1920. In 1921, Hajj Amin al-Husseini, a member of an old Palestinian Arab family, was appointed Grand Mufti of Jerusalem. Husseini was rabidly anti-Zionist, and used his great power and the vast resources available to him as the ultimate controller of the Muslim religious endowment in Jerusalem (the *waqf*), to thwart Jewish attempts to gain greater access to the Temple Mount.[26] The Palestinians of that era developed a deep mistrust of Jewish intentions regarding the *Haram al-Sharif*, based on the numerous Jewish attempts to purchase or to barter control of the Western Wall and their awareness of Jewish paintings showing the Dome of the Rock with a Star of David at its top. These suspicions went hand in hand with their fears that the Jews intended to seize the Temple Mount in order to build the third Jewish temple on the site.[27] During the British Mandate period, up to the Israeli War of Independence of 1948, Jerusalem experienced dramatic growth of its Jewish population (Mazar gives the 1967 population of the city as 263,000, with 200,000 Jews),[28] as well as expanded building activity. All of this exacerbated the suspicion and indeed the hatred that the Palestinian population felt toward the Jews. Riots were a staple of those times, with the most severe outbreak occurring in August of 1929, caused by the "extension of Jewish ritual rights at the Western Wall."[29] Hundreds of Jews and Arabs were killed in these riots, and the Jewish population of Hebron had to be evacuated.[30]

With the expansion of the Jewish population of Jerusalem during these times, a conflict arose between the essentially secularist aims of Zionism and the religious, indeed Messianic longings of religious Jews, who viewed the return to the Land of Israel as the fulfillment of ancient prophecy. Central to these prophecies was the Temple, and central to the Temple was the belief that the coming of the Messiah would be coeval with the rebuilding of the Temple. Thus the tremendous pressure within the Jewish community to gain access to the remains of the ancient Temple. However, this was not so simple, because Rabbinic law, *Halakha,* forbade any Jew to enter upon the Temple Mount itself, because it was a ritually unclean place, associated with corpses killed during the destruction of the Second Temple. More recent interpretations within Jewish religious legal circles have decreed that Jews could enter the sacred precincts if the exact dimensions and plan of the Second Temple could be determined.

In the early 1970s, Rabbi Shlomo Goren, then the Ashkenazic Chief Rabbi of Israel, decreed that Jews could enter the *haram* if the exact precincts of the Second Temple could be determined. Some years earlier he had undertaken to ascertain what these measurements were, which parts of the Temple Mount did not belong to the ancient Temple, and were therefore open to Jews. However, his Sephardic counterpart as Chief Rabbi, Ovadia Yosef, determined that Jews could not enter the Temple Mount unless the dimensions of the Temple were determined, but that furthermore Jewish law did not authorize any person to make such a determination.[31]

A sign is now posted at the Western Gate of the Temple Mount: "Notice and Warning—Entrance to the Area of the Temple Mount is Forbidden to Everyone by Jewish law Owing to the Sacredness of the Place—the Chief Rabbinate of Israel."[32]

With respect to the Western (Wailing) Wall, *ritual* access is allowed by Jewish law, and indeed it has always been a place of pilgrimage for Jews because Suleiman the Magnificent made it possible for Jews to gain greater access to the Wall as a result of his restoration activities in the city.[33] However, the activities of the Grand Mufti during the Mandate period constantly hindered and harassed Jewish efforts to come to the Wall for prayer.[34] After 1967, with the unification of Jerusalem under Israeli control, all restrictions against Jewish ritual access to the Western Wall were abolished, but at the same time the Israeli Knesset ruled that the Muslims had sole ritual control of the Temple Mount itself.[35] In 1977, Moshe Dayan was appointed foreign minister of Israel, and as one of the conditions of his acceptance he demanded that the Islamic *waqf* should retain control of the Temple Mount.[36] According to other reports, Moshe Dayan had already asserted his authority, as Defense Minister in 1967, to insist that the *waqf* should retain control over Muslim holy sites in Jerusalem.[37]

The underlying religious law of control of and access to religious sites in Jerusalem has been governed by what is known as the Status Quo since a *firman* (decree) of the Ottoman sultan Abdul Majid in 1852. This *firman* "granted the various religious communities shared rights in the holy places, demarcating which areas came under whose control and establishing time schedules for officiating in areas shared by more than one religious group." The Status Quo was incorporated into "the 1856 Paris Peace Convention Treaty, the 1878 Treaty of Berlin, the 1919 Versailles Peace Treaty, and the British mandate government's 1922 Palestine Order-in-Council."[38]

The primary conflict over the Status Quo is obviously centered around the Temple Mount, which has undergone a number of changes, with constant conflict between the Israeli authorities and the Palestine Authority over access, supervision of building, restoration, or archaeological activities.

The Israeli removal of the Muslim inhabitants at the Western Wall on June 10, 1967, and the subsequent building of the plaza adjacent to the Western Wall, is one of the most dramatic changes that has occurred in the Status Quo. The Israelis also have many complaints regarding the handling of access by the *waqf*, and regarding accusations of unsafe, unlawful, and secret excavations, removals, renovations, and rebuildings, particularly underneath the Temple Mount, by *waqf* authorities.[39] Recently, following renewed access by non-Muslims to the esplanade following the most intense period of the 2000 Intifada, both Israelis and Palestinians have complained about the possibility that the Status Quo is being altered, "on the ground," by, from the point of view of each side, attempts by the other to limit access, or to increase access over what was allowed under the Status Quo. An American rabbi was quoted as saying that now, with increased access, the groups were getting larger, and their access on the esplanade itself was increasing, with more freedom to explore. "We're really trying to establish a different status quo, I think."[40]

On November 29, 1947, the United Nations General Assembly voted unanimously to approve the creation of two states within British Mandate territory, an Arabic state and Jewish state (UN Resolution 181). At midnight on May 14, 1948, the new State of Israel was declared by the Provisional Government. A coalition of Arab armies invaded the new state on May 15, 1948, thus setting in motion the first Arab-Israeli war. The war ended one year later with a cease-fire on April 3, 1949. Jerusalem was divided in this agreement, with East Jerusalem under the control of the Hashemite Kingdom of Jordan, and West Jerusalem under the control of Israel. Even though the cease-fire agreement allowed Jews access to the Western Wall for prayers, the Arab side never honored this agreement.[41]

In 1964, in preparation for the visit to Jerusalem by Pope Paul VI, King Hussein of Jordan initiated a renovation of the Dome of the Rock, which including replacing the Iznik tiles with new tiles, also from workshops in Iznik, Turkey, covering the dome itself with gilt aluminum, and replacing the dome of the Al-Aqsa mosque with silvered aluminum.[42]

With the Israeli victory in the Six Day War of June 5–10, 1967, and the subsequent unification of the city of Jerusalem under Israeli control, there has been a resurgence of excavation activity around the Temple Mount.[43] Additionally, there was an increase in Muslim suspicion of the motives of the excavations, which are carried out mostly by Israelis, Americans, British, and European excavators. The Muslim authorities have opposed all archaeological activity around the Temple Mount, and have indeed complained to the United Nations Educational, Scientific and Cultural Organization (UNESCO) authorities that the excavations carried out

Wailing Wall of the Jews, Jerusalem, 1857. Robertson, Beato & Co., Photographer. Albumen print. 31.5 × 26.5 cm. on mount 46 × 38 cm. The Dorot Jewish Division, The New York Public Library, Astor, Lenox and Tilden Foundations.

along the base of the southern retaining wall were for the purpose of bringing down the walls of the entire Temple Mount, so that the Temple of Jerusalem could be rebuilt.[44] Furthermore, it is an article of faith of the Palestine Authority that there never was a Jewish temple at this site, and that "the idea of a Jewish origin in Jerusalem is a myth used to justify conquest and occupation."[45]

The loss of Jerusalem to Islamic control is one of the greatest catastrophes to befall Islam, from an Islamic perspective. After all, Islamic entities had controlled Jerusalem from 638 to 1099 c.e., then, following the Crusader interlude of control from 1099 to 1187, Islamic control resumed from 1187 to 1917, when Allenby entered the city. Soon after the fall of the city to Israeli forces in June of 1967, the Muslim residents of the Maghribi (Western) district of Jerusalem, bordering the Western Wall, were ordered to leave their houses by the Israeli authorities. Their houses were demolished in order to make space for the wide plaza that now extends outward from the Western Wall, the place where many national religious and patriotic Israeli events occur.[46]

> For believing Muslims, Jerusalem's fall to the Prophet's armies [in 638] proved the superiority of their faith to that of their Abrahamic predecessors. Inside the Dome of the Rock, the magnificent structure marking the place from which the prophet Muhammad was believed to have ascended to heaven, the beautiful calligraphy is directed specifically against the divinity of Jesus and Christian Trinitarian speculation.... Jewish sovereignty here is more than a stain on Arab honor; it is a challenge to Islamic belief itself.[47]

On their part, the Muslims, who control the Temple Mount through the *waqf* have carried out a number of building activities around and within the Temple Mount. The most extensive of these came in 1998 with the construction of a mosque in the name of Marwan, the father of the Umayyad Caliph who built the Dome of the Rock, 'Abd al-Malik, in the area of Solomon's Stables.[48] Solomon's Stables is an area of huge vaults some 600 square yards (500 square meters), underneath the surface of the Temple Mount in the southeastern corner. These vaults, "supported by eighty-eight pillars resting on massive Herodian blocks and divided into twelve rows of galleries" were originally storage areas of the Second Temple. They were taken over as stables by the Crusaders in the time of Baldwin II (King of Jerusalem 1118–1131 C.E.).[49] Saladin closed off this area following his conquest of Jerusalem in 1187, which included seven arches that provided access to the Solomon's Stables area in antiquity. Two of the arches were reopened by the Muslim authorities for access to the mosque, and the tunnel that leads northwards from the Triple Gate, along the southern wall, was also employed to provide access to the mosque.[50]

According to a report in the *New York Times*, although the *waqf* authorities control all activity on the Temple Mount, there is an implicit acceptance of Israeli authority and control. This same article asserts that, in the construction of the Marwan mosque, the construction crews were forced to stop construction after they had cleared two of the seven arches that give access into the mosque. The Israeli authorities had authorized that only two of the arches could be opened.[51]

Protestant evangelicals and other forms of conservative Christianity in the United States strongly support the State of Israel and are committed to all forms of archaeological excavation, biblical scholarship, and cooperation

273 Jerusalem: Mosque d'Omar interieur. Felix Bonfils, Photographer. *Palestine and Egypt, March 1894*. Plate 17. Albumen print, 22.5 × 28.5 cm. Photography Collection, Miriam and Ira D. Wallach Division of Art, Prints, and Photographs, The New York Public Library, Astor, Lenox and Tilden Foundations.

between and among Israeli scholars, archaeologists, politicians, and Jewish religious leaders, which confirm their literal interpretations of the Bible, Old and New Testaments. From the point of view of conservative American Christianity, the Zionist movement, and the subsequent founding of the State of Israel constitute direct and concrete fulfillments of biblical prophecy, namely that the Jews will be restored to their ancient God-given and God-promised homeland. According to this view, the fulfillment of this ancient promise is the single most important and auspicious sign of the Second Coming of Jesus and the onset of the Millennium.

Despite the narrow victory in the Yom Kippur War of 1973, the Israeli victories in the wars of 1948, 1967, and 1973 are viewed as little short of miraculous, "concrete demonstrations that the end times were near, the Second Coming of the Risen Christ was at hand, and the ultimate and final victory over the powers of evil was already beginning."[52] Then-President Jimmy Carter was quoted in 1976 as saying: "I think the establishment of

Israel...is a fulfillment of biblical prophecy. I think God wants the Jews to have a place to live."[53]

They [that is, American evangelists and their followers] and the members of their tours listened to Israeli archaeologists and Middle Eastern specialists and spoke with Israeli politicians and prime ministers. Each tour attempted to demonstrate Israel's role in the continuing unfolding of God's plan, the progress of salvation, in which they, or the members of and contributors to their ministries were playing a direct role.[54]

According to Griessman, all Protestant fundamentalist groups adhere to "four sets of beliefs [that] have important implications for Jews and Zionism: *literalism, particularism, millennialism, and evangelism.*"[55] Of these two, literalism and millennialism are most important in the understanding of conservative Christianity's views of Zionism and of the State of Israel. Literalism means that the Bible, in the King James translation, is the "divinely inspired and inerrant word of God" (Southern Baptist Convention). The second view, millennialism, refers to the Second Coming of Christ, central to which is the rebuilding of the Temple of Jerusalem, that is, the Third Temple. Before all these events can transpire, however, the Jews must be returned to their ancestral homeland, in fulfillment of prophecy. This has been a major theme of fundamentalist Christian commentators and believers since at least the nineteenth century. In 1918, a prominent pastor of the American Church in Jerusalem, the Reverend A. E. Thompson, said:

The capture of Jerusalem is one of those events to which students or prophecy have been looking forward for many years. Even before Great Britain took possession of Egypt, there were keen-sighted seers who foresaw the day when God would use the Anglo-Saxon peoples to restore Jerusalem...when the city was captured, we felt very confident we could put one hand upon this great event which had stirred the heart of the whole Christian world, and, laying open our Bible at many places in the prophets, say, as confidently as Peter on the day of Pentecost, 'This is that which was spoken by the prophets.'[56]

Similar pronouncements have been made at each stage of the Israeli-Arab conflicts of the past 50 years. Writing in 1956, Fuller Theological Seminary professor Wilbur M. Smith wrote: "The promise to Israel of Palestine as a permanent possession is at no time cancelled....The promises regarding Canaan were made to one nation, Israel, and to no other."[57] And following the Israeli conquest of Jerusalem in 1967, L. Nelson, Bell, executive editor of Christianity Today wrote: "[the conquest of Jerusalem to Jewish forces] gives a student of the Bible a thrill and a renewed faith in the accuracy and validity of the Bible."[58]

The authors of one of the perennial best-selling Christian fundamentalist books, *The Late, Great Planet Earth,* Hal Lindsey and C. C. Carlson, gave a timeline for the countdown to Armageddon: "1) The nation of Israel is established in Palestine (Fulfilled—May 14, 1948); 2) Jerusalem is repossessed (Fulfilled—June, 1967); 3) The Jewish Temple is rebuilt on Mount Moriah (Future); 4) Russia invades the Middle East (Future); 5) The Battle of Armageddon is fought (Future); 6) The Second Coming of Christ occurs (Future); 7) The 'spiritual' restoration of Israel begins' (Future)."[59] As to the central problem associated with rebuilding the Jewish Temple, the presence of the Dome of the Rock, Lindsey and Carlson dismissed it by saying:

> There is one major problem barring the construction of a Third Temple. The obstacle is the second holiest place of the Moslem faith, the Dome of the Rock. This is believed to be built squarely in the middle of the old temple site. Obstacle or no obstacle, it is certain that the Temple will be rebuilt; Prophecy demands it.[60]

There is always a historical connection to fundamentalist apocalypticism. During the height of the Cold War, that connection was Russia, that is the Soviet Union, which was always regarded as being the kingdom of "Gog and Magog," which would come out of the north countries to attack Israel in the last great cataclysmic war that would precede the Second Coming of Jesus and inaugurate the Millennium.[61] Ironically, with the fall of the Soviet Union and the receding of Russia somewhat from the international stage, Russia has also receded from its apocalyptic role as the evil kingdom that would oppose Israel before the coming of the Messiah. That role has now been taken over by Islam, which, before 1989 and the fall of the Soviet Union, and before the events of the 1990s, culminating in 9/11/2001, was always viewed as a kind of afterthought. As the quotation from *The Late Great Planet Earth* implies, an "obstacle" that would be easily removed by God's hand, working through the State of Israel, when the time came.

There is also great irony in the close relationship between American fundamentalist Christians and Israel, creating a situation of "strange bedfellows." The strangeness comes from the fact that fundamentalist Christians view all those who have not taken on the name of Christ as lost. These Christians have essentially a conversionist agenda toward Jews and toward all "non-saved" people (which can include other, non-saved, non-born-again Christians). [62] It is a situation of two groups, who have fundamentally opposing worldviews and goals, but who agree on one central goal that, for the time being, is sufficient to cause them to overlook all the other differences. Such a bond can also create certain cynicisms, and indeed there are ample examples of American Christians and Israelis cynically using each other. Israel is after all, a modern nation-state, founded on Zionist principles that were basically Socialist and secularist. The coming of ANY Messiah is hardly an article of faith of most Israelis, a matter to which most are willing to "leave in the hands of God," and indeed many Israelis view the idea of a Third Temple with alarm, sarcasm, and disdain. [63] However, the financial, spiritual, and most importantly, political support that American Christians provide the State of Israel is the key to the continued viability, dynamism, and indeed the survival, of the State of Israel. [64]

There is within Israel a Zionist, fundamentalist, nationalist "Third Temple" organization that has considerable influence on Israeli politics and on Temple Mount-related views and policies. That group is the "Temple Mount Faithful," founded in 1967 by Gershon Salomon, with its primary goal to assert full Jewish/Israeli control over the Temple Mount, and to build the Third Temple there, because, "whoever controls the Temple Mount has rights over the land of Israel." [65] Since the Knesset in 1967 had approved the Law for the Preservation of the Holy Places, which placed the Temple Mount under Muslim control, this defined the Temple Mount as "the last and only piece of real estate outside direct Israeli sovereignty." [66] The group has both messianic and non-messianic members and views, and has non-practicing and practicing Jews within its membership. [67] The Temple Mount Faithful has established close ties with American fundamentalist Christian organizations, all with a view to building the Third Temple, which for the Christians would signal the Second Coming of Jesus, while for the Temple Mount Faithful it would signal "the reinstitution of sacrificial worship." [68]

The Faithful of the Temple Mount attempted to enter the esplanade on October 8, 1990, at the Festival of Sukkot, setting off riots in which 17 Palestinians were killed and more than 100 wounded. Various reports indicated that the Palestinians were brought to the site specifically to ward off the Faithful of the Temple Mount (who numbered some 50 people), and that, in the ensuing chaos, the Palestinians began throwing rocks down from atop the Western Wall. The police responded with live ammunition. Salomon was quoted as saying: "We shall continue our struggle until the Israeli flag is flying from the Dome of the Rock." [69]

Yet another Messianic group that is centered on the Temple Mount is the Yeshivat Ataret-Cohanim, founded in the 1930s. Its founder was Chief Rabbi of Palestine, Avraham Yitzhak ha-Cohen Kook. One of the main activities of this group has been to study the laws relating to Temple sacrifice, in readiness for the building of the Third Temple. In addition, this group has purchased houses in the old Jewish Quarter, and in adjacent areas, as a prelude to preparing Jerusalem for the Messianic age to come. Both the Faithful of the Temple Mount and the Yeshivat Ataret-Cohanim received large grants from American evangelicals.[70] A board member of one of the American groups, the Jerusalem Temple Foundation, was quoted as saying that "we know there was gentile involvement in the financing and building of both the First and Second Temples. So why not the third?" This group gave financial support to Yeshivat Ataret-Cohanim on the grounds that "the rituals of the Temple were being studied in 'preparation for the construction of the Third Temple in Jerusalem.'"[71]

It would be too easy to say that all of these problems will be "solved by God," although that is exactly what many on all sides of this crisis think and say. We have the seemingly insuperable problem of the coalescence of what is arguably the most sacred site in the world with the clash of two of the most ancient and unyielding religions of the world, Judaism and Islam. With the third member of the "Judaeo-Christian-Islamic" tradition playing a major role in the controversy, it is difficult to see how this crisis can be solved peacefully. And yet, that is exactly what apocalypticism is all about—violence, *apocalyptic* violence. The Messianic age cannot be ushered in without cataclysmic violence, according to the apocalyptic writings of all three religions. It is certainly true that there are major factions in all three religions that are trying to "jump start" the Millennium, to perpetrate an act that will provoke the "Second Coming." We are led ineluctably to W. B. Yeats "*The Second Coming*"

> Turning and turning in the widening gyre
> The falcon cannot hear the falconer;
> Things fall apart; the centre cannot hold;
> Mere anarchy is loosed upon the world,
> The blood-dimmed tide is loosed, and everywhere
> The ceremony of innocence is drowned;
> The best lack all conviction, while the worst
> Are full of passionate intensity.
> Surely some revelation is at hand;
> Surely the Second Coming is at hand.

The Second Coming! Hardly are those words out
When a vast image out of *Spiritus Mundi*
Troubles my sight: somewhere in the sands of the desert
A shape with lion body and the head of a man,
A gaze blank and pitiless as the sun,
Is moving its slow thighs, while all about it
Reel shadows of the indignant desert birds.
The darkness drops again; but now I know
That twenty centuries of stony sleep
Were vexed to nightmare by a rocking cradle,
And what rough beast, its hour come round at last,
Slouches towards Bethlehem to be born?

CHAPTER 8

The Temple of the Future

The Influence of the Temple of Jerusalem on the
Apocalyptic Ideas of Judaism, Christianity, and Islam

The "future" from the point of view of the Judaeo-Christian-Islamic traditions can mean only one thing: the end of the world as we know it, the judgment and destruction of the wicked, the coming of the Messiah, and the inauguration of a perfect world. This future is known within theological writing by two Greek-based words, "apocalyptic," and "eschatology." Apocalyptic comes from Greek *apokalupto*, meaning to disclose, to reveal, to unmask, particularly to disclose "divine mysteries."[1] The title of the last book of the New Testament is the *Apocalypse* (The Revelation to John). The first word of the Book of Revelation is *apokalypsis*, "The Revelation of Jesus Christ, which God gave him to show to his servants what must soon take place" (*apokalypsis Iesou Christou* Revelation 1:1). The word also means "revelation," and it is this sense in which it is used in the Pauline books of the New Testament: "For I did not receive it [the gospel] from man, nor was I taught it, but it came through a revelation of Jesus Christ" (Galatians 1:12).[2] "This revelation, as expressed in Paul's gospel, is not only of the immediate powers of God, but also of his future purposes; it reveals his wrath to the wicked, to the righteous his justice and the things he has prepared for them; it is thus a revelation of the long-secret mystery of his will."[3]

The second word, "eschatology," comes from Greek *eschatos,* the basic meaning of which is the "farthest," "uttermost," "extreme." Of time, it means "the last," "the end," "the end of time." The neuter Greek word *eschaton,* "the last," "for the last time," comes into English as "Eschaton," "the end," and plays an enormous role in biblical theology as "Eschatology," "the science of the last things," namely, the end of the world, the destruction of the wicked, the judgment, the resurrection, and the ushering in of the Messianic Age.[4] Apocalyptic is a kind of scripture or pseudo-scripture that predicts and describes the events leading up to the end-time, thus it has a "historical" basis, whereas eschatology describes the specific, prescribed theological events of the final age.

Within the Judaeo-Christian-Islamic religious traditions, the apocalyptic, eschatological traditions are centered in and on the Temple Mount in Jerusalem. The catastrophic events of the Last Days, of the time preceding the end, the time before the ushering in of the Messianic Era will play themselves out in Jerusalem, in and on and around the Temple Mount. The Judaeo-Christian traditions both foresee a Third Temple, a Messianic temple, which is described primarily in the Books of Ezekiel in the Hebrew Bible and of the Revelation of John in the New Testament. In each of these cases, the Temple is the Heavenly Temple, not to be built by hands, but that already exists fully "built" in Heaven, and will come down to earth in the Messianic age.[5] The Islamic tradition cannot of course envision a "Third Temple," because to a large extent, particularly within the Palestinian community, an ancient, pre-Dome of the Rock temple on the Temple Mount is denied. Furthermore, the Dome of the Rock is the permanent shrine sitting atop the Temple Mount from the Islamic perspective. But the events of the End of Time within the Muslim tradition still focus on the Temple Mount.[6] The focal point of this chapter will be the "canonical" depictions of the End Time within the three traditions. I have discussed non-biblical, pseudepigraphal apocalypses in other chapters, placing them more within their ancient settings as we discussed the early Jewish and Christian responses to the destruction of the Second Temple.

The primary text of Jewish apocalyptic within the Hebrew Bible is the Book of Ezekiel, chapters 40–48, "The Law of the Temple."[7] We will add to this later Qumran Scrolls that comprise the text known as "The Songs of the Sabbath Sacrifice," and "A Vision of the New Jerusalem."[8] We have discussed the Temple Scroll, and the Pseudepigraphical Apocalyptic texts in Chapter 3, but will reprise these themes here following our discussion of Ezekiel 40–48.

Ezekiel 40–48, which are connected with the oracles that form Ezekiel 33–39, forms the greatest extended apocalyptic text within the Hebrew

Bible. As is the case with apocalyptic in general, the Messianic age is preceded by an era of cataclysmic violence, warfare, and bloodshed. This future period is outlined with great, terrifying, and bloody detail as part of the oracle that comprises chapters 38–39, that is, those chapters that immediately precede the climactic description of the temple of the Messianic age.[9] According to this oracle, the people of the Land of Israel will be invaded and threatened with annihilation by a force referred to as "Gog, of the land of Magog, the chief prince of Meshech and Tubal" (Ezekiel 38:2). These names have been variously interpreted, but all fit into the pattern of northerly peoples of the Iron Age II period (1000–586 B.C.E.), including ethnic groups centered in Anatolia. For example Meshech has been identified with Assyrian *Mushku*, Tubal with Assyrian *Tabal*, both located in the area of the Taurus Mountains of Asia Minor/Anatolia. The origins of the names Gog and Magog have been much debated, with no certain known ancient correspondences.[10] In any case, these and other named peoples are addressed directly by the prophet through the divine oracle:

> After many days you will be mustered; in the latter years you will go against the land that is restored from war, the land where many people were gathered from many nations upon the mountains of Israel, which had been a continual waste; its people were brought out from the nations and now dwell securely, all of them. You will advance, coming on like a storm, you will be like a cloud covering the land, you and all your hordes, and many peoples with you. (Ezekiel 38:8–9)

The invading armies will be met with the terrible wrath of God, and will be utterly annihilated, at the end of which there will be a sacrificial meal in which the flesh and blood of the defeated warriors will be consumed by the birds and beasts (Ezekiel 39:17–20). This sets the stage for the introduction of the Messianic temple of Ezekiel 40–48, a time when

> "I will set my glory among the nations; and all the nations shall see my judgment which I have executed, and my hand which I have laid on them" (Ezekiel 39:21). "The house of Israel shall know that I am the Lord their God, from that day forward "(Ezekiel 39:22). "I will restore the fortunes of Jacob, and have mercy upon the whole house of Israel" (39:25); "…when they dwell securely in their land with none to make them afraid, when I have brought them back from the peoples and gathered them from their enemies' lands…." (39:26–27); "…I sent them into exile among the nations, and then gathered them into their own land. I will leave none of them remaining among the nations any more." (39:28)

The text (Ezekiel 40–48) has been subjected to extensive form-critical and historical-critical examination, which is summarized in Tuell.[11] For our purposes, we will treat it as a unified whole, which indeed must have been its ancient origin and intent. We will be guided in part by the interpretation of the greatest authority on the Temple of Jerusalem, Busink.[12]

Before we enter the details of the text however, we must examine the circumstances surrounding the inception of Ezekiel's vision, which counts as perhaps the archetypal apocalyptic vision of the biblical tradition, one that had enormous and profound influence on all that followed it as the destiny and influence of the Temple unfolded.[13] Then, from this point of view, we must state that one of the most significant scholarly treatments of this vision is that of Susan Niditch, writing in 1986.[14] Niditch has located this vision within what I feel is its only proper setting, "a visionary context" which encompasses our understanding of Tibetan Buddhist-based cosmic mandala visions. In these visions, the world in which we live is expanded to its true cosmic setting, and, by extension, that category of visionary revelation that we understand by the term shamanism.

Ezekiel's vision occurs within a shamanistic setting. Eliade's definition of shamanism is that of "an archaic technique of ecstasy." "Techniques of ecstasy, mystical journey to the sky, descent to the underworld, conversations with God, semidivine beings, and the souls of the dead, and so on."[15] "Without ecstasy, there is no shamanism."[16]

...on that very day, the hand of the Lord was upon me, and brought me in the visions of God into the land of Israel, and set me down upon a very high mountain, on which was a structure like a city opposite me. When he brought me there, behold, there was a man, whose appearance was like bronze, with a line of flax and a measuring reed in his hand; and he was standing in the gateway. And he said to me, 'Son of man, look with your eyes, and hear with your ears, and set your mind upon all that I shall show you, for you were brought here in order that I might show it to you; declare all that you see to the house of Israel. (Ezekiel 40:1–4)

Eliade's definition of shamanism is that it is a "technique of ecstasy."[17] It often involves "magical flight." "Hence any ecstatic cannot be considered a shaman; the shaman specializes in a trance during which his soul is believed to leave his body and ascend to the sky or descend to the underworld."[18] Furthermore, "All over the world, indeed, shamans and sorcerers are credited with power to fly, to cover immense distances in a twinkling, and to become invisible."[19] The "shamanic vocation or initiation is directly connected with ascent to the sky."[20] Indeed, it is flight that constitutes the essence and definition of "ecstasy."[21]

We see techniques of ecstasy in the *Merkabah* (Chariot) and Ascent (*Hekhalot*) literature of the Old and New Testament Pseudepigrapha. The processes by which the seers attained an ecstatic state, prior to their ascent, included the endless repetition of certain words or formulae or sounds, and reciting hymns while their heads were placed between their knees, as was the case with the ecstatic Elijah, as recorded in the Hebrew Bible: "So Ahab went up to eat and to drink. And Elijah went up to the top of Carmel; and he bowed himself down upon the earth, and put his face between his knees" (I Kings 18:42).[22]

The fact that the Merkabah trances were confined to a small elite within society suggests that their modern analogue would be shamanistic trance. In shamanistic societies trance is confined to a few and it serves two purposes: First, it marks off the trance-subjects as special and distinctive within the group; and, second, it is an integral part of the role these people play toward society.[23]

We see in what direction Yoga and the other Indian techniques of meditation elaborated the ecstatic experiences and magical prowesses belonging to an immemorial spiritual heritage. However this may be, the secret of magical flight is also known to Indian alchemy. And the same miracle is so common among the Buddhist arhats that *arahant* yielded the Singhalese verb *rahatve*, "to disappear," "to pass instantaneously from one place to another." The *dakinis*, fairy sorceresses who play an important role in some tantric schools, are called in Mongolian "they who walk through the air," and in Tibetan "they who go to the sky." Magical flight and ascending to the sky by means of a ladder or rope are also frequent motifs in Tibet, where they are not necessarily borrowed from India, the more so since they are documented in the Bon-po traditions or in traditions deriving from them. In addition, as we shall soon see, the same motifs play a considerable role in Chinese magical beliefs and folklore, and they are also found almost everywhere in the archaic world.[24]

Ezekiel 40–48 is an oracle, not a mundane account of the measuring of the temple area in Jerusalem by a prophet who could carry out the measuring process because he had lived in Jerusalem and worked in the Temple as a priest (Ezekiel 1:3). At the same time, however, the measurements are rooted in the reality of the temple, just as "Students of modern spirit movements note that the phenomena seen in trance states are dependent upon the seer's real-life experience and the religious tradition with which he is familiar."[25] Thus it is that scholars use the information from Ezekiel's temple descriptions to understand the actual measurements and other architectural and ritual details of the Temple of Solomon, as we have done in this book.

The Temple described by the Prophet Ezekiel is virtually identical with the Solomonic Temple, with a few relatively minor changes. Ezekiel does not give the height of the walls, which are given in the I Kings account of the Temple of Solomon.[26] A major difference between the two temples is the absence of the Ark of the Covenant in Ezekiel's descriptions, because it disappeared in the Babylonian destructions of 587 B.C.E. In Ezekiel's plan, the *heikal* (the nave or sanctuary) and the Most Holy Place, the *debir* are made equally holy, whereas in the Temple of Solomon the *debir*, because it contained the Ark of the Covenant and the Cherubim, was the supremely holy place, without any peer.[27]

The feature of the mountain in the vision of Ezekiel (40:2), "...and set me down upon a very high mountain, on which was a structure like a city opposite me" brings us to the cosmic mountain-temple, which stands at the center of temple building all over the ancient world, and of the Messianic city-temple that we will meet again in the Revelation of John.[28] I have written about this at length for almost 25 years now. "The temple is the architectural embodiment of the cosmic mountain." "This perception is very common in the OT, as is well known and is seen in such passages as Isa. 2:2 and Ps. 48:2. These conceptions of Zion as a holy mountain go back ultimately to the inner-Israelite experience at what is probably *the* holy, cosmic mountain of religious literature, Sinai. The Temple of Solomon would seem ultimately to be little more than the architectural realization and the ritual enlargement of the Sinai experience."[29]

"*The architecture of the temple projects the building both as a mountain and as a structure based upon a heavenly model....* The mountain and the temple are inseparable. The sacredness of the one (the mountain) passes over onto and defines the sacredness of the other (the temple). All of those features which cause or create or determine the sacredness of the mountain are attached to the temple, and *determine its architecture, its symbolism, and its ritual.*"[30]

Having established this connection between the shamanistic journey of the prophet from Babylonian Exile to Jerusalem (April 28, 573 B.C.E.—the matter-of-fact mention of the date establishes the historical connectedness of Israelite apocalyptic prophecy), with the mountain-temple of the holy city, we now come to that final, essential element in apocalyptic: the means or medium through which the revelation of the heavenly plan is vouchsafed to the prophet: "When he brought me there, behold, there was a man, whose appearance was like bronze, with a line of flax and a measuring reed in his hand" (Ezekiel 40:3). The "pattern" or *tabnit* of the heavenly temple was revealed to Moses on Mount Sinai by God himself. The prophet cannot know what the architectural plan of the temple should be, whether this is the actual earthly Tabernacle in the Wilderness, the

Temple of Solomon, or the Messianic temple that will be built in the New Age, when the entire city of Jerusalem will become the celestial city.

There must be mediation between heaven and earth, and, in this case, the mediator is the heavenly being "whose appearance was like bronze." "The plan and measurements of the temple are revealed by God to the king [or prophet], and the plan must be carefully carried out."[31] The language of Ezekiel 40:4: "And the man said to me: 'Son of man, look with your eyes, and hear with your ears, and set your mind upon all that I will show you, for you were brought here in order that I might show it to you," is very close to that of Exodus 25:9: "According to all that I show you concerning the pattern (Hebrew *tabnit*) of the tabernacle, and of all its furniture, so shall you make it."[32]

Van Buren writes that "every new temple, as distinct from a mere shrine or chapel, was founded in accordance with precisely ordained rites," which in ancient Sumer were known as "the ordinances and ritual of Eridu."[33] When King Gudea of Lagash (2150–2125 b.c.e.) went into the temple in order to receive a dream regarding the temple he wanted to build for the god Ningirsu, "He was shown a lapis-lazuli tablet with the temple plan on it, and was given a sacred brick mould which contained the bricks to be used in the building."[34] Thus Ezekiel is engaged in a process that, has been interpreted by some commentators as a mundane architectural measuring process, from a much later date than implied here.[35] We shall see, however, that in the context of an oracle revealed to him by a heavenly messenger, and on a project that (described by me in an earlier publication as "sacred surveying"[36]) has cosmic significance for the House of Israel.

The Temple Vision of Ezekiel forms the following parts: (1) the opening, describing the origin and nature of the ecstatic vision, (Ezekiel 40:1–4); (2) the description of the measuring process, and adumbration of the architectural plan of the Temple, in which the prophet is guided by the angelic being (Ezekiel 40:5–42:20); (3) The Glory of the Lord enters the Temple through the East gate and fills the Temple (Ezekiel 43:1–4)[37]; (4) the command to Ezekiel to proclaim the vision of the Temple to the people of Israel, to make everything known to them, which constitutes the Law of the Temple (Ezekiel 43:12) to the people of Israel; (5) the description of the altar of burnt offering and its ordinances (Ezekiel 43:13–27)[38]; (6) the closing of the Eastern gate forever, now that the Lord has entered it; the Law and ordinances of the Temple and of the Temple priesthood; the clothing, grooming, and marriage practices of the priesthood. The restriction of the priesthood to the "Sons of Zadok," as is the case in the Qumran community[39] (Ezekiel 44:1–31); (7) the distribution of land for the Holy Precinct and the priesthood and for the larger city, comprising an area of 8.3 square miles (Ezekiel 45:1–8); (8) the law of cereal and burnt offerings (Ezekiel 45:10–25); (9) the law of the Prince, the *nasi*,[40] the Messianic figure who will finance, direct, and inspire the sacrificial program of the Messianic era Temple. "David my servant shall be their prince for ever" (Ezekiel 37:25, 37:15–28); (10) The sanctifying waters of life that flow out from underneath the threshold of the Temple that give life (trees of life) and fertility to the entire Land of Israel (Ezekiel 37)[41]; (11) The allotment of the land to the Tribes of Israel, the circumference of the city—18,000 cubits, and the new name of the Messianic city of Jerusalem: "The Lord is There" (*Yahweh-shammah*) (Ezekiel 48 and 48:35).[42]

The most eloquent summation that we have of the Ezekielian and the Qumran views of the temple of the future is that of Corbin.[43] "The *Book of Ezekiel* appears indeed to be that which, more than any other offers us the perfect *Imago Templi*. This is further confirmed by the fact that it was the book on which the Essene Community of Qumran modeled its own conception of the Temple....For Ezekiel, as for the Community of Qumran, the vision of the Temple unfolds into a drama whose starting-point is the ruin the Temple and the reasons for it, and whose culmination is a vision of the New Temple, the building of which is the prelude to the apotheosis of a cosmic restoration."[44] "In the course of these long visionary chapters Ezekiel's *Imago Templi* is defined: the image of a supernatural Temple beyond our time and our space. It is not to be confused, therefore, with the second Temple, built by Zerubbabel in 151 B.C."[45]

"In short, Ezekiel's vision of the new Temple sets before us the Temple's celestial archetype, or, in other words, the celestial Temple as the archetype—a concept which reappears frequently in later apocalyptic literature. In its nature the new Temple—the city-Temple—is supra-terrestrial, and it is envisioned "as the frame of a city" (Ezekiel 40:2)."[46]

There are among the Qumran texts a group of fragments which, taken together, are called "A Vision of the New Jerusalem" by Wise, Abegg, Jr., and Cook,[47] and "The New Jerusalem" by Vermes.[48] These texts, written mostly in Aramaic, and dating to the turn of the era,[49] "are all inspired by Ezekiel xl–xlviii."[50] They give "a detailed description of a Jerusalem-to-be given by an angel to an unknown recipient quite in the manner of Ezekiel's vision, but differing in many details. No description of the temple itself survives in the fragments, but the temple is mentioned several times."[51] "The reactualization of Ezekiel's theology of the Temple is itself a remarkable instance of the spiritual hermeneutics practiced at Qumran."[52]

These texts describe a vast city—Jerusalem itself as a vast temple city, as we will see in Revelation 21. The angelic messenger is measuring with a reed, exactly as in Ezekiel's vision.

Yigael Yadin disagrees with the views quoted above from Henry Corbin, according to which Corbin sees both the Ezekiel and the Qumran Temple Scroll temples as eschatological temples. Yadin holds that the Temple described in the Temple Scroll (11QT) was intended by the Essenes not as a future temple, but as one to be built now, by them, and is distinct from the eschatological Temple:

> In fact, the author of the scroll is quite explicit that he is discussing the Temple to be built one day by the Children of Israel, and not the eschatological Temple. This statement pertaining to the commands for the construction of the Temple proper and preparation of its furnishings is presented after the festival offerings are enumerated: 'And I will consecrate my [t]emple by my glory, (the temple) on which I will settle/my glory, until the day of blessing on which I will create my temple/and establish it for myself for all times, according to the covenant which I have made with Jacob at Bethel' (Col. XXIX:8–10).[53]

In other words, there are two Temples mentioned in this passage, the one described in the Temple Scroll, which should be built by the Essenes, just as God commanded Moses to build the Tabernacle, which he then subsequently built, and the eschatological Temple to follow, "until the day of blessing on which I will create my temple." "Our author [i.e., the author of the Temple Scroll—11QT] believed in the heavenly Temple, as well as the future Temple that God would eventually bring into being. In the scroll, however, he is concerned with God's law on the Temple, which refers to the earthly Temple of the present, the only one of the three that was to be man-made."[54]

The Qumran/Dead Sea Scroll texts mentioned above however, "The New Jerusalem"/"A Vision of the New Jerusalem," are distinct from the Temple Scroll itself, are much more in the spirit and content of the vision of Ezekiel, and must therefore be accounted to the Qumran communities' visions of the Messianic-era, eschatological Temple, the same as that of Ezekiel.

There is one more final issue to discuss here, and that is the relationship between the Temple of Solomon, The Temple of Ezekiel, and the Temple of the Qumran Temple Scroll (11QT). Based on Yadin's studies and summary, there are many similarities between the Temples of Ezekiel and that of the Temple Scroll, along with stark differences. Yadin believed that the author of the Temple Scroll was quite familiar with Ezekiel's vision, and even used some of his terminology. There are differences with regard to the number of courts between the two, with the placement of altar and

Temple within the courts, the numbers of gates in the courts, and other distinctions. Ezekiel's visionary plan does not have installations such as the House of the Laver and the House of the Utensils, which are present in the Temple Scroll. Yadin has no answer as to why there should be differing plans of, as it were, one and the same Temple, the Temple of Jerusalem, irrespective of which era of the world's history to which it should belong. Yadin writes, "that the explanation may lie in the different purposes of the two Temples. The one in the scroll purports to be the Temple which the Children of Israel are commanded to build. The one in the vision of Ezekiel is the Temple of the future which the Lord himself will create. The two, therefore, need not be identical."[55]

Temple-Related Apocalyptic Ideas in Christianity

"The last chapters (40–48) of the *Book of Ezekiel* clearly demonstrate the ideal of the city-temple, anticipating the heavenly Jerusalem of the Johannine Apocalypse. The city-temple assumes the dimension of a cosmic restoration."[56] The Revelation to John (The Apocalypse) reflects the same apocalyptic typology as the Temple Vision of Ezekiel:

> I John, your brother, who share with you in Jesus the tribulation and the kingdom and the patient endurance, was on the island called Patmos on account of the word of God and the testimony of Jesus. I was in the Spirit on the Lord's day, and I heard behind me a loud voice like a trumpet saying, 'Write what you see in a book and send it to the seven churches, to Ephesus and to Smyrna and to Pergamum and to Thyatira and to Sardis and to Philadelphia and to Laodicea.' Then I turned to see the voice that was speaking to me, and on turning I saw seven golden lampstands, and in the midst of the lampstands one like a son of man, clothed with a long robe and with a golden girdle round his breast; his head and his hair were white as white wool, white as snow; his eyes were like a flame of fire, his feet were like burnished bronze, refined as in a furnace, and his voice was like the sound of many waters; in his right hand he held seven stars, from his mouth issued a sharp two-edged sword, and his face was like the sun shining in full strength (Revelation 1:9–16).

This incandescent vision of the risen Jesus Christ to John inaugurated the series of oracles that John was shown, including the scroll sealed with seven seals (Revelation 5:1), which the Lamb was worthy to unseal, one by one, thus revealing the destiny and judgment of the world. With the opening of each seal, some form of chaos, bloodshed, or, alternatively, salvation, was revealed. John was then given the scroll and told to eat it, which he did. The scroll was sweet in his mouth, but bitter in his stomach, a sign that he should continue to prophesy the judgments which would come upon the earth (Revelation 10:8–11).

At this point, John "was given a measuring rod like a staff," and was told "rise and measure the temple of God and the altar and those who worship there, but do not measure the court outside the temple; leave that out, for it is given over to the nations, and they will trample over the holy city for forty-two months." (Revelation 11:1–2). This chapter ends with the *leitmotif* that will be expanded and realized in the final visions of the book: "Then God's temple in heaven was opened, and the ark of his covenant was seen within his temple; and there were flashes of lightning, voices, peals of thunder, an earthquake, and heavy hail" (Revelation 11:19). Thus within Revelation the Heavenly Temple is at the center of the oracles, much as is the case in the Apocalypses. There is no other place in the canons of either the Hebrew Bible or the New Testament where we get such a vivid description of the Heavenly Temple.[57]

As in Ezekiel, the establishment of the heavenly, Messianic temple on earth is preceded by chaos, turmoil, and vast slaughters, which are detailed in chapters 12 through 20. Chapter 20 ends with the judgment of the dead before the "great white throne and him who sat upon it" (Revelation 20:11). And "Then I saw a new heaven and a new earth; for the first heaven and the first earth had passed away, and the sea was no more. And I saw the holy city of Jerusalem, coming down out of heaven from God" (Revelation 21:1–2). The REAL temple and the REAL city exist in full form in heaven. Just as the temple is "a copy of a celestial work of architecture,"[58] so also "The Heavenly Jerusalem was created by God at the same time as Paradise, hence *in aeternum.* The city of Jerusalem was only an approximate reproduction of the transcendent model; it could be polluted by man, but the model was incorruptible, for it was not involved in time."[59] "Sennacherib built Nineveh according to the 'plan established from most distant times in the configuration of the Heavens.'"[60] Thus both cities and temples exist in heaven in full architectural form, and are revealed to the king or the prophet on earth in a vision. During this vision, the king or prophet is shown the heavenly "pattern," which forms the blueprint for what is built on earth, always after the heavenly model for[61] "the earthly sanctuary is situated at the *nadir* of the celestial Temple, which is at its *zenith*."[62] The language of Revelation is largely the language of the Temple in heaven.[63]

At this point in the narrative, John reprises the shamanistic experience of Ezekiel, and is led away in spirit into a "great high mountain" by one of the angels, and shown "the holy city of Jerusalem coming down out of heaven from God" (Revelation 21:9–10). The jewel-like radiance of the city is evident, and its walls and gates are described (Revelation 21:11–14). Then, "he who talked to me had a measuring rod of gold to measure the city and its gates and its walls" (Revelation 21:15). This is the city that has descended from the heavens. Finally, the *denouement:* "And I saw no temple in the city, for its temple is the Lord God the Almighty and the Lamb. And the city has no need of sun or moon to shine upon it, for the glory of God it its light, and its lamp is the Lamb" (Revelation 21:22–23).

> Now, in contradistinction to the historical plus millennial periods of the earth, when the temple existed as a copy on earth of the heavenly temple, a 'piece of heaven on earth,' there will no longer be any temple. The need for it will have disappeared with the presence on the renewed earth of the Father himself. Heaven, the Real, will have been brought down to earth in the form of the New Jerusalem, and the entire city is now suffused with the saving, paradisiacal symbols that in the period of earthly history were limited to the rather smallish temple itself.[64]

As was the case in Ezekiel's description of the Messianic temple:

> Then he showed me the river of water of life, bright as crystal, flowing from the throne of God and of the Lamb through the middle of the street of the city; also, on either side of the river, the tree of life with its twelve kinds of fruit, yielding its fruit each month; and the leaves of the tree were for the healing of the nations (Revelation 22:1–2).[65]

Muslim Apocalyptic

The Qur'an itself contains many apocalyptic Suras and passages, and can indeed be viewed as a whole as an apocalyptic scripture because it constantly admonishes the faithful, and refers to the various signs of the end of the world, and to death, the judgment, and the resurrection.[66] For example Sura 81, called "Shrouded in Darkness," begins "When the sun is shrouded in darkness, when the stars are dimmed, when the mountains are set in motion…when hell is made to blaze and paradise is brought near" (Qur'an 81:1–3, 12–13). Sura 82, "Torn Apart," begins "When the sky is torn apart, when the stars are scattered, when the seas burst forth, when graves are turned inside out, each soul will know what it has done and what it has left undone…the good will live in bliss, and the wicked will burn in Fire. They will enter it on the Day of Judgment and they will find no escape. What will explain to you what the Day of Judgment is?" (Qur'an 82:1–5, 13–18). Other strongly apocalyptic Suras are 56 ("That Which is Coming"), 75 ("The Resurrection"), 80 ("He Frowned"), 83 ("Those Who Give Short Measure"), 84 ("Ripped Apart"), 89 ("Daybreak"): 21–30, 99 ("The Earthquake"), and 101 ("The Crashing Blow").[67] The time of the End of the World was not named in the Qur'an, as is the case in the Judeo-Christian scriptures: "They ask you [Prophet] about the Hour, saying 'When will it arrive?' but how can you tell [them]? Its time is known only to your Lord; you are only sent to warn those who fear it" (Qur'an 79:42–45). At the same time, there is no extended apocalyptic narrative Sura or section in the Qur'an that would be comparable to the passages in Ezekiel and Revelation that we have discussed, or that compare to other apocalyptic sections of the Hebrew Bible such as Zechariah 12–14, or the Book of Daniel, or to the extended apocalyptic passages in the New Testament.[68] Cook defines the Qur'an "as an eschatological book and not an apocalyptic book."[69] That means that the Prophet Muhammad was more concerned with the Day, the End, and the events associated with that Day, the Hour, such as the catastrophic natural calamities, the judgment, and the resurrection, which relates to eschatology (the science of the end time), than with the lengthy historical or pseudo-historical sequence of events that will precede the end itself.[70] "This would indicate…that Muhammed believed in the immediacy of the end to such an extent that the whole issue of apocalyptic 'future history' was a moot one for him."[71]

The largest body of extended or narrative Islamic apocalyptic material after the Qur'an itself, comes from the *hadith* (traditions). The *hadith* (plural *ahadith*) are compilations of sayings that are attributed to the Prophet, and are accompanied by an *isnad*, or chain, that is, the chain of transmission of authorities that takes the saying back to the Prophet Muhammad. Within Sunni Islam, the two primary and most authoritative collections of *hadith* are that of al-Bukhari, compiled in 857 c.e., and that of Muslim, compiled in 862/63 c.e.[72] The Prophet Muhammad died in 632 c.e. Within this context, the definition of Cook of Islamic apocalyptic is: "Muslim apocalyptic is a genre of literature presented in the form of a *hadith* purporting to convey information about the period of time leading up to the end of the world, or to give the impression that the historical events occurring in the contemporary present are an integral part of this finale."[73]

During approximately the first two centuries of Islam, there was a great amount of borrowing and interchange of biblical and (mostly Christian) apocalyptic material that went into Islamic sources and appear in varying forms in *hadith*. However, there was also a borrowing of Islamic material by Jewish and Christian writers.[74] The Book of Daniel, for example, was

228 • The Temple of Jerusalem

widely known, read, and quoted among Muslim apocalyptic thinkers and writers, and existed in many different forms, excerpts, and traditions, and, for example, was "in the hands of both the Byzantines and Muslims, who used them to ascertain the future and to plan out battles."[75] The Book of Revelation is quoted extensively in early Muslim apocalyptic literature, particularly the images of the cruelty, barbarism, general insecurity, and the catastrophic conditions that will accompany the end of the world.[76]

There is a lengthy, connected section on the events leading up to the end of the world in the *Sahih* (the collection of *hadith*) of Muslim, and we are going to rely on that group of traditions to outline what we can reliably say is a mainstream account of Sunni Muslim apocalyptic traditions.[77] The title of this "book" within the collection of Muslim is *Kitab al-Fitan wa Ashrat as-Sa'ah*, *The Book Pertaining to the Turmoil and Portents of the Last Hour*.[78] The word *Fitan* of the title comes from Arabic *fitna*, which means "a burning with fire, a melting of (metals) in order to separate or distinguish the bad from the good, a means whereby the condition of *aman* is evinced in respect of good or evil, punishment, chastisement, conflict among people, faction, and sedition, discord, dissension, difference of opinions, a misleading, causing to err, seduction, temptation."[79] In other words, a *Kitab al-Fitan* is a "Book of Tribulations," a book outlining the events leading up to the Last Hour, the events through which the righteous will be refined and separated out from the evil, "before the Last Day."[80]

One of the central features of The Book Pertaining to the Turmoil and Portents of the Last Hour is the tradition of the ten Signs of the Hour. These are outlined in Hadith 6931. The signs are (1) smoke (Qur'an 44:10: "[Prophet], watch out for the Day when the sky brings forth clouds of smoke for all to see."); (2) *Dajjal* (the Antichrist, about which more later); (3) the beast (Qur'an 27:82: "When the verdict is given against them, We shall bring a creature out of the earth, which will tell them that people had no faith in Our revelations."); (4) the rising of the sun from the west; (5) the descent of Jesus, son of Mary; (6) the Gog and Magog; (7, 8, 9) land slides in three places, one in the east, one in the west, and one in Arabia; and (10) fire burning forth from the Yemen.[81]

The Book Pertaining to the Turmoil and Portents of the Last Hour places great emphasis on the turmoil and chaos of that time, and of the overwhelming amount of bloodshed. Before the Last Hour can come, massacres will take place in which Muslims will be pitted against Muslims (Hadith 6902). "The Last Hour will not come unless there is much bloodshed. They said: 'What is *harj*? Thereupon he said: 'Bloodshed, bloodshed.'" (Hadith 6903). The Muslim community will be vast upon the earth, and will be protected from external enemies and natural calamities, but not from enemies from within (Hadith 6904). The *jizya* tax (levied upon non-Muslims in the Islamic Caliphate) will not be remitted, because everyone will have to become Muslim (Hadith 6923).

The "Romans" (that is, Christians) will also become dominant, and there will be terrible battles and bloodshed pitting the "Romans" against the Muslims. The Muslims will be massacred by the Romans, but in the end will be saved by Allah (Hadith 6927). Many Muslims will revert to polytheism and the Ka'ba will be destroyed by Christians or by polytheists (Hadith 6944, 6951, 6953, 7023). The Jews will attack the Muslims, and the Muslims will hunt down and kill the Jews, to the point at which every stone and every tree will speak out and reveal that a Jew is hiding behind it (Hadith 6979–6985).

At this point the *Dajjal*, the Antichrist, will appear. The *Dajjal* cannot be killed by ordinary means (Hadith 6990, 6991). The *Dajjal* is a Jew (Hadith 6995), a young man, childless (Ibid); his right eye is blind while his left eye is like a floating grape, and he has the word *kafir* (infidel, unbeliever) written on his forehead ("which every Muslim would be able to read"—Hadith 7009), is a liar, and has thick, twisted hair (Hadith 7005–7015). He will remain on the earth for 40 days or months or years ("For forty days, one day like a year and one day like a month and one day like a week and the rest of the days would be like your days"—Hadith 7015). The *Dajjal* will walk upon the earth like a cloud driven by the wind (Hadith 7015), inviting people to accept wrong religion. He would bring great treasure to those who accepted him, while those who reject him would dwindle.

At this point, Allah will send Jesus, the son of Mary to kill the *Dajjal* near modern-day Tel Aviv (Ancient Lydda, Arabic Ludd, Hebrew Lod—Hadith 7015, 7023). Jesus will "descend at the white minaret in the eastern side of Damascus wearing two garments lightly dyed with saffron and placing his hands on the wings of two Angels" (Hadith 7015). There will then be peace among people for seven years, after which "Allah would send a cold wind from the side of Syria that none would survive upon the earth having a speck of good in him or faith in him but he would die" (Hadith 7023). Only the wicked, the immoral, and the beastly will survive. Then the two trumpets will sound, signifying the Day of Resurrection, at which time people will be judged, with 999 out of 1,000 going to hell (Qur'an 39:67–75—Hadith 7023). Hadith 7055 indicates that there will be an interval of 40 (months?, years?) between the blowing of the first and second trumpets.

A central feature of Muslim apocalyptic as with Jewish, is the role of Gog and Magog. We are introduced to Gog (a "chief prince of Meschech and Tubal"—Ezekiel 38:2–3) and Magog (a place name—Ezekiel 38:2) in the Ezekielian apocalypse. Gog and Magog appear in the Qur'an in two places: Sura 18—The Cave—"the apocalypse of Islam,"[82] and in Sura 21:96. In Sura 18, Gog and Magog (Arabic *Yajuj* and *Majuj*) are introduced as part of an Alexander the Great legend. Alexander, called *Dhu 'l-Qarnayn* ("the two-horned one"), was given power by God to build an iron barrier in the gap between two mountains in order to keep Gog and Magog imprisoned behind the barrier, so that they could not escape and wreak havoc on the earth. Gog and Magog are forced to stay behind this barrier until the Last Day, when "On that Day, We shall let them surge against each other like waves and then the Trumpet will be blown and We shall gather them all together. We shall show Hell to the disbelievers." (Qur'an 18:83–102).[83]

The Hadith of the *Kitab al-Fitan wa Ashrat as-Sahih* of Muslim states that the barrier will be opened, "because of the turmoil which is near at hand as the barrier of Gog and Magog has been opened" (Hadith 6883). Gog and Magog would swarm over the lands, reaching as far as Lake Tiberias, where they would besiege Jesus and his companions. Jesus and his companions will supplicate Allah, who will send insects to attack Gog and Magog, whose slaughter would be so great as to cause unbearable stench. Jesus, the Apostle of Allah, would then again beseech Allah, who would send down birds who would remove the corpses of Gog and Magog, after which the earth would be cleansed with rain, restored to great fertility, and be shining like a mirror (Hadith 7015).

Jerusalem, "is seen in Muslim apocalyptic circles as the messianic capital."[84] We have seen how in the Hadith Jesus will kill the Antichrist, the *Dajjal,* near modern-day Tel Aviv. Gog and Magog will reach within a few miles of Jerusalem before they are destroyed. The Qur'an situates the call of the second trumpet, announcing the Resurrection, from "a nearby place" (Qur'an 50:41). Muslim tradition further interprets "a nearby place" as "the rock of Jerusalem (*sakhr bayt al-maqdis*), on the grounds that Jerusalem is "the place on earth nearest to heaven."[85]

The modern-day tradition of Muslim apocalyptic writing places virtually all its emphasis on Jerusalem and its holy places as the central places in the drama of the End Time. It is for this reason that there is great Muslim despair over the extent to which the holy places are controlled by Israel. "Thus the end of the world literally cannot take place until Israel is removed and a Muslim state is put in its place."[86] We have already seen that this kind of thinking is also characteristic of conservative Jewish views of the Temple Mount. "For this reason there is a striking emotional similarity between Jewish and Muslim messianic expectations. Both Jews and Muslims feel that they are incredibly and frustratingly close to the realization of their goals. For many religious Jews, it is incomprehensible that the

Third Temple cannot be built upon the Temple Mount, the area of the Dome of the Rock, because control over it was won during the 1967 war. Israel reigns over the Temple Mount but does not rule over it....In a way, the very tenuousness of each side's control of this sensitive site contributes significantly to apocalyptic expectation."[87]

At the same time, contemporary Muslim apocalyptic writing pays very close attention to the apocalyptic writings of the Hebrew Bible and to the New Testament, particularly to the Books of Ezekiel and Daniel, and to the Revelation of John. These writings are read very closely and intertwined with traditional Muslim apocalyptic, such as was outlined above. The various symbols of these writings, so well known to conservative Jewish and Christian commentators, are placed completely within the events of contemporary history and interpreted from a Muslim perspective. Thus the "saints, the people of the Most High" of Daniel 7:27, are the Muslims.[88] The Jews of Israel are Gog and Magog.[89] The Antichrist is associated with Israel, the United States, Great Britain, the West, or with world Zionism.[90] The people of Messianic-era Jerusalem of whom the Revelation writes that: "There will be no more night. They will not need the light of a lamp or the light of the sun, for the Lord God will give them light. And they will reign forever and ever" (Revelation 22:5). They "will be Muslims and they will reign forever, since the Antichrist and his followers and all the liars will be killed. The meaning of this is that the victorious side at the end of time will be the camp of Islam and Islam alone."[91] "Fundamentally, 'Abdallah reads the Bible as a Palestinian document instead of as a Jewish one."[92]

One could say that Jerusalem and its Temple stand at the center of history, past, present, and future. If one counters that the drama of the Jerusalem story is little known in the vast hinterlands of Asia, and that the events that have roiled the Middle East and the West for approximately the last 3,000 years create barely a ripple in further Asia, we could say that the power of the apocalyptic visions that surround Jerusalem and its Temple is such that it can engulf the rest of a world that is otherwise dismayed at the intimate entanglement of a religious apocalyptic vision with the brutal realities of contemporary politics. Every religion has an apocalyptic tradition, an end-of-the-world scenario, but no other tradition or traditions experience the intertwining of this tradition with a contemporary political situation. In other religious traditions, the apocalypse, the eschaton, have lost much of their meaning, and have been pushed into the background by the inexorable march forward of secularization. How can such ideas continue to hold on to the imaginations and passions of a twenty-first-century world? But so it is, nevertheless. We cannot come out from under the spell of "Next Year in Jerusalem."

Notes

Chapter 1

1. Lundquist, 1982; see the summary in Dever, 2005, pp. 277–279.
2. Kapelrud, 1963.
3. Atkinson, 2000, p. 901; Ben-Dov, 2002, pp. 52–53.
4. Haran, 1985, pp. 198–201; Chyutin, 2006, pp. 39, 42.
5. Haran, 1985, pp. 15–16.
6. See Eliade, 1987, p. 26.
7. Zevit, 2002, pp. 76–77.
8. Strachan, 2003, pp. 9–10.
9. ANET, 1969, p. 265.
10. Amiet, 1980, pp. 527–528.
11. Eliade, 1987, p. 26.
12. ANET 1969, pp. 328–329.
13. Haran, 1985, p. 198.
14. Stricker, 1955.
15. Keel, 1997, p. 116; Milgrom, 1970, pp. 44–46.
16. Keel, 1997, pp. 115–116.
17. Lundquist, 1983, pp. 205–212.
18. Clifford, 1984, pp. 112, 114, 107–124.

19. Ben-Dov, 2002, pp. 32–35, 40–43, 47–48, 50–51.

20. Bell, 1997, p. 133—regarding Egyptian temples. Also Lundquist, 1983.

21. Kapelrud, 1963; Lundquist 1982, pp. 288–290.

22. Freedman, 1981, p. 26; see also Chyutin, 2006, pp. 35–36 on "The Meeting Tent Tabernacle As a Model of the Cosmos"; Elior, 2005, pp. 64–71; Cross, 1984, pp. 93–94; Clifford, 1984, p. 119: "Dualism, or correspondence between heavenly and earthly or between primal event and present celebration was pervasive in Canaanite and biblical civilizations and must be taken seriously. The Temple on Mount Zion is the copy of the real palace in the heavenly world"; see also Macrae, 1984, pp. 177–181, for views of the heavenly temple in the Gnostic Nag Hammadi literature; see also Hurowitz, 1992, pp. 168–170.

23. Patai, 1967, pp. 130–131.

24. Patai, p. 131.

25. Lundquist, 1993, p. 13; Chyutin, 2006. pp. 193–196; Proverbs 8:22–31; see also Hurowitz, 1992, pp. 326–327.

26. Lundquist, 1990; Michell, 2000.

27. Kapelrud 1963, pp. 59–60; Chyutin, 2006, pp. 39–40.

28. For an explanation of the passages referenced in this paragraph, see Cross, 1984, pp. 97–102: "The [Ugaritic] 'temple of Ba'l' and the 'tent of El' thus symbolize alternate political ideologies. In the rise of kingship in Israel there were those who wished Israel's old constitution to limit kingship and its cultic trappings, but others were ready to embrace Canaanite ideology of the divine king and his dynastic shrine" (p. 98).

29. Clements, 1965, passim.

30. ANET, 1969, p. 268.

31. Zevit, 2002, pp. 78–79.

32. Von Simson, 1989, p. 97.

33. ANET, 1969, p. 268; Hurowitz, 1992, pp. 171–223.

34. Holladay, 1971, p. 156.

35. ANET, 1969, p. 283.

36. Boyd, 2000, p. 1100.

37. Byrne, 2000, p. 990.

38. Boyd, 2000, pp. 463–464; http://www.fas.harvard.edu/semitic/HOAI/adultmain.cgi?article=weaving.htm.

39. Haran, 1985, p.160.

40. Fritz, 1987, p. 39.

41. 1 Kings 6:14–22; Cogan, 2001, p. 243–244; Dever, 2005, pp. 96–98.

42. Waterman, 1943, pp. 285, 292.

43. Cogan, 2001, pp. 316–318; but see Millard, 1989, pp. 20–29, 31, 34, and Kitchen, 1989, p. 30.

44. Bell, 1997, p. 284.

45. Keil and Delitzsch, 1989, Vol. 3, p. 117.

46. Haig, 1899, pp. 551–552.

47. Chan, 1994, pp. 105, 114.

48. Zevit, 2001, pp. 169–170; Irwin, 2000, p. 299; Chyutin, 2006, pp. 198–199.

49. Lundquist, 1993, p. 7.

50. Corbin, 1986, pp. 218–223.

51. Wright, 1985, Vol. 1, p. 256.

52. Lundquist, 1993.

53. Charlesworth, 1983, Volume 1.

54. Exodus 34:23; Wright, 1985, Vol. 1, p. 254.

55. Skarsaune, 2002, pp. 88–91.

56. Cogan, 2001, pp. 234, 238, commentary to I Kings 6:4; see also Chyutin, 2006, pp. 135–136.

57. Cogan, 2001, p. 238.

58. Waterman, 1943; for the Annex structure as well as Solomon's palace, the House of the Forest of Lebanon (1 Kings 7:2–5), and the Hall of Pillars (1 Kings 7:6) as well as the treasure-house nature of these structures, see Chyutin, 2006, pp. 62–65, 104–112.

59. Cogan, 2001, pp. 238–239; Lundquist, 1982, p. 276.

60. 2 Kings 18:15–16—Haran, 1985, pp. 284–286.

61. Lundquist, 1982, pp. 294–295; Carol L. Meyers understands the *ulam* within the context of Near Eastern courtyards: "Thus pillars [i.e. Jachin and Boaz] at its entry stand within the realm of gate posts, marking the entryway to the larger domain of the deity, which includes court as well as house proper." Meyers, 1984, pp. 139–140. "The courtyard of the temple was thus the focus of 'public' involvement with the temple, the place of sacrifice, of justice, of song and dance, of procession." Ibid., p. 141; see also Chyutin, 2006, pp. 72–76.

62. Ouellette, 1976, p. 10.

63. Keel, 1997, pp. 164–165; Ouellette, 1976, p. 8 and Figure 4.

64. Lundquist, 1982, pp. 293–295; Carol L. Meyers, 1984, pp. 145–147.

65. Lundquist, 1982, pp. 293–295; Keel, 1997, p. 164.

66. Gardiner, 1957, p. 489; Arnold 2003, p. 183; Chyutin, 2006, p. 202.

67. Ben-Dov, 2002, pp. 194–198.

68. Rosen-Ayalon, 1975, p. 95 (Plan of Islamic-era Temple Mount); Prawer, 1975, p. 105 (Plan of Crusader-era Temple Mount); Avigad, 1975, p. 17; Kaufman, 1981; against Kaufman see Ritmeyer, 1992, p. 64, note 28.

69. Ritmeyer, 1992, 1996.

70. Ritmeyer, 1992, pp. 30–31, 44; Grabar, 2006, p. 38, has argued that the great size of the rubble over the rock massif in the time of the construction of the Dome of the Rock in the late seventh century c.e. may provide partial proof that this was indeed the site of the earlier Temples.

71. Michell, 2000, pp. 14–22, with plans, and bibliography of Kaufman's work, p. 70.

72. Patai, 1967, pp. 54–104; Keel, 1997, pp. 136–140.

73. Keel, 1997, pp. 130–135; "... the Temple precincts were divided into a succession of progressively more sacred zones culminating in the innermost sanctuary, the *devir*, or Holy of Holies, where the Divine Presence (or *shechinah*, to use the

later rabbinic terminology) resided." Branham, 1992, pp. 377–378. Mishnah *Kelim* 1:8,9 gives "…a detailed account of areas that increased in sanctity from greater Israel to the Holy of Holies in the Temple." Branham, 1992, p. 378, note 8.

74. Psalms 118:19–20; Keel, 1997, pp. 134–135.

75. Lundquist, 1993, p. 7; Smith, 1978, pp. 112–115.

76. Bell, 1997, p. 133.

77. New Oxford Annotated Bible, Notes to 2 Chronicles 3:1–17; Newsom, 1985, p. 54.

78. Waterman, 1943, p. 291; Chyutin interprets the sacred space at the west end of the Temple as divided into two discreet spaces: the debir or Oracle, the upper section, open to the *heikal,* through which the Cherubim "peered," as it were, and the lower section, the *qodesh ha qodashim,* or Holy of Holies, where the Ark stood, with the poles visible, and leaning upon the parapet of the wall dividing the sacred space from the *heikal,* Chyutin, 2006, pp. 66–71; Elior, 2005, p. 66: "In biblical tradition, the cherubim marked the place of Deity's self-revelation in the desert sanctuary, they adorned the laver stands in the Temple court and stood in the Holy of Holies. They are mentioned again in the ornamentation of the cloth strips for the desert sanctuary, the engravings on the Temple walls, and the decorations of the curtain in the Temple, in other traditions, they were part of the winged divine retinue and served as guardians of the Garden of Eden." And see Elior, 2005, pp. 66–81; Lewis, 2005, pp. 103–105 (referring to the article by H. Niehr, "In Search of YHWH's Cult Statue in the First Temple," In *The Image and the Book: Iconic Cults, Aniconism, and the Rise of Book Religion in Israel and the Ancient Near East,* edited by Karel van der Toorn, Leuven: Uitgeverij Peeters, 1997. Niehr contends "that Yahweh had a cult statue [in the Holy of Holies] and that his adherents regularly viewed Yahweh's image in cult processions similar to those in Mesopotamia and Egypt," Lewis, 2005, pp. 95–97, 105.

79. CAD, Volume 8, K, p. 216.

80. Illustrations of examples from ancient Near Eastern sculptures in Keel, 1997, pp. 169–173. See also ANEP, 1969, pp. 212–217, and Ben-Dov, 2002, p. 53.

81. I Kings 7:12; Keel, 1997, pp. 128–130; for a more extensive discussion of the courts see Chyutin, 2006, pp. 83–98, 102–104.

82. Davies, 1943, pp. 53–54, and Rosellini, 1832–1844, Vol. 2, Plate 50.

83. Otto, p. 56.

84. Davies, p. 53.

85. Birch, 1880–1902; L. W. King, 1915.

86. Ezekiel 47:1–2; Lundquist, 1983, pp. 208–209.

87. Lundquist, 1997, p. 327; Hurowitz, 1992, pp. 131–167, 224–259.

88. Yadin, 1983, Vol. 2, p. 6.

89. Hayward, 1996, p. 50; "The old tabernacle was received, as it were, into the temple, thereby accommodating the scruples aroused by the relocation from tabernacle to temple (cf. 2 Sam 7:1–7). The development was thus similar to that in Egypt, where the old chapels were taken over in the great temple complexes," Keel, 1997, pp. 162–163; "Almost in every aspect we may discuss, the MTTT (= Meeting

Tent Tabernacle Temple) is a miniature portable version of Solomon's Temple,"
Chyutin, 2006, p. 79, and pp. 77–79; Cross, 1984, p. 93; "In fact, Israel's temple
incorporated compromises between the older traditions of the league tent-shrine
and the dynastic temple of Canaanite kingship. The portable Ark with its cherubim became the 'center piece,' usurping the place of the divine image of Canaanite
temples. According to one tradition [1 Kings 8:4 = 2 Chronicles 5:5] the Tent of
Meeting was taken up and placed in the Temple," Cross, 1984, p. 98; Hurowitz,
1992, pp. 264–266.

90. Clements, 1965, p. 111.
91. Clements, 1965, pp. 111–122.
92. Haran, 1985, pp. 5–6.
93. Haran, 1985, pp. 189–204; Cross, 1984.
94. Haran, 1985.
95. Busink, 1970, Vol. 1, pp. 198, 283–284.
96. Ritmeyer, 1996, p. 72.
97. Busink, 1970, Vol. 1, p. 198; according to Chyutin, 2006, pp. 69–70, the
poles could not be removed so that "the priests, who are forbidden to enter the Holy
of Holies but are allowed to enter the Holy [the *heikal*], are aware of the presence of the Ark because its staves, which may not be removed from its rings, are
visible in 'the face of the Oracle' under the Cherubim's wings, which are visible
too," p. 70.
98. Haran, 1985, p. 61.
99. Haran, 1985, pp. 58–61.
100. Haran, 1985, pp. 238–239.
101. Haran, 1985.
102. I Samuel 14:41–42; Dozeman, 2000, p. 1349.
103. Haran, 1985, pp. 173–174.
104. Haran 1985, pp. 59–60.
105. Referred to by Menahem Haran as "The Material Gradation," 1985, p. 158.
106. Haran, 1985, pp. 163–164.
107. Haran, 1985, p. 26.
108. Haran, 1985, p. 291.
109. Lundquist, 1982, pp. 296–297; Hurowitz, 1992, pp. 260–277.
110. 1 Kings 8:62–66; but see the comments of Cogan, 2001, p. 289.
111. Cogan, 2001, p. 388.
112. 1 Kings 15:18—Cogan, 2001, pp. 397–400.
113. Cogan and Tadmor, 1988, p. 140.
114. Cogan and Tadmor, 1988, p. 158.
115. Cogan and Tadmor, 1988, p. 190.
116. Cogan and Tadmor, 1988, p. 189.
117. 2 Kings 16:17–18; Cogan and Tadmor, 1988, pp. 186–194.
118. Lenchak, 2000, pp. 586–587.
119. ANET, 1969, p. 288.
120. ANET, 1969, p. 288.

121. Cogan and Tadmor, 1988, p. 236.
122. Cogan and Tadmor, 1988, p. 268, quoting the literature.
123. Haran, 1985, pp. 280–284.
124. Stevenson, 2001, pp. 175–176.
125. Cogan and Tadmor, 1988, pp. 293–296.
126. Cogan and Tadmor, 1988, pp. 293–296.
127. 2 Kings 23:1–3; Lundquist, 1982, p. 295.
128. Lundquist, 1982, pp. 293–297.

Chapter 2

1. Cogan, 2001, p. 263.
2. *New York Times*, December 28, 2004, p. B2; *New York Times*, December 30, 2004, p. A3.
3. Wright, 1985, Vol. 1, pp. 215–216, 225; Zevit, 2001, pp. 81–84; Lewis, 2005, pp. 69–79.
4. Reymond, 1969; David, 1981, pp. 1–7.
5. Freedman and Lundquist, 1979; Orthmann, 1997, Vol. 1, p. 492.
6. Lundquist, 1982.
7. ANET, 1969, pp. 483–490.
8. Wright, 1985, Vol. 1, pp. 225–237; Keel, 1997, pp. 151–154.
9. Lundquist, 1982, pp. 294–295.
10. Wood, 1985, pp. 192–193.
11. Keel, 1997, p. 161.
12. Keel, 1997, p. 161.
13. Keel, 1997, pp. 151–159.
14. Wright , 1985, Vol. II, Illustrations 123–182.
15. ANET, 1969, pp. 262–263; ANEP, 1969, p. 4.
16. Seger, 1997, Vol. 5, pp. 19–23; Tappy, 2000, p. 1202. The figurine is illustrated in Toombs, 1992, Vol. 5, pp. 1182–1183; Dever, 2005, pp. 167–170, has an excellent summary of the history of the interpretation of this temple.
17. Ezekiel 40:5, with notes in *The New Oxford Annotated Bible With Apocrypha* and Wright, 1978, Vol. 4, p. 1089.
18. Toombs, 1992, Vol. 5, p. 1181.
19. Wright, 1978, Vol. 4, pp. 1085, 1089; Toombs, 1992, Vol. 5, p. 1182.
20. Yadin, 1977, Vol. 3, pp. 838 [the temple plans], 845–849.
21. Yadin, 1976, Vol. 2, p. 474.
22. Illustration in Yadin, 1976, Vol. 2, p. 479.
23. Yadin, 1976, Vol. 2, pp. 480–481; Ben-Tor, 1997, Vol. 3, pp. 3–4.
24. Yadin, 1976, Vol. 2, p. 481.
25. Illustrated in Yadin, 1976, Vol. 2, p. 479; for all of the above relating to Hazor, Yadin, 1976, Vol. 2, pp. 474–495.
26. Wright, 1985, Vol. 1, p. 235.

27. Approximately ninth to seventh centuries B.C.E.—Zevit, 2001, p. 163.

28. Aharoni, 1975, Vol. 1, p. 86.

29. Exodus 20:25; 27:1; Aharoni, 1975, Vol. 1, pp. 84–86; Herzog, 1997, Vol. 1, pp. 174–175; Zevit 2001, pp. 159–161.

30. Wright, 1985, Vol. 1, p. 237, Vol. 2, Fig. 164.

31. For recent discussion see Zevit, 2001, pp. 156–171; see also Dever, 2005, pp. 170–175 for a summary of views and interpretations of this temple; Milgrom, 1970, pp. 43–44 (note 166).

32. 2 Kings 18:22; Herzog, 1997, Vol. 1, p. 175; Aharoni attributes this phase to King Josiah—Aharoni, 1975, Vol. 1, p. 86.

33. Cogan, 2001, p. 263.

34. Keel, 1997, p. 164; ANEP, 1969, pp. 195, 320.

35. Reeves, 1995, p. 197.

36. Reeves, 1995, p. 197.

37. Song of Solomon 8:2; Keel, 1997, p. 164.

38. de Vries, 1984, p. 371.

39. Lundquist, 1988, p. 300; Chyutin, 2006, pp. 72–76.

40. Keel, 1997, p. 164.

41. Lundquist, 1983, pp. 208–209.

42. Orthmann, 1997, Vol. 1, pp. 491–492.

43. Amiet, 1980, p. 484.

44. Matthiae, 1997, Vol. 2, p. 182.

45. Photograph of the table of offerings in Wood, 1985, p. 192; reconstruction of the temples in Wood, Ibid., and Margueron, 1997, Vol. 5, p. 168; Margueron and Sigrist, 1997, Vol. 2, pp. 236–239.

46. Amiet, 1980, p. 493.

47. For a discussion of Solomon's palace and the House of the Forest of Lebanon in the light of ancient Near Eastern building patterns and with relevant parallels, see Matthiae, 1997; and see Chyutin, 2006, pp. 104–112.

48. Keel, 1997, p. 161.

49. Abou 'Assaf, 1997, Vol. 1, p. 34.

50. 'Ain Dara' plan in Abou 'Assaf, 1990, p. 21.

51. Abu 'Assaf, 1997, Vol. 1, p. 35.

52. I Kings 6:5–6; Cogan, 2001, pp. 238–239, 252.

53. Abu 'Assaf, 1997, Vol. 1, p. 35; Abu 'Assaf, 1990, Tafel 16–18.

54. I Kings 6:6; Abou 'Assaf, 1990, p. 18.

55. Abou 'Assaf, 1990, p. 18.

56. Abou 'Assaf, 1990, p. 18.

57. Borchardt, 1938.

58. Abou 'Assaf, 1990, p. 17.

59. Abu 'Assaf, 1990, Tafel 10,c.

60. Bloch-Smith, 2002, p. 90; Lewis, 2005, p. 105; "While the man was standing beside me, I heard one speaking to me out of the temple; and he said

to me, 'Son of Man, this is the place of the soles of my feet, where I will dwell in the midst of the people of Israel forever'" (Ezekiel 43:6–7).

61. Abu 'Assaf, 1990, Tafel 43–46.

62. Bloch-Smith, 2002, p. 90.

63. Zevit, 2001, pp. 316–317; see Dever, 2005, p. 97: "Of particular significance is the well-preserved Aramaic temple of 'Ain Der'a in northwestern Syria, which exhibits more than 50 almost exact parallels with the Jerusalem Temple described in Kings."

64. Loud, 1939, pp. 1–13, Plate 4; Lewis, 2005, pp. 95–97.

65. Zevit, 2001, pp. 123–138.

66. Keel, 1997, pp. 162–171.

67. Keel, 1997, pp. 160, 162.

68. See Uphill, 1984, for an Egyptologist who accepts this connection.

69. Bietak, 1996, p. 36.

70. Bietak, 1986, pp. 247–248.

71. Bietak, 1996, p. 36.

72. Bietak, 1986, pp. 250–251.

73. Petrie, 1901, Part 2, p. 21 and Plate X,2; see also Keel, 1997, p. 160.

74. Petrie, 1901, Part 2, p. 21.

75. ANEP, 1969, pp. 171, 308.

76. Carol L. Meyers, 1984, pp. 142–143.

77. Gardiner, 1957, p. 494; for a reconstruction of the archaic shrine at Hierankonpolis, see Wilkinson, 2000, p. 17.

78. David, 1981, p. 4.

79. Kemp, 1989, pp. 92–93, 100, 101.

80. Kemp, 1989, p. 88.

81. Keel, 1997, pp. 167–168.

82. Morgenstern, 1942–1943.

83. Haran, 1985, pp. 194–204.

84. Haran, 1985, pp. 189–204.

85. Morgenstern, 1942–1943, pp. 153–265.

86. Catalog no. 261; Carter, 1933, Vol. 3, pp. 31–46, Plates II, VI; Reeves, 1995, pp. 133–134; ANEP, 1969, pp. 185, 316.

87. Reeves, 1995, p. 133.

88. Carter, 1933, Vol. 3, p. 42.

89. Carter, 1933, Vol. 3, p. 42.

90. Fox, 1951, Plate 39.

91. See, for example, from the Tomb of Neferhotep in Thebes, illustrated in Keel, 1997, p. 124.

92. Kitchen, 1975, Vol. 1, pp. 619–626.

93. Calverley and Broome, 1933, Vol. 1, Plate 7.

94. Calverley and Broome, 1935, Vol. 2, Plate 11.

95. Busink, 1970, Vol. 1, p. 283–284, based on 1 Kings 8:7.

96. Busink, 1970, Vol. 1, p. 198; and see now Chyutin, 2006, pp. 69–70.
97. Keel, pp. 269–280.
98. David, 1981, p. 63; redrawn in Keel, 1997, pp. 167–168.
99. Cogan, 2001, p. 246.

Chapter 3

1. ANET, 1969, p. 316.
2. Myers, 1965, pp. 5–6.
3. ANET, 1969, p. 316.
4. Myers, 1965, p. 70.
5. Meyers, 1965, pp. 15–16.
6. Meyers, 1965, p. 26.
7. Meyers, 1965, p. 28.
8. Meyers, 1992, p. 363.
9. ANET, 1969, p. 316.
10. Lundquist, 1983, pp. 205–219.
11. Lundquist, 1983, p. 212.
12. Lundquist, 1983, pp. 201–219; Myers, 1992, p. 363.
13. Lundquist, 1982, pp. 271–297; Chyutin calls the Temple of Solomon a "King's Temple," and the Second Temple a "Priests' Temple," Chyutin, 2006, pp. 55, 103, 143.
14. Meyers, 1992, p. 364.
15. Meyers, 1992, p. 364.
16. McCarthy, 1983, p. 89.
17. McCarthy, 1983, p. 90; Cohen, 1982, p 55: "In the Maccabean period the temple's illegitimacy was revealed to all. It was profaned by a gentile monarch and by the wicked priests. True, it was regained by the Jews, but without a prophet to guide them and without miracles to authenticate their actions, who could be sure that the temple was really purified?"; Elior, 2005, pp. 214–215.
18. Elior, 2005, pp. 8–10, 194–196.
19. Hayward, 1996, p. 18.
20. Hayward, 1996, pp. 20, 22.
21. Hayward, 1996, p. 20.
22. Hayward, 1996, p. 22.
23. Hayward, 1996, p. 20.
24. Hayward, 1996, p. 23.
25. Hayward, 1996, pp. 26–27.
26. Shutt, 1985, pp. 7–34.
27. Andrew, 1913, Volume 2, pp. 83–89, 104.
28. Shutt, 1985, Vol. 2, p. 18.
29. Shutt, 1985, Vol. 2, p. 18.
30. Shutt, 1985, Vol. 2, p. 18.

31. Hayward, 1996, pp. 30–31; Chyutin, 2006, p. 147, strongly favors the view that there were major changes and improvements to the Temple during the Hasmonean period.

32. Hayward, 1996, p. 28; see Mazar, Cornfeld, and Freedman, 1975, pp. 176–178, 210–212, for descriptions and discussions of the water supply, Hezekiah's Tunnel, the Gihon Spring, the Siloam Pool, and the systems of cisterns. See also Gibson and Jacobson, 1996.

33. Lundquist, 1983, p. 208.

34. Hayward, 1996, p. 32.

35. Hayward, 1996, p. 29.

36. Hayward, 1996, p. 30.

37. Andrew, 1913, Volume 2, p. 104.

38. Hayward, p. 28.

39. Hayward, p. 29.

40. Knohl, 1996, p. 21.

41. Hayward, pp. 32–34.

42. Ben-Dov, 2002, pp. 91–95; Tsafrir, 1975, pp. 85–86.

43. Andrew, 1913, Volume 2, pp. 104–105.

44. Hayward, 1996, pp. 38–72.

45. Hayward, 1996, p. 38.

46. Hayward, 1996, p. 42.

47. Barker, 1999, pp. 101–104.

48. Yadin, 1985.

49. Milgrom, 1984, p. 132.

50. Yadin, 1985, pp. 112–115; Elior, 2005, pp. 215–216.

51. Vermes, 2004, p. 192; Schiffman, 1994, p. 111; Chyutin, 2006, p. 125: "The description of the Temple in the Temple Scroll constitutes an integral part of the religious codex of the Qumran sect, and the commandment to build the Temple parallels the commandment to build the Tabernacle. The style of the description of the Temple and its dimensions is accompanied by expressions such as 'and you will build', 'and you will make', or 'make' and 'clad' in the imperative— divine commandments which generally open a description of the new building element…only the descriptions of Noah's Ark and the MTT [= Meeting Tent Tabernacle] are presented as being structures that were built according to a divine commandment."

52. Wise, Abegg Jr., and Cook, 2005, p. 594.

53. Wise, Abegg Jr., and Cook, 2005, p. 594.

54. Milgrom, 1984, p. 131.

55. Yadin, 1983, Vol. 2, p. 135.

56. Cogan, 2001, p. 240.

57. Yadin, 1983, Vol. 2, pp. 137–139.

58. Yadin, 1983, Vol. 2, p. 149.

59. Yadin, 1983, Vol. 2, p. 141.

60. Yadin, 1983, Vol. 2, pp. 142–143.

61. Yadin, 1983, Vol. 2, pp. 144–147; Yadin, 1985, pp. 136–139.

62. Yadin, 1985, pp. 137–138.

63. Yadin, 1983, Vol. 1, pp. 237–238.

64. Yadin, 1983, Vol. 2, pp. 150–151; Yadin, 1985, pp. 140–145; Yadin, 1983, Vol. 1, pp. 235–239; for proposed reconstructions of the temple of the *Temple Scroll* see Yadin, 1985, between pp. 140–145.

65. Milgrom 1984, pp. 125–133.

66. Charlesworth, 1983, Vol. 1, pp. ix–xiii.

67. Lundquist, 2000; Barker, "Beyond the Veil of the Temple. The High Priestly Origin of the Apocalypses."

68. Lundquist, 1993.

69. Gartner, 1965; Reynolds, 1998.

70. Isaac, 1983, Vol. 1.

71. Lundquist, 1982, p. 274; Elior, 2005, pp. 247–249; Bloch-Smith, 2002, pp. 85–87.

72. Lundquist, 1984, p. 66.

73. Wintermute, 1985, p. 73.

74. Lundquist, 1983, p. 216.

75. Wintermute, 1985, Vol. 2.

76. Corbin, 1986, p. 296; Elior, 2005, pp. 6–7, 59, 206–207, 216, 218–220.

77. Anderson, 1983, Vol. 1, p. 114.

78. Lundquist, 1983, p. 208.

79. Anderson, 1983, Vol. 1, p. 136.

80. Anderson, 1983, Vol. 1, p. 138.

81. Siliotti, 2004, pp. 52–57.

82. Alexander, 1983, Vol. 1.

83. Alexander, 1983, Vol. 1, p. 256.

84. Alexander, 1983, Vol. 1, p. 296.

85. Alexander, 1983, Vol. 1, p. 296.

86. Alexander, 1983, Vol. 1, p. 296.

87. Wintermute, 1985, Vol. 2, p. 113; Hayward, 1996, p. 87.

88. Hayward, 1996, p. 88.

89. Hayward, 1996, p. 90.

90. Hayward, 1996, p. 90.

91. Hayward, 1996, p. 102.

92. Weiss, Abegg Jr., and Cook, 2005, pp. 462–475.

93. Vermes, 2004, pp. 329–339.

94. Newsom, 1985; De Conick, 1999, pp. 316–317.

95. Vermes, 2004, p. 329; Wise, Abegg Jr., and Cook, 2005, pp. 463–464.

96. De Conick, 1999, p. 316.

97. Vermes, 2004, p. 329.

98. Newsom, 1985, p. 59.

99. Wise, Abegg Jr., and Cook, 2005, pp. 470–471.

100. Wise, Abegg Jr., and Cook, 2005, p. 471.

101. Wise, Abegg Jr., and Cook, 2005, p. 472.

102. Wise, Abegg Jr. and Cook, 2005, p. 473.

103. Wise, Abegg Jr., and Cook, 2005, p. 475.

104. Corbin, 1986, p. 323.

105. Newsom, 1985, p. 52; "Merkabah terminology is found in a hymn-fragment in the Dead Sea Scrolls, where the angels praise 'the Image of the Throne of the Chariot' (Strugnell). Members of the sect combined ideas concerning the song of the angels, who stand before the Chariot, with other ideas about the names and duties of the angels, and all this is common to the sect of Qumran and to later traditions of the *ma'aseh merkabah*" [the Throne on its Chariot, as described in Ezekiel 1]: see Scholem, 1974, pp. 13, 10–14; Elior, 2005, pp. 72–73, 79–81, 218.

106. Lundquist, 1983, p. 216; Lundquist, 2000, pp. 28–30.

107. Marcus and Wikgren, Translators, *Jewish Antiquities*, Books XV–XVII, pp. 206–207; all translations from the Mishnah are from Danby, 1933, unless otherwise noted.

108. Richardson, 2000, pp. 579–584; Mandell, 2000, pp. 555–556.

109. Meyers, 1992, p. 365.

110. Marcus and Wikgren, Translators, *Jewish Antiquities*, pp. 206–207.

111. Meyers, 1992, pp. 364–365.

112. Ritmeyer, 1992, p. 33.

113. Quoted in Marcus and Wikgren, Translators, *Jewish Antiquities*, Books XV–XVII, p. 193; Chyutin, 2006, p. 86: South wall = 280 meters; East = 485 meters; North = 315 meters; West = 485 meters.

114. Schwartz, 2002, p. 85.

115. Ben-Dov, 2002, p. 103.

116. Meyers, 1992, p. 365.

117. Meyers, 1992, p. 365.

118. Gibson and Jacobson, 1996, p. vii.

119. Meyers, 1992, p. 365.

120. Tsafrir, 1975, p. 85; Ritmeyer, 1992, pp. 38–39; Silberman, 1989, p. 60.

121. Ritmeyer, 1992, pp. 37–43.

122. Photographs of these columns, now supporting a cupola of the vestibule/entrance of the western Huldah gate, underneath the Al-Aqsa Mosque, and in the vestibule of the Golden Gate in the eastern wall, can be seen in Mazar, Cornfeld, and Freedman, 1975, pp. 141, 150.

123. For a reconstruction of the Royal Portico, see Ben-Dov, 2002, p. 108; and see Mazar, 1975, pp. 26–27.

124. *Jewish Antiquities* XV, 411–417; *Jewish War* V, 190–192.

125. Mazar, Cornfeld, and Freedman, 1975, p. 126; Ben-Dov, 2002, pp. 126–129, 132.

126. Skarsaune, 2002, p. 83.

127. Schwartz writes that "there were 35 courses of ashlars at the southeast corner, giving it a spectacular height of 138 feet above bedrock" Schwartz, 2002, p. 91.

128. Ben-Dov, 2002, p. 134—with the illustration of a partially preserved Hebrew inscription attesting to this practice found as the foot of this corner of the wall; see also Mazar, Cornfeld, and Freedman, 1975, p. 13; Ritmeyer and Ritmeyer, 1989, p. 34, for a photograph of the inscription plus a suggested restoration showing it in its original place at the southwestern corner.

129. Mazar, 1975, p. 30.

130. Mazar, Cornfeld, and Freedman, 1975, p. 146.

131. Ritmeyer and Ritmeyer, 1989, p. 39.

132. Reconstructed in Ben-Dov, 2002, p. 107; for a photograph of this passageway from 1902, see Gibson and Jacobson, 1996, p. 255, and for a drawing from 1864, p. 245.

133. Some authorities view the triple gate as having been reserved for priests—Ritmeyer, 1993, p. 67.

134. Ritmeyer and Ritmeyer, 1989, pp. 38–39, with photographs and drawings.

135. Mazar, Cornfeld, and Freedman, 1975, pp. 124, 140–146; Mazar, 1975, pp. 28–29, 31; Ben-Dov, 2002, p. 107; Gibson and Jacobson, 1996, p. 256; Ritmeyer and Ritmeyer, 1989, pp. 38–39.

136. *Jewish Antiquities* XV, 410; for reconstruction and photograph see Ben-Dov, 2002, pp. 104–105; Mazar, Cornfeld, Freedman, 1975, pp. 132, 134; Mazar, 1976, pp. 26–27.

137. Mazar, Cornfeld, and Freedman, 1975, pp. 133–134.

138. Ben-Dov, 2002, p. 107, for elevation showing levels at the time of Herod, during the Umayyad period, and today.

139. Mazar, Cornfeld and Freedman, 1975, p. 134.

140. Mazar, Cornfeld and Freedman, 1975, p. 134.

141. For a reconstruction of the street, see Ben-Dov, 2002, p. 110; for a diagram of the gates along the western wall see Mazar, Cornfeld and Freedman, 1975, p. 129.

142. Mazar, Cornfeld and Freedman, 1975, pp. 148–152.

143. Asher's theory, with plans, and bibliography, described in Michell, 2000, pp. 14–21, 70; Grabar, 2006, p. 32, writes that "there can be no doubt that the rather striking remains of an originally Herodian gate existed in this location in the seventh century."

144. Busink, Vol. 2, pp. 1250–1251, with Abb. 253—p. 1179.

145. Mazar, Cornfeld, and Freedman, 1975, between pp. 96–97, p. 130; Ben-Dov, 2002, pp. 353–356.

146. Mazar, Cornfeld, and Freedman, 1975, p. 118.

147. Marcus and Wikgren, Translators, *Jewish Antiquities*, XV, pp. 202–203; this inscription, and another partial one, are illustrated in Mazar, Cornfeld, and Freedman, 1975, p. 114; Branham, 1992, pp. 377–378.

148. Edersheim, 1994, p. 27.

149. Lundquist, 1993, pp. 20–21, with illustration.

150. Ritmeyer, 1993, pp. 62, 64–65; for the strikingly Egyptian-like reproduction of the Qumran Temple of the Temple Scroll, see Yadin, 1985, between pp. 140–145.

151. Wilkinson, 2000, pp. 204–207.
152. Edersheim, 1994, p. 24: "...the principal entrance to the Temple"; for the court gates in general, see Chyutin, 2006, pp. 159–160.
153. Busink, Vol. 2, p. 1251.
154. Ritmeyer, 1993, p. 62.
155. John 8:1–4; Mazar, Cornfeld, and Freedman, 1975, p. 118.
156. Luke 21:1–3; Mazar, Cornfeld, and Freedman, 1975, pp. 117–118.
157. Mazar, Cornfeld, and Freedman, 1975, p. 116.
158. Mazar, Cornfeld, and Freedman, 1975, p. 117; *Middoth 5*, 4.
159. Edersheim, 1994, pp. 113–114, 120–130.
160. Hayward, 1996, p. 28.
161. 1975, p. 129.
162. 1996.
163. Mazar, Cornfeld, and Freedman, 1975, p. 114.
164. Mazar, Cornfeld, and Freedman, 1975, p. 115.
165. Filson, 1944, p. 82; Chyutin, 2006, pp. 203–204.
166. Parry, 1994, p. 423; Edersheim, 1994, p. 34; Yadin, 1983, Vol. 2, pp. 27–28.
167. Yadin, 1983, Vol. 2, pp, 27–28.
168. Mazar, Cornfeld, and Freedman, 1975, p. 115.
169. *Middoth* 3, 1; *Jewish War* V, 225; Edersheim, 1994, pp. 30–31.
170. Edersehim, 1994, p. 32.
171. Yadin, 1983, Vol. 2, pp. 143–147.
172. Yadin, 1983, Vol. 2, p. 147.
173. Ritmeyer, 1993, p. 67.
174. Yadin, 1983, Vol. 2, pp. 133–135.
175. Yadin, 1983, Vol. 2, p. 135.
176. Branham, 1992, pp. 380–382.
177. M. Avi-Yonah, 1968, p. 327, quoting Alice Muehsam.
178. Avi-Yonah, pp. 327–328.
179. Avi-Yonah, pp. 327–335, with Plates I-IV; Chyutin, 2006, pp. 126, 134, 162–167 (with Figure 5.6).
180. Branham, 1992, pp. 377–379 (photo on p. 378); Mazar, Cornfeld, and Freedman, 1975, pp. 20–21 (photo on p. 21), 235–236; Ben-Dov, 2002, pp. 143–146 (drawing on p. 143).
181. Stevenson, 2001, p. 173; Chyutin, 2006, p. 158.
182. Fine and Meyers, 1997, Vol. 5, p. 121 (Figure 4); Hachlili, 1976, p. 49 (Figure 9).
183. 1975, pp. 106–111.
184. *De Vita Mosis* II, 117–121, in Hayward, 1996, pp. 113–114.
185. Hayward, 1996, pp. 114–118.
186. Hayward, 1996, p. 113.
187. *De Vita Mosis* II, 122–123, in Hayward, 1996, p. 114.
188. Hayward, 1996, p. 140.

189. Lundquist, 1983, p. 211; Lundquist, 1993, pp. 11–12; Lundquist, 2000, pp. 29–30; Hammerton-Kelly, 1970, pp. 1–15.

190. *Quis Heres* 196–197 in Hayward, 1996, pp. 120–121.

191. Schwartz, 2002, p. 124.

192. Schwartz, 2002, p. 124.

193. Mazar, Cornfeld, and Freedman, 1975, pp. 88–93; Ben-Dov, 2002, pp. 132–135; Brandon, 1957, pp. 154–166.

194. Ben-Dov, 2002, pp. 132–139.

195. Mazar, Cornfeld, and Freedman, 1975, p. 92; Scholem, 1974, p. 246.

196. Mazar, Cornfeld, and Freedman, 1975, p. 137; see also Ben-Dov, 2002, p. 139.

197. Smith, 1978, p. 118.

198. Mishnah *Aboth*, from Danby, 1933, quoted in Smith, 1978, p. 118.

199. Smith, 1978, p. 118; Patai, 1967, pp. 118–125.

Chapter 4

1. *Jewish Antiquities* XVIII, 14–15, in Feldman, 1965, p. 13.

2. *Jewish Antiquities* XVIII, 16–17, in Feldman, 1965, pp. 13–15; see also *Jewish War* II, 165, in Thackeray, 1997, p. 387.

3. *Jewish Antiquities* XIII, 297, in Marcus, VII, p. 377; all translations from the Mishnah are from Herbert Danby, *The Mishnah,* unless otherwise noted; Danby, *The Mishnah,* pp. XVIII–XIX.

4. Ibid., p. XIII.

5. Cohen, 1982, p. 51, and pp. 49–50, 52–53, 59.

6. Danby, 1933, p. XIV.

7. Ben-Dov, 2002, pp. 132–134.

8. *Avot of Rabbi Nathan* 4, from Judah Goldin, 1967, pp. 35–36, quoted in Skarsaune, 2002, p. 104.

9. Danby, 1933, *The Mishnah,* Tractate *Aboth* 1, pp. 446–447, xvii.

10. Skarsaune, 2002, p. 119.

11. Danby, *The Mishnah,* pp. xx–xi.

12. Ibid., pp. xiii, xxviii.

13. Ibid., pp. xxi–xxii.

14. Ibid., p. xvi.

15. Ibid., p. xvi.

16. Quoted in Neusner, 1979, p. 118; see S.G.F. Brandon, *The Fall of Jerusalem and the Christian Church,* p. 167; there are three Pseudepigraphic Apocalypses, those of 4 Ezra, 2 Baruch, and the Apocalypse of Abraham, that are widely thought to have been written in the interval following the destruction of the Temple in 70 C.E. and the Bar Kochba revolt in 135 C.E., and to actually reflect the primary theological responses of the Jews of Palestine to the destruction and the tumult that followed, as well as the apocalyptic oracles that were inspired by

that event. See Kolenkow, 1982, Mueller, 1982, Metzger, 1983, Klijn, 1983, and Rubinkiewicz, 1983.

17. Neusner, 1979, p. 118; Cohen, 1982, pp. 45–46.

18. Neusner, 1979, pp. 109–110.

19. Ibid., pp. 109–110, 119, 124.

20. "Mishnah addresses a world in which the cult is tied inextricably to Jerusalem and the Holy Land." Ibid., p. 124; "One temple for the one God," according to Josephus in *Contra Apionem* 2:193, quoted in Cohen, 1982, pp. 54, 57.

21. Neusner, 1979, pp. 121, 120–122; Cohen, 1984, p. 165; "Robert Goldenberg writes that despite the rise of the synagogue as a religious institution, rabbinic commentaries constantly betray a yearning for the old system of the Temple, insisting that it has only been 'submerged' temporarily, awaiting its inevitable restoration in Jerusalem on the Temple Mount." See Branham, 1992, p. 383; "They expected the temple to be rebuilt shortly (in 'seventy years') and part of their sectarian legacy was interest in this legislation." Cohen, 1982, p. 56.

22. Neusner, 1979, p. 122.

23. Russell, 1937, p. 172.

24. Skarsaune, 2002, p. 123.

25. Cohen, 1984, p. 153; Filson, 1944, p. 79; Skarsaune, 2002, p. 123; Levine, 1996, pp. 426–429.

26. Cohen, 1984, p. 153.

27. Skarsaune, 2002, p. 124; Levine, 1996, pp. 438–443; According to the Theodotus Inscription, a pre-70 c.e. Greek inscription found south of the Temple Mount, the purposes of the synagogue were to recite the Torah, study the commandments, and provide for lodging for pilgrims. Prayer is not mentioned in this inscription. See Branham, 1992, p. 387 with Figure 21 (p. 388), and Fine and Meyers, 1997, Vol. 5, p. 118.

28. Filson, 1944, p. 78; Edersheim, 1994, p. 12 (460–480 synagogues in Jerusalem); John Wilkinson estimates the number at 365 synagogues in Jerusalem, quoted in Eric M. Meyers, 1980, p. 97. But Meyers views these as "nothing more than 'meeting places.'"

29. Cohen, 1984, pp. 154–155, 171 (note 6); Filson, 1944, pp. 79, 83–85.

30. Talmud *Sotah*, end, quoted in Cohen, 1984, pp. 163–164, 173 (note 31).

31. Cohen, 1984, p. 165.

32. Quoted in Cohen, 1984, pp. 165–166, and 173 (note 35).

33. Stevenson, 2001, p. 168—emphasis in original; Lundquist, 1982.

34. Cohen, 1984, pp. 170, 174 (note 49).

35. Levine, 1996, p. 446.

36. Levine, 1996, p. 446.

37. Levine, 1996, pp. 446–447; Eric M. Meyers, 1980, p. 100.

38. Levine, 1996, p. 446; Eric M. Meyers, 1980, p. 100; the *lulav* (*lulab*) is the long, thin palm branch, tied together with willow and myrtle branches, used in the "Joy of the House of Water Drawing" at the time of the Feast of Tabernacles. The *ethrog*, or citron was used in conjunction with the *lulab*. See Patai,

1967, pp. 24–53; the festival of the "Joy of the House of Water Drawing" was a Fall season rain-making ceremony. The *lulab* and the *ethrog* were symbols of immortality: Goodenough 1964, Vol. 9:1, p. 71, and of fertility, healing, renewal and triumph: Patai, 1967, pp. 25–41.

39. Filson, 1944, p. 84; Eric M. Meyers, 1980, p. 100.
40. Branham, 1992, p. 387.
41. Quoted in Ibid.
42. White, 1997, Vol. 2, p. 174.
43. Ibid., p. 176.
44. Ibid.
45. Fine and Meyers, p. 122.
46. Ibid., p. 122; "The third-century Dura Europos synagogue paintings represent the earliest continuous narrative cycle of biblical images known in art. Not until the fifth century do we find similar complex and elaborate narrative cycles of biblical images in church art," Gutmann, 1988, p. 25.
47. Wischnitzer, 1971, pp. 367–373. A color photograph of the West wall can be seen in Goodenough, Vol. 11, Plate I.
48. Wischnitzer, 1971, pp. 367–368; Branham, 1992, pp. 378–379; Kraeling, 1956, pp. 59–60.
49. Kraeling, 1956, pp. 60–61; see also Goodenough, 1964, Vol. 9, pp. 68–71.
50. Kraeling, 1956, p. 58; Wischnitzer, 1971, p. 367.
51. Goodenough, 1964, Vol. 9, p. 65.
52. Hachlili, 1976, pp. 48–49, Figure 9; Fine and Meyers, 1997, Vol., 5, p. 121, Figure 4.
53. Fine and Meyers, 1997, Vol. 5, p. 122.
54. Hachlili, 1976, p. 43.
55. Kraeling, 1956, pp. 60, and 54–61; Hachlili, 1976, p. 43.
56. Fine and Meyers, 1997, Vol. 5, p. 120, Figure 2.
57. Lundquist, 1993, pp. 11, 56–57.
58. Elior, 1997, p. 222; Alexander, 1983, Vol. 1, pp. 235–236.
59. De Conick, 1999, p. 312.
60. Lundquist, 2000, p. 34.
61. Elior, 1999, p. 222.
62. De Conick, 1999 , p. 312.
63. Newsom, 1985, pp. 59–72.
64. Barker, 1999, pp. 98–99.
65. Elior, 1999, p. 223; Lundquist, 1990, pp. 435–436; Hamblin, 1994, pp. 440–444.
66. Lundquist, 1983, pp. 218–219.
67. Scholem, 1974, p. 11; Alexander, 1983, Vol. 1, p. 240.
68. Newsom, 1985, pp. 59–60; and see Chapter 3, The Second Temple, above; Alexander, 1983, Vol. 1, pp. 247–249.
69. Elior, 1999, p. 220; Alexander, 1983, Vol. 1, p. 240.
70. Elior, 1999, pp. 242–243.

71. Newsom, 1985, p. 60.
72. Ibid., p. 61.
73. Ibid., p. 65.
74. Newsom, 1985, p. 65.
75. *Hagigah* 2:1 in Danby, 1933, pp. 212–213.
76. Scholem, 1974, p. 12; Elior, 2005, pp. 218–220.
77. Elior, p. 243.
78. Elior, 1999, pp. 243–245.
79. Alexander, 1983, Vol. 1, pp. 224–225, 231; Scholem, 1974, pp. 8–21, 377–381.
80. Scholem, 1974, p. 10.
81. Ibid., p. 16.
82. Alexander, 1983, Vol. 1, p. 264; Scholem, 1974, pp. 377–381.
83. Ibid., pp. 23–28, 42–46.
84. Ibid., pp. 23, 26–28.
85. Halevi, 2005, p. 37; Hamblin, 1994, pp. 444–461.
86. Lancaster, 2006, p. 79; Scholem, 1974, p. 46.
87. Scholem, 1974, p. 25.
88. Ibid., pp. 24–25; Lancaster, 2006, p. 52.
89. Scholem, 1974, p. 23; Lancaster, 2006, pp. 175–176.
90. Scholem, 1974, pp. 57, 232–235; Scholem, 1977, pp. xviii–xxi.
91. Scholem, 1974, pp. 88–89; Lancaster, 2006, p. 26.
92. Scholem, 1974, p. 89.
93. Scholem, 1974, p. 100.
94. Ibid., p. 106; Halevi, 2005, pp. 5–12, 40–41.
95. Lancaster, 2006, pp. 48–50.
96. Scholem, 1974, p. 214.
97. Scholem, 1977, p. 7.
98. Patai, 1967, pp. 85–86.
99. Lundquist, 1984, p. 57.
100. Scholem, 1977, p. 7.
101. Patai, 1967, pp. 84–85.
102. Lancaster, 2006, pp. 149–151.
103. Quoted in Lancaster, 2006, pp. 152–153.
104. Patai, 1967, pp. 91, 116, 126.
105. Scholem, 1974, p. 31.
106. Ibid.
107. Ibid., pp. 111–112; Patai, 1967, p. 89.
108. Lancaster, 2006, pp. 85–86, 117–118.
109. Ibid., pp. 85–86.
110. Ibid., pp. 85–86.
111. Patai, 1967, p. 92.
112. Scholem, 1974, p. 213.

113.   Patai, 1967, pp. 92–93; Smith, 1978, pp. 120–121, 124: "The room is decorated with myrtle, forming a marriage canopy for the intercourse of the deity and
his bride, for the reuniting of the totality of the deity. The mother of the house
is kissed in a ritual which Luria [in the Kabbalistic practices of Isaac Luria—
1534–1572—Scholem, 1974, pp. 420–428] states has 'deep mystical significance'
and is homologized to the Bride of God through a recitation of Psalms 31. She
begins the ceremony by lighting the Sabbath candles, shielding her eyes from the
light which shone on the first day (the light which was still visible in the Jerusalem
Temple, the light which shattered into sparks in the kabbalistic myth)." p. 125:
"Next, the absolutely indispensable act of the Friday evening service is performed:
the chanting of a hymn celebrating the *hieros gamos* of the deity on high and the
exiled Bride, which takes place before the visionary eyes of the family—an act of
intercourse which for one brief ritual moment reunites the shattered deity, which
for a brief moment ends the exile and translates each home into the Center of
blessing and fertility which stood in the days of old." But see Smith's comments
in 1978, p. 128, "Afterword." Dever, 2005, surveys the evidence for the worship of a
mother goddess in the folk and official religions of ancient Canaan and Israel, and
bridges the gap between the ancient evidence and that of Kabbalah, showing the
continuities that exist over this vast time period. See especially pp. 207–208, 301,
303, 313.

114.   Patai, 1967, p. 231.

115.   Ibid., p. 232; and see Elior, 2005, pp. 67–68, 159–164, 219–220.

Chapter 5

1.   Skarsaune, 2002, p. 101; Gartner, 1965, pp. 47–122.

2.   Edersheim, 1994, pp. 113–114, 120–130.

3.   Skarsaune, 2002, pp. 100–101; Brown, 2002; Macrae, 1984, pp. 186–187,
is skeptical that Luke had any real or accurate knowledge of or direct experience
with the Temple.

4.   Skarsaune, 2002, p. 421.

5.   De Conick, 2001, p. 241; and see Reynolds, 1998.

6.   Nibley, 1959, 1960.

7.   Edersheim, 1994, p. 24.

8.   Skarsaune, 2002, pp. 147–178.

9.   Ben-Dov, 2002, p. 139.

10.   Ben-Dov, 2002, p. 141, illustrated on p. 139; "Many treasures from the
Temple of Herod were taken to Rome, as depicted on the Arch of Titus, and were
placed in a Temple of Peace in Rome, built by Emperor Vespasian," Campbell,
1981, p. 6.

11.   Mazar, Cornfeld, and Freedman, 1975, p. 235.

12.   Illustrated in Ben-Dov, 2002, p. 143; see also Mazar, Cornfeld, and Freedman, 1975, pp. 20–22, 235–236.

13. Ousterhout, 1990, p. 47, and illustration Figure 4.

14. Ben-Dov, 2002, pp. 143–147.

15. Mazar, Cornfeld, and Freedman, 1975, p. 236.

16. Mazar, Cornfeld, and Freedman, 1975, p. 236.

17. Nibley, 1959, p. 113.

18. Branham, 1992, p. 382; Mazar, Cornfeld, and Freedman, 1975, p. 244; plan of original building, relationship of original to Byzantine-era location of Golgotha, and plan of the church at the time of Emperor Justinian in Ben-Dov, 2002, pp. 148, 149, 156.

19. Hirschberg, 1953, p. 333.

20. Nibley, 1959, pp. 114–115, 120–121.

21. Eusebius, quoted in Nibley, 1959, p. 112.

22. Branham, 1992, p. 382.

23. Ousterhout, 1990, p. 44.

24. Ousterhout, 1990, p. 45.

25. Branham, 1992, p. 380.

26. Quoted in Branham, 1992, p. 380.

27. Branham, 1992, pp. 380–382.

28. Sylvester John Saller, quoted in Branham, 1992, p. 381.

29. Branham, 1992, p. 382, note 45.

30. Gibson and Jacobson, 1996, pp. 287–288; Hirschberg, 1953, pp. 322–323.

31. Krinsky, 1970, p. 4.

32. Pliny, quoted in Nibley, 1959, p. 115.

33. Nibley, 1959, pp. 115–117.

34. Mazar, Cornfeld, and Freedman, 1975, pp. 248–254.

35. Ben-Dov, 2002, pp. 161–162; Mazar, Cornfeld, and Freedman, 1975, p. 256; Nibley, 1959, pp. 114–115.

36. Ben-Dov, 2002, p. 161; Mazar, Cornfeld, and Freedman, 1975, pp. 22–23, 257–260.

37. Krinsky, 1970.

38. Krinsky, 1970, pp. 14–17 with Plates 4–5.

39. Krinsky, 1970, pp. 16–17, with Plate 4.

40. Krinsky, 1970, p. 19 with Plate 6c.

41. Ferber, 1976, p. 25–26 with Figure 9.

42. Ferber, 1976, p. 27 with Figure 10—emphasis in original.

43. Ferber, 1976, p. 28, with Figure 10.

44. Ferber, 1976, pp. 28–28, with Figure 10.

45. Ferber, 1976, p. 29, with Figure 10.

46. Cahn, 1976, pp. 46–47, with Figure 16; Krinsky, 1970, p. 14, with Plate 3b.

47. Cahn, 1976, pp. 47–48.

48. Read, 1999, pp. 82–83; Hillenbrand, 1999, pp. 63–66.

49. Read, 1999, p. 91.

50. Read, 1999, pp. 91–92; Nibley, 1960, pp. 229–230; Ritmeyer, 1996, pp. 52–53; Hillenbrand, 1999, pp. 286–291.

51. Corbin, 1986, pp. 345–350.

52. Corbin, 1986, pp. 349–350.

53. Corbin, 1996, pp. 347–348.

54. Corbin, 1986, p. 353; Read, 1999, pp. 304–305.

55. Ritmeyer, 1996, p. 53; Hillenbrand, 1999, pp. 286–291, with photograph p. 289 showing the Crusader grille around the central rock. Upon the defeat of Crusader Jerusalem in 1187 by Saladin, the victorious Muslims felt the need to formally purify the Dome of the Rock and the al-Aqsa mosque from what they viewed as Frankish (that is, Crusader), filth and defilement, Hillenbrand, 1999, pp. 298–301; see also Grabar, 2006, pp. 159–169 for a summary of Crusader activities and architectural and design changes on the esplanade.

56. Gibson and Jacobson, 1996, p. 287.

57. Corbin, 1986, pp. 346–352.

58. Weston, 1957; Cowen, 1979, pp. 99–103; Jung and Von Franz, 1998; Barb, 1956.

59. Von Simson, 1989, p. xviii.

60. Knight and Lomas, 1996; Gardner, 2003, pp. 217–271; Corbin, 1986, pp. 350–354.

61. Burckhardt, 1996, pp. 75–82.

62. Burckhardt, 1996, pp. 105–113, 127–130; Cowen, 1979, p. 102; Bony, 1983, pp. 13 (with note 8, p. 466), 17 (with notes 13, 14, pp. 467–468), 306.

63. He wrote a treatise supporting the creation of the Order—Read, 1999, pp. 101–106.

64. His preaching was instrumental in propelling forward the Second Crusade, which began in 1145, one year following the dedication of the St-Denis choir—Read, 1999, pp. 116–124.

65. Von Simson, 1989, pp. 43–48, 56–58.

66. Corbin, 1986, p. 269.

67. Corbin, 1986, p. 339.

68. Ibid., p. 341.

69. Ibid., p. 342.

70. Ibid., p. 344.

71. Ibid., pp. 345–350.

72. Ibid., pp. 348–350.

73. Corbin, p. 341.

74. Corbin, p. 341.

75. Corbin, pp. 341–342.

76. Corbin, p. 354.

77. Guenon, 1995, pp. 57–66.

78. Geunon, pp. 65–66; Hamblin, 1994, pp. 461–464; Barker, "The Secret Tradition."

79. *The Secret Rituals of the O.T.O.*, pp. 17–18.

80. *The Secret Rituals of the O.T.O.*, pp. 14–21.

81. Ibid., pp. 26–33.

82. Francis King, 1973, pp. 70–75.
83. Francis King, 1973, p. 211.
84. Francis King, 2002, p. 95; see also Bogdan, 2007, pp. 148–168.
85. Faulkner, 2005, pp. 158–163.
86. Meyer, 1987, pp. 1–14, 157–196; Skarsaune, 2002, p. 246.
87. Meyer, 1987, p. 189.
88. Marvin Meyer and Richard Smith, 1994, pp. 66–68.
89. Compton, 1990, p. 613.
90. Compton, 1990, pp. 615–616, Figure 2.
91. J. K. Elliott, 1993, pp. 195–196.
92. Compton, 1990, pp. 611–642.
93. Urban, 1997, pp. 7–8.
94. Meyer, 1987; Hall, 2003, pp. 39–78; Ebeling, 2007; Bogdan, 2007, pp. 51–66.
95. Curl, 2005, pp. 110–112, 115, 117, 128, 134, 136, 150, 159, 195; Curran, 2007, pp. 231–234, 245–277, 252, 254.
96. Barker, 1999, pp. 104–105.
97. De Conick, 2001, pp. 234–235.
98. Elior, 1999, pp. 247.
99. Elior, 1999, pp. 248–254; Scholem, 1974, pp. 17–18; Hamblin, 1994.
100. Quoted in De Conick, 2001, p. 235.
101. De Conick, 2001, p. 234.
102. De Conick, 2001, p. 234, quoting from The Gospel of Philip.
103. Alexander, 1983, Vol. 1, p. 237; see Macrae, 1984, for additional views on the heavenly temple within the Gnostic Nag Hammadi literature.
104. Barker, 1999, pp. 93–111.
105. Hall, 2003, p. 237.
106. A. E. Waite, quoted in Hall, 2003, p. 454; Corbin, 1986, pp. 350–353.
107. Frankl, 1945, p. 46.
108. Frankl, 1945, p. 46.
109. Frankl, 1946, p. 47.
110. Von Simson, 1989, p. 14.
111. "Freemasonry," *Man, Myth, and Magic*, 1995, Vol. 7, p. 952.
112. Urban, 1997, pp. 15–16.
113. Urban, 1997, p. 26.
114. Urban, 1997, p. 28; Bogdan, 2007, pp. 67–94.
115. Von Simson, 1989, p. 11; Critchlow, Carroll, and Lee, 1973, p. 12; Bony, 1983, pp. 377–378.
116. Von Simson, 1989, p. 8.
117. Hans Sedlmayr, referenced in Von Simson, 1989, p. 10.
118. Cowen, 1992, pp. 7–8.
119. Panofsky, 1979, pp. 64–65.
120. Von Simson, 1989, pp. 95–96; "It follows that if Rome is equated with Jerusalem then its major church will be compared to the Temple," Campbell, 1981, p. 3.

121. Stookey, 1969, pp. 35–36.

122. Stookey, 1969, p. 36.

123. De Conick, 2001, pp. 244–245.

124. Quoted in De Conick, 2001, p. 245.

125. Von Simson, 1989, p. 109; Bony writes that "While the classic two-tower facades were based on a city gate concept, the church entrance being seen as representing the gates to the Heavenly Jerusalem, Saint-Nicaise [Reims, began 1231] would seem to have been meant to evoke another kind of symbolic transposition, that of an announcement of the Holy of Holies, of the inner sanctuary contained within the church, through the projecting onto the façade of a choir-screen motif," Bony, 1983, p. 384. In his note (28) to this passage, Bony writes that "The process of formation of Romanesque and Gothic two-tower façade cannot be reduced exclusively to the City-Gate or Palace-Gate sources which are at the origin of the Syrian type.... However, the City-Gate concept never lost its significance and was sometimes revived most literally, as at Lincoln Cathedral in the 1080's, where the pattern of a triple archway was based on imitation of a triumphal gate of the type of the Golden Gate of Constantinople," p. 525. It seems to be a small step from seeing the twin towers of Gothic Cathedrals as originating from Near Eastern City-Gate influences, to seeing the actual materialization in the Middle Ages of the twin pillars that stood in front of the Temple of Solomon, Jachin and Boaz.

126. Von Simson, 1989, pp. 113–114.

127. Burckhardt, 1996, p. 58.

128. Quoted in Von Simson, 1989, p. 100.

129. Von Simson, 1989, p. 101.

130. Quoted in Burchkardt, 1996, p. 43; see also Stookey, 1969, pp. 38–39.

131. Burckhardt, 1996, p. 35.

132. Burckhardt, 1996, p. 69, with photographs on pp. 50, 68, 86–87.

133. Burckhardt, 1996, p. 70; Lundquist, 2002, pp. 685–686.

134. Critchlow, Carroll, and Lee, 1973, p. 12; Guenon, 1995, p. 142.

135. Guenon, 1995, p. 270.

136. Critchlow, Carroll, and Lee, 1973, p. 12; Lundquist, 2002, p. 665.

137. Nibley, 1959, pp. 118–119.

Chapter 6

1. Soucek, 1976, pp. 73–123.

2. Khoury, 1993, p. 60.

3. Soucek, 1976, p. 88.

4. Busse, 2003, Vol. 3, p. 2.

5. Ben-Dov, 2002, p. 171.

6. Grabar, 1996, p. 112.

7. Busse, 2003, Vol. 3, p. 2.

8. Soucek, 1976, p. 77.

9. Lundquist, 1993, pp. 8–9, 14–15; Wheeler, 2006, pp. 28–29, 85–86; Hawting, 2003, p. 78.

10. Hirschberg, 1953, pp. 321–335.

11. Hirschberg, 1953, p. 342.

12. Rabbat, 1989, p. 14.

13. Qur'an 2:142–150 (all translations from the Qur'an are from Koran. English. 2004, unless otherwise noted); Glubb, 1998, pp. 136, 170–171; Busse, 2003, Vol. 3, p. 3.

14. Qur'an 17:1; Glubb, 1998, p. 136.

15. Glubb, 1998, p. 136.

16. Glubb, 1998, p. 136; Soucek, 1976, pp. 99–111; Sells, 2001, Vol. 1, pp. 176–181; for the most famous painting of this scene, from the *Khamsa* of Nizami (1540 CE), see Bloom and Blair, 1997, p. 343.

17. Hirschberg, 1953, p. 331; Flood, 1999, p. 326.

18. Flood, 1999, pp. 326–327.

19. Flood, 1999, 312–313; for a photograph of the *mihrab* located in the cave, see Grabar, 2006, p. 135 (Figure 40), and pp. 133–136.

20. Hirschberg, 1953, p. 322; Patai, 1967, pp. 130–132.

21. Widengren, 1955, p. 117; Hirschberg, 1953, pp. 339–340.

22. Nibley, 1959, pp. 118–119.

23. Grabar, 1996, p. 47.

24. Grabar, 1996, p. 47.

25. Soucek, 1976, p. 91; Hirschberg, 1953, p. 320; Grabar, 1996, pp. 47–48.

26. Ben-Dov, 2002, pp. 170, 178.

27. Grabar, 1996, p. 48; Kaplony, 2002, p. 50; see also Flood, 1999, pp. 322–323, 326.

28. Grabar, 1996, p. 111; Rabbat, 1989, p. 15.

29. Mazar, Cornfeld, and Freedman, 1975, p. 261; Grabar, 1996, pp. 49–50.

30. Grabar, 1996, p. 50.

31. Mazar, Cornfeld, and Freedman, 1975, p. 266; Ben-Dov, 2002, pp. 173–174.

32. Grabar, 1996, p. 51.

33. Grabar, 1996, p. 52.

34. Grabar, 1996, p. 52.

35. Mazar, Cornfeld, and Freedman, 1975, p. 262.

36. Soucek, 1976, pp. 94–111; see Grabar, 2006, pp. 114–119, on the question of the possible influence of the Temple of Solomon on the building of the Dome of the Rock, and on the general awareness of the Temple of Solomon in the Muslim community at the time of the building of the Dome.

37. Quoted in Grabar, 1996, p. 53; Shams al-Din al-Maqdisi given as the correct spelling of this person's name, in Grabar, 2006, p. 124.

38. Grabar, 1996, p. 104.

39. Grabar, 1996, p. 52.

40. Mazar, Cornfeld, and Freedman, 1975, p. 262.

41. St. Laurent and Riedelmayer, 1993, p. 76.
42. Mazar, Cornfeld, and Freedman, 1975, p. 262.
43. Mazar, Cornfeld, and Freedman, 1975, p. 262.
44. Grabar, 1996, p. 110.
45. Grabar, 1996, pp. 109–110.
46. Grabar, 1996, p. 107.
47. Soucek, 1976, p. 96.
48. Soucek, 1976, p. 96.
49. Soucek, 1976, p. 97.
50. Soucek, 1976, pp. 86–88, 95–99; see also Grabar, 2006, pp. 77–89; "A vision of Paradise is particularly meaningful in Jerusalem in the last decades of the seventh century, as Jerusalem was to be the site of the Resurrection, which would begin on the Mount of Olives and in the ravine separating it from the city proper," Grabar, 2006, p. 116.
51. Grabar, 1996, pp. 59–62.
52. Goitein, 1966, p. 139.
53. Grabar, 1996, pp. 62–63.
54. Kaplony, 2002, p. 41–42; Elad, 1992, pp. 35–36.
55. Lawlor, 1982, pp. 74–79.
56. Kaplony, 2002, pp. 44–46.
57. Kaplony, 2002, p. 45.
58. Lundquist, 1983; Lundquist, 1993.
59. Freedman and Frey, 2002, pp. 646–647.
60. Sharon, 1992, pp. 56–67; Cook, 2002, pp. 54–55, 66.

Chapter 7

1. Alfoldi, 1947.
2. Ben Dov, 2002, pp. 243–245.
3. Bloom and Blair, 1997, p. 395.
4. Bloom and Blair, 1997, pp. 298–302.
5. Ben-Dov, 2002, pp. 251–253; photograph in Bloom and Blair, 1997, pp. 26–27.
6. Ben-Dov, 2002, p. 246; Grabar, 2006, pp. 191–196, with Figure 50, p. 1970.
7. Ben-Dov, 2002, p. 253.
8. Ben-Dov, 2002, pp. 246, 256–257.
9. Ben-Dov, 2002, pp. 265; Mazar, Cornfeld, and Freedman, 1975, p. 288.
10. Mazar, Cornfeld, and Freedman, 1975, p. 289.
11. Mazar, Cornfeld, and Freedman, 1975, pp. 289–290.
12. Ben-Dov, 2002, pp. 265–266.
13. Mazar, Cornfeld, and Freedman, 1975, pp. 290–291; Ben-Dov, 2002, pp. 267–276.
14. Mazar, Cornfeld, and Freedman, 1975, p. 291.

15. Gibson and Jacobson, 1996, p. 12.

16. Gibson and Jacobson, 1996, p. 14.

17. Gibson and Jacobson, 1996, p. 15.

18. Gibson and Jacobson, 1996, p. 20.

19. Gibson and Jacobson, 1996, pp. 20–21.

20. 1996, p. 23; Ben-Dov, 2002, pp. 280–281.

21. Ben-Dov, 2002, pp. 281–287.

22. Mazar, Cornfeld, and Freedman, 1975, p. 293.

23. Ben-Dov, 2002, p. 288.

24. Ben-Dov, 2002, p. 288.

25. Ben-Dov, 2002, p. 289.

26. Ben-Dov, pp. 290–297; Freidland and Hecht, 1998b, p. 141.

27. Friedland and Hecht, 1998b, p. 141.

28. Mazar, Cornfeld, and Freedman, 1975, p. 293.

29. Friedland and Hecht, 1998b, p. 140.

30. Freidland and Hecht, 1998b, p. 140.

31. Friedland and Hecht, 1998b, pp. 119–121.

32. Friedland and Hecht, 1998b, pp. 120–121; Ben-Dov, 2002, pp. 295–297.

33. Ben-Dov, 2002, pp. 294–295.

34. Ben-Dov, 2002, pp. 292–293; Friedland and Hecht, 1998a, p. 149.

35. Friedland and Hecht, 1998b, p. 119.

36. Friedland and Hecht, 1998b, p. 120.

37. Orme Jr., 1999, p. A4; Emmett, 1997, pp. 24–25.

38. Emmett, 1997, pp. 19–20; Friedland and Hecht, 1998a, pp. 146–147.

39. Shanks, 2005, pp. 14–15.

40. Quoted in Bennett, 2003, p. A8.

41. Ben-Dov, 2002, pp. 304–309.

42. Ben-Dov, 2002, pp. 309–311.

43. Summarized in Ben-Dov, 2002, pp. 327–328, and Bahat, 1997, Vol. 3, pp. 224–238.

44. Ben-Dov, 2002, pp. 322–330.

45. Steven Erlanger, 2005, p. A4.

46. Armstrong, 1998, p. 10; Emmett, 1997, p. 24.

47. Friedland and Hecht, 1998a, p. 148.

48. Ben-Dov, 2002, pp. 354–355.

49. Mazar, Cornfeld, and Freedman, 1975, p. 276.

50. Plan and photographs in Ben-Dov, 2002, p. 354–355.

51. Orme Jr., 1999, p. A4.

52. Friedland and Hecht, 1998a, p. 151.

53. Griessman, 1976, p. 197.

54. Friedland and Hecht, 1998a, p. 151.

55. Griessman, 1976, p. 200, emphasis in the original.

56. Quoted in Griessman, 1976, p. 204.

57. Quoted in Griessman, 1976, p. 204.

58. Quoted in Griessman, 1976, p. 204.
59. Quoted in Griessman, 1976, pp. 206–207.
60. Quoted in Griessman, 1976, p. 207.
61. Griessman, 1976, p. 207.
62. Griessman, 1976, pp. 209–211.
63. According to statistics quoted in Armstrong, 1998, p. 8, 30% of Israelis in a 1996 poll supported the activities of the Temple Mount Faithful.
64. Armstrong, 1998, pp. 8; Friedland and Hecht 1998a, pp. 149, 151–157, 161; Friedland and Hecht, 1998b, p. 126.
65. Quoted in Heilman, 1994, p. 189; Don-Yehiya, 1994, p. 280; according to Don-Yehiya, the group was founded "immediately after the Six Day War"—1994, p. 280, whereas Friedland and Hecht state that the Temple Mount Faithful was founded in 1982–1998a, p. 155, and in 1981–1998b, p. 122.
66. Friedland and Hecht, 1998a, p. 155.
67. Don-Yehiya, 1994, pp. 280–281; Friedland and Hecht, 1998a, p. 156.
68. Friedland and Hecht, 1998a, p. 156.
69. Friedland and Hecht, 1998b, pp. 103–104, 122.
70. Friedland and Hecht, 1998a, pp. 155–156.
71. Friedland and Hecht, 1998a, pp. 156–157.

Chapter 8

1. Liddell, 1996, p. 201; Funkenstein, 1985.
2. Morton Smith, 1983, p. 15; Christopher R. Smith, "The Structure of the Book of Revelation in Light of Apocalyptic Literary Conventions," p. 379 (citing the definitions of John J. Collins and Adela Yarbro Collins).
3. Smith, 1983, p. 15; Tord Olsson, 1983, pp. 22–28; Youngblood, 1988, p. 215.
4. Liddell, 1996, 699–700.
5. R. G. Hammerton-Kelly, "The Temple and the Origins of Jewish Apocalyptic." *Vetus Testamentum* 20 (1970), pp. 5–8; "The true temple, to be revealed at the eschaton, was present in heaven. It had been seen by Ezekiel." Hammerton-Kelly, p. 13; Lawrence H. Schiffman, "The Theology of the Temple Scroll." *The Jewish Quarterly Review* 85 (1994), p. 118: "The concept behind our passage in the Temple Scroll is clearly connected with the interpretation which this scroll had of the dream of Jacob and the ladder. For the author, the dream indicated the notion of a connection between heaven and earth, a temple, but one to be constructed by God himself"; Gartner, 1965, p. 17.
6. Cook, 2005.
7. Tuell, 1992.
8. Wise, Abegg Jr., and Cook, 2005, pp. 462–475, 557–563; Newson, 1985; Corbin, 1986, pp. 284–292.
9. Niditch locates chapters 37–39, leading on to 40–48 as part of a classic, ancient near Eastern "Chaos Cosmos" scenario, in which the battle with and victory over evil of chapters 38–39 (Chaos) leads on to the founding of the Temple

building, the classic Cosmos/Creation symbol. Niditch, 1986, pp. 220–223. In Eli-adean terms, this constitutes a "founding of the world, the ultimate hierophany, the founding of a sacred space," the "cosmicization" of a territory, the transformation of a territory from chaos to cosmos, because, "The profound reason for all these symbols is clear: the temple is the image of the sanctified world. The holiness of the temple sanctifies both the cosmos and cosmic time. Therefore, the temple represents the original state of the world: the pure world that was not worn out by time or sullied by an invasion of the profane." "The Prestige of the Cosmogonic Myth." *Diogenes* 23 (1958), pp. 1–13.

10. *The New Oxford Annotated Bible with the Apocrypha,* Revised Standard Version, p. 1049; Julie Galambush, 2000, pp. 517–518; Paul L. Redditt, 2000, p. 888; Paul J. Kissling, 2000, p. 1340.

11. Tuell, 1992, pp. 1–17.

12. Busink , 2, pp. 701–775.

13. R. G. Hammerton-Kelly, "The Temple and the Origins of Jewish Apoc-alyptic," pp. 1–15.

14. Niditch, 1986.

15. Eliade, 1964, pp. 143.

16. Dominik Schroder, quoted in Waida, p. 223.

17. Eliade, 1964, p. 4.

18. Ibid., p. 5.

19. Ibid., p. 140.

20. Ibid., p. 141.

21. Ibid., p. 154; Martha Himmelfarb uses the term "Ascent Apocalypses." Himmelfarb, 1991, pp. 79–90.

22. Alexander, 1983, Vol. 1, p. 233.

23. Alexander, 1983, Vol., 1, pp. 238–239.

24. Eliade, 1964, p. 410.

25. Niditch, p. 215.

26. Busink, 2, pp. 773–774, Abb. (Figures) 186, 187.

27. Busink, 2, pp. 754–757, 775, Abb. (Figures) 189, 190, 191.

28. Corbin, 1986, pp. 289–291.

29. Lundquist, 1983, pp. 207.

30. Lundquist 2000, pp. 29–30 (emphasis in the original).

31. Lundquist, 1983, p. 211.

32. R. G. Hammerton-Kelly, "The Temple and the Origins of Jewish Apoc-alyptic," pp. 1–15.

33. Van Buren, 1952, pp. 294.

34. Lundquist, 1983, p. 211.

35. Tuell, 1992, pp. 6–7, referring to C. C. Torrey.

36. Lundquist, 1993, p. 13.

37. The description of the East gate parallels that of the excavated city gates at Megiddo, Hazor, and Gezer in Palestine. Busink, 2, pp. 713–721, Abb. (Fig-ures) 179, 180.

38. The description of this altar fits that of a Babylonian ziggurat, Busink, 2, pp. 730–736, Abb. (Figure) 182.

39. Gartner, 1965, pp. 4–5.

40. Tuell, 103–120; the Messiah will return on the ninth of Ab, the date of the destruction of the Temple of Solomon and of the Second Temple: Scholem, 1974, p. 246.

41. "The temple is often associated with the waters of life which flow forth from a spring within the building itself—or rather the temple is viewed as incorporating within itself or as having been built upon such a spring. The reason that such springs exist in temples is that they are perceived as the primeval waters of creation, Nun in Egypt, Abzu in Mesopotamia. The temple is founded upon and stands in contact with the primeval waters." Lundquist, 1983, p. 208; Corbin, 1986, pp. 287–288, 290–291; Margaret Barker, *On Earth as it is in Heaven,* pp. 28–31.

42. Henry Corbin, 1986, pp. 284–292; Chyutin, 2006, pp. 168–178.

43. Corbin, Ibid.

44. Ibid., p. 284.

45. Ibid., pp. 285–286.

46. Ibid., p. 291.

47. 2005, pp. 557–563.

48. 2004, pp. 607–610.

49. Vermes, 2004, p. 607.

50. Vermes, 2004, p. 607.

51. Wise, Abegg, Jr., and Cook, 2005, p. 558.

52. Corbin, 1986, p. 312; see also Chyutin, 2006, pp. 180–184.

53. Yigael Yadin, *The Temple Scroll* 1, p. 183; Yigael Yadin, *The Temple Scroll, The Hidden Law of the Dead Sea Sect,* pp. 112–115.

54. Yigael Yadin, *The Temple Scroll: The Hidden Law of the Dead Sea Sect,* pp. 114, 146; Lawrence H. Schiffman, "The Theology of the Temple Scroll," pp. 115–117.

55. Yadin, Ibid., pp. 165–167; Chyutin, 2006, pp. 169–178; see also, for a general discussion of Jewish apocalyptic, Funkenstein, 1985, pp. 50–53.

56. Corbin, 1986, p. 289; Christopher R. Smith, "The Structure of the Book or Revelation in Light of Apocalyptic Literary Conventions," pp. 373–393.

57. Stevenson, 2001, pp. 231–237.

58. Eliade, 1987, p. 58; Lundquist, 1993, pp. 11–12.

59. Eliade, 1987, pp. 60–61.

60. Ibid., p. 59.

61. Corbin, 1986, pp. 281, 291, 298–299 (regarding the Pseudepigrapha), 323, 326, 358, 360.

62. Ibid., p. 281.

63. Stevenson, 2001, p. 2.

64. Lundquist, 1990, p. 435; Stevenson, 2001, pp. 268–270.

65. Margaret Barker, *On Earth as it is in Heaven,* pp. 28–31, 71–72; it is also true that, in Christian eschatology, the Mount of Olives is the place thought to

be nearest to heaven, and it became a favored place to die and be buried. Jesus will return to the earth in His Second Coming to the exact same spot on the Mount of Olives from where he ascended into heaven (Acts 1:11). The antichrist will be defeated by Jesus himself on the Mount of Olives. See Limor, 1998, pp. 13–22; "A vision of Paradise [in the Dome of the Rock] is particularly meaningful in Jerusalem in the last decades of the seventh century. Jerusalem was to be the site of the Resurrection, which would begin on the Mount of Olives and in the ravine separating it from the city proper. This had been an area of tombs for many centuries, and all three monotheistic faiths were ripe with announcements of the end of time," Grabar, 2006, p. 116; for a general discussion of Christian apocalyptic, see Funkenstein, 1985, pp. 53–58.

66. Leemhuis, 2001, pp. 111–112; "The Koran is not like the Bible, historical; running from Genesis to Apocalypse. The Koran is altogether apocalyptic." Norman O. Brown, "The Apocalypse of Islam," p. 166.

67. Leemhuis, Ibid., p. 112.

68. Neal Robinson, 2001, pp. 108–109.

69. Cook, 2002, pp. 9, 301.

70. Ibid., pp. 301–302.

71. Ibid., p. 301.

72. Glubb, 2001, pp. 17–18; Juynboll, 2002, pp. 376–377.

73. Cook, 2002, p. 1.

74. Ibid., pp. 2–3.

75. Ibid., pp. 7–8.

76. Ibid., p. 10–11.

77. Muslim, 4, pp. 1493–1528 (Chapters MCXC–MCCXV—Hadith 6881–7057—all references to Hadith are from this source); Leemhuis, 2001, p. 114.

78. Muslim, 4, p. 1493.

79. E. W. Lane, *Arabic-English Lexicon,* quoted in Cook, 2002, p. 20.

80. Cook, 2002, pp. 20–21.

81. Robinson, 2001, p. 110.

82. Louis Massignon, quoted in Norman O. Brown, p. 155.

83. Lewinstein, 2002, pp. 331–333.

84. Cook, 2002, p. 172; "As already mentioned, there have been conflicting views amongst Muslim scholars over the centuries on the relative merits of the Holy Cities of Mecca and Medina as opposed to Jerusalem, but the Palestinian writer al-Muqaddasi (d. 387/997), speaking with pride of his native city, sums up the pro-Jerusalem viewpoint: 'The province of Syria is in the first rank, the Land of the Prophets, the dwelling-place of the saints, the first *qibla*; the site of the Night Journey and the Gathering.' Then he turns to Jerusalem itself: 'Mecca and Medina derive their high position from the Ka'ba and the Prophet, but on the Day of Judgement they will both be brought to Jerusalem," Hillenbrand, 1999, p. 149.

85. Leemhuis, 2001, p. 114; Jewish tradition also views the Temple as the nearest point on earth to heaven. Whereas the earth in general is the equivalent

of a walking distance of five hundred years, the "upper Temple" and the "lower Temple" are a mere eighteen miles apart. See Patai, 1967, pp. 110, 131.

86. Cook, 2005, p. 22.
87. Ibid., pp. 22–23.
88. Ibid., p. 42.
89. Ibid., p. 47.
90. Ibid., pp. 184–189.
91. Ibid., p. 39, quoting Sa'id Ayyub.
92. Ibid., p. 45.

Bibliography

Abbreviations

ANEP   *The Ancient Near East in Pictures Relating to the Old Testament.* 2nd ed. with Supplement, by James B. Pritchard.

ANET   *Ancient Near Eastern Texts Relating to the Old Testament.* Edited by James B. Pritchard; Translators and Annotators, W. F. Albright et al. 3rd ed, with suppl. Princeton: Princeton University Press, 1969.

CAD   *The Assyrian Dictionary.* Editorial Board Ignace J. Gelb et al. Chicago: Oriental Institute, 1956–.

Abou Assaf, Ali. "'Ain Dara'." In *The Oxford Encyclopedia of Archaeology in the Near East.* Eric M. Meyers, Editor-in-Chief. Prepared under the Auspices of the American Schools of Oriental Research. Vol. 1. New York: Oxford University Press, 1997, 33–35.

Abou Assaf, Ali. *Der Tempel von Ain Dara.* Damaszener Forschungen, Bd. 3. Mainz am Rhein: P. v. Zabern 1990.

Aharoni, Y. "Arad." In *Encyclopedia of Archaeological Excavations in the Holy Land.* Edited by Michael Avi-Yonah. Vol. 1. London: Oxford University Press, 1975, 86–89.

Alexander, P. "3 (Hebrew Apocalypse of) Enoch (Fifth to Sixth Century A.D.)." In *Old Testament Pseudepigrapha*. Edited by James H. Charlesworth. Vol. 1, 1983, 223–315.

Alfoldi, A. "On the Foundation of Constantinople: A Few Notes." In *The Journal of Roman Studies* 37, parts 1, 2 (1947):10–16.

Amiet, Pierre. *Art of the Ancient Near East*. Translated by John Shepley and Claude Choquet. Edited by Naomi Noble Richard. New York: H. H. Abrams, 1980.

Amikam, Elad. "Why Did 'Abd al-Malik Build the Dome of the Rock? A Re-examination of the Muslim Sources." In *Bayt al-Maqdis*. Oxford Studies in Islamic Art, 9. Oxford: New York: Published by Oxford University Press for the Board of Faculty of Oriental Studies, University of Oxford, c1992–c1999. Vol. 1, 1992, 33–58.

Anderson, F. I. "2 (Slavonic Apocalypse of) Enoch (Late First Century A.D.)." In *Old Testament Pseudepigrapha*. Edited by James H. Charlesworth. Vol. 1 (1983), 91–221.

Andrews, Herbert T. "The Letter of Aristeas." In *The Apocrypha and Pseudepigrapha of the Old Testament in English*. With Introductions and Explanatory Notes to the Several Books. Edited in Conjunction with Many Scholars by R. H. Charles. Vol. 2. *Pseudepigrapha*. Oxford: Clarendon Press, 1913, 83–122.

Armstrong, Karen. "The Holiness of Jerusalem: Asset or Burden?" In *Journal of Palestine Studies* 27, no. 3 (Spring 1998): 5–19.

Arnold, Dieter. *The Encyclopedia of Ancient Egyptian Architecture*. Translated by Sabine H. Gardiner and Helen Strudwick. Edited by Nigel and Helen Strudwick. Princeton: Princeton University Press, 2003.

Atkinson, Kenneth. "Millo." In *Eerdmans Dictionary of the Bible*. David Noel Freedman, Editor-in-Chief, Allen C. Myers, Associate Editor, Astrid B. Beck, Managing Editor. Grand Rapids, MI: W. B. Eerdman's, 2000, 901.

Avigad, N. "The Architecture of Jerusalem in the Second Temple Period." In *Jerusalem Revealed: Archaeology in the Holy City, 1968–1974*. Edited by Y. Yadin, Associate Editor, E. Stern. English Translation and Abridgement by R. Grafman. Jerusalem: Israel Exploration Society, 1975, 14–20.

Avi-Yonah, M. "The Façade of Herod's Temple, An Attempted Reconstruction." In *Religions in Antiquity: Essays in Memory of Erwin Ramsdell Goodenough*. Edited by Jacob Neusner. Studies in the History of Religions; Supplements to Numen, 14. Leiden: E. J. Brill, 1968, 326–335.

Bahat, Dan. "Jerusalem." In *The Oxford Encyclopedia of Archaeology in the Near East*. Eric M. Meyers, Editor-in-Chief. Prepared under the Auspices of the American Schools of Oriental Research. Vol. 3. New York: Oxford University Press, 1997, 224–238.

Barb, A. A. "Mensa Sacra: The Round Table and the Holy Grail." In *Journal of the Warburg and Courtauld Institutes* 19, no. 1–2 (January/June 1956): 40–67.

Barker, Margaret. "Beyond the Veil of the Temple: The High Priestly Origin of the Apocalypses." http://www.marquette.edu/maqom/veil.

Barker, Margaret. "The High Priest and the Worship of Jesus." In *The Jewish Roots of Christological Monotheism: Papers from the St. Andrews Conference on the Historical Origins of the Worship of Jesus.* Supplements to the Journal for the Study of Judaism, v. 63. Edited by Carey C. Newman, James R. Davila, Gladys S. Lewis. Leiden, Boston: Brill, 1999, 93–111.

Barker, Margaret. *On Earth as it is in Heaven: Temple Symbolism in the New Testament.* Edinburgh: T&T Clark, 1995.

Barker, Margaret. "The Secret Tradition." http://www.marquette.edu/maqom/tradition1.

Bell, Lanny. "The New Kingdom 'Divine' Temple: The Example of Luxor." In *Temples of Ancient Egypt.* Edited by Byron E. Shafer. Ithaca, NY: Cornell University Press, 1997, 124–184.

Ben-Dov, M. *Historical Atlas of Jerusalem.* Translated by David Louvish. New York: Continuum, 2002.

Ben-Tor, Amnon. "Hazor." In *The Oxford Encyclopedia of Archaeology in the Near East.* Eric M. Meyers, Editor-in-Chief. Prepared under the Auspices of the American Schools of Oriental Research. Vol. 3. New York: Oxford University Press, 1997, 1–5.

Bennet, James. "Jerusalem Holy Sites a Tense Crossroads Again." *The New York Times.* August 29, 2003.

Bietak, Manfred. *Avaris and Piramesse: Archaeological Exploration in the Eastern Nile Delta.* Mortimer Wheeler Archaeological Lecture, 1979. Oxford: Oxford University Press, 1981.

Bietak, Manfred. *Avaris, the Capital of the Hyksos: Recent Excavations at Tell el-Daba.* The First Raymond and Beverly Sackler Foundation Distinguished Lecture in Egyptology. London: Published by British Museum Press for the Trustees of the British Museum, 1996.

Birch, Samuel. *The Bronze Ornaments of the Palace Gates of Balawat (Shalmaneser II, BCE 859–825).* Edited, with an Introduction, by Samuel Birch, with Descriptions and Translations by Theophilus G. Pinches. London: Society of Biblical Archaeology, 1880–[1902].

Bloch-Smith, Elizabeth. "Solomon's Temple: The Politics of Ritual Space." In *Sacred Time, Sacred Place: Archaeology and the Religion of Israel.* Edited by Barry M. Gittlen. Winona Lake, IN: Eisenbrauns, 2002, 83–94.

Bloom, Jonathan. *Islamic Arts.* Jonathan Bloom and Sheila Blair. London: Phaidon Press, 1997.

Bogdan, Henrik. *Western Esotericism and Rituals of Initiation.* SUNY Series in Western Esoteric Traditions. Albany: State University of New York Press, 2007.

Bony, Jean. *French Gothic Architecture of the 12th and 13th Centuries*. California Studies in the History of Art, 20. Berkeley, CA: University of California Press, 1983.

Borchardt, Ludwig. *Agyptische Tempel mit Umgang*, Mit Zeichnungen von Herbert Ricke. Beitrage zur Agyptischen Bauforschung und Altertumskunde, Heft 2. Cairo: n.p.: 1938.

Boyd, Mary Petrina. "Purple." In *Eerdmans Dictionary of the Bible*. David Noel Freedman, Editor-in-Chief, Allen C. Myers, Associate Editor, Astrid B. Beck, Managing Editor. Grand Rapids, MI: Eerdmans, 2000, 1100.

Brandon, S.G.F. *The Fall of Jerusalem and the Christian Church: A Study of the Effects of the Jewish Overthrow of A.D. 70 on Christianity*. London: S.P.C.K., 1951.

Branham, Joan R. "Sacred Space under Erasure in Ancient Synagogues and Early Churches." In *The Art Bulletin* 74, no. 3 (September 1992): 375–394.

Brown, Norman O. "The Apocalypse of Islam." In *Social Text* 8 (Winter 1983–1984): 155–171.

Brown, S. Kent. "The Temple in Luke and Acts." In *Revelation, Reason, and Faith: Essays in Honor of Truman G. Madsen*. Edited by Donald W. Parry, Daniel Peterson, and Stephen D. Ricks. Provo, UT: Foundation for Ancient Research and Mormon Studies, Brigham Young University Press, 2002, 615–633.

Bryne, Ryan. "Ophir." In *Eerdmans Dictionary of the Bible*. David Noel Freedman, Editor-in-Chief, Allen C. Myers, Associate Editor, Astrid B. Beck, Managing Editor. Grand Rapids, MI: Eerdmans, 2000, 990.

Burckhardt, Titus. *Chartres and the Birth of the Cathedral*. Translated by William Stoddert. Foreword by Keith Critchlow. Bloomington, IN: World Wisdom Books, 1996.

Busink, Th. A. *Der Tempel von Jerusalem, von Salomo bis Herodes; eine Archaologisch-Historische Studie unter Berucksichtigung des Westsemitischen Tempelbaus*. Studia Francisci Scholten Memoriae Dictata, Vol. 3. 2 Vols. Bd. 1. Der Tempel Salomos. Bd. 2. Von Ezechiel bis Middot. Leiden: Brill, 1970–1980.

Busse, Heribert. "Jerusalem." In *Encyclopedia of the Qur'an*. Jane Dammen McAuliffe, General Editor. Leiden: Brill, 2003. Vol. 3, 2–7.

Cahn, Walter. "Solomonic Elements in Romanesque Art." In *The Temple of Solomon: Archaeological Fact and Medieval Tradition in Christian, Islamic and Jewish Art*. Edited by Joseph Gutmann. No. 3 of American Academy *The Temple of Solomon: Archaeological Fact and Medieval Tradition in Christian* of Religion Society of Biblical Literature Religion and the Arts, edited by Anthony Yu and Joseph Gutmann. Missoula, MT: Scholars Press, 1976, 45–72.

Campbell, Ian. "The New St. Peters: Basilica or Temple?" In *Oxford Art Journal* 4, No. 1 (July 1981): 3–8.

Carter, Howard. *The Tomb of Tut-Ankh-Amen: Discovered by the Late Earl of Carnarvon and Howard Carter.* With Appendices by Douglas E. Derry. Vol. 3, with 156 Illustrations from Photographs by Harry Burton. London: Cassell and Company, Ltd., 1933.

Chan, Victor. *Tibet Handbook.* Chico, CA: Moon Publications, 1994.

Charlesworth, James H. "Introduction for the General Reader." In *The Old Testament Pseudepigrapha.* Edited by James H. Charlesworth. Vol. 1 (1983): xxi–xxxiv.

Charlesworth, James H. *The Old Testament Pseudepigrapha.* Edited by James H. Charlesworth. 2 Vols. Vol. 1. Apocalyptic Literature and Testaments. Vol. 2. Expansions of the "Old Testament" and Legends, Wisdom and Philosophical Literature, Prayers, Psalms, and Odes, Fragments of Lost Judeo-Hellenistic Works. Garden City, NY: Doubleday, 1983–1985.

Chyutin, Michael. *Architecture and Utopia in the Temple Era.* Translated by Richard Flantz. Library of Second Temple Studies 58. Edited by Lester L. Grabbe. New York and London: T & T Clark, 2006.

Clements, R. E. *God and Temple.* Oxford: B. Blackwell, 1965.

Clifford, Richard J. "The Temple and the Holy Mountain." In *The Temple in Antiquity: Ancient Records and Modern Perspectives.* Edited, with an Introductory Essay by Truman G. Madsen. Religious Studies Monograph Series, Vol. 9. Provo, UT: Religious Studies Center, Brigham Young University; Salt Lake City, UT: Produced and Distributed by Bookcraft, 1984, 107–124.

Cogan, Mordechai. *I Kings: A New Translation with Introduction and Commentary.* The Anchor Bible, Vol. 10. New York: Doubleday, 2001.

Cogan, Mordechai and Hayim Tadmor. *II Kings: A New Translation,* with Introduction and Commentary by Mordechai Cogan and Hayim Tadmor. The Anchor Bible, Vol. 11. Garden City, NY: Doubleday, 1988.

Cohen, Shaye J.D. "The Temple and the Synagogue." In *The Temple in Antiquity: Ancient Records and Modern Perspectives.* Edited, with an Introductory Essay by Truman G. Madsen. Religious Studies Monograph Series, Vol. 9. Provo, UT: Religious Studies Center, Brigham Young University; Salt Lake City, UT: Produced and Distributed by Bookcraft, 1984, 151–174.

Cohen, Shaye J. D. "Yavneh Revisited: Pharisees, Rabbis and the End of Jewish Sectarianism." In *Society of Biblical Literature 1982 Seminar Papers.* Edited by Kent Harold Richards. Chico, CA: Scholars Press, 1982, 45–61.

Compton, Todd M. "The Handclasp and Embrace as Tokens of Recognition." In *By Study and Also By Faith: Essays in Honor of Hugh W. Nibley on the Occasion of His Eightieth Birthday, 27 March 1990.* Edited by John M. Lundquist, Stephen D. Ricks. Salt Lake City, UT: Deseret Book; Provo, UT: Foundation for Ancient Research and Mormon Studies, 1990. Vol. 1, 611–642.

Cook, David. *Contemporary Muslim Apocalyptic Literature.* Religion and Politics. Syracuse, NY: Syracuse University Press, 2005.

Cook, David. *Studies in Muslim Apocalyptic.* Studies in Late Antiquity and Early Islam, 21. Princeton: Princeton University Press, 2002.

Corbin, Henry. *Temple and Contemplation.* Translated by Philip Sherrard with the Assistance of Liadain Sherrard. Islamic Texts and Contexts. London; New York: KPI in Association with Islamic Publications, 1986.

Cowen, Painton. *Rose Windows.* Photography by the Author. Art and Imagination. New York: Thames and Hudson, 1979.

Critchlow, Keith, Jane Carroll, and Llewylyn Vaughn Lee. "Chartres Maze: A Model of the Universe?" In *Architectural Association Quarterly* 5 (1973): 11–20.

Cross, Frank Moore, Jr. "The Priestly Tabernacle in the Light of Recent Research." In *The Temple in Antiquity: Ancient Records and Modern Perspectives.* Edited, with an Introductory Essay by Truman G. Madsen. Religious Studies Monograph Series, Vol. 9. Provo UT: Religious Studies Center, Brigham Young University; Salt Lake City, UT: Produced and Distributed by Bookcraft, 1984, 91–105.

Curl, James Stevens. *The Egyptian Revival: Ancient Egypt as the Inspiration for Design Motifs in the West.* Rev. and enl. Ed. of *Egyptomania.* 1994. Abingdon, England; New York: Routledge, 2005.

Curran, Brian. *The Egyptian Renaissance: The Afterlife of Ancient Egypt in Early Modern Italy.* Chicago: The University of Chicago Press, 2007.

Danby, Herbert. *The Mishnah.* Translated from the Hebrew with Introduction and Brief Explanatory Notes, by Herbert Danby. Oxford: Oxford University Press, 1933.

David, Rosalie A. *A Guide to Religious Ritual at Abydos.* Egyptology Series. Modern Egyptology Series. Warminster, Wilts, England: Aris & Phillips, 1981.

Davies, Norman de Garis. *The Tomb of Rekh-mi-Re at Thebes.* Publications of the Metropolitan Museum of Art, Egyptian Expedition. Edited by Ludlow Bull...with the Assistance of Nora E. Scott, Vol. XI. New York: The Plantin Press, 1943.

De Conick, April D. "Heavenly Temple Traditions and Valentinian Worship." In *The Jewish Roots of Christological Monotheism: Papers from the St. Andrews Conference on the Historical Origins of the Worship of Jesus.* Supplements to the Journal for the Study of Judaism, v. 63. Edited by Carey C. Newman, James R. Davila, Gladys S. Lewis. Leiden, Boston: Brill, 1999, 308–341.

De Conick, April D. "The True Mysteries: Sacramentalism in the 'Gospel of Philip.'" In *Vigiliae Christianae* 55, no. 3 (2001): 225–261.

Dever, William G. *Did God Have a Wife?: Archaeology and Folk Religion in Ancient Israel.* Grand Rapids, MI: W. B. Eerdmans Pub. Co., 2005.

Don-Yehiya, Eliezer. "The Book and the Sword: The Nationalist Yeshivot and Political Radicalism in Israel." In *Accounting for Fundamentalisms: The Dynamic Character of Movements*. The Fundamentalism Project, 4. Edited by Martin E. Marty and R. Scott Appleby. Sponsored by the American Academy of Arts and Sciences. Chicago: University of Chicago Press, 1994, 264–302.

Dozeman, Thomas B. "Urim and Thummim." In *Eerdmans Dictionary of the Bible*. David Noel Freedman, Editor-in-Chief, Allen C. Myers, Associate Editor, Astrid B. Beck, Managing Editor. Grand Rapids, MI: Eerdmans, 2000, 1349.

Ebeling, Florian. *The Secret History of Hermes Trismegistus: Hermeticism from Ancient to Modern Times*. Translated by David Lorton. Foreword by Jan Assmann. Ithaca: Cornell University Press, 2007.

Edersheim, Alfred. *The Temple: Its Ministry and Services*. Updated ed. Peabody, MA: Hendrickson, 1994.

Eerdmans Dictionary of the Bible. David Noel Freedman, Editor-In-Chief; Allan C. Myers, Associate Editor; Astrid B. Beck, Managing Editor. Grand Rapids, MI: W. B. Eerdmans, 2000.

Eliade, Mircea. "The Prestige of the Cosmogonic Myth." In *Diogenes* 23 (1958): 1–13.

Eliade, Mircea. *The Sacred and the Profane: The Nature of Religion*. Translated by Willard R. Trask. San Diego, CA: A Harvest Book, Harcourt Inc., 1987.

Eliade, Mircea. *Shamanism: Archaic Techniques of Ecstacy*. Translated by Willard R. Trask. Bollingen Series 76. New York: Bollingen Foundation, 1964.

Elior, Rachel. "From Earthly Temple to Heavenly Shrine." In *The Jewish Roots of Christological Monotheism: Papers from the St. Andrews Conference on the Historical Origins of the Worship of Jesus*. Supplements to the Journal for the Study of Judaism, v. 63. Edited by Carey C. Newman, James R. Davila, Gladys S. Lewis. Leiden, Boston: Brill, 1999, 217–267.

Elior, Rachel. *The Three Temples: On the Emergence of Jewish Mysticism*. Translated by David Louvish. Oxford; Portland, OR: The Littman Library of Jewish Civilization, 2005.

Elliott, J. K., trans. *The Apocryphal New Testament: A Collection of Apocryphal Christian Literature in an English Translation*. Rev. and newly translated ed. of *Apocryphal New Testament*. Translated by Montague Rhodes James. 1924. Oxford: Clarendon Press, 1993.

Emmett, Chad F. "The Status Quo Solution for Jerusalem." In *Journal of Palestine Studies* 26, no. 2 (Winter 1997): 16–28.

Erlanger, Steven. "Digging Deep for Proof of an Ancient Jewish Capital." In *The New York Times*. August 5, 2005.

Faulkner, Raymond O., transl. *Ancient Egyptian Book of the Dead*. Translated by Raymond O. Faulkner, With an Introduction by James P. Allen. New York: Barnes & Noble, 2005.

Ferber, Stanley. "The Temple of Solomon in Early Christian and Byzantine Art." In *The Temple of Solomon: Archaeological Fact and Medieval Tradition in Christian, Islamic and Jewish Art*. Edited by Joseph Gutmann. No. 3 of American Academy *The Temple of Solomon: Archaeological Fact and Medieval Tradition in Christian* of Religion Society of Biblical Literature Religion and the Arts, edited by Anthony Yu and Joseph Gutmann. Missoula, MT: Scholars Press, 1976, 21–43.

Filson, Floyd. "Temple, Synagogue, and Church." In *The Biblical Archaeologist* 7, no. 4 (December 1944): 77–88.

Fine, Steven and Eric M. Meyers. "Synagogues." In *The Oxford Encyclopedia of Archaeology in the Near East*. Eric M. Meyers, Editor-in-Chief. Prepared under the Auspices of the American Schools of Oriental Research. Vol. 5. New York: Oxford University Press, 1997, 118–123.

Flood, Finbarr Barry. "Light in Stone. The Commemoration of the Prophet in Umayyad Architecture." In *Bayt al-Maqdis*. Oxford Studies in Islamic Art, 9. Oxford: New York: Published by Oxford University Press for the Board of Faculty of Oriental Studies, University of Oxford, c1992–c1999. Vol. 2, 1999, 311–359.

Fox, Penelope. *Tutankhamun's Treasure*. London, New York: Oxford University Press, 1951.

Frankl, Paul. "The Secret of the Medieval Masons, With an Explanation of Stornaloco's Formula by Erwin Panofsky." In *Art Bulletin* 27 (1945): 46–60.

Freedman, David Noel. *Archaeological Reports from the Tabqa Dam Project—Euphrates Valley, Syria*. Edited by David Noel Freedman with the Assistance of John M. Lundquist. Annual of the American Schools of Oriental Research, vol. 44. Cambridge, MA: American Schools of Oriental Research, 1979.

Freedman, David Noel. "Temple Without Hands." In *Temples and High Places in Biblical Times:Proceedings of the Colloquium in Honor of the Centennial of Hebrew Union College—Jewish Institute of Religion*. Edited by Avraham Biran. Jerusalem: Nelson Glueck School of Biblical Archaeology of Hebrew Union College—Jewish Institute of Religion, 1981, 21–30.

Freedman, David Noel and Rebecca L. Frey. "The Dome of the Rock." In *Revelation, Reason, and Faith: Essays in Honor of Truman G. Madsen*. Edited by Donald W. Parry, Daniel Peterson, and Stephen D. Ricks. Provo, UT: Foundation for Ancient Research and Mormon Studies, Brigham Young University Press, 2002, 635–649.

"Freemasonry." In *Man, Myth & Magic: The Illustrated Encyclopedia of Mythology, Religion, and the Unknown*. New ed. Editor-in-Chief Richard Cavendish, Editorial Board, C. A. Burland et al. New ed. Edited and Compiled by Richard Cavendish and Brian Innes. New York: M. Cavendish, 1997, Vol. 7, 951–956.

Friedland, Roger and Richard Hecht. "The Symbol and the Stone: Jerusalem at the Millennium." In *Annals of the American Academy of Political and Social Science* Vol. 558, Americans and Religions in the Twenty-First Century (July 1998): 144–162.

Friedland, Roger and Richard Hecht. "The Bodies of Nations: A Comparative Study of Religious Violence in Jerusalem and Ayodhya." In *History of Religions* 38, no. 2 (November 1998): 101–149.

Fritz, Folkmar. "What Can Archaeology Tell Us About Solomon's Temple?" In *Biblical Archaeology Review* 13, no. 4 (July/August 1987): 38–49.

Funkenstein, Amos. "A Schedule for the End of the World: The Origins and Persistence of the Apocalyptic Mentality." In *Visions of Apocalypse: End or Rebirth?* Edited by Saul Friedlander, Gerald Holton, Leo Marx, and Eugene Skolnikoff. New York: Holmes and Meier, 1985, 44–60.

Galambush, Julie. "Gog, Magog." In *Eerdmans Dictionary of the Bible*. David Noel Freedman, Editor-in-Chief, Allen C. Myers, Associate Editor, Astrid B. Beck, Managing Editor. Grand Rapids, MI: Eerdmans, 2000, 517–518.

Gardiner, Alan Henderson, Sir. *Egyptian Grammar, Being an Introduction to the Study of Hieroglyphs*. 3rd ed., rev. London: Published on Behalf of the Griffith Institute, Ashmolean Museum, Oxford, by Oxford University Press, 1957.

Gardiner, Alan Henderson, Sir. *The Temple of King Sethos I at Abydos*. Copied by Amice M. Calverley wit the Assistance of Myrtle F. Broome, and Edited by Alan H. Gardiner. London: The Egypt Exploration Society; Chicago: The University of Chicago Press, 1933–1958. 4 Vols.

Gardner, Laurence. *Lost Secrets of the Sacred Ark: Amazing Revelations of the Incredible Power of Gold*. New York: Barnes & Noble, 2003.

Gartner, Bertil E. *The Temple and the Community in Qumran and the New Testament: A Comparative Study in the Temple Symbolism of the Qumran Texts and the New Testament*. Society for New Testament Studies. Monograph Series, 1. Cambridge: University Press, 1965.

Gibson, Shimon. *Below the Temple Mount in Jerusalem: A Sourcebook on the Cisterns, Subterranean Chambers and Conduits of the Haram al-Sharif*. Shimon Gibson, David M. Jacobson. BAR International Series, 637. Oxford, England: Tempus Reparatum, 1996.

Glubb, John Bagot (Glubb Pasha). *The Life and Times of Muhammad*. First Cooper Square Press ed. New York: Cooper Square Press, 2001. Reprint New York: Stein & Day, 1970.

Goitein, S. D. *Studies in Islamic History and Institutions*. Leiden: E. J. Brill, 1966.

Goodenough, Erwin Ramsdell. *Jewish Symbols in the Greco-Roman Period*. Vols. 9–11: *Symbolism in the Dura Synagogue*. Bollingen Series 37. New York: Pantheon Books, 1964.

Grabar, Oleg. *The Dome of the Rock*. Cambridge, MA: The Belknap Press of Harvard University, 2006.

Grabar, Oleg. *The Shape of the Holy: Early Islamic Jerusalem*. With Contributions by Mohammad al-Asad, Abeer Audeh, Said Nuseibeh. Princeton: Princeton University Press, 1996.

Griessman, B. Eugene. "Philo-Semitism and Protestant Fundamentalism: the Unlikely Zionists." In *Phylon* 37, no. 3 (3rd Quarter 1976): 197–211.

Guenon, Rene. *Fundamental Symbols: The Universal Language of Sacred Science*. Translated by Alvin Moore. Compiled and Edited by Michel Valson. Revised and Edited by Martin Lings. Cambridge, UK: Quinta Essentia, 1995.

Gutmann, Joseph. "The Dura Europos Synagogue Paintings and Their Influence on Later Christian and Jewish Art." In *Artibus et Historiae* 9, no. 17 (1988): 25–29.

Hachlili, Rachel. "The Niche and the Ark in Ancient Synagogues." In *Bulletin of the American Schools of Oriental Research*, no. 223 (October 1976): 43–53.

Haig, M. R. "Correspondence." In *Geographical Journal* (1899): 551–552.

Halevi, Z'ev Ben Shimon [i.e. Warren Kenton]. *Kabbalah, Tradition of Hidden Knowledge*. Art and Imagination. London: Thames and Hudson, 2005.

Hall, Manly Palmer. *The Secret Teachings of All Ages: An Encyclopedic Outline of Masonic, Hermetic, Qabbalistic, and Rosicrucian Symbolical Philosophy: Being an Interpretation of the Secret Teachings Concealed Within the Rituals, Allegories, and Mysteries of the Ages*. Reader's ed. New York: Jeremy P. Tarcher/Penguin, 2003.

Hamblin, William J. "Temple Motifs in Jewish Mysticism." In *Temples of the Ancient World: Ritual and Symbolism*. Edited by Donald W. Parry. Illustrations directed by Michael P. Lyon. Salt lake City, UT: Deseret Book Co.; Provo, UT: Foundation for Ancient Research and Mormon Studies, 440–476.

Hammerton-Kelly, R. G. "The Temple and the Origins of Jewish Apocalyptic." In *Vetus Testamentum* 20, fasc. 1 (January 1970): 1–15.

Haran, Menahem. *Temples and Temple-Service in Ancient Israel: An Inquiry into the Character of Cult Phenomena and the Historical Setting of the Priestly School*. Winona Lake, IN: Eisenbrauns, 1985.

Hawting, Gerald R. "Ka'ba." In *Encyclopedia of the Qur'an*. Jane Dammen McAuliffe, General Editor. Leiden: Brill, 2003. Vol. 3, 75–80.

Hayward, C.T.R. *The Jewish Temple: A Non-Biblical Sourcebook*, edited by C.T.R. Hayward. London; New York: Routledge, 1996.

Heilman, Samuel C. "Quiescent and Active Fundamentalisms: The Jewish Cases." In *Accounting for Fundamentalisms: The Dynamic Character of Movements*. The Fundamentalism Project, 4. Edited by Martin E. Marty and R. Scott Appleby. Sponsored by the American Academy of Arts and Sciences. Chicago: University of Chicago Press, 1994, 173–196.

Herzog, Ze'ev. "Arad: Iron Age Period." In *The Oxford Encyclopedia of Archaeology in the Near East.* Eric M. Meyers, Editor-in-Chief. Prepared under the Auspices of the American Schools of Oriental Research. Vol. 1. New York: Oxford University Press, 1997, 174–176.

Hillenbrand, Carole. *The Crusades: Islamic Perspectives.* Chicago: Fitzroy Dearborn Publishers, 1999.

Himmelfarb, Martha. "Revelation and Rapture: The Transformation of the Visionary in the Ascent Apocalypses." In *Mysteries and Revelations: Apocalyptic Studies Since the Uppsala Colloquium.* Edited by John J. Collins and James H. Charlesworth. Sheffield, England: JSOT Press, 1991, 79–90.

Hirschberg, J.W. "The Sources of Moslem Tradition Concerning Jerusalem." In *Rocznik Orientalistyczny* 17 (1951–1952): 314–350.

Holladay, William Lee. *A Concise Hebrew and Aramaic Lexicon of the Old Testament, based upon the Lexical Work of Ludwig Koehler and Walter Baumgartner.* Grand Rapids, MI: Eerdmans, 1971.

Hurowitz, Victor (Avigdor). *I have Built You an Exalted House: Temple Building in the Bible in the Light of Mesopotamian and Northwest Semitic Writings.* Journal for the Study of the Old Testament Supplement Series 115. JSOT/ASOR Monograph Series 5. Sheffield, England: JSOT Press, 1992.

Irwin, Brian P. "Cubit." In *Eerdmans Dictionary of the Bible.* David Noel Freedman, Editor-in-Chief, Allen C. Myers, Associate Editor, Astrid B. Beck, Managing Editor. Grand Rapids, MI: Eerdmans, 2000, 299.

Isaac, E. "1 (Ethiopic Apocalypse of) Enoch (Second Century B.C.—1st Century A.D.)." In *Old Testament Pseudepigrapha.* Edited by James H. Charlesworth. Vol. 1, 1983, 5–89.

Josephus, Flavius. *Jewish Antiquities.* With an English Translation by H. St. John Thackeray. 7 Volumes. The Loeb Classical Library, 242, 281, 326, 410, 433, 456. 1. Books I-IV. 2. Books V-VIII, With an English Translation by H. St. John Thackeray and Ralph Marcus. 3. Books IX-XI, with an English Translation by Ralph Marcus. 4. Books XII-XIV. 5. Books XV-XVII, with an English Translation by Ralph Marcus. Completed by Allen Wikgren. 6. Books XVIII-XIX, with an English Translation by Louis H. Feldman. 7. Book XX. General Index, with an English Translation by Louis H. Feldman. Cambridge, MA: Harvard University Press, 1930–1965 (1986–1996 printing).

Josephus, Flavius. *The Jewish War.* With an English Translation by H. St. John Thackeray. The Loeb Classical Library, 203, 210, 487. 3 Vols. 1. Books I-II. 2. Books III–IV. 3. Books V–VII. Cambridge, MA: Harvard University Press, 1927 (1997 printing).

Jung, Emma and Marie-Louise Von Franz. *The Grail Legend.* 2nd ed. Translated by Andrea Davis. Mythos. Princeton, NJ: Princeton University Press, 1998.

Juynboll, G.H.A. "Hadith and the Qur'an." In *Encyclopedia of the Qur'an.* Jane Dammen McAuliffe, General Editor. Leiden: Brill, 2002. Vol. 2, 376–396.

Kapelrud, Arvid. "Temple Building, A Task for Gods and Kings." *Orientalia* 32 (1963): 56–62.

Kaplony, Andreas. *The Haram of Jerusalem, 324–1099: Temple, Friday Mosque, Area of Spiritual Power.* Freiburger Islamstudien, 22. Stuttgart: Franz Steiner Verlag, 2002.

Kaufman, Asher S. "The Eastern Wall of the Second Temple at Jerusalem Revealed." In *Biblical Archaeology Review* 44, no. 2 (Spring 1981): 108–115.

Keel, Othmar. *The Symbolism of the Biblical World: Ancient Near Eastern Iconography and the Book of Psalms.* Translated by Timothy J. Hallett. Winona Lake, IN: Eisenbrauns, 1997.

Keil, Carl Friedrich. *Commentary on the Old Testament,* C. F. Keil and F. Delitzsch. Translated by James Martin et al. 10 vols. Vol. 3. 1 and 2 Kings, 1 and 2 Chronicles, Ezra, Nehemiah, Esther. Peabody, MA: Hendrickson, 1989.

Kemp, Barry J. *Ancient Egypt: Anatomy of a Civilization.* London; New York: Routledge, 1989.

Khoury, Nuha N.N. "The Dome of the Rock, the Ka'ba, and Ghumdan: Arab Myths and Umayyad Monuments." Essays in Honor of Oleg Grabar Contributed by His Students. In *Muqarnas* 10 (1993): 57–66.

King, Francis, ed. *The Secret Rituals of the O.T.O.* Edited and Introduced by Francis King. London: Daniel, 1973.

King, Francis. *Sexuality, Magic and Perversion.* Los Angeles, CA: Feral House, 2002.

King, L. W., ed. *Bronze Reliefs from the Gates of Shalmaneser, King of Assyria, B.C. 860–825 . . . with 80 Plates.* London: Printed by Order of the Trustees of the British Museum, 1915.

Kissling, Paul J. "Tubal." In *Eerdmans Dictionary of the Bible.* David Noel Freedman, Editor-in-Chief, Allen C. Myers, Associate Editor, Astrid B. Beck, Managing Editor. Grand Rapids, MI: Eerdmans, 2000, 1340.

Kitchen, Kenneth A. "Barke." In *Lexikon der Agyptologie.* Edited by Wolgang Helck and Eberhard Otto. Wiesbaden: O. Harrassowitz, 1973–. Vol. 1 (1975): 619–625.

Kitchen, Kenneth A. "Where Did Solomon's Gold Go?" *Biblical Archaeology Review* 15, no. 3 (May/June 1989): 30.

Klijn, A.F.J. "2 (Syriac Apocalypse of) Baruch (early Second Century A.D.)." In *Old Testament Pseudepigrapha.* Edited by James H. Charlesworth. Vol. 1 (1983), 615–652.

Knight, Christopher and Robert Lomas. *The Hiram Key: Pharaohs, Freemasons and the Discovery of the Secret Scrolls of Jesus.* Gloucester, MA: Fair Winds press, 1996.

Knohl, Israel. "Between Voice and Silence: The Relationship between Prayer and Temple Cult." In *Journal of Biblical Literature* 115, no. 1 (Spring 1996): 17–30.

Kolenkow, Anitra Bingham. "The Fall of the Temple and the Coming of the End: The Spectrum and Process of Apocalyptic Argument in 2 Baruch." In *Society of Biblical Literature 1982 Seminar Papers*. Edited by Kent Harold Richards. Chico, CA: Scholars Press, 1982, 243–250.

Koran. English. *The Quran: A New Translation*. M.A.S. Abdel Haleem. New York: Oxford University Press, 2004.

Kraeling, Carl H. *The Synagogue*. Yale University. The Excavations at Dura-Europos. Final Report. No. 8, Pt. 1. With Contributions by C. C. Torrey, C. B. Welles, and B. Geiger. New Haven: Yale University Press, 1956.

Krinsky, Carol Herselle. "Representations of the Temple of Jerusalem Before 1500." In *Journal of the Warburg and Courtauld Institutes* 33 (1970): 1–19.

Lancaster, Brian L. *The Essence of Kabbalah*. Royston, Hertfordshire, England: Eagle Editions Limited, 2006.

Lawlor, Robert. *Sacred Geometry: Philosophy and Practice*. Art and Imagination. London: Thames and Hudson, 1982.

Leemhuis, Frederik. "Apocalypse." In *Encyclopedia of the Qur'an*. Jane Dammen McAuliffe, General Editor. Leiden: Brill, 2001. Vol. 1, 111–114.

Lenchak, Timothy A. "Hezekiah." In *Eerdmans Dictionary of the Bible*. David Noel Freedman, Editor-in-Chief, Allen C. Myers, Associate Editor, Astrid B. Beck, Managing Editor. Grand Rapids, MI: Eerdmans, 2000, 586.

Levine, Lee I. "The Nature and Origin of the Palestinian Synagogue Reconsidered." In *Journal of Biblical Literature* 115, No. 3 (Autumn 1996): 425–448.

Lewis, Theodore J. "Syro-Palestinian Iconography and Divine Images." In *Cult Image and Divine Representation in the Ancient Near East*. Edited by Neal H. Walls. No. 10 in American Schools of Oriental Research Books Series, edited by Brian B. Schmidt. Boston, MA: American Schools of Oriental Research, 2005, 69–107.

Liddell, Henry George. *A Greek-English Lexicon*. Compiled by Henry George Liddell and Robert Scott. 9th ed., Rev. and Augm. Throughout by Sir Henry Stuart Jones with the Assistance of Roderick McKenzie and with the Cooperation of Many Scholars. Oxford: Clarendon Press, 1996.

Limor, Ora. "The Place of the End of Days: Eschatological Geography in Jerusalem." In *The Real and Ideal Jerusalem in Jewish, Christian, and Islamic Art: Studies in Honor of Bezalel Narkiss on the Occasion of His Seventieth Birthday*. Edited by Bianca Kuhnel. Jewish Art. Jerusalem: Center for Jewish Art, Hebrew University of Jerusalem, 1998, 13–22.

Loud, Gordon. *The Megiddo Ivories*. The University of Chicago Oriental Institute Publications, Vol. 52. Chicago: University of Chicago Press, 1939.

Lundquist, John M. "Biblical Temple." In *The Oxford Encyclopedia of Archaeology in the Near East*. Eric M. Meyers, Editor-in-Chief. Prepared under the Auspices of the American Schools of Oriental Research. Vol. 1. New York: Oxford University Press, 1997, 324–330.

Lundquist, John M. "The Common Temple Ideology of the Ancient Near East." In *The Temple in Antiquity: Ancient Records and Modern Perspectives*. Edited by Truman G. Madsen. Religious Studies Monograph Series, Vol. 9. Provo, UT: Religious Studies Center, Brigham Young University; Salt Lake City, UT: Produced and Distributed by Bookcraft, 1984, 53–76.

Lundquist, John M. "Fundamentals of Temple Ideology from Eastern Traditions." In *Revelation, Reason, and Faith: Essays in Honor of Truman G. Madsen*. Edited by Donald W. Parry, Daniel Peterson, and Stephen D. Ricks. Provo, UT: Foundation for Ancient Research and Mormon Studies, Brigham Young University Press, 2002, 651–701.

Lundquist, John M. "Legitimizing Role of the Temple in the Origin of the State." In *Society of Biblical Literature 1982 Seminar Papers*. Edited by Kent Harold Richards. Chico, CA: Scholars Press, 1982, 271–297.

Lundquist, John M. "New Light on the Temple Ideology." In *East and West* 50, nos. 1–4 (December 2000): 9–42.

Lundquist, John M. *The Temple: Meeting Place of Heaven and Earth*. Art and Imagination. New York: Thames and Hudson, 1993.

Lundquist, John M. "What is a Temple? A Preliminary Typology." In *The Quest for the Kingdom of God: Studies in Honor of George E. Mendenhall*. Edited by H. B. Huffmon, F. A. Spina, and A.R.W. Green. Winona Lake, IN: Eisenbrauns, 1983, 205–219.

Lundquist, John M. "What is Reality?" In *By Study and Also by Faith: Essays in Honor of Hugh W. Nibley on the Occasion of His Eightieth Birthday, 27 March, 1990*. Edited by John M. Lundquist and Stephen D. Ricks. Salt Lake City, UT: Deseret Book; Provo, UT: Foundation for Ancient Research and Mormon Studies, 1990, 428–438.

Macrae, George. "The Temple As a House of Revelation in the Nag Hammadi Texts." In *The Temple in Antiquity: Ancient Records and Modern Perspectives*. Edited, with an Introductory Essay by Truman G. Madsen. Religious Studies Monograph Series, Vol. 9. Provo, UT: Religious Studies Center, Brigham Young University; Salt Lake City, UT: Produced and Distributed by Bookcraft, 1984, 175–190.

Mandell, Sara R. "Hasmoneans." In *Eerdmans Dictionary of the Bible*. David Noel Freedman, Editor-in-Chief, Allen C. Myers, Associate Editor, Astrid B. Beck, Managing Editor. Grand Rapids, MI: Eerdmans, 2000, 555–556.

Margueron, Jean-Claude. "Temples: Mesopotamian Temples." Translated by Nancy Leinwand. In *The Oxford Encyclopedia of Archaeology in the Near*

East. Eric M. Meyers, Editor-in-Chief. Prepared under the Auspices of the American Schools of Oriental Research. Vol. 5. New York: Oxford University Press, 1997, 165–169.

Margueron, Jean Claude and Marcel Sigrist. "Emar." Translated by Nancy Leinwand and Monique Fecteau. In *The Oxford Encyclopedia of Archaeology in the Near East.* Eric M. Meyers, Editor-in-Chief. Prepared under the Auspices of the American Schools of Oriental Research. Vol. 2. New York: Oxford University Press, 1997, 236–239.

Matthiae, Paolo. "Ebla." In *The Oxford Encyclopedia of Archaeology in the Near East.* Eric M. Meyers. Editor-in-Chief. Prepared under the Auspices of the American Schools of Oriental Research. Vol. 2. New York: Oxford University Press, 1997, 180–183.

Matthiae, Paolo. "Some Notes About Solomon's Palace and Ramesside Architectural Culture." In *L'Impero Ramesside: Convegno Internazionale in Onore di Sergio Donadoni.* Vicino Oriente—Quaderno 1. Rome: Universita degli Studi di Roma "La Sapienza," 1997, 117–130.

Mazar, B. "The Archaeological Excavations near the Temple Mount." In *Jerusalem Revealed: Archaeology in the Holy City, 1968–1974.* Edited by Y. Yadin, Associate Editor, E. Stern. English Translation and Abridgement by R. Grafman. Jerusalem: Israel Exploration Society, 1975, 25–40.

Mazar, Benjamin. *The Mountain of the Lord.* Benjamin Mazar, Assisted by Gaalyah Cornfeld; D. N. Freedman Consultant. Garden City, NY: Doubleday, 1975.

McCarthy, Dennis J. "Covenant in Narratives from late OT Times." In *The Quest for the Kingdom of God: Studies in Honor of George E. Mendenhall.* Edited by H. B. Huffmon, F. A. Spina, and A.R.W. Green. Winona Lake, IN: Eisenbrauns, 1983, 77–94.

Metzger, B. M. "The Fourth Book of Ezra (Late First Century A.D.)." In *Old Testament Pseudepigrapha.* Edited by James H. Charlesworth. Vol. 1 (1983), 517–559.

Meyer, Marvin, General Editor. *Ancient Christian Magic: Coptic Texts of Ritual Power.* Marvin Meyer, General Editor, Richard Smith, Associate Editor, Meal Kelsey, Managing Editor. San Francisco: HarperSanFrancisco, 1994.

Meyer, Marvin, Editor. *The Ancient Mysteries: A Sourcebook: Sacred Texts of the Mystery Religions of the Ancient Mediterranean World.* San Francisco: Harper & Row, 1987.

Meyers, Carol. "Jachin and Boaz in Religious and Political Perspective." In *The Temple in Antiquity: Ancient Records and Modern Perspectives.* Edited by Truman G. Madsen. Religious Studies Monograph Series, Vol. 9. Provo, UT: Religious Studies Center, Brigham Young University; Salt Lake City, UT: Produced and Distributed by Bookcraft, 1984, 135–150.

Meyers, Carol. "Temple, Jerusalem." In *The Anchor Bible Dictionary*. David Noel Freedman Editor-in-Chief, Associate Editors Gary A. Herion, David F. Graf, John David Pleins, Managing Editor Astrid B. Beck. New York: Doubleday, 1992. Vol. 6, 350–369.

Meyers, Eric M. "Ancient Synagogues in Galilee: Their Religious and Cultural Setting." In *The Biblical Archaeologist* 43, no. 2 (Spring 1980): 97–108.

Michell, John. *The Temple at Jerusalem: a Revelation*. York Beach, ME: Samuel Weiser, Inc., 2000.

Milgrom, Jacob. "New Temple Festivals in the Temple Scroll." In *The Temple in Antiquity: Ancient Records and Modern Perspectives*. Edited by Truman G. Madsen. Religious Studies Monograph Series, Vol. 9. Provo, UT: Religious Studies Center, Brigham Young University; Salt Lake City, UT: Produced and Distributed by Bookcraft, 1984, 125–133.

Milgrom, Jacob. *Studies in Levitical Terminology*, I: *The Encroacher and the Levite. The Term 'Aboda*. University of California Publications. Near Eastern Studies, Volume 14. Berkeley: CA: University of California Press, 1970.

Millard, Alan R. "Does the Bible Exaggerate King Solomon's Wealth?" *Biblical Archaeology Review* 15, no. 3 (May/June 1989): 20–29, 31, 34.

Morgenstern, Julian. "The Ark, the Ephod, and the Tent of Meeting." In *Hebrew Union College Annual* 17 (1942–1943): 153–266.

Mueller, James R. "The Apocalypse of Abraham and the Destruction of the Second Jewish Temple." In *Society of Biblical Literature 1982 Seminar Papers*. Edited by Kent Harold Richards. Chico, CA: Scholars Press, 1982, 341–349.

Muslim ibn al-Hajjaj al-Qurashi, ca. 821–875 [Muslim ibn al-Hajjaj al-Qushayri]. *Sahih Muslim; Being Traditions of the Sayings and Doings of the Prophet Muhamad as Narrated by His Companions and Compiled Under the title al-Jami-us-sahih, by Imam Muslim*. Rendered into English by Abdul Hamid Siddiqi, with Explanatory Notes and Brief Biographical Sketches of Major Narrators. Vol. 4. Lahore: Sh. Muhammad Ashraf, 1978.

Myers, Jacob M. *Ezra, Nehemiah*. Introduction, Translation, and Notes by Jacob M. Meyers. The Anchor Bible, 14. Garden City, NY: Doubleday, 1965.

Neusner, Jacob. "Map Without Territory: Mishnah's System of Sacrifice and Sanctuary." In *History of Religions* 19, no. 2 (November 1979): 103–127.

Newsom, Carol. *Songs of the Sabbath Sacrifice: A Critical Edition*. Harvard Semitic Studies, vol. 27. Atlanta, GA: Scholars Press, 1985.

Nibley, Hugh. "Christian Envy of the Temple." In *The Jewish Quarterly Review*, New Ser., 50, no. 2 (Oct. 1959): 97–123; 50, no. 3 (January 1960): 229–240.

Niditch, Susan. "Ezekiel 40–48 in a Visionary Context." In *The Catholic Biblical Quarterly* 48, no. 2 (1986): 208–224.

The Old Testament Pseudepigrapha, 1st ed. Vol. 1. Apocalyptic Literature and Testaments. Vol. 2. Expansions of the 'Old Testament' and Legends, Wisdom, and Philosophical Literature, Prayers, Psalms, and Odes, Fragments of Lost Judeo-Hellenistic Works. edited by James H. Charlesworth. Garden City, NY: Doubleday, 1983–1985.

Olsson, Tord, "The Apocalyptic Activity: The Case of Jamasp Namag." In *Apocalypticism in the Mediterranean World and the Near East: Proceedings of the International Colloquium on Apocalypticism, Uppsala, August 12–17, 1979.* Tubingen: Mohr, 1983, 21–49.

Orme, William A. Jr. "Bulldozer Hits a Nerve, and the Old City Jumps." In *The New York Times,* December 21, 1999.

Orthmann, Winfried. "Tell Chuera." In *The Oxford Encyclopedia of Archaeology in the Near East.* Eric M. Meyers, Editor-in-Chief. Prepared under the Auspices of the American Schools of Oriental Research. Vol. 1. New York: Oxford University Press, 1997, 491–492.

Otto, Eberhard. *Ancient Egyptian Art: The Cults of Osiris and Amon.* Translated by Kate Bosse Griffiths. Photographs by Max Hirmer. New York: Harry N. Abrams, Inc, Publishers, n.d.

Ouellette, Jean. "The Basic Structure of Solomon" Temple and Archaeological Research." In *The Temple of Solomon: Archaeological Fact and Medieval Tradition in Christian, Islamic and Jewish Art.* Edited by Joseph Gutmann. No. 3 of American Academy *The Temple of Solomon: Archaeological Fact and Medieval Tradition in Christian* of Religion Society of Biblical Literature Religion and the Arts, edited by Anthony Yu and Joseph Gutmann. Missoula, MT: Scholars Press, 1976, 1–20.

Ousterhout, Robert. "The Temple, the Sepulchre, and the Martyrion of the Savior." In *Gesta* 29, no. 1 (1990): 44–53.

Panofsky, Erwin, Editor and Translator. *Abbot Suger on the Abbey Church of St.-Denis and its Art Treasures.* 2nd ed. by Gerda Panofsky-Soergel. Princeton: Princeton University Press, 1979.

Parry, Donald W. "Demarcation between Sacred Space and Profane Space: The Temple of Herod Model." In *Temples of the Ancient World: Ritual and Symbolism.* Edited by Donald W. Parry. Illustrations directed by Michael P. Lyon. Salt lake City, UT: Deseret Book Co.; Provo, UT: Foundation for Ancient Research and Mormon Studies, 413–439.

Patai, Raphael. *Man and Temple in Ancient Jewish Myth and Ritual,* 2nd enl. Ed. with a New Introduction and Postscript. New York: KTAV Publishing House, Inc., 1967.

Petrie, W. M. Flinders. *The Royal Tombs of the Earliest Dynasties,* with a Chapter by F. Ll. Griffith. Twenty First Memoir of The Egypt Exploration Fund.

Part 2. London: The Offices of the Egypt Exploration Fund and Kegan Paul, Trench, Trubner & Co., 1901.

Prawer, J. "Jerusalem in Crusader Days." In *Jerusalem Revealed: Archaeology in the Holy City, 1968–1974*. Edited by Y. Yadin, Associate Editor, E. Stern. English Translation and Abridgement by R. Grafman. Jerusalem: Israel Exploration Society, 1975, 102–108.

Rabbat, Nasser. "The Meaning of the Umayyad Dome of the Rock." In *Muqarnas* 6 (1989):12–21.

Read, Piers Paul. *The Templars.* Cambridge, MA: Da Capo Press, 1999.

Redditt, Paul L. "Meshech." In *Eerdmans Dictionary of the Bible*. David Noel Freedman, Editor-in-Chief, Allen C. Myers, Associate Editor, Astrid B. Beck, Managing Editor. Grand Rapids, MI: Eerdmans, 2000, 888.

Reeves, C. N. *The Complete Tutankhamun: The King, The Tomb, The Royal Treasure,* foreword by the Seventh Earl of Carnarvon. 1st pbk. ed. London; New York: Thames and Hudson, 1995.

Reymond, E.A.E. *The Mythical Origin of the Egyptian Temple.* Manchester, England: Manchester University Press; New York: Barnes & Noble, 1969.

Reynolds, Edwin. "The Sanctuary Terminology in Hebrews." In *Asia Adventist Seminary Studies* 1 (1998): 63–83.

Richardson, Peter. "Herod (Family)." In *Eerdmans Dictionary of the Bible*. David Noel Freedman, Editor-in-Chief, Allen C. Myers, Associate Editor, Astrid B. Beck, Managing Editor. Grand Rapids, MI: Eerdmans, 2000, 579–584.

Ritmeyer, Kathleen. "Herod's Temple in East Anglia." In *Biblical Archaeology Review* 19, no. 5 (September/October 1993): 62–67, 90.

Ritmeyer, Kathleen and Leen Ritmeyer. "Reconstructing Herod's Temple Mount in Jerusalem." In *Biblical Archaeology Review* 15 (November/December 1989): 23–42.

Ritmeyer, Leen. "The Ark of the Covenant: Where it Stood in Solomon's Temple." In *Biblical Archaeology Review* 22 (Jan./Feb. 1996): 46–55, 70–73.

Ritmeyer, Leen. "Locating the Original Temple Mount." In *Biblical Archaeology Review* 18, no. 2 (March/April 1992): 24–45, 64–65.

Robins, Gay. "Cult Statues in Ancient Egypt." In *Cult Image and Divine Representation in the Ancient Near East.* Edited by Neal H. Walls. No. 10 in American Schools of Oriental Research Books Series. Edited by Brian B. Schmidt. Boston, MA: American Schools of Oriental Research, 2005, 1–12.

Robinson, Neal. "Antichrist." In *Encyclopedia of the Qur'an.* Jane Dammen McAuliffe, General Editor. Leiden: Brill, 2001. Vol. 1, 107–111.

Rosellini, Ippolito. *I Monumenti dell'Egitto e della Nubia.* Vol. II: *Monumenti Civili.* Pisa: 1834.

Rosen-Ayalon, M. "The Islamic Architecture of Jerusalem." In *Jerusalem Revealed: Archaeology in the Holy City, 1968–1974.* Edited by Y. Yadin, Associate Editor,

E. Stern. English Translation and Abridgement by R. Grafman. Jerusalem: Israel Exploration Society, 1975, 92–96.

Rubinkiewicz, R. "Apocalypse of Abraham (First to Second Century A.D.)." Revised and Notes Added by H. G. Lunt. In *Old Testament Pseudepigrapha.* Edited by James H. Charlesworth. Vol. I (1983), 681–705.

Russell, A. G. "The Jews, the Roman Empire, and Christianity, A.D. 50–180." In *Greece & Rome* 6, no. 18 (May 1937): 170–178.

Scholem, Gershom. *Kabbalah.* Library of Jewish Knowledge. New York: Quadrangle/New York Times Book Co., 1974.

Scholem, Gershom. *Zohar: The Book of Splendor. Basic Readings from the Kabbalah.* Selected and Edited by Gershom Scholem. New York: Schocken Books, 1977.

Schiffman, Lawrence H. "The Theology of the Temple Scroll." In *The Jewish Quarterly Review,* New ser. 85, no. 1–2, Papers on the Dead Sea Scrolls (July October 1994): 109–123.

Schwartz, Max. *The Biblical Engineer: How the Temple in Jerusalem was Built.* Hoboken, NJ: KTAV Publishing House, Inc., 2002.

Seger, Joe D. "Shechem." In *The Oxford Encyclopedia of Archaeology in the Near East.* Eric M. Meyers, Editor-in-Chief. Prepared under the Auspices of the American Schools of Oriental Research. Vol. 5. New York: Oxford University Press, 1997, 19–23.

Sells, Michael. "Ascension." In *Encyclopedia of the Qur'an.* Jane Dammen McAuliffe, General Editor. Leiden: Brill, 2001. Vol. 1, 176–181.

Shanks, Hershel. "Sifting the Temple Mount Dump." In *Biblical Archaeology Review* 31, no. 4 (July August 2005): 14–15.

Sharon, Moshe. "The 'Praises of Jerusalem' as a Source for the Early History of Islam.'" In *Bibliotheca Orientalis* 49, no. 1–2 (January March 1992): 56–67.

Shutt, R.J.H. "Letter of Aristeas, A New Translation and Introduction." In *The Old Testament Pseudepigrapha.* Edited by James H. Charlesworth. Vol. 2, 1985, 7–34.

Silberman, Neil Asher. "Glossary: Stones in Many Shapes and Sizes: Ashlars, Bosses, Margins, Headers and Stretchers." In *Biblical Archaeology Review* 15 (July/August 1989): 59–60.

Siliotti, Alberto. *The Illustrated Guide to the Valley of the Kings and the Theban Necropolises and Temples.* Cairo: The American University in Cairo Press, 2004.

Simson, Otto Georg von. *The Gothic Cathedral: Origins of Gothic Architecture and the Medieval Concept of Order.* Bollingen Series XLVIII. Princeton, NJ: Princeton University Press, 1989.

Skarsaune, Oskar. *In the Shadow of the Temple: Jewish Influences on Early Christianity.* Downers Grove, IL: InterVarsity Press, 2002.

Smith, Christopher R. "The Structure of the Book of Revelation in Light of Apocalyptic Literary Conventions." In *Novum Testamentum* 36, fasc. 4 (October 1994): 373–393.

Smith, Jonathan Z. "Earth and Gods." In *Map is Not Territory*. Studies in Judaism in Late Antiquity. Leiden: D. J. Brill, 1978, 104–129.

Smith, Morton. "On the History of *apokalypto* and *apocalypsis*." In *Apocalypticism in the Mediterranean World and the Near East: Proceedings of the International Colloquium on Apocalypticism, Uppsala, August 12–17, 1979*. Tubingen: Mohr, 1983, 9–20.

Soucek, Priscilla. "The Temple of Solomon in Islamic Legend and Art." In *The Temple of Solomon: Archaeological Fact and Medieval Tradition in Christian, Islamic and Jewish Art*. Edited by Joseph Gutmann. No. 3 of American Academy *The Temple of Solomon: Archaeological Fact and Medieval Tradition in Christian* of Religion Society of Biblical Literature Religion and the Arts, edited by Anthony Yu and Joseph Gutmann. Missoula, MT: Scholars Press, 1976, 73–123.

St. Laurent, Beatrice and Andras Riedlmayer. "Restorations of Jerusalem and the Dome of the Rock and Their Political Significance, 1537–1928." Essays in Honor of Oleg Grabar Contributed by His Students. In *Muqarnas* 10 (1993): 76–84.

Stevenson, Gregory. *Power and Place: Temple and Identity in the Book of Revelation*. No. 107 of *Beihefte zur Zeitschrift fur die Neutestamentliche Wissenschaft und die Kunde der alteren Kirche*. Edited by Michael Wolter. Berlin; New York: Walter de Gruyter, 2001.

Stookey, Laurence Hull. "The Gothic Cathedral as the Heavenly Jerusalem: Liturgical and Theological Sources." In *Gesta* 8, no. 1 (1969): 35–41.

Strachan, Gordon. *Chartres: Sacred Geometry, Sacred Space*. With Architectural Drawings by Oliver Perceval. Edinburgh: Floris, 2003.

Stricker, B. H. "The Origin of the Greek Theatre." *Journal of Egyptian Archaeology* 41 (1955): 34–47.

Tappy, Ron E. "Shechem." In *Eerdmans Dictionary of the Bible*. David Noel Freedman, Editor-in-Chief, Allen C. Myers, Associate Editor, Astrid B. Beck, Managing Editor. Grand Rapids, MI: Eerdmans, 2000, 1200–1203.

Toombs, Lawrence E. "Shechem." In *The Anchor Bible Dictionary*. David Noel Freedman, Editor-in-Chief; Associate Editors Gary A. Herion, David F. Graf, John David Pleins, Managing Editor Astrid B. Beck. Vol. 5. New York: Doubleday, 1992, 1174–1186.

Treasures of the Holy Land: Ancient Art from the Israel Museum. New York: Metropolitan Museum of Art, 1986.

Tsafrir, Y. "The Location of the Seleucid Akra in Jerusalem." In *Jerusalem Revealed: Archaeology in the Holy City, 1968–1974*. English Translation and

Abridgment by R. Grafman. Editor Y. Yadin, Associate Editor E. Stern. Jerusalem: Israel Exploration Society, 1975, 85–86.

Tuell, Steven Shawn. *The Law of the Temple in Ezekiel 40–48.* Harvard Semitic Museum. Harvard Semitic Monographs, Edited by Frank Moore Cross, 49. Atlanta, GA: Scholars Press, 1992.

Uphill, Eric. *The Temples of Per Ramesses.* Warminster, England: Aris & Phillips, 1984.

Urban, Hugh B. "Elitism and Esotericism: Strategies of Secrecy and Power in South Indian Tantra and French Freemasonry." In *Numen* 44, no 1 (January 1997): 1–38.

Van Buren., E. Douglas. "Foundation Rites for a New Temple." *Orientalia* 21 (1952) 293–306.

Vermes, Geza. *The Complete Dead Sea Scrolls in English.* Rev. Ed. London: Penguin Books, 2004.

Vries, Ad de. *Dictionary of Symbols and Imagery.* Amsterdam: North-Holland Pub. Co.; New York: Distributors for the U.S.A. and Canada, Elsevier Science Pub. Co., 1984.

Waida, Manabu. "Problems of Central Asian and Siberian Shamanism." In *Numen* 30, fasc. 2 (December 1983): 215–239.

Wasserstrom, Steven M. *Religion after Religion: Gershom Scholem, Mircea Eliade, and Henry Corbin at Eranos.* Princeton, NJ: Princeton University Press, 1999.

Waterman, Leroy. "The Damaged 'Blueprints' of the Temple of Solomon." In *Journal of Near Eastern Studies* 2 (1943): 284–294.

Weston, Jessie L. *From Ritual to Romance: An Account of the Holy Grail from Ancient Ritual to Christian Symbol.* Garden City, NY: Doubleday, 1957.

Wheeler, Brannon M. *Mecca and Eden: Ritual, Relics, and Territory in Islam.* Chicago: University of Chicago Press, 2006.

White, L. Michael. "Dura-Europos." In *The Oxford Encyclopedia of Archaeology in the Near East.* Eric M. Meyers, Editor-in-Chief. Prepared under the Auspices of the American Schools of Oriental Research. Vol. 2. New York: Oxford University Press, 1997, 173–178.

Widengren, Geo. *Muhammad, the Apostle of God, and His Ascension.* King and Savior, V. Uppsala Universitets Arsskrift 1955:1. Acta Universitatis Upsaliensis. Uppsala: A. B. Lundequistska Bokhandeln, 1955.

Wilkinson, Richard H. *The Complete Temples of Ancient Egypt.* New York: Thames & Hudson, 2000.

Wintermute, O.S. "Jubilees (Second Century B.C.)." In *Old Testament Pseudepigrapha.* Edited by James H. Charlesworth. Vol. 2, 1985, 35–51.

Wischnitzer, Rachel. "The 'Closed Temple' Panel in the Synagogue of Dura-Europos." In *Journal of the American Oriental Society* 91, no. 3 (Jul/Sep 1971): 367–378.

Wise, Michael O., Martin G. Abegg Jr., and Edward M. Cook. *The Dead Sea Scrolls: A New Translation.* Rev. Ed. San Francisco: Harper San Francisco, 2005.

Wood, Michael. *World Atlas of Archaeology.* Foreword by Michael Wood. London: M. Beazley, 1985.

Wright, G. E. "Shechem." In *Encyclopedia of Archaeological Excavations in the Holy Land.* Edited by Michael Avi-Yonah. Vol. 4. London: Oxford University Press, 1978, 1083–1094.

Wright, G.R.H. *Ancient Building in South Syria and Palestine.* Handbuch der Orientalistik. Siebente Abteilung, Kunst und Archaeologie; 1. Bd. Der Alte Vordere Orient, 2. Abschnitt, Die Denkmaler, B. Vorderasien, Lfg. 3. 2 vols. Leiden: E. J. Brill, 1985.

Yadin, Yigael. "Hazor." In *Encyclopedia of Archaeological Excavations in the Holy Land.* Edited by Michael Avi-Yonah. Vol. 2. London: Oxford University Press, 1976, 474–495

Yadin, Yigael. *The Temple Scroll.* Edited by Yigael Yadin. 3 vols. In 4. Vol. 1. Introduction. Vol. 2. Text and Commentary. Vol. 3. Plates and Text. Supplementary Plates 2 vols. Jerusalem: Israel Exploration Society; Institute of Archaeology of the Hebrew University of Jerusalem; Shrine of the Book, 1983.

Yadin, Yigael. *The Temple Scroll: The Hidden Law of the Dead Sea Sect.* New York: Random House, 1985.

Youngblood, Ronald. "A Holistic Typology of Prophecy and Apocalyptic." In *Israel's Apostasy and Restoration: Essays in Honor of Roland K. Harrison.* Edited by Avraham Gileadi. Frand Rapids, MI: Baker Book House, 1988, 213–221.

Zevit, Ziony. "Preamble to a Temple Tour." In *Sacred Time, Sacred Place: Archaeology and The Religion of Israel.* Edited by Barry M. Gittlen. Winona Lake: IN: Eisenbrauns, 2002, 73–81.

Zevit, Ziony. *The Religions of Ancient Israel: A Synthesis of Parallactic Approaches.* London: Continuum, 2001.

Index

About the Author

JOHN M. LUNDQUIST is The Susan and Douglas Dillon Chief Librarian of the Asian and Middle Eastern Division, The Research Libraries—Humanities and Social Sciences Library, New York Public Library. He has written many books and has written pieces for *The New York Times* Travel section.